NOFX

is

"Fat Mike" Burkett

Eric Melvin

Erik "Smelly" Sandin

Aaron "El Hefe" Abeyta

NOFX

The Hepatitis Bathtub and Other Stories

NOFX with Jeff Alulis

DA CAPO PRESS

A Member of the Perseus Books Group

Editorial production by Lori Hobkirk at the Book Factory
Set in 11 point Adobe Jenson Pro

Cataloging-in-Publication data for this book is available from
the Library of Congress.
ISBN: 978-0-306-82477-7 (hard cover)
ISBN: 978-0-306-82478-4 (e-book)

Published by Da Capo Press
A Member of the Perseus Books Group
www.dacapopress.com

Da Capo Press books are available at special discounts for bulk
purchases in the U.S. by corporations, institutions, and other organizations.
For more information, please contact the Special Markets Department at the
Perseus Books Group, 2300 Chestnut Street, Suite 200, Philadelphia,
PA 19103, or call (800) 810-4145, ext. 5000,
or e-mail special.markets@perseusbooks.com.

10 9 8 7 6 5 4

This book is dedicated to all the people
who died within its pages:

All of our grandparents, Bob Baxter, John Macias, Jordan
Hiller, Rich Rosemus, Stevo Jensen, Tim Yohannan, El Duce,
Dave Allen, Lynn Strait, Mike Maklychalk from Anti-Krieg,
Dana McCarty, Bomber Manzullo, Jimmy Dread, Bob Lush,
Quake, Misfit, Carlton, Susan, Suzy, Bill Bartell, the kid we
met in Minneapolis after that D.O.A. show, Buddy Arnold,
Shannon Hoon, Mikey Welsh, Jim Cherry, Brian from the
Fulton house, Henry Abeyta, Hefe's mom, Melvin's mom,
Mike's parents, and Tony Sly

1

Mike

The first time I drank piss was on a fire escape overlooking downtown Los Angeles. In the course of testing my sexual boundaries, my then-girlfriend (and now my wife), Soma, asked me if I had ever drunk another person's pee, and I said no. It wasn't something I was into, but how do you know if you don't try? We were hanging out on the fire escape of her loft apartment; she told me to take my clothes off and lie down. The cold steel dug into my naked back as she squatted over me. She started pissing on my chest and then moved up to my mouth. I could hear the overflow splatter on the sidewalk below.

Soma later sampled my pee backstage during a show we played with No Use For A Name. Before our encore, I went to the bathroom to do some coke with No Use's Tony Sly. I had to pee, but as I was about to aim for the toilet, Soma got down on her knees and opened her mouth. Tony watched as I redirected my stream and said, "You guys are just made for each other, aren't you?"

1

It really doesn't taste as bad as you'd think. It's certainly better than whiskey. It's like strong oolong tea. At least that's what hers tastes like. She made me taste my own once, and it tasted bitter and horrible from all the shit I put into my body. Soma is definitely getting the worse end of the deal.

Like many of the weird things Soma and I have done, it wasn't a turn-on in the traditional sense. The dominant/submissive element was super cool, but pee drinking in and of itself was more about being punk and doing the things you're not supposed to do. During our shows, I would sometimes finish drinking my usual vodka and soda, and our drum tech, Jay, would mix me a new drink. Soma would intercept it, squat behind my amplifier, and make a little pee cocktail. El Hefe's wife watched her do it once and immediately turned around and walked to the opposite side of the stage. I would tell the crowd or our friends on the side of the stage what was in my drink, and no one would believe me . . . until they took a sip.

The side effect of my continued boundary pushing is that somewhere along the way my Weirdness Barometer broke. Once you get over the shock of drinking someone's pee, drinking it the fourth or fifth time isn't weird anymore. But it's still very weird to the majority of the non-pee-drinking public. So my perception of what's fucked up and what's acceptable to discuss in mixed company has become somewhat skewed. I've told people about the time I tied a girl down and milked her, and they've said, "That's so fucked up." I've had to stop myself and wonder if maybe I crossed a line, either in my behavior or in my selection of anecdotes to share publicly.

You tell me:

NOFX played a gig in England, and one of our crew guys brought a female friend to the show. She'd recently had a baby, so we started talking about breastfeeding, and the conversation turned (as it tends to do when I'm involved) to kinky sex. She told me her fantasy about being tied up in a barn and getting milked like a cow.

She had been trapped at home as a single mom for so long, this was her chance to cut loose. I asked Jay to grab some rope, duct tape, and my "special" bag from the bus. I told the girl that if she wanted to go for it she could meet me upstairs in our dressing room in fifteen minutes.

Fifteen minutes later—on the dot—there was a knock at the dressing room door.

I put her facedown on a table and hog-tied her wrists and ankles. Her tits hung over the edge of the table, and I tied a rope around them so they were bulging out. I gagged her and started milking. I had never milked anything before. I had to ungag her for a second so she could explain how to squeeze and pull properly. Once I got the hang of it, the milk started to flow. I saved it in a plastic cup and added some ice and vodka. It was my first nipple-fresh White Russian.

I took a few sips and forced her to drink some, too. It tasted awful. But, as you may have figured out by now, it wasn't about how it tasted.

Later that night on the tour bus I told the band about my evening. I expected them to dig my White Russian Human Milking story, but instead of laughter and smiles I got a bunch of awkward looks and raised eyebrows. They told me I should probably keep that particular story to myself.

But here we are . . .

◆ ◆ ◆

My parents took me to a porno movie when I was four years old.

It was the early '70s, and porn still played in decent-sized theaters. One sunny California afternoon, we walked into such a theater on Ventura Boulevard near the Topanga Bowl bowling alley. There was a tractor on the screen, and then there was some sort of sex act I was way too young to understand. I guess my parents started to feel awkward because we left just as it was getting interesting.

We never spoke about it again. I'll never know why they thought it was a good idea to take me there. But it's one of the only memories I have from when my parents were still married.

My dad was a traveling shoe salesman who was on the road most of the year, so there was barely any difference between how often I saw him before and after my parents split up. He moved into an adults-only apartment building, and I stayed with him every other weekend, but I couldn't leave the apartment. He played volleyball, drank, and smoked pot with his buddies by the pool, and I sat inside and watched seaweed creatures on *Night Gallery*. Those were my weekends with my dad.

Years later, when I was in my thirties, he told me he never really wanted to have me over. He worked hard all week and wanted time to himself to party and get laid. I was only "invited" because my mom insisted he spend time with me. It suddenly made sense why he and I had never bonded, and I always held some resentment toward him that never fully dissipated. I was never abused. I was never beaten. I was just neglected. I suppose it could've been worse.

I spent most of my childhood at my mother's apartment in Beverly Hills. In the interest of accuracy, I should point out that there's Beverly Hills—which is full of mega-mansions and European sports cars—and there's the

Flats of Beverly Hills, a neighborhood south of Wilshire Boulevard that housed all the people who cleaned the mega-mansions and parked the European sports cars.

My mom found work as a manicurist and moved us to the Flats to get me into a good school district and expose me to the upper crust, in the hopes that some class and sophistication would rub off. As it turned out, the affluent parents on the other side of Wilshire welcomed the opportunity for their kids to mingle with the lower class, in the hopes of subliminally suggesting, "Work hard, or you'll end up being a manicurist!" It was a symbiotic relationship that allowed for a surprising lack of class discrimination. I never felt out of place or looked down upon by any of the other kids because there were no barriers between our stations in life. One night I'd sleep over at a friend's apartment and four siblings would literally be sharing the same bed, the next night I'd sleep over at a friend's mansion that had previously hosted the Shah of Iran. It was normal.

I had a friend named Eddie Machtinger who had an elevator in his house. He'd wait until the maid got in and then shut off the power to the whole house, leaving the maid trapped. It's the kind of prank you can only play when you're raised in Beverly Hills.

In the summers, I went to camp with kids like Josh Brolin, the Nelson brothers and their sister, Tracy (from the show *Square Pegs*), and the kid who played Willie from *Little House on the Prairie*. Strangely enough, it was there, at an upscale mountain ranch nestled in the Sierra Nevadas, that I was first exposed to punk rock.

My parents unintentionally raised me as a musical illiterate. They had a grand total of two record albums: Herb Alpert's *Whipped Cream & Other Delights* and the soundtrack to Barbra Streisand's *Funny Girl*. And they didn't even really listen to those; I think they just had them so they could seem normal when their friends came over. I didn't even discover the Beatles until I was in college.

The first music I remember getting excited about was the soundtrack to *The Rocky Horror Picture Show*. I caught it on cable when I was in fifth grade, and the next time it aired I held a tape recorder up to the TV speaker and taped the whole thing. I listened to it a hundred times, over and over, and went to see it live several times in Hollywood (and once in St. Louis, randomly enough).

By the time I was twelve my father had remarried, and I had a new baby half-sister, so when I would stay at my dad's house his seventeen-year-old neighbor would come over to babysit. She would play me Rush and Led

Zeppelin and Black Sabbath; she turned me on to the idea of just sitting back and listening to music for its own sake. She also poured me my first real drink: Kahlúa and milk. Now that's a good drink to turn a kid into an alcoholic. Tastes like chocolate milk!

So, anyway, back to the life-changing introduction to punk: Mountain Meadow Ranch in Susanville, California. The summer of 1981.

Each week the camp would have a dance, and the DJ (who I later came to know as Joe Escalante from the Vandals) would spin the usual disco fare. But one night he slipped in "Who Killed Bambi?" by the Sex Pistols and "Beat on the Brat" by the Ramones. I don't know what it was about those songs—maybe it was just because they stood out so starkly among Donna Summer and the Bee Gees—but when I got home at the end of the summer I immediately went to Rhino Records and asked the clerk, "Do you know a song called 'Beat on the Brat with a Baseball Bat'?" He chuckled and sold me the first Ramones album on cassette. To be honest, I really only liked three or four of the songs on it. But this "punk" thing was intriguing.

Eddie Machtinger—my elevator saboteur friend—met up with me one night soon after that to go to a movie. Once we were safely out of my mom's earshot, he said, "You know what? Let's go see this band play. I heard them—they're really good." So instead of taking the bus to Westwood, we took the bus to Hollywood to see Killing Joke at the Whisky a Go-Go.

Having never been to a punk show before, we had no idea what to expect. We showed up way too early and walked in as soon as they opened the doors. We went up to the balcony, ordered fries and Cokes from the bar, and stationed ourselves at a table in the far corner.

As first shows go, this was a weird one. Kommunity FK was the opener, and they were awful, but we stuck it out and waited for the headliner. Killing Joke was like nothing I'd ever heard before—pounding and relentless and loud as fuck. Everyone on the dance floor was slamming into each other. I didn't know what to make of it at the time; slam dancing had not yet been splattered all over the media, at least not any media I was paying attention to. Eddie wanted to go down into the pit. I said, "I'm not going down there!" But he went down and got into the mix anyway. He had a blast that night.

I, on the other hand, was scared shitless. Two skinheads stood directly behind me while Eddie was gone. They were taking drags off their cigarettes and slowly, deliberately blowing smoke down the back of my neck, trying to freak me out. Well, it fucking worked. We were 14 years old. We were in Hollywood after midnight. We were surrounded by creepy older kids slamming into each other like lunatics. And we stuck out like sore thumbs: I was wearing shorts and a pink Izod polo shirt. (I thought we were going to the movies!)

It was frightening and violent and uncomfortable and bizarre. So, naturally, when Eddie called me the following week and said, "There's another band playing called X," I immediately agreed to return to the Whisky. We showed up at the same time, sat at the same table, and placed the same order for fries and Cokes. But this time I hoped to fit in a bit better, so I wore a blue Izod shirt instead and put a safety pin through the little alligator logo.

That was how it began. I started going to shows all the time, picked up what records I could at Rhino, and bought a PiL pin to cover up the little horse on my other polo shirts. Not that I had any idea who or what a "PiL" was. I was a total poser (and was called out as such many times). I just took cues from the people I saw at shows and the older punks at my school. I bought a Buzzcocks shirt but had never heard the Buzzcocks. I bought a Dead Kennedys shirt; never heard Dead Kennedys. The music was almost secondary. I liked watching X, but it was more about the attitude and the craziness of the crowd and how dangerous it all seemed.

That's what kept me coming back. It certainly wasn't PiL. They were fucking terrible.

2

Smelly

If you follow my family tree on my mom's side, you'll end up back in Northern Ireland at the turn of the twentieth century, in a small fishing village called Culdaff. The legend goes that my great-great-grandfather owned a fleet of fishing boats and was the king ding-a-ling of the town. The English, as part of their policy of fucking with the Irish, decided they were going to take a chunk of everyone's fishing catch to feed the English people, which left the town without enough food or money.

My great-great-grandfather stopped making money, but he kept paying his workers out of his own pocket so they wouldn't starve. He did so until he was flat broke. And then he killed himself.

Two generations later, my grandfather emigrated from Ireland to Canada, joined the Canadian army, and ended up on a battleship headed for the French port city of Dieppe. The Dieppe Raid was an experiment by the

Allied Forces during World War II to see if they could capture and hold a major Nazi-occupied port before launching a larger operation like the one at Normandy.

The Germans were tipped off, and the Allies were unprepared. My grandfather was part of the first wave of the attack. He made it past the beach and into town but was taken down by a sniper. Five thousand Canadian soldiers stormed Dieppe; 3,367 were killed or wounded, including my grandfather, who sustained 14 gunshot wounds, was hit by shrapnel from explosives, and ended up in a German POW camp for two years.

But he survived. He made it back to Canada, was awarded over a dozen medals, and married my grandmother—a Scottish immigrant who performed as a showgirl in the Canadian version of the USO. He was a big, jolly guy who liked to drink, and he stomped around like Frankenstein because of his steel hip, his fucked-up foot, and his total lack of a left knee. He died in his early fifties when his injuries finally caught up with him.

That was my mom's side of the family. My dad doesn't talk about his family history much, so his side is more of a mystery. I can kind of understand why, based on the stories I've been able to piece together.

My sister somehow heard a story about a time when my father's father took my dad and his brother to a movie theater during the day. He sat them down and said, "Don't move, I'll be back later." He never came back. My dad and his brother were so scared of their abusive, alcoholic father that they actually stayed put for hours. My dad didn't even want to leave his seat to go to the bathroom. I have no idea how long he sat there in a puddle of his own urine.

I only know one other story about my grandfather: he was bludgeoned to death in a bar fight when my dad was ten years old. That one sentence is every detail I have to offer about the incident.

My father's mother was a sweet old lady who spoiled me whenever she could and even covered for me when I got into an accident while driving her car before I had a license. But she was also an alcoholic and, in her later years, a hoarder. She would go to the Pic 'N' Save across the street from her house and buy a hundred of those little green baskets for storing strawberries. She didn't have any strawberries to store; she just stacked the baskets up in a corner. Sometimes an older person might buy a magnifying glass to help them read—my grandmother would buy forty of them and leave them in a pile on the floor. Her tiny house was filled with old newspapers, magazines, knick-knacks, and bits of trash she couldn't bring herself to throw away. Her garage was filled to the ceiling with boxes of garbage.

As a kid I thought it was pretty cool that my grandmother had mounds of buried treasure I could climb around in. And I didn't see anything wrong with her asking me to mix her rum and Cokes, or how she always made herself a drink the minute she stepped through the door when she visited my parents. But I eventually realized her alcoholism and hoarding were symptoms of deeper mental problems. When my grandfather died, I don't think my grandmother was emotionally or financially equipped to raise my dad and his brother on her own.

Recently I was teasing my dad about how he never bought me a new bike when I was a kid and how I had to assemble my own bike from pieces I dug out of the trash. He told me to suck it up and reminded me that he didn't even have a single toy until he was twelve. After his dad died, he lived out of a suitcase as he was shuffled around to various family members, eventually finding a home with his Uncle John and Aunt Florence somewhere in upstate New York. They were a truly sweet couple that loved nature and hiking, and they took good care of my dad. I have fond memories of family trips to visit them; Uncle John would teach us about plants, Aunt Florence would read us Steinbeck, and my dad would truly relax in their presence.

But my dad's scars ran deep from those unstable, toyless, faintly detailed early years. Whatever he endured, it closed him off emotionally.

My parents met on a blind date and married young because my mom was pregnant with me at age seventeen. They settled in La Crescenta, which is like a suburb of a suburb of Los Angeles—it's as far north as you can get before hitting the Angeles National Forest. Four years after I was born, my mom gave birth to my sister Heather, and our cousin Terry moved in since he was at risk of being put into foster care.* My mom worked at the library of our elementary school and later got a job as the school's secretary; my dad did welding and plumbing jobs out of our garage and later opened his own plumbing shop up the street from our house.

My dad tried his best, but unfortunately his best included heavy drinking and regular doses of verbal and mental abuse. I was never beaten (aside from the occasional smack upside the head for insubordination), but I was also never hugged. I don't remember my dad hugging me even once when I was a kid. I never heard "I love you," ever. And whatever I did, I didn't do it right.

"Goddammit, Erik! What the fuck's wrong with you?"

---

*Terry was my dad's brother's kid. When my dad saw my uncle falling short as a father, he must've seen himself in Terry. Whatever the faults were in our family, my dad knew Terry was better off with us than lost in the system, and I'll always admire him for selflessly opening his home to the kid that I would come to consider my brother.

Today my dad is a completely different person, but the dad I grew up with terrified me. All the kids in the neighborhood were scared of him, too. He was 6-foot-4, 220 pounds, always angry, and usually drunk. When he'd come home from work, I would run into my closet and sit in the dark, listening to him storm through the house, bellowing "Erik!" at the top of his lungs. I'd listen to the anger grow and grow, until I had no choice but to come out, at which point he'd make me pull weeds or chop wood until he was satisfied.

I was always twitchy and jumpy because I never knew what to expect. Was I about to get yelled at or would I be ignored? Being ignored sucked but was usually preferable. One day he and his friends were having a few drinks in our garage (which was still his plumbing shop at the time). He called me in, and as soon as I entered he grabbed the waistband of my underwear, hooked me to a crane that he used to pick up pipes, and zipped me up into the air. I twisted like a piñata in front of his howling beer buddies, humiliated for his amusement.

All I wanted was to be accepted; all I got was belittled. Another time he summoned me while he was drinking with his friends in our living room.

"Get in here! Tell me a dirty joke."

"No, I'm gonna get in trouble . . ."

"You're not gonna get in trouble, it's fine, just tell me a dirty joke!"

"No, I don't want to!"

Finally he convinced me, and I told him my best fourth-grade-level knee-slapper:

"This lady has two dogs—one is named 'Titswiggle' and the other one's called 'Seymour.' One day she's taking a shower and the dogs get outside. So she runs outside naked, yelling, 'Seymour, Titswiggle! Seymour, Titswiggle!'"

My dad's friends laughed. My dad didn't. With fire in his eyes, he grabbed me by the back of my neck, dragged me into the bathroom, and washed my mouth out with soap.

Mom was always the peacemaker. She was an expert at shoveling things under the rug and pretending everything was okay, which was how she coped with her own father's alcoholism when she was growing up. She warned me when my dad was drunk or in a bad mood so I could make myself scarce. And whatever emotional support my dad didn't provide, my mom did her best to make up for it.

My parents, of course, had their own problems. Lying in bed at night, I would hear them screaming at each other. My dad held our house hostage with his hostility and it definitely took its toll on my mom.

One afternoon when I was seven, my mom grabbed my sister, my cousin Terry, and me and herded us into the family van. She was crying.

"What's the matter, mom?"

"Nothing, everything's fine."

"Where are we going?"

"I don't know. We're just gonna go away."

She drove and drove, crying and sobbing. I still don't know what set her off. All I know is she must have felt so fucking trapped. She never had her own life. She married my dad when she was eighteen, and here she was at twenty-five, trying to raise three kids while taking endless emotional abuse from a raging alcoholic.

We parked on top of a hill overlooking the city. Day drifted into night, and we all stayed quiet in the back seat while my mom sobbed. We were gone for at least four or five hours. As far as I know, that was the closest she ever came to leaving him. I don't remember going home, but we eventually ended up there. Even at age seven I felt bad for my mom. She never had a chance. We were all stuck.

◆ ◆ ◆

I don't want to shy away from the reality of how my dad's behavior affected me, but I don't think of him as a villain. Whatever struggles we had, there was a far darker struggle happening inside.

When I was ten years old my mom developed an infection that required emergency surgery, and she was in the hospital for over a week. I was sheltered from the details, but I overheard something about "the size of a grapefruit," which is never good. I get the sense she was closer to checking out for good than I would've wanted to know.

One night while she was hospitalized I awoke to a crash from the kitchen. I opened my bedroom door to find my dad, pulling all of our pots and pans out of the cabinets and hurling them to the ground. He had opened up a cupboard while making himself a late dinner and some of the pans fell out. It was the final straw of frustration that broke him after shouldering so much stress about my mom's condition. He cracked and tore the kitchen apart.

After the outburst he slumped to the floor, bawling. It was the only time I ever saw my dad break down. He was utterly helpless without my mom, and the prospect of raising my sister and me alone was probably scarier to him than his looming presence ever was to me. I stood in the darkness and watched him cry.

We would clash countless times over the following years, but in that moment, from the doorway of my bedroom, I saw him for what he truly was: a lost and troubled soul.

3

Melvin

The statistics may contradict me, but L.A. seemed safer back in the early '70s. I grew up in an apartment complex near the corner of Melrose and La Brea, and I walked home from elementary school on my own almost every day. There was an Italian place along the way, and whenever the chef would see me walk by he'd come out and give me a roll and some butter. Sometimes I'd stop at Winchell's or the candy store for something sweet, then I'd ride my bike and play with my friends until the streetlights came on. I rode the bus to Mann's Chinese Theater to see the original *Gone in 60 Seconds*, and the ride only cost a quarter. I sound like Grandpa Simpson—am I really that old?

I had plenty of friends, but I spent a lot of time by myself. One of my favorite games was climbing onto the roof of our garage and then going from rooftop to tree branch to fence to rooftop all the way down the block, never touching the ground. I would cross to the next block and find more garages and fences and rooftops to traverse, and I'd repeat the whole process until I ended up at this one particular orange tree. I'd reward myself with an orange and make my way back home, feeling invincible. From the perspective of a ten-year-old, I had the city wired.

It was an idyllic middle-class childhood. My parents were happily married, we took regular family vacations, I played little league and flag football. So it came as a bit of a surprise to my folks when, in fifth grade, my grades suddenly plummeted and I emotionally withdrew. I had been a good student and a happy kid my whole life, so this change in attitude seemed to come from nowhere.

After failing to solve this mystery on their own, my parents started driving me out to Brentwood once a week to see a therapist. I would sit in his office for an hour and he'd prod me with questions. Mostly I'd shrug him off with one-word answers or mumble, "I dunno." He put me through a series of tests, which I actually thought were fun. I interpreted inkblots and rearranged blocks to form specific shapes, and he eventually surmised there was nothing techni-cally wrong with my brain. In fact, he told my parents I was a pretty smart kid. After a few months, my parents stopped taking me to therapy, and for the next two decades they remained puzzled by my sudden shift of emotions.

Looking back, it started with a fight in the schoolyard.

It wasn't my fight—I was watching the new kid in school take a beating from a much bigger kid. I felt bad for the new kid. He was quiet and socially awkward, and he didn't seem like he wanted trouble. Since it was the end of the day, the parents were there to pick up their children. The new kid's fa-ther broke through the crowd and pulled the bully off his son. We all thought the fight was over, but then the new kid's dad held the bully's arms behind his back and shouted, "Punch him!" The son backed down, but the father insisted. "Punch him back! Hit him now!" The son sheepishly dis-obeyed and the scene fizzled out. It seems pretty horrible and fucked up to think about it now—a thirty-something-year-old man holding a ten-year-old boy's arms behind his back for a beating. But at the time I thought it was so cool. I wished my own dad and I had that kind of relationship. My dad helped me with schoolwork, took me camping, and built model rockets with me. But this other kid's dad was like a tough-guy superhero.

And he had a badass Trans Am. One day on my way home from school I saw him working on it in a nearby alley. It was sleek and black, with a glimmering gold Firebird logo on the propped-open hood. He greeted me and indulged my curiosity about the car for a while and then invited me in-side his apartment.

Up to that point, trusting adults had worked out pretty well. They gave me free rolls and taught me martial arts and sometimes took me to Disney-land. So I had no reason to think anything unseemly would happen in that apartment. That's probably why I didn't immediately bolt out the door when he said, "You know, I've seen you at school. And I always wondered what you would look like naked." It weirded me out a bit, but I didn't really comprehend what was about to happen. "Do you wanna show me what you look like when you're naked?" he asked.

I reluctantly showed him. And that's where my memory starts to get a bit foggy.

I don't think he got naked, and I don't think he fucked me, but I seem to have blocked out a lot of the encounter. I remember his hands wandering around my body and touching my genitals. I remember him asking me if it felt good and if I liked the way he was touching me. I remember looking at the door and wishing I was on the other side of it. And I remember wondering, "If I scream, will anyone hear me?"

He said he wanted to put his penis in my mouth, and I said I didn't want to do that. I said I wanted to leave, but he wouldn't let me go until I agreed to kiss him goodbye. He shoved his tongue into my mouth. His breath tasted like stale cigarettes. The kiss seemed endless, but I endured it and held back tears, hoping he would keep his word. He demanded a second kiss in the stairwell as I was leaving, but finally he set me free.

I went home and told no one.

It wasn't until I was in my mid-thirties that I told a brief and somewhat sanitized version of this story to my mom, but I've never revealed this much detail about that day to anyone—including my family and my band mates—until now. It was a horrible experience, but compared to what so many other children go through it could've been so much worse. I can at least appreciate the fact that there was strength in that little boy; he spoke up for himself and found courage when he needed it. But that courage didn't prevent the experience from taking a heavy emotional toll.

The dad and son moved away soon after. Maybe I wasn't the only one who went into that apartment. Maybe one of his other guests didn't keep his mouth shut like I did.

I don't remember their names. And they showed up in the middle of the school year and left before it was over, so the son doesn't exist in any of the class photos. They were ghosts. And they haunted me for years.

4

Smelly

One hugely positive aspect of growing up with my dad was his love of music. He cheaped out on every item in our house except for the stereo, and he started his weekend mornings by blasting Zeppelin, Cream, and Hendrix from huge, powerful speakers. Music was my dad's escape, and it quickly became mine, too.

I'd come home from school and thumb through my dad's enormous record collection, which contained as much early jazz and blues as it did rock 'n' roll. I would strap on the headphones, drop the needle on Pink Floyd's *Ummagumma*, and lie on the floor, diving into a world of psychedelic sound. I would fall asleep in the middle of the afternoon listening to the Who's *Tommy*, and at night I'd pass out in my bedroom listening to David Bowie on my little clock radio.

When I was thirteen I was flipping through some magazine and saw a blurb about punk rock that featured a picture of the Dead Boys. They were all greasy and slimy. They were dressed weird, and they looked . . . well, dead. Cheetah Chrome's skin was as pale as a corpse. It was creepy and bizarre and different from anything I'd seen on even the scariest Led Zeppelin album cover. I had no idea what the band sounded like, but I was already a fan.

During one of my family's weekly Sunday outings to the local swap meet, I came across the Dead Boys' *Young Loud and Snotty* album on cassette. I snuck it into my pocket and walked away. I stole my first punk album—how punk is that? I went home, and there it was on the very first track: *I don't need anyone / Don't need no mom and dad / Don't need no pretty face / Don't need no human race.*

Fucking. Rad.

Around that time, a kid named Lee moved to my neighborhood. He was tough and beat up other kids—he had that same scary appeal as that photo of the Dead Boys, so I befriended him. The Dead Boys had already sent me down a path of digging into alternative forms of music, but the deepest I got was Oingo Boingo. Lee introduced me to Dead Kennedys, Red Kross, the Germs, the Weirdos, and Rodney on the Roq. He told me if you had long hair and went to a punk show they would beat you up for being a hippie and cut your hair off with a broken bottle. It didn't sound so far-fetched; I found an article about punk in my uncle's *Penthouse* magazine that claimed punks were having sex in people's driveways and stabbing each other for fun. The photos showed people with bloody noses and shaved heads slamming into each other and fighting. I couldn't get enough of it.

Media hysteria about punk was standard at the time. Shows like *Donahue* fed off the fear of punk to boost their ratings. Punks like to cut themselves with razor blades and sacrifice animals! They knock down old ladies in front of grocery stores and steal their beer! If your kid gets into this music they'll end up in prison! It's violence and chaos!

Violence and chaos may have scared someone like my mom, but it had the opposite effect on me. I wanted the violence and chaos and razor blades and public sex and stolen beer! I cut my hair, drew the Germs logo on my shoes, and started hanging out with high school seniors with Mohawks.

In December 1981, one of my older friends found out about a punk show at Godzilla's, featuring Shattered Faith and China White. I don't know if I had heard either of those bands before the show, but it didn't matter—I was fucking going. Godzilla's was a DIY venue way out in the Valley founded by Shawn and Mark Stern of BYO Records. It was a far hike for the L.A. crowd, but it was only ten minutes from my house.

The whole week leading up to the show, Lee* was psyching me up: "Friday night! Get ready! Friday night!" And he was also psyching me out: "You're gonna get fucking beat up! You better be fucking ready!" The angst and anxiety gradually rolled to a boil.

Our group pulled into the parking lot the night of the show, and we pounded vodka and orange juice behind a dumpster while waiting for the bands to start. My older friends always teased me for being a poser, but now I was at an actual punk show, about to pop my cherry and become a real punker. My stomach was full of some very non-punk butterflies, and I'm sure it showed. Like when I cockily announced, "Finally, I'm around some other people like me!" and a couple in their twenties walked by and laughed at me.

I was young. I was shitfaced. I was ready to go inside.

There were band names and graffiti spray-painted on the walls behind the stage, and holes kicked in the walls of the bathroom. It was like the inmates had taken over the asylum. I was too hammered to know who was on stage or whether they were even playing actual songs, but it was the greatest sound I'd ever heard.

---

*Interesting tidbit: Lee banged my mom's best friend when he was in high school. He was eighteen and she was forty. They're still together.

I went down to the edge of the pit and some random guy grabbed me and chucked me into the middle of the dance floor. I could barely walk, let alone slam dance. I got clocked in the head and my skull rang out: BONGGGG-GGG! I felt like a pinball bouncing between a furious set of bumpers. I was being punched and pushed from all directions. Someone grabbed my shirt and it tore halfway down the back. This wasn't anything like the practice slam dancing I had done in my bedroom—I got completely pummeled.

I finally escaped the pit and stumbled, dazed and panting, back into the lobby area. I had survived my trial by fire. I was no longer a poser. I was a punker. I was bruised from being hit, and my fingers hurt from hitting others. In the morning I would be hungover and in deep shit with my mom for lying to her about where I'd been. I didn't care. I didn't need no pretty face. I didn't need no human race.

I shouted at the top of my lungs:
"FUCK LED ZEPPELIN!!!"

5

Melvin

Partial deafness due to cannon fire was an occupational hazard during World War I, especially when you were the guy who tended to the horses that towed around all the cannons. There's some painful irony in the fact that my grandfather, Willy Muchnick, moved to America to find better opportunities than those available in Eastern Europe and then was sent right back to Eastern Europe as part of the U.S. Army in order to earn his citizenship. With his service complete (and his hearing forever damaged) he settled in Ohio, brought over a bunch of other relatives, and, to better assimilate, changed his last name from Muchnick to Melvin.

Because my grandfather came from the Ukraine, English was his second language. He didn't want his sons to have accents, so he purposely didn't speak to them very much. The unintended result was that my dad learned not to talk much either, and the general quiet demeanor of the Melvin men was ultimately passed on to me as well.

My mom was more verbal than my dad but equally as economical with her words. Her mother was a nurse, and I guess watching people die from time to time turned her a bit morbid, so she passed down a certain harshness to my mother. I'm not saying we were a cold, emotionless, silent family. We just kept most of our thoughts to ourselves. And we internalized emotions and experiences (like, for instance, being molested) that maybe would've been healthier to share.

Beyond that, I was hugged, I was encouraged, I was told I was loved. I was extremely lucky to be born a Melvin. But I only learned to appropriately express that sentiment over the past few years.

Willy Melvin (or Grandpa Bill, as I knew him) owned a movie theater in Cleveland in the '50s where my dad worked as an usher and my mom was the popcorn girl and doesn't that sound like the beginning of the cutest story ever? It almost ended when my dad moved to California to go to college for engineering, but thankfully he convinced my mom to move out and marry him soon after. For the next forty years he worked on classified projects for companies like Aerospace, McDonnell Douglas, Boeing, and Hughes. Possibly for satellites, possibly for doomsday devices—who knows? His ingrained silence was an asset to his career.

My mom was the artist of the family. She eventually became an illustrator, painter, and ceramicist, and when I was younger she was very much into singing and playing guitar. She only knew a handful of songs, but she played her Martin acoustic for my sister and me, and I sat and listened to her practice all the time. The guitar became a focal point of my young life. Even though we were Jewish we celebrated Christmas every year, and after a while my mom started placing our presents around her guitar case rather than a tree.

Sometimes I talk to people who are intimidated by the idea of learning guitar, but it was such a familiar object to me that it seemed inevitable I would pick it up. My mom befriended a well-known folk musician named Bob Baxter and worked as an accountant at his guitar shop and performance space in Santa Monica. Soon enough I was learning the chords to "Yellow Submarine" from one of the instructors.

I hated it. I didn't have any finger strength or calluses, and the strings on the acoustic hurt my fingers, so I grew impatient, quit, and didn't pick up a guitar again for years.

Not that I didn't love music. I listened to my parents' collection of mellow '70s records, like Carole King, James Taylor, and Elton John. As I grew older, my friends turned me on to ELO, Queen, and Kiss (the latter was a little too harsh for me, having been nurtured by folk rock for so many years). When I was thirteen or fourteen my parents enrolled me in an after-school program at the Jewish Community Center, and one of the counselors introduced me to Adam and the Ants and the Go-Go's (and took me on different occasions to see both at the Greek Theatre in L.A.). I latched onto the new wave trend of the early '80s, thinking I was listening to punk rock. That summer, I went to day camp at the JCC and at the end of the season we took a trip to Magic Mountain. To mark the occasion, I painted a white stripe across my eyes, just like Adam Ant. While we were waiting in line for one of the roller coasters, some older, fat guy sneered at me and said, "Punk is junk." I was intimidated and scared, but it felt cool to be an outsider.

When I returned to school in the fall, all my friends looked and acted different. They told me they had been going to these things called "gigs" at a place called Godzilla's out in the Valley. Some of them had shaved their heads. My friend Bob Bonehead showed up to school wearing his pants inside out and his hair chopped into a Mohawk. My friend David Lustgarten played me the Circle Jerks' *Group Sex* record and said, "What if you became a punk right now?" We both laughed at the absurdity of the idea.

Group Sex opened my eyes to what punk really was. I still love that record. The time signatures and the lyrics and the furious speed of it all wasn't just a novelty, it was something that marked me permanently. I never knew music like that was allowed by law. I discovered all the English punk stuff next. I was a huuuuuge Crass fan. If you want to talk about a different sound, Crass was as far from Elton John as you could get. I had no clue what they were talking about half the time with their heavily layered references to British politics, but it was still so fucking cool.

Around that time, I befriended an older punk named Ed Brown, who had a souped-up flat-black Dodge Charger. He drove me to my first gigs, speeding the whole way and disregarding all stop signs. It's a wonder we weren't killed. A few years later, one of the temporary singers for NOFX died at one of the very same intersections we blew through to get to my first-ever punk show.

Despite my Ukrainian heritage I had never been to the Ukrainian Cultural Center on Melrose and Vermont, but that's where I experienced one of the most important cultural moments of my life. From the outside, the building looked like a medieval castle, with terra-cotta tiling and dramatic arched windows. The inside looked like a church, with art deco columns lining the walls, a curved ceiling, and a former movie-palace stage framed by velvet curtains.

The priests in charge of my conversion: Bad Brains. I'm pretty sure it was their first performance in Los Angeles. Ed wasn't planning on sticking around to watch them. It sounded like a silly name for a serious band, so we decided just to watch the openers: Jodie Foster's Army, the Lewd, and Bad Religion, each of whom put on sets with enough volume and energy to sufficiently push me further down the road of punk rock. During the show, I ran into my friend Benny, and we grabbed each other by the shoulders, screamed into each other's faces, and pulled each other into the slam pit. We spun through a blender of humanity and got clocked in the face and kicked in the legs, and we bounced out covered in bruises. And then we went back in again.

Ed told me we'd stick around for the first Bad Brains song just to check them out. But anyone who saw Bad Brains in the early '80s probably knows that once that first song started we weren't going anywhere.

The singer, H. R., was a blur. He ran all over the stage, throwing himself to the ground and then flinging himself back up again. He pulled off standing back flips and handsprings right on beat, all to the sound of the fastest, most amazing punk music I'd ever heard.*

I shaved my head within days. That was the show that officially made me a punk rocker.

My parents never said anything about my torn jeans or missing hair— like I said, we just didn't talk about that kind of stuff—but not everyone was so accepting. The day after I shaved my head a friend at school introduced me to a big, olive-skinned, square-jawed kid with intense eyes and an Israeli name. He was part of the Jewish Defense League, so I said, "That's cool, I'm Jewish, too."

"You look like a skinhead to me."

"I'm not a skinhead."

"I think you're lying."

He grabbed me by my collar and slammed me against the wall, almost lifting me off the ground. "Prove it!"

I opened my mouth and the traditional Hebrew blessing for the wine came spilling out in song:

"Baruuuuch ata Adonaiiii . . ."

As I finished the blessing he released his grip and smoothed out my shirt.

"All right. My mistake."

Maybe I should've just stuck with the Adam Ant makeup.

---

*Apparently Henry Rollins joined Bad Brains on stage to close out the night by singing "Pay to Cum," but I had no idea who he was at the time, so I wasn't as excited as everyone else in the crowd.

6

Mike

One night at Mountain Meadow Ranch summer camp someone stole some Bacardi from the owner's house, and we all mixed it into our sodas. It was my first time drinking with people my age. Super fun times.

I went back to the cabin to go to the bathroom, and while I was gone everyone else got busted and kicked out the next day.

This would prove to be a theme in my life: dumb fucking luck. When I was a kid, I owned a tabletop football game. An electric motor vibrated the board and your little plastic players moved randomly in every direction. You could only control one player at a time via a small magnet under the board. I feel like I'm that one player with the magnet under him. I don't believe in God, and I don't believe in destiny, but I can't shake the feeling that there's possibly a race of mole people living in the Earth's core playing a world-sized game of electric football and using some huge magnet to somehow always guide me to safety through the chaos.

Exhibit A is merely the fact that I survived the early '80s punk scene in Los Angeles without hospitalization or any major visible scars.

Southern California has produced some of the best music and the most famous legends in punk history. It was, and still is, the biggest punk scene in the world. But if the '80s L.A. scene was known for one thing above all else, it was violence. It's funny how some of us romanticize that era. I guess that's because it was so fun and exciting . . . to those of us who managed to keep our original teeth.

L.A. had the only scene populated by actual punk gangs. The Suicidals were from Venice Beach, spawned by the band Suicidal Tendencies. The Family was led by John Macias from the band Circle One. FFF was from the Valley, the L.A. Death Squad (L.A.D.S. for short) was from Hollywood . . . there were enough of them to fill a whole book of their own.

With gangs come rivalries, so basically every five or ten minutes at any given punk show people were beating each other to a bloody pulp. Bystanders got it just as bad as gangsters: once, the drummer from my first band was drinking from a water fountain at a Scream/Subhumans show and someone bashed his head from behind and fully ruined his mouth. Another time, my friends Eric and Albert were beaten with golf clubs outside the Olympic Auditorium. Once, we found Skinhead Ed (who would later become the singer for Royal Crown Revue) knocked unconscious in an alley behind the Cathay de Grande.

Everyone was on the wrong side of a beat-down sooner or later. It was just our reality. A lot of the people joining the scene weren't just doing it for the music or the fashion; they also wanted to kick the shit out of people without suffering any consequences. It was a scene with no rules taking place in DIY venues in the weirdest parts of the city. There were no cops around, and on the rare occasion when there were security guards they were usually friends with the thugs. Who was going to stop them?

My scrapes were relatively minor. At a backyard party hosted by the band Neighborhood Watch, a bunch of Suicidals jumped me and chopped off the Darby Crash rat tail I had been cultivating, but that was more friendly hazing than unchecked aggression. In front of the Cathay de Grande, a guy I knew named Bob Bonehead shoved me to the ground and stole my boom box, but that was more getting-money-for-heroin than spiteful robbery. And there was the GBH show at Perkins Palace where Mike Knox from the band Rigor Mortis grabbed me and head-butted me out of nowhere, but that was more . . . actually, that one was just because Mike Knox didn't like me.

Mostly, I had a lot of near misses. One night my friend Steve and I were outside a show, and Shawn MD from FFF (who had just gotten out of prison) walked up and asked Steve for a sip of his beer. Steve handed over his bottle; Shawn used it to bash Steve in the mouth. Three of Steve's teeth splintered into fragments, and his mouth overflowed with blood. I went with him to the hospital, but he had to drive himself: We had taken his car to the show, and I didn't know how to drive a stick.

It turned out Mike Knox had seen me from across the street and told Shawn to go fuck me up, but Shawn thought he was pointing at Steve. Thank you, magnet-wielding mole people.

One of the reasons I managed to go mostly unscathed was because I had friends in all the different gangs. At various times, I was invited to join the Suicidals, the L.A.D.S., and FFF, but I figured I was better off as an independent. Once I was walking with three of my Suicidal friends when ten L.A.D.S. started a brawl with them. I just stood by and watched. No one cared enough to beat up some random bystander, and there was no way I was going to put a permanent target on my back by picking a side. On the flipside, my best friend from third grade, Jordan Hiller,* went on to join FFF and was dead a year later.

---

*I knew Jordan from growing up in Beverly Hills. I went over to his house one day, and Jon Voight was playing Ping-Pong in the backyard. We played, and he beat me. But it was close.

Of course, the friendships that kept me safe weren't always string-free. One night I was picking up some friends to go to a Circle Jerks show, and Mike Muir from Suicidal Tendencies got into my car. This was huge for a sixteen-year-old punker, so it took some energy for me to play it cool as we drove from L.A. down to a venue called Flashdance in Anaheim. I don't know if Mike cared so much about seeing the show as he did about selling Suicidal Tendencies shirts to the audience afterward out of the trunk of my car.

On the way home, Mike made me speed the whole way, yelling at me to "Take it up to 90!" Whatever he would've done to me had I disobeyed would have paled in comparison to a mere speeding ticket, so I kept my mouth shut and floored it. When we finally got back to L.A., we stopped at a taco place. After we ate, we were walking back to the car when some guy rolled up on a Vespa. Without a word, or any provocation, or even the smallest break in his stride, Mike bitch-slapped the guy as hard as he could and knocked him off his scooter. No one said anything; we just thought, "Fuck!" to ourselves as we got in the car and drove away.

My casual friendship with John Macias from Circle One and the Family was even scarier. John was an infamously violent figure in the scene who was eventually shot and killed by police in 1991. John didn't "get into fights," John just "beat the fuck out of people." I watched him throw someone off a 15-foot drop at a construction site near the Whisky a Go-Go, and no one else watching was surprised or shocked.

When NOFX first started we played with Circle One a few times, and for some reason John took a liking to Eric Melvin and me. So one night when Circle One and the Vandals were playing together at a rented hall in a rough part of South Central, John asked us to hang outside while his band played to make sure no one's cars got broken into. Which was ridiculous because we were sixteen-year-olds who looked like twelve-year-olds; no way were we going to intimidate any potential criminals.

Eric and I were alone outside once the show started, until two members of the Family came out of the hall with a girl slung over their shoulders. She was obviously wasted, but she grabbed Eric Melvin, looked into his eyes and said, very clearly, "Help me."

I should maybe mention that members of the Family often wore military green and black face paint as part of their gang uniform. These guys were not only part of one of the most vicious gangs in L.A., but they also looked like Arnold Schwarzenegger in *Predator*.

One of them pointed at Eric and said, "You didn't see a fucking thing." And they took the girl down a dark stairwell behind the hall into the basement.

I wish I could say we helped that girl, but we knew the consequences could've been fatal if we'd tried. Even if we had called the police, we knew they wouldn't be in any hurry to help out some punks in South Central. And if they did show up everyone would've known exactly who called them, and we would've paid the price for ratting.

So we just went back into the show. The Vandals were performing, and the singer, Stevo, was standing on stage without pants on, flossing his genitals with a studded belt. Everyone in the room was laughing. Eric and I just stood there with blank looks on our faces, feeling worthless.

I may not have any visible scars from those days, but I've got demons. The guilt and shame of not helping that girl will always sting. If I could go back in time, I'm not sure that we could've done anything differently, but I'm haunted by it to this day either way. I'm sure Eric is, too.

I couldn't tell you what her face looked like, but I can still see her hand clamped on Melvin's shoulder. This was the punk scene we were a part of.

7

Smelly

I was always drawn to the dark side. Whether it was the punks at Godzilla's, or the bikers in my neighborhood, or the *Afterschool Specials* where Johnny smokes marijuana and gets swirling diamonds in his eyes and thinks he's a chicken and jumps off a building, it always aroused curiosity instead of fear.

I was destined to be a drinker. My dad gave me the first sip off any beer I fetched him as a kid, and I was sneaking booze by age ten. Drugs were much more intriguing.

Some of my dad's friends lived in a trailer parked in our backyard, and I knew they smoked pot in there. One day when I knew they were out, I went in and found their bong. I had no idea how it worked, so I tried putting my mouth over the mouthpiece and sucking in air. Then I sucked on the stem of the bowl and got a mouthful of burnt ashes. I coughed it all out, picked the grit from my teeth, and decided to do more research.

Soon after, my friend Mark brought over a pipe and showed me how to light it. I turned into a total stoner overnight. I didn't even get high the first few times; I just loved the idea of a stoner identity. It was all about "Hey!

Look at me! I'm the cool counterculture guy doing drugs!" so I smoked whenever I could, but it's hard to be a stoner when you're not actually getting stoned.

I had a steady supply of weed from my aunt and uncle, who lived next door to us, and happened to be bikers and drug dealers. They had a huge horizontal freezer filled with hundreds of one-pound bags of pot, so I skimmed a bit from each bag every time I babysat my cousins and it supplied me for years. It was their weed that finally kicked my ass after a good amount of posing. I was walking down the street while smoking with some buddies when everything started moving in freeze frames. It was like the sun had turned into an enormous, slow-acting strobe light and every moment existed on its own, disconnected from the moment before and after it. Now we were talking! (Although I was so high I was unable to actually talk.)

When I got to junior high, I smoked every day before and after school. I even made my own pipe in woodshop class and smoked *during* school. I grew my own marijuana plant in the back of my closet in this little plastic terrarium that originally contained a Venus flytrap (a random gift from my packrat grandma), and I had a Styrofoam cooler buried in my backyard filled with drug paraphernalia.

The pot turned into cross tops. The cross tops turned into Quaaludes. The Quaaludes turned into amyl nitrate. It was the classic experimentation and progression that I was ineffectively warned about on all those corny *Afterschool Specials*. And all of this before I was thirteen years old.

As I graduated from junior high to high school, I also graduated from pot and pills to acid. When I was fifteen my friend Monica and I took the bus into Hollywood to shop for records. I don't remember where I got the acid, but I remember walking along Hollywood Boulevard and laughing at everything. Some homeless guy was bugging us for change, and I was cracking up. The hilarity didn't subside until several hours later when we were at her parents' house. I started to feel paranoid because I knew her parents were home, and I was afraid they'd know I was high.

As I sat in the kitchen, I heard a ruckus coming toward me and my senses went to full alert. In ran two seven-year-old twin dwarves. I wasn't hallucinating: Monica's brothers were actually identical twin dwarves! I freaked out. "OH MY FUCKING . . . AHHHH . . . SCARED . . . WHAT THE FUCK'S GOING ON?!"

Monica tried to calm me down. "Be cool, be cool!" Then her mom came into the kitchen. I knew her mom didn't like me—she had probably seen the same *Donahue* show about punk as my mom did—and that escalated the paranoia. The dwarf kids were running around, the mom was staring daggers at me. I got up and bolted.

My mind convinced me I couldn't walk home on the usual streets because my parents might drive by and bust me, so I hopped a fence and climbed into a 12-foot-deep cement drainage trench that I knew would eventually lead me home. The trench, however, ran past the yard of a juvenile detention facility, and thirty or forty kids came running up to the fence at the edge of the yard. They were throwing rocks, shaking the fence, and shouting, "Fuck you!" from 12 feet over my head. I was whimpering like a frightened puppy. I ran to my mom's friend Dee Dee's* house. She was an artist and a hippie; I knew she'd be cool. I showed up at her door with tears streaming down my face.

"I'm on acid, I can't fucking handle it. I need to sit down and relax."

"Sit down, honey, it's okay, everything will be cool. You're in a safe place."

She talked me down from the mindfuck overload of the dwarves and Monica's mom and the drainage trench and walked me through the rest of my trip for the next three hours.

It was such a fucking frightening experience, you'd think I would have sworn off acid forever. But like everything else that was designed to push me away, it only drew me closer. Just like with that first punk show, I had been through the spin cycle and survived. And I wanted to go again.

Instead of taking my chances in the outside world, I would just go to Dee Dee's house and do acid with her son Josh, so I was always in a safe place. She never supplied it, but she let us do it safely under her roof. I was dropping acid at least once a week, and over the years the good trips outnumbered the bad. I remember once watching a freckle on my arm turn into an ant, crawl to the tip of my finger, turn into a droplet of water, drip upward, cause a ripple pattern on the ceiling, which turned into a swirl, out of which emerged a horse that drifted toward my face, and when I was nose to nose with the horse, the skin peeled away from its head until I was staring into its skull.

Life on the dark side was fucking cool.

---

*Interesting tidbit: Dee Dee illustrated the flames on the cover of the Dead Kennedys' *Give Me Convenience or Give Me Death* album. She was also the one who slept with Lee.

8

Melvin

Chuck Norris taught my dad karate.

Well, technically, Chuck Norris's partner, Pat Johnson, taught my dad a Korean martial art called Tang Soo Do, but Chuck taught a few of the classes my dad was in, and Pat was the guy who played the referee in *The Karate Kid*, so that's still pretty cool.

Before he was a movie star, Chuck opened a small chain of karate studios in Southern California, and my dad regularly attended classes at the Mid-Wilshire location. I wish I could brag that Chuck (or even Pat) taught me, too, but I was only nine or ten when my dad started bringing me along to the studio, and a separate instructor taught the kids.

Since Chuck was tight with Bruce Lee, the students from all of Chuck's studios were part of an exhibition to celebrate the premiere of one of Bruce's movies at (where else?) the Chinese Theater on Hollywood Boulevard. They closed off local traffic for the occasion and had one of those Chinese dragons weaving down the street while I, and several dozen of my fellow students, showed off our Tang Soo Do skills in the middle of it all. We weren't really organized or doing any of our drills in unison or anything; we were just randomly kicking, punching, and blocking the air. We felt like badasses, but we probably looked spastic and ridiculous.

I can only think that it was my Tang Soo Do training that gave me the confidence to continue exploring the L.A. punk scene, because I can't think of any logical reason why a kid with my skinny teenage frame would've otherwise felt safe at a place like the Olympic Auditorium.

The Olympic was a massive concrete sports arena with 55-foot ceilings and room for over 7,000 people. It was constructed for the 1932 Olympic Games in Los Angeles, and before it became a nerve center for the the '80s hardcore punk scene it hosted dozens of historic boxing matches and was used as a filming location for movies like *Rocky* and *Raging Bull*.

This was fitting because every time there was a punk show at the Olympic, someone was getting knocked out. Even before you walked inside there were probably at least two guys duking it out in the parking lot. One night I watched from the balcony as a swarm of Suicidals ganged up on one guy on the venue floor. It was just fists and elbows and arms, and no one was even trying to stop them. It was a massacre.

And at the end of the night the police helicopters circled overhead, and sometimes you'd have to dodge billy clubs on the way to your car. It wasn't a place for normal, sane people. I'm thankful I avoided any serious tangles down there because my Tang Soo Do green belt probably wouldn't have amounted to much.

It certainly didn't help when I was running from the cops after the infamous Dead Kennedys riot at the Longshoremen's Hall in Wilmington. When the DKs finished, the cops were waiting for us in two lines on either side of the back exit. People were trying to leave and the cops whaled on us as we ran out. A billy club cracked me on the hand as I ran the gauntlet and it stayed swollen for a week. My hand was covering my head, so that club could've landed in a far worse place. In fact, I watched in horror as other people suffered that exact fate.

But I kept coming back for more. As much as the scene was plagued by bloodthirsty psychopaths and barbaric cops, it was also populated by a fascinating cast of characters. People sometimes say Mohawks are part of a punk rock "uniform," but no two Mohawks were alike. Everyone spun the punk rock style his or her own way. Plus, you know, the music was pretty good.

It was the three-chord simplicity of punk that gave me the confidence to pick up a guitar again. My friend Benny showed me how to play a power chord with two fingers. I made a $25 down payment on a Randy Rhoads model Charvel owned by an acquaintance at school, but when I couldn't come up with the rest of the cash, he took the guitar back and kept my money. Later I bought a $170 Peavey guitar with a natural woodgrain finish and a black pickguard with money I had saved from lifeguarding at the Jewish Community Center pool, and Benny and I started our first band.

Okay, "band" might be a strong word. We didn't have a name, we didn't write any songs, we didn't have a drummer, bassist, or singer, and we never performed publicly. It was really just the two of us hanging out at Benny's house, showing each other guitar parts we had figured out from Black Flag and Descendents records. But we called it a band, and who are you to say we weren't one?

The problem was that Benny lived way out in Eagle Rock and I didn't have my driver's license. I wanted to start a real band, with real songs and real gigs. I was sick of the older kids at Fairfax High laughing at my friends and me and calling us posers. I read the scene reports in *Maximum Rocknroll*, where punks from around the country wrote about the bands, clubs, and drama in their area. I wanted to get on the road and explore exotic places like Texas and Florida and Idaho.

My friend Dylan was a drummer, so he was my first recruit. Dylan knew a straight edge punk kid named Steve from Orange County who was supposed to start singing for a band called America's Hardcore. We convinced him to sing for us instead. And Dylan knew another musician who could fill the last remaining slot in our lineup:

"I'll call a guy I know named Mike. He plays bass."

Mike during the False Alarm days.

9

Mike

Chris, Mitch, and I wanted to get laid. There was a punk girl named Laura at our school, so we figured we could start a band, get her to sing, and somehow, in the process, convince her to sleep with one of us. Mitch's dad bought

Eric Melvin.

him a guitar for Christmas, so Chris said he'd play the drums, and I volunteered to play bass.

I bought a used Hondo II bass and a Fender amp at a guitar shop on Sunset, and we started jamming under the name PTA. But Mitch never really learned the guitar, so he just played on one string. And Chris ditched us to join Mike Knox's band, Rigor Mortis. And we had no PA. So the whole Laura plan never panned out.

I figured being in a band would still eventually help me get laid, so I started a new group with my friend Floyd as the singer/guitarist and our friend Justin on drums. We called ourselves False Alarm, and you could almost say we were a real band because we actually played one show.

We managed to write and record nine horrible hardcore songs and send a tape to *Maximum Rocknroll* for review. Tim Yohannan wrote, "I can't hear the words for shit as they're spit out at 150 mph and subjected to the kind of recording techniques that were probably used in the 1920s," and then he went on to (rightfully) mock one of the songs Floyd had written called "Fags Suck."

We booked a show at a cool underground punk venue called the Anti-Club, but Floyd's mom found out about it and wouldn't let us play, so we

Eric Sandin.

had to cancel. So our first—and what would turn out to be our only—gig was at a house party in Beverly Hills.

We performed our nine songs, and people were polite enough to watch us, but apparently they didn't feel the need to humor us by dancing. But the one cool thing that came out of that night was meeting my first girlfriend, Natalie.

I guess she had a thing for sloppy Jewish musicians, because right after we played she pulled me behind a bush and made out with me. In hindsight, I should've probably known that she'd eventually cheat on me and nearly get me killed, but none of that mattered to my sixteen-year-old virgin self. Being in a band was starting to pay off.*

+   +   +

My mom couldn't help but notice my spiked hair, weird friends, and the occasional black eyes and bruises. She was upset that her plan to move me to Beverly Hills and keep me on the straight and narrow had somehow backfired. I think her breaking point was probably when I called her from the Wilcox jail.

My friends and I were drinking in the alley behind the Cathay de Grande before a Personality Crisis show when four police cars surrounded us. As they rounded us up, Bob Bonehead (the "friend" who stole my boom box for drug money) tossed some heroin on the ground in front of me so he wouldn't get caught with it in his pocket. The cops found the heroin, assumed it was mine, and slapped the cuffs on me. They took us all to jail, and mom was my only out.

There I was, sitting with all these junkies and punks on a bench when my mom walked in, threw her purse at me, and launched into a rant: "What the fuck are you doing?! Why are you out so late?! I told you about this stuff!" The cops, junkies, and punks were all cracking up.

But in classic Mike-always-squeaks-by fashion, they dropped the charges and let her take me home. It was a Friday night before a holiday weekend. Everyone else was locked up through Tuesday. So who's laughing now?

My mom forbade me to return to the Cathay after that, and she put me in therapy. I disregarded her order to stay away from punk shows, but I agreed to the therapy. What teenage kid doesn't have problems that could use a little talking out? For about six months I vented about my issues with my dad and everything else that was weighing me down. Then things took a turn . . .

---

*False Alarm only lasted for a few months. After I left I didn't speak to Justin again for almost thirty years. He's a hairdresser now. Floyd kept the band going for a while, and they released a CD, which is advertised as "featuring Fat Mike from NOFX!" even though I didn't play a note on the album. Floyd is currently a lawyer, so I'm guessing it would be pointless to sue.

After that first False Alarm show, Natalie and I continued making out on a regular basis, and then one night after a Peter and the Test Tube Babies show she came back to my mom's apartment to spend the night. We were kissing on the bed, and I nervously started to put my penis inside her vagina. She stopped me and said, "I'm on my period." I said, "That's okay," because, seriously ladies: guys do not give a shit. Especially when they're mere centimeters away from becoming a non-virgin. She explained, "I gotta take my tampon out," but I just said, "Let's do this!" and started fucking her. After five minutes or so she said, "This feels awesome, but I gotta take this tampon out. It's too weird."

She went to the bathroom while I looked down at my blood-soaked dick and thought, "Yeahhhh!" All was right in the world. Except for Natalie's vagina. Her tampon was wedged inside her and she had to go to the hospital the next morning to have it removed. Whoops.

Two therapy sessions after losing my virginity, my psychiatric problems seemed to completely disappear.

◆　◆　◆

Natalie was a tough chick. She ran with an all-female gang called the Girls Brigade. They beat up other girls and stole their shoes and purses. And she was wild: We fucked in cars, we fucked at construction sites, and she once gave me a blowjob under a table at the Cathay while Crucifix played. I was a teenager in love.

I even sort of defended her honor when I found her ex-boyfriend pulling her hair with one hand and slapping her with the other outside a show in the Valley. He was a member of FFF and a gnarly dude. But I gathered enough courage to walk up and say, "Um, can you stop doing that?"

He shoved her away and suddenly I was surrounded by a dozen FFF members. He punched me in the face and I went down. Two other guys tried to grab me but I somehow slipped away and ran to my friend's car. I dove through his open window and he drove off. Considering the circumstances, this was the height of '80s L.A. punk chivalry.

So you can imagine how crushed I was when, four months into our relationship, some Suicidals threw me against a wall at the Olympic and said, "If you ever talk to Natalie again we're gonna kill you." That's how she broke up with me.

I had no idea anything was wrong between us. After we "broke up" I ran into her outside the Olympic. She screeched, "What the fuck are you doing here?!" took off her spiked belt, and whipped me repeatedly with the buckle. In no time, we drew a crowd of probably a hundred people. I knew if I hit her back I would be destroyed by the salivating wolves surrounding us. They were all waiting for the smallest excuse to tear me to pieces, so I just ran as fast and as far as I could.

They say you never forget your first kiss. They say you never forget your first lay. I say you never forget the first time you get the shit beat out of you in public by a sixteen-year-old girl.

10

Smelly

I was always tall, but as a kid I felt skinny and weak, and I wrestled with a lot of inferiority issues. Dealing with my dad and riding a bike that was pieced together from garbage didn't help. I dealt with it all through humor and became the class clown. If someone dared me to drink a Taco Bell cup full of muddy gutter water, I chugged it down for the laughs. If someone dared me to leap off a roof, I risked life and limb for acceptance.

So when I stepped up from drug user to drug dealer it wasn't so much because I needed the money. I wanted validation.

I would skim handfuls of pot from my aunt and uncle's massive freezer stash and sell it to my fellow junior high students. One of my friends' moms had undergone several surgeries, so she had hundreds of pills that we stole and sold, and when I started doing acid I bought sheets at a time and subsidized my own habit by selling a portion of the sheets to my friends.

I was making a few hundred bucks a week, which was a significant amount of money for a fourteen-year-old, but I couldn't spend any of it because I knew my parents would notice if I suddenly had a new bike they didn't pay for. So I wasted most of the cash down at the arcade, or just bought more drugs.

My dad wanted to instill a solid work ethic in me, so I had summer jobs starting at age ten. I began with a paper route, then from age eleven to thirteen I swept up at a woodworking shop for a dollar an hour. At fourteen I worked as a janitor at a factory. In high school I worked on an assembly line putting vitamin bottles on a conveyor belt for eight hours a day like I was in *Laverne and Shirley*, but without the laugh track. I only made three bucks an hour, so I couldn't mask any big drug-money purchases with my legitimate income, but I went out on a limb for one big ticket item: a used drum set.

I took guitar lessons for a year when I was eight, but the teacher had me learning "Skip to My Lou" and "A Horse with No Name" when all I wanted to play was Kiss and Black Sabbath, so I walked away with only four chords under my belt. Years later when Lee and his friends wanted to start a punk rock band they all knew more chords than I did, so they told me to play drums instead.

I found a shitty kit for 200 bucks and set it up in the laundry room. I didn't have cymbal stands, so I nailed ropes from the floor to the ceiling and rested my crash and hi-hat cymbals on knots tied in the middle. When I hit the crash it would swing away and then back toward me, so while I was playing I had to dodge it like one of those double-end punching bags they use to train boxers.

My friend Dan showed me a basic drum beat, but I never took any lessons. I listened to records and learned by ear, and I mimicked what I saw drummers doing on (the then-brand-new) MTV. I picked it up surprisingly fast, and thankfully most punk drumbeats were simple enough for me to copy. I knew playing drums was my key to being in a band, which was the key to being a part of the punk scene, which was the key to more validation and acceptance, so I poured myself into it. Drumming was fun, but I could've just as easily poured myself into playing bass or keyboards or a fucking jaw harp. I just wanted to belong.

The Acid Tommy Experience (or was it the Tommy Acid Experience?) was me on drums, Lee and Dan on guitar, and a guy we called Flipper (because he really liked the band Flipper) on bass. I don't know if we ever had a singer. We mixed MC5 and Stooges covers with classic rock stuff like Iron Butterfly. We played a few parties, but by "party" I mean like ten of our weird friends drinking beer at someone's house. Mostly we just jammed in the laundry room.

The older guys in the band went away to college the next year, but by my sophomore year of high school I had been going to punk shows pretty regularly and had gotten good enough at drumming that a girl I had dated put me in touch with an established local band called Caustic Cause.

Caustic Cause could fucking play. They were in their thirties and were really talented musicians, and I was just some sixteen-year-old with cymbals tied to the ceiling. So it was a huge compliment when they deemed me competent enough not only to join their band but also to be worthy of them driving out to La Crescenta to practice at my house, since my mom wouldn't drive me to their practice space. My drumming skills accelerated rapidly because it was so much easier to jam with people who knew what they were doing, and of course because I wanted to keep up with their skills and expectations.

I don't remember my first time on stage with them—none of our shows were all that spectacular. We played in random bars and maybe once at Madame Wong's (a legendary restaurant in Chinatown that hosted every now-famous L.A. punk, new wave, and hair-metal band in their early days). No one really remembers Caustic Cause these days, but at the time people were impressed when I dropped the name of my band.

Despite the fun and the talent and the always-sought-after validation, after a year and a half I slowly lost interest in Caustic Cause. Their style was more old school, and I was more into the L.A. hardcore sound, like Black Flag and Wasted Youth. Plus they were all way older than me with wives and families. I wanted to play with people who were closer to my own age so we could hang out as friends rather than just as band mates.

And I always felt like they were doing too much coke. At one practice, the singer, out of nowhere, yelled, "I'LL FUCK YOU UP!" and then rushed the bass player and beat the fuck out of him.

So when I met a guy named Mike who was exactly my age and who liked the same music as I did and who (at the time) didn't do excessive amounts of coke, I was tempted to jump ship.

But I didn't.

◆ ◆ ◆

My memories of early punk shows are scattered and faded, but I distinctly remember going to see Black Flag and the Bangs (before they became the Bangles) at a club called the Cathay de Grande.

It was a matinee show, and I was drunk. So drunk, in fact, that the room was spinning. I grabbed hold of the bar to steady myself and stuck my fingers down my throat so I could hopefully throw up some of the alcohol I no longer wanted inside me. Security saw me attempting to ruin the carpet and 86'd me out the front door in classic headfirst fashion.

I wobbled down the street by the club and randomly bumped into El Duce, singer for the notoriously offensive band the Mentors, who looked like the result of a failed experiment to create a human-walrus hybrid. I was a fan of his band, so I started slurring some speech his way. El Duce responded by sticking his finger up his nose, withdrawing a sizable booger, and jamming said booger into my mouth. I spat it out and stumbled away.

I found some hedges to pee in nearby, but I lost my balance and fell backward with my dick still in my hand, peeing all over myself. My head landed on the edge of the curb, and as I rolled over in pain I looked into the gutter and saw a dead baby bird maybe an inch from my face. It must have just hatched: no feathers, just translucent skin and bulging eyes. As gross as it was, I couldn't summon the strength to move. I lay there face to face with it for hours.

My friends found me when the show was over and scraped me off the pavement. Boogers on my breath, piss all over my clothes, and a dead bird for a pillow. That's how I'll always remember the Cathay de Grande.

◆ ◆ ◆

I'm sure other people had way worse childhoods than I did (even within my own neighborhood), but it's worth mentioning for this next part that I never had a skateboard growing up.

Okay, that's not entirely true: My folks bought me one of those plastic boards made for little kids for like four bucks at the local swap meet, but I couldn't ride something like that off a ramp or around the streets.

When I was working as a sweeper at the woodworking shop, they sometimes let me fuck around with the equipment, so I took a heavy piece of mahogany that was intended to be a cabinet door, cut it to the approximate shape of a skateboard, attached the cheapest trucks and wheels I could find, and glued tuna-can lids to the base of the tail so it would withstand grinding. It worked—technically—but it was mortifying when I showed up to skate with my friends, who all had brand-new boards (or at least store-bought boards where the tail flipped up, unlike mine, which was defiantly flat).

Skate parks popped up everywhere in Southern California in the late '70s. One opened less than half a mile from my house, literally across the street from my dad's plumbing shop. My parents wouldn't allow me to have a membership to the park, so every day after elementary school I'd go to my dad's shop to work for a couple hours and stare through the fence, watching every other kid in the world have fun on their Alva, Sims, and Logan Earth Ski decks. Even if I had been allowed to join them, I would've felt like a character out of *Gummo* walking in with my cabinet-door-and-tuna-can-lid monstrosity.

And that's why today, more than thirty years after the fact, I have such a vivid memory of meeting Fat Mike.

I was hanging outside the Cathay de Grande when a scrawny kid with funny hair skated by on a special-edition Black Flag skateboard. It was decorated with an original Raymond Pettibon design that featured a leaping demon surrounded by dozens of Black Flag logos. It both taunted and tempted me, and it looked like it was fresh out of the box. It was everything cool and everything I coveted. I complimented him on it, and he let me try it out. It was like touching God's boob.

We chatted for a while. He told me his name was Mike and he was in a band called False Alarm, and I casually bragged that I was drumming for Caustic Cause. He said he was looking for a new drummer and gave me his phone number. We kept in touch, but I could never jam with him because my parents wouldn't drive me to practice in Beverly Hills (which today I understand since it would have been at least an hour drive each way in L.A. traffic).

I liked Mike, though. We loved the same bands and had similar senses of humor, so we talked on the phone about music and met up at shows. We were good friends in no time.

My first meeting with Eric Melvin didn't involve skateboards, so I remember it less distinctly, but he told me he was in a new band with Mike, and they wanted me to join. I was noncommittal at first, but Melvin told me Steve from America's Hardcore was singing with them, so I said, "Okay!" I dug America's Hardcore, and Mike, Melvin, and I all had driver's licenses by that point so practicing was no longer a geographical challenge.

I showed up to practice, but Steve never did. And Mike and Melvin were fucking terrible musicians. It was clear I would be taking a huge step backward if I left Caustic Cause to join them. But I meshed with Melvin as well as I did with Mike, and we'd all get together, ride skateboards and listen to music. Friendship started to take precedence over musicianship.

Until we played our first show.

11

Melvin

Steve's excuse for never showing up to the first practice was that he couldn't get a ride up from Orange County. Dylan quit after the first practice with no excuse offered; Mike and I could've easily walked away as well, but Mike said he'd call a guy named Erik who played drums in Caustic Cause.

Erik kind of blew us off about joining the band, but one night I ran into him at the Olympic Auditorium and introduced myself. He was carrying around a pair of drumsticks because he had lied his way into the show by convincing the people at the door he was drumming for one of the bands. It was only a quick hello. I told him Steve from America's Hardcore was going to be our singer, which was a double bluff: Not only had Steve skipped our first and only practice, I don't think he had performed with America's

Hardcore at that point. But it seemed to pique Erik's interest enough to at least show up to one of our practices.

Steve flaked out on the second practice as well. I'm not sure he ever intended to join us, but for a long time, even after we started playing gigs, I kept thinking he'd eventually show up and be our singer. I don't think Erik was as deluded about Steve as I was, and he must have noticed that Mike and I (especially I) were absolutely clueless about how to play our instruments, but I think he just enjoyed hanging out with us.

I knew we weren't good. I knew songs like "Ant Attack" were never going to make us popular. But I thought we'd somehow get better. I didn't know it would take eight years, but I knew we had to write our first terrible song in order to write our next slightly better song. I was willing to put in the necessary work to get our band on the road so we could start having adventures. Writing quality music and playing guitar well were secondary concerns at best.

That's probably why I was in such an ill-advised rush to get us on stage that first night at the Cathay de Grande, even though Steve had still never made it to any of our practices, we barely had any songs, and Mike was totally wasted.

12

Mike

If there's one club in L.A. that would be considered the most significant in NOFX history, it would probably be the Cathay de Grande. It sat at the corner of Argyle and Selma and they had three or four punk shows every week (and on Tuesday nights it only cost a buck to get in). It ran for four or five years, and an unattributed source on Wikipedia called it "the most dangerous club in America."

That's where I met Erik Sandin.

I was skateboarding outside the Cathay one night, and Erik complimented me on my Black Flag deck. Admittedly a cool board, but he really seemed to drool over it for some reason.

We got to talking about skateboards and music, and he mentioned he played drums in Caustic Cause. Justin had left False Alarm, so Floyd and I had been on the lookout for a replacement. I invited Erik to join our band, but his mom wouldn't drive him to Beverly Hills for practice.

Sometime later I got a call out of nowhere from a guy named Steve who was supposed to be the new singer for a well-known Valley band called America's Hardcore. Erik had passed him my number and told him I played bass, so he asked if I wanted to jam with him and a few friends. I showed up to rehearsal and met the drummer, Dylan, and the guitarist, Eric Melvin.

Melvin and I brought in two songs each, and we fleshed them out as instrumental numbers. Maybe we would've written some vocal parts if we'd had a PA for Steve to sing through, but at least we were off to a pretty good start. Then Steve quit after the first practice. We played our instrumental songs at a house party within a few weeks, and Dylan quit soon after that.

Melvin and I hit it off famously, though, and asked Erik Sandin once again to join us as a drummer. We agreed to rehearse on his side of town in order to seal the deal. His dad had a plumbing workshop near their house where we could make a ton of noise. We came up with four songs in a day or two, and we called ourselves NOFX.

I've always hated the name. It was a rip-off of a Boston band called Negative FX that had recently broken up. Eric and Erik liked that name and suggested NOFX. I said, "It sounds just like Negative FX." They said, "No, it's different." In fairness, I didn't really have any better ideas. I wanted to call us the Banned, but it was two against one. I thought, "Whatever . . . it's not like it's going to be something I'll have to live with for the rest of my life."

Within a week of that stupid decision I found myself beer-bonging a 40-ounce malt liquor outside a Justice League show at the Cathay de Grande. Erik Sandin knew the Justice League guys, so after they were done he asked them if his new band could jump up and play a few songs on their equipment.

I believe it was Elie Wiesel who said, "The opposite of love is not hate, it's indifference." We were so bad we didn't even earn the crowd's boos. No one slam-danced out of pity. No one clapped out of politeness. They just stared at us for a bit and then walked away.

That was the first NOFX show.

I don't know how we ever got booked at the Cathay again, but we played four or five more shows there (including the farewell party when the venue finally closed) and opened for bands like Adrenaline O.D., the F.U.'s, Iron Cross, Sin 34, and Reagan Youth.* All of our performances were met with the same deafening apathy. We never played to more than ten people, and we never made more than five bucks. Except for one night when the club booked too many bands: we made thirteen dollars for agreeing *not* to play.

Something I've learned from having my own record label and meeting so many bands over the years is that everyone thinks their band is good, regardless of any evidence to the contrary. We were no different. It didn't matter that we couldn't get booked anywhere other than the Cathay, or that we never got a single compliment, or that we were being paid more to leave a show quietly than to perform. I listened to our demo a hundred times. We were fucking great!

---

*Reagan Youth stayed at my mom's apartment once when she was away for the weekend. I took them to Capitol Records to master their first record, and I drove them to the Olympic, where they opened for Dead Kennedys. In front of 3,500 punk rockers they opened their set with a cover of "War Pigs" by Black Sabbath—all eight minutes of it. The crowd was dumbfounded, and I was floored. It was maybe the biggest show they ever played, and they opened with Black Sabbath because fuck you. They only had a twenty-five-minute set, and they used eight minutes of it to do that song. It was one of the most important lessons about punk I've ever learned: You can't just get up on stage and do what the crowd wants you to do. You always have to throw them off a little bit. It's been a key part of my philosophy with NOFX ever since. And it's why some people love us and some people hate us, even if they just walked out of the same show.

13

Smelly

I once met a gorgeous California girl with perfect Farrah Fawcett hair named Sandra at the park near my house. I gathered the courage to ask her to ride bikes with me, and shockingly she agreed. We pedaled along with the sun shining on our faces—if it had been a movie there would've been an upbeat '70s folk music soundtrack and lots of dissolves.

And then it hit me: I had to take a shit.

We were miles from my house, but the gurgles in my gut were sending a very clear message: "This is happening right now, whether you like it or not." Mercifully, the bike path ran past a little outhouse thing, so I excused myself and hoped I could handle things quietly.

I whipped my pants off, sat down, and let loose. But what I didn't realize was that the tail of my oversized mesh football jersey had not cleared the drop zone. I released a couple quarts of pudding out of my ass, and at least a full pint or so was unknowingly retained by my shirttail.

After I finished, I thought I would give Sandra a little sexy treat by exiting the outhouse with my shirt off. So I grabbed my shirt collar and pulled the shirt up over my head. As I was pulling, I could feel something heavy dragging along my back. And then up my neck. And then through my hair. And then down my forehead and the bridge of my nose.

I realized what it was when I looked at the unnaturally brown shirttail after it was off. I had shit running from my ass to my nose, like the stripe on the back of a skunk. There was no sink or mirror in the outhouse. It was Game Over. The sense of humiliation was so intense I felt like I was having an out-of-body experience. I walked out and, without a single word, got on my bike and rode home. I never saw Sandra again.

Even that was less embarrassing than the first NOFX show.

◆ ◆ ◆

We didn't have a show booked; we were just hanging out at the Cathay de Grande like always. Melvin was friends with the band on stage and somehow thought it would be a good idea to ask them if his new band, which had only begun a couple weeks prior and whose singer had spent the evening beer-bonging in the parking lot, could get up on stage and play a few songs on their equipment.

I don't know if I've properly underscored just how bad Mike and Melvin were at their instruments at the time, but they were seriously awful. Being shitfaced did not enhance Mike's abilities, and Melvin trying to mask his shyness by monkeying with his amp and rarely facing the audience did not help his performance. I don't like making excuses for myself, but I was handed two drumsticks that were so chewed up I got gnarly blisters by the end of our first song. Even if we had written the best songs in the world, we still would've sounded like shit.

We had not written the best songs in the world. Somewhere in the middle of the second song I realized what a horrible band we were. The crowd just stared at us blankly as we embarrassed ourselves for six back-to-back songs.

Mike was only slightly less drunk at the next couple of bad shows we played, so Melvin and I talked about kicking him out. That idea may have been sparked by Melvin's girlfriend, Chelsea, who wanted to replace him. I can't imagine where my life would've led if we'd followed through with it.

Even though the shows sucked, I was impressed by Mike's songwriting. I remember being on the phone with some chick that I was trying to woo and bragging about my band. I thought I would impress her by reading our totally deep lyrics to the song "No Problems."

Sitting by yourself
No friends are near
You got a needle in one hand
And in the other one a beer

It had the exact opposite effect from what I'd intended. I probably had a shot at sleeping with her until I read her our lyrics and blew it.

For the first few months we played with the same handful of equally bad bands at small bars and smaller parties, and every time we finished our set I felt a little bit embarrassed. Once we played a show at this rented rehearsal space and afterward some heavy metal dude in his twenties came up to me and said, "You're a good drummer. You're the only thing good about that band. The rest, they just suck!"

Every instinct I had should have pushed me away from NOFX, but inexplicably I stayed with them. We were having fun. It was music I liked with guys my own age. I told Caustic Cause I was leaving to play with my new band.

They didn't make much of a fuss. Punk bands weren't building careers back then, so they didn't see it as a tragedy that they were losing a drummer, and I didn't see it as a bad financial move to start working with an untalented new band with zero reputation.

I just wanted to play loud, fast music with my buddies. And occasionally ride their skateboards.

Recording at Mystic Studios.

14

Mike

We convinced Don Bolles, the drummer from the Germs, to produce our demo. And by that I mean we met him at the Cathay one night and offered to pay him gas money to sit in the studio for a few hours the next day while we live-tracked nine songs that were all out of tune.

I wrote most of the lyrics because no one else bothered. One of our songs was a theme song of sorts, simply titled "NOFX":

> *Play for punks, not for cash*
> *Our music's fast, but it's not trash*
> *The lyrics are what we believe*
> *We dress on stage as we do on the street*
> *We're NOFX*

They may not be the most sophisticated or clever lyrics I've ever written, but the song still defines us pretty well. Except maybe I'd change that first line to "Play for punks AND for cash." It has admittedly been a long time since we were paid thirteen dollars not to perform.

Aside from the Cathay, the only gigs we could find in L.A. were house parties, which are generally known for having very loose booking standards. We played with some metal band at a Beverly Hills high school party (which was attended by Pauly Shore and Bob Dylan's daughter), and we played to twenty people in a driveway in La Crescenta while one of Erik Sandin's friends beat up one of my friends. But once we had a demo tape I was able to send it out to people and get us shows out of town, so in the spring of 1985, without any record released, we set out on our first actual four-date tour.

First stop: Reno, Nevada. This was easily the best show we played up to that point, and the best show we would play for the next three or four years.

Driving from L.A. to Reno takes about eight hours on a good day. It took us closer to twelve because we had to drive through snowstorms as we went over the Sierra Nevadas. We were in Eric Melvin's parents' station wagon, which had no rear windshield, so we had to wrap ourselves in blankets to keep warm as the snow flew around inside the car.

It was worth braving the cold—the crowd actually liked us. We opened for local legends 7 Seconds and played in front of about three hundred people who slammed the whole time. It was the first time we'd gotten any sort of reaction from a crowd, let alone a positive one. We sold $150 worth of T-shirts, and I even managed to get laid. We stayed with a gay guy named Chris from Positive Force whose only rule was that we couldn't bring any girls over to his house. I brought a girl back anyway, and she left in the morning before Chris woke up, so I thought I'd gotten away with it, but then Chris found her panties on the couch and freaked out on us. It would not be the last time NOFX was kicked out of someone's house.

From there we headed to Boise, Idaho, and Ashland, Oregon, and played some smaller shows at house parties, and then on to Portland,

Oregon, for a show at the Satyricon. There were about twenty-five people at that show, all of whom seemed to like us (except for Tom from Poison Idea, who said our version of "138" was the worst Misfits cover he had ever heard). An all-female band called 69 Ways also played, and I ended up sleeping with one of them, so I came home thinking, "Fuck! A four-day tour, and I got laid twice? We have to do this again!"

It was the best time we could've asked for. Partying, staying on floors, playing music, hanging with friends, getting laid . . . what more could three teenage punks want? We immediately booked another tour for that summer.

And then Erik quit.

15

Smelly

Mike had a theory that Don Bolles wanted to fuck me and that's why Don had agreed to produce our demo. All I remember is that he asked for fifteen bucks to fill his van with gas; beyond that I don't know if he was in the room while we were recording. Still, "produced by Don Bolles from the Germs" was a nice way to trick people into listening to our shitty demo tape.

I put an ad in the back of *Flipside* magazine with my address that said if you sent us a blank tape and a stamped envelope we would make a copy of our demo and send it back for free. I probably got a hundred or so blank tapes in the mail—I had a grocery bag full of them—but I'm a lazy turd so I don't think I returned half of them.

You hear about bands like Black Flag who practiced for hours and blanketed L.A. with flyers for shows and toured relentlessly in pursuit of establishing themselves. We were not Black Flag. We couldn't even be bothered to tune before a recording session. And we certainly didn't arouse the same response from our audience as Black Flag did. Of the fifty demos I sent out, I never got word back from anyone who thought it was any good. They probably erased their tape so they could put something better on it.

But apparently the demo was enough to get us several shows out of town in the spring of '85. We loaded our gear, ourselves, and Melvin's girlfriend Chelsea into Melvin's parents' station wagon, which had a broken frame, so it always felt like the car was drifting all over the place. We didn't care, though. We stopped in the mountains and threw snowballs at each other and we jammed the Subhumans on the tape deck the whole way to Reno, Nevada.

We opened for Reno's hometown heroes, 7 Seconds, and it was not only the biggest show we'd ever played but the best. People were slamming and stage diving, Mike and Melvin were feeding off the energy, and there was a girl in the front row making up her own lyrics as she pretended to sing along. Unlike every other show up to that point, I was not embarrassed when I left the stage.

We stayed that night with a pimply faced, redheaded gay guy who hated girls and said his only rule was that we couldn't bring girls over. Mike violated that rule. I was about to fall asleep on the couch when I heard an unmistakable rhythmic squishing sound and looked down to see Mike fucking his new friend right next to me on the floor. I watched them go at it for while and thought, "Good job, buddy!"

The closest I came to getting laid on that trip was before our show in Portland, Oregon, when the guy who sang for the opening band threatened to rape me.

We had set up a show at the now-legendary Satyricon with a local band called the Oily Bloodmen. The singer, Rich,* had offered to put us up for the night. When we pulled into town, we knocked on his door and met Rich for the first time. He was a scary-looking fat guy with curly red hair and eyes that went in two different directions. His house was filthy and smelled like death—it was like something out of *Silence of the Lambs*. Immediately, I looked at Mike, Mel, and Chelsea, and we all wordlessly communicated that we would not be sleeping there that night. But before we could make an excuse, we ended up walking around town with Rich. Out of the blue he turned to me and said, "You ever been fisted in the ass, son?"

None of us knew what to say. I think I responded with a meek "Dude . . . " But he kept fucking with me: "Oh, I'm gonna fuck you hard. There's a gay bar around the corner—we're gonna tie you up and shove a baseball bat up your ass." I was scared to death.

I pulled Mike aside as soon as I found a private moment and said, "I'm not staying with him. We gotta go!" It was like having Charles Manson in my head, pulling my brain apart. He would act all friendly one minute and then, when no one was looking, he would glare at me with an "I'm going to kill you" look.

After a half hour or so, Rich said, "Nah, kid, I'm just fucking with you, man. I ain't gonna fuck you up the ass!" I smiled with relief. I should've

---

*Deceased 2001; apparent drug overdose.

known he was just joking around. And then he said, "No, but yeah, I am gonna fucking kill you."

The Oily Bloodmen played before us that night, and Rich's creepiness turned out to be a big asset on stage because they were really good. They had a supportive local crowd of about forty people cheering them on. We went on after them: crickets. I was back to being embarrassed.

The guys from Poison Idea agreed to let us stay with them that night, so we partied after the show at their house. Melvin, Chelsea, and I took acid and sat out in the front yard, watching the stars and clouds move and swirl and dance in the sky. There was a bicycle leaned up against a house across the street, and in its shadow I saw a woman pedaling the bike and going nowhere.

We ended up back inside, planted around the TV, watching some nature show about chimpanzees. Melvin was sitting off to the side with his legs crossed and his mouth hanging slightly open. I looked at him, and then back at the TV . . . and then back at him . . . and then back at the TV . . . and the acid made it all clear to me: "Melvin is a fucking ape!"

I hate to mock one of the best friends I've ever had, but seriously: the dude looks like a monkey. If you look at his facial features and bone structure and then look at a chimpanzee (especially back in those days when Melvin had a shaved head, and especially when you're high as fuck on acid) you will see a striking resemblance. "Oh my god! Melvin's a fucking ape! He's the missing link!" I didn't say any of this out loud; I was just piecing the mysteries of the universe together in my head. But sometime later I called him "ape face" and Mike fucking died of laughter.

As the sun was coming up up and my brain was concluding, "We're all just creatures of this planet . . . we came from apes . . . look at Melvin, he's one of them!" this insanely hot girl named Paula curled up with me on the couch. She reached over and grabbed my crotch and said, "You wanna get out of here?"

I got in her car and went to her house, but when it came time to pull the trigger I couldn't do it. She was twenty-five and I was eighteen, which is a world of difference. I had only had sex with a few girls and I was intimidated. The acid made me whimper, "I gotta girlfriend." I regret it to this day. If I were to make an anti-drug commercial, I wouldn't bother talking about the potential for prison, poverty, or addiction. I would just show a picture of Paula and explain how drugs cockblocked me that night.

As I said, Rich was the closest I got. He and I actually became friends later on. Nice guy.

16

Melvin

These days Mike is mostly the captain of the NOFX ship, but I was the one in charge of booking our first tour. From day one my goal was to hit the road, and now I had a band to do it with. I wanted to see all those exciting, exotic places I'd been reading about in *Maximum Rocknroll*. Like Boise, Idaho.

I sent out letters and demo tapes to a few dozen promoters, and a guy from Boise offered us $200 to play a show in his garage. I got out a map, figured out an efficient route, and piled everyone into my parents' wood-paneled 1972 Ford Country Squire station wagon.

About a week before the tour I was driving around with my amp in the back seat, and it tilted somehow and broke out the back window, so we drove from Los Angeles to Reno, Nevada, with a heavy sheet of plastic duct-taped in the window's place. It was bearable until we had to cross the Sierra Nevadas and got caught in a late-season snowstorm.

I had some snow chains in the car for just such an occasion. But I had never put snow chains on a car before. My fingers went numb trying to figure out how to attach the chains while the other guys threw snowballs at each other and trucks flew by, blowing snow all over us. And then a cop pulled up.

He asked what we were doing, and I explained about the chains. He laughed and told us that it was only snowing at the summit of the mountain. If we had driven for ten more minutes we would've been out of the snow completely.

But we took the journey in stride because we were all so excited to get to Reno for our first official out-of-town gig, opening for 7 Seconds.

The only problem was we weren't actually booked. When I called a promoter in Reno to find us a show he said he had just booked the 7 Seconds show and didn't want to book anything else around the same time. I asked if we could open for 7 Seconds, and he said, "I'll ask. We'll see," and never called me back. So we were never actually confirmed as an opener for 7 Seconds—a fact that Mike and Erik are probably discovering for the first time in this book. We just showed up.

The promoter couldn't believe we were there.

"What are you guys doing here? I never told you you were confirmed!"

"I know, but can't we just play anyway?"

He must've pitied us for how naïve I was and how far we had driven, because he grumbled, "You can play for half an hour right after doors open."

As far as Mike and Erik knew, we were booked the whole time. We look back on that night now and think of it fondly as the first time we played a show to a big, responsive crowd. But it could've just as easily been the night where Melvin dragged everyone all the way to fucking Reno through a snowstorm for a show that wasn't even booked, and we mocked him mercilessly for the rest of his life.

17

Smelly

In L.A., we always played with the same four or five bands who were all just as bad as we were, but when we got back from tour I felt like we had separated ourselves from the pack. We were a "touring" band now! We may still have been getting blank stares from our audience, but at least we were doing it outside of our local comfort zone.

We had also recorded some songs for some compilation records: a horrible cover of "Iron Man" for some cover comp, a song that was under a minute long for a *Party or Go Home* comp full of songs that had to be less than sixty seconds, and a song called "Cops and Donuts" for a comp called *Copulation*. Then we laid down tracks for our first real seven-inch EP.

Things seemed to be happening for us. So of course that was the moment I picked to quit the band.

I was a stubborn kid. When I told Mike and Melvin I had a family vacation planned around the same time as our second tour, I felt insulted that they weren't willing to work around my schedule, but they wondered why the two of them had to change plans for only one of me. It wasn't a big fight or anything; I just sat down with them and said I had to quit.

I was stubborn, and I was not smart. Why did I want to go on vacation with my family anyway? You know what we did on vacations? We drove for hundreds of miles while my parents screamed at each other over directions and maps. And at the end of it we didn't visit Wally World, we visited fucking steel refineries and factories because my dad was fascinated by all the machinery. There were, admittedly, some pleasantly calm moments of fishing and canoeing, but there were way more stressful moments of being yelled

Newsletter

HI*!*

THIS LETTER HAS BEEN SENT TO YOU TO TELL YOU ABOUT A GREAT BAND FROM LOS ANGELES, WELL, WE THINK SO ANYWAY. WE ARE No F-X AND WE'VE BEEN PLAYING FOR A BIT OVER A YEAR. WE JUST GOT BACK FROM OUR FIRST TOUR THROUGH NEVADA, OREGON, AND IDAHO. WE ARE PLANNING A NATIONWIDE TOUR THIS SUMMER BUT WE NEED A LOT MORE EXPOSER FOR THIS TOUR TO COME OUT AS GOOD AS OUR FIRST ONE. WE HAVE ONE TRACK ON MYSTIC RECORDS' PARTY ANIMAL COMP. AND ONE ON THEIR COVERS COMP. WE JUST RECORDED A SONG FOR THEIR COPULATION II, CALLED COPS 'N' DONUTS. IN A WEEK OR TWO WE ARE GOING TO RECORD A 7 SONG, 7" E.P.

THIS LETTER IS MERELY TO INFORM YOU OF OUR BAND'S EXISTENCE. WE HAVE MANY MORE THINGS TO SAY, TOO MANY TO FIT ON THIS PAPER, SO IF YOU ARE INTERESTED IN WRITING US, WE WOULD GLADLY WRITE BACK. IF YOU WRITE FOR A FANZINE WE WOULD LOVE TO DO AN INTERVIEW (BY MAIL, PROBABLY)

No F-X 225 N. IRVING BL., LA, CA 90004

PLEASE WRITE BACK TO US, BECAUSE WE WANT TO TELL EVERYONE ABOUT OUR BAND AND OUR SUMMER/NATIONWIDE TOUR.

THANX, ERIC/GUITAR MIKE/BASS/VOCALS ERIK/DRUMS

OUR FAVORITE BANDS, MUTILATE YOUR FAVORITE SONGS!! 20 bands!

at about improperly tying up the canoe. Taking acid under the stars and getting hit on by twenty-five-year-old chicks was infinitely preferable. But I had my stupid pride.

The worst part was that NOFX found a new drummer pretty quickly. The guy's name was Matt from a band called Fatal Error; he had dreads and looked cool. I was still friends with Mike and Melvin, so I dropped by practice one day to check him out (and maybe pee on my territory a little bit). The guy fucking ripped. It was like seeing your ex-girlfriend with a hotter, richer, manlier dude. I was so bummed. Especially when my parents ultimately canceled our vacation and it turned out I had quit over nothing. NOFX left for tour, and I was left in the dust.

I still had some good memories, though. So when the first NOFX 7-inch hit the stores I figured I could at least brag about once being in the band. The day it was released I ran to the record store the minute school was over to pick up a copy. On the back cover there were photos of Mike, Melvin, and their new drummer, Scott (I guess Matt quit before they left for tour, too). All of their names were in big, bold print. Scrawled next to a tiny asterisk it said, "All songs played by Erik Sandin, our former drummer." I went straight to Melvin's house to beat his ass.

I marched down his street, I balled up my fists, I knocked on his door ... but when I looked in my buddy's eyes I couldn't do it. I had gone there with the express purpose of knocking him out because I felt so angry and rejected and disrespected, but I couldn't hit my little monkey friend. I got in his face and told him he had narrowly avoided a beating. He started spewing excuses. "I didn't do it, Scott did it! He took it down to the art place to get it duplicated!" I knew that was bullshit: Melvin was always in charge of artwork stuff in the early days.* But how can you be mad at Eric Melvin? He is, quite possibly, the sweetest guy in the universe. I suppose I could've gone over to Mike's house to punch him instead, but he lived kinda far and it was getting late.

I stewed on it all night. All of my friends, my family, everyone knew I was in that band. I had been on tour with them, we had played all these shows and written all these songs and done all that work. And all I had to show for it was an asterisk. I was humiliated, even though I had brought it upon myself: I was the dipshit that quit the band.

To this day, though, I'll come across a copy of that old 7-inch and think, "Those dicks."

---

*And he admitted it years later.

18

Melvin

I was lucky I had a screen door between Erik and me when he came to my house that night. I pretended the lock was busted and I couldn't let him in because I could tell he was angling to leave me with at least a black eye.

But I was only half-lying when I blamed Scott for putting his picture on the cover of the 7-inch. Scott worked at some photo place that could shoot our negatives for free, so it made more sense to put him on the cover and cash in his favor rather than spend out of pocket to include Erik's photo when we were pretty sure he was never coming back.

So Scott was, indeed, in charge of assembling the artwork, but Mike and I fully knew that Erik's name would just be an asterisk in the corner.

Sorry, buddy. Shouldn't have quit, dude!

19

Mike

I bought a beat-up Dodge van for 1,500 bucks so we could tour again immediately. There was a flower shop near my apartment that used the same type of van for deliveries, so one night Melvin and I took a screwdriver and stole the brake lights and all the other spare parts we needed off their van in order to make ours street legal. And as we traveled, we saved money on gas by having Melvin siphon it from other cars. I suppose it was karma that caused us to break down at least five times on that summer's tour.

When most bands start touring, their crowds slowly begin to grow. Our tours seemed to have the opposite effect. We headed back to Reno and Ashland two months after our first trip there, and no one showed up. From 1985 to 1989 almost every crowd we played to got smaller each time we returned to a city.

Erik's family had decided to take a vacation to Mexico or Idaho or something, but I was determined to get back on the road and hopefully get laid again. After a handful of auditions we found a guy named Scott Sellers to play drums and headed out for a full summer's worth of poorly attended shows across the United States. We literally played to four people at a club in Detroit called Blondie's. They all left after the first song.

Our first show with Scott. Kids were very interested in something. Just not us. (Check out Murray Bowles on the bottom right . . . NOT taking our picture.)

Cabaret Voltaire in Houston.

Sitting room only in New Orleans.

Green Bay, Wisconsin. Seriously: Have you ever seen so many pictures of people sitting down at punk shows?

The Metroplex in Atlanta, opening for Articles of Faith.

20

Melvin

I understood the concept of how to siphon gas, but I had never done it before. If we'd had a clear tube to work with maybe I could've seen when the gas was about to reach my lips and avoided sucking in a mouthful of 87 octane, but we were using a regular garden hose, so I inhaled at least four or five gasoline swigs on that first full U.S. tour.

Between no one showing up to our gigs and our van rebelling against us on a daily basis, the tour could've been considered a disaster if we hadn't had so much fun. When we couldn't fill dates, we'd set up our gear in a basement or a local park and play impromptu gigs. We stayed at my uncle's house in Cleveland for five days and did a backyard show for my aunt and cousins. Playing music was its own reward and was worth eating shit on some nights.

At least to us—maybe not to any of our audiences. There's a photo from our "show" in my uncle's backyard: my six-year-old cousin Danny is joking around for the camera, grimacing and plugging his ears with his fingers.

Yeah . . . joking around . . .

Uncle Harry's house in Aurora, Ohio.

✦ ✦ ✦

I led a secret life as an Eagle Scout and an avid Dungeons & Dragons player as a teen. I still have all my old D&D books—I don't care if you call me a nerd, I think they're cool. When I was fifteen I invited one of my gaming friends, Dave Reed, to a family holiday party at my aunt and uncle's house. My dad's brother's wife came from a huge Irish family, so their parties were always populated with more brothers and sisters and little kids and half-cousins-once-removed than I could possibly name.

At a party the year before, I couldn't help but notice the soft brown hair, narrow hips, and all-around general hotness of my dad's brother's wife's brother's new twenty-five-year-old surfer/hippie chick girlfriend. Like any good D&D nerd I was reading a lot of sci-fi/fantasy novels at the time, even at parties. She noticed me reading *Stranger in a Strange Land* and excitedly struck up a conversation with me about it. I didn't think much of it until later at dinner, when we were sitting next to each other. She leaned over to whisper something to me and then breathed heavily into my ear.

It sent a chill through my body that my fifteen-year-old self had no idea how to interpret. That chill sat in my memory until the next year's party, unlike her name. "Distinctly Non-Blood-Related-Aunt's Brother's Girl-friend" is a bit of a mouthful, so I'll just call her Gillian after one of the characters in *Stranger in a Strange Land*. Gillian invited me outside with her, and Dave came along, not yet understanding the concept of a wingman. Gillian had been nursing a glass of wine for a while, but she suddenly gulped down the last of it and politely asked Dave if he would get her a refill.

As the door closed behind Dave, Gillian grabbed my hand and said, "Come on!" pulling me into the backyard of the house next door. She sat down on a chaise lounge and asked, "Would you like to kiss me?"

"Okay . . ."

And there I was, making out with a twenty-five-year-old.

This is the stuff of fantasy for most fifteen-year-olds, but I have to admit I was a little freaked out. I wasn't prepared for it, and I wasn't old enough to understand it. If you think about the same scenario with the genders reversed it seems way creepier. But I'm not saying I wasn't turned on.

Clothes came off and Gillian grabbed my dick and put it inside her. In the midst of losing my virginity I heard Dave's squeaky voice from the other side of the fence: "Guys?"

I did my best to ignore him, but a minute later I heard my mom calling. "Eric? Where are you?"

I stopped. "Fuck, it's my mom!"

"It's okay, come on!"

Gillian pulled me further behind the neighbor's house. She backed up against a wall and spread her legs. I tried to fuck her while standing, but I could still hear my mom and Dave calling for me. "Eric? Eric!" Dave Reed, if you're reading this, I nominate you for the title of World's Worst Wingman.

I pulled my pants up and ran back into my aunt's yard, acting as nonchalantly as any fifteen-year-old could who had just run 20 yards after fucking his semi-uncle's girlfriend. They asked where I'd been, and I don't remember what excuse I gave them, but I'm sure neither of them bought it. We all returned to the party and pretended everything was normal.

At the end of the night, Gillian gave me her phone number. I stashed it at the bottom of a drawer for a long time, too scared to actually use it. But when the holidays rolled around the next year I was more eager than usual to uphold our family tradition of celebrating at my aunt's.

My parents decided we weren't going back. They never gave a reason. Soon after, I gathered the courage to call Gillian, but the phone number had gone missing. I can't say for certain that my mom figured out what was going on, but I never saw Gillian again.

I thought about her for years afterward. If I knew her name I could at least look her up online, but I could never figure out a way to get that information out of my aunt or uncle that wasn't extremely awkward.

◆   ◆   ◆

A girlfriend or two later I was at a house party somewhere near L.A., drinking beer with a cute bleached blonde named Chelsea. Her short hair and boots made her look like a skinhead, while her heavy makeup and brown roots made her look like a chola. Either way, I was digging her, and she must've been digging me, because we soon ended up alone in one of the bedrooms.

We had been fucking for a while on somebody's bed and she was on top of me. She paused for a moment, looked down, and said, "I'm sorry . . . what was your name again?"

We both laughed and a relationship was born. But the way it began should've maybe been a clue that it wasn't going to be a healthy one.

Chelsea's dad was a biker, her mom was a biker's old lady with missing and jagged teeth, and her brother was was part of the FFF gang. They lived a half hour west of L.A. near a town called Rosemead, and when I visited they'd invite me to stay for mac-and-cheese dinners. Her dad offered me cans of Coors while he worked on his motorcycle. They were sweet, friendly people but a far cry from the kind of people I grew up with. Chelsea once showed me a Polaroid she found of her mom's mouth around her dad's cock. I winced at the thought of those teeth being anywhere near anyone's sensitive parts, but I guess her dad was enjoying himself enough to commemorate the occasion.

As nice as they were, it was a turbulent environment that left Chelsea with some rough edges. She was temperamental—to say the least—and she always stirred up drama. It was always "I don't like the way that chick is looking at me," or some other perceived slight that would escalate into yelling and/or slapping. Sometimes she would straight up pick fights, like when she told Mike, "That fag devil lock you got isn't doing you any good," and then slapped him and grabbed his hair when he told her to shut up. Mike looked up at me and asked, "What am I supposed to do here?"

"Do what you need to do. She's fucking with you."

He socked her in the gut and she still didn't let go; he had to claw her in the face to break free.

I've been involved in only a handful of fights in my life, and I think it's fair to say most of them were because of Chelsea. She picked some stupid fight with our drummer Scott on our first U.S. tour. I was driving the van when I heard the familiar din of Chelsea's nagging from the backseat, followed by "Fuck you, Scott!" and a slap.

I yelled, "Fuck you, guys! Cut it out!" and turned around to see Scott cocking his arm back in preparation for a punch. I pulled over, but the van wasn't fully stopped when I jumped out of the driver's seat into the back and attacked Scott. We grappled with each other as the van slowly strayed back toward the highway. Mike grabbed the wheel and threw the van into park. The unnatural grinding sound from the transmission broke up the fight (and probably had something to do with one or more of our many breakdowns).

The tour after that was a winter run to Texas with a different guy named Scott on drums and my friend Dave Allen filling in as our singer. We were on stage playing in Dallas on New Year's Eve, and Chelsea was frantically yelling and signaling to me from the side of the stage. She was pointing at her face, which seemed all red, and then pointing at some guy next to her. I attempted to read her lips:

"He hit me!"

I instinctively yanked off my guitar, ran across the stage, and pounced on the guy. I knocked him to the ground and we traded punches as we rolled off the stage onto the floor. He ended up on top of me, but Mike tore through the tangled crowd to pull the guy off.

"You fucker! You hit my girlfriend!"

"No I didn't!"

"Chelsea, what happened?"

She clarified: "He kissed me."

I ended up being angrier at Chelsea than I was at the guy. She and I ar-gued for the rest of the night—I don't remember if we finished our set.

The worst, though, was a show in Bakersfield when Chelsea picked a fight with some girl who looked at her the wrong way. They started shoving each other, then the girl's boyfriend put his hands on Chelsea.

Again, instinct took over; I threw a single punch and broke the guy's nose. He cupped his hands to his face, and they quickly filled with blood. What the fuck did I just do? My anger instantly sublimated into remorse.

"Oh fuck! I'm going to go get you some ice!"

Somebody grabbed me. "Leave him alone! You hurt him enough already!"

I got him some ice anyway. Someone told me later that the guy was an asshole, and this wasn't the first time his nose had been broken at a show, but it didn't matter. What was this girl doing to me? And why was I letting her do it? It was time to break up.

And then she told me she was pregnant.

We had a long talk about what to do. I was nineteen, she was seventeen, and we were both still living with our parents. We didn't know anything about raising a kid. We barely understood that breaking random people's noses wasn't an appropriate way to spend a Saturday evening.

It was like in *Fast Times at Ridgemont High*: $200 and a ride, except I paid the total for the abortion and waited for her at the clinic. Forty minutes after her appointment began, she came out crying. She told me about the blood that came out and how they told her to expect more bleeding in the future.

The weight of the experience finally pushed our relationship to the breaking point, but it also bonded us. We remained friends after breaking up, and we still talk from time to time. She has a family of her own now; one of her three kids is even a NOFX fan.

I can't imagine how different both of our lives would be if she had kept that kid. In all likelihood, NOFX would only be remembered by a single, awful 7-inch record (or more realistically, not remembered at all), because my priorities would've been elsewhere. I would've gotten a shitty job and settled into a routine of constant fighting and living in fucking Rosemead. And we still probably would've eventually broken up.

I never told my parents about any of it. And yet again, the band will be reading this story for the first time in these pages. It was another heavy secret that I hoisted onto my shoulders and carried around for years.

Opening for the Descendents (with Dave Allen on vocals).

21

Mike

When my friend Noah was nearly stabbed to death, I realized it was probably time for me to leave L.A. Noah was more of a casual punk fan—he was on the Beverly Hills High football team and not really involved with the scene—but he and I went together to see the Dickies at the Music Machine in Santa Monica just before NOFX went on our summer tour. I guess he stuck out from the rest of the crowd because some Suicidals zeroed in on us outside of the show. My Suicidal friend Bruno stepped in and vouched for us, so I thought we were in the clear. I went inside, but Noah stayed outside, and a little while later another friend came up to me and said, "Dude, your friend's out there. He's fucked up."

I went outside and discovered Noah on the ground with blood squirting out of his chest. Apparently the Suicidals fucked with him again, so he took off running, and they chased him down like feral dogs. I helped load him into Eddie Machtinger's car, and Eddie drove him to the hospital. He had been stabbed in the lung; the doctors were barely able to save his life. He never played football again.

Around the same time, I was sitting outside the Cathay during a show, and some gangsters were beating up some random Mohawked dude in a parking lot 100 feet away. It was the typical, nightly, 20-on-1 scuffle, until someone jumped on the Mohawked guy's neck. The crowd around him froze, and then everyone scattered. The guy just lay there limp on the asphalt.

I liked punk rock, and I liked being in a band, but I didn't like the idea of getting killed over it. It had become far too normal to go to a show and have someone walk up and say, "Oh, by the way, they took your friend to the hospital."

I was going to college one way or the other. Even though my parents weren't religious, they were still Jewish, and in a Jewish family it's not "Are you going to college?" it's "Which college are you going to?" I had been accepted to USC and San Francisco State, so when I saw my chance to move north, I took it.

I majored in Social Science with a minor in Human Sexuality and met a girl named Wendie. Her dad was a rich dude, but he decided at some point to stop paying her college expenses, so she moved into my dorm room soon after we started dating. She became a bike messenger to cover her tuition, and we ended up moving into a house with some of her new colleagues.

Being a bike messenger is less of a job and more of a lifestyle. We had six or eight people living with us (I'm not sure if you count the one who got busted selling acid through the mail and went to jail for twenty years), and they all partied constantly.

I have a lot of fond memories from those days. Once, Wendie dragged me to see the Red Hot Chili Peppers at San Jose State University, and we couldn't find parking. We stole a parking pass from a van with an open window and, feeling mischievous, stole a suitcase from the back of the van as well. When we got home we opened the case to find a hat with a whale sticking out of it, an American-flag kilt, some leather wader pants . . . these were the outfits the Chili Peppers had worn in all their promo photos and on stage for their whole *Freaky Styley* tour. They were known for their goofy costumes—I had wondered why that night they chose to perform in just jeans and T-shirts.

I wore the whale hat and Wendie wore the kilt for a while, but eventually everything got lost or disappeared. Which is a shame because all that stuff would probably be pretty valuable now.*

Things with Wendie went south after she had a couple of nasty accidents on her bike. She cracked her head open during one of them, and her behavior took a sharp turn toward crazy. She was angry and moody all the time, and she constantly picked fights with me.

One day I found a note on my van. Some girl named Erin Kelly saw that I had "NOFX" spray painted on the side of the van and noticed that NOFX was playing in Santa Barbara that weekend. She wondered if she might be able to hitch a ride south to meet a friend. Erin would later describe this as the most uncomfortable drive of her life, because Wendie and I blasted music at top volume to try to cover up the fact that we were arguing the whole trip. Erin chose to purchase a bus ticket back to San Francisco rather than ride with us again.

The final straw with Wendie was at a Verbal Abuse show in Berkeley. We went with a group of seven friends and I managed to get five people in for free. But two of Wendie's friends couldn't get in, so she was furious that they had to pay the five-dollar cover. She kept screaming at me and I just kept walking away from her. I had just finished a 40-ouncer of Olde English 800, and the moment I opened a second one she knocked the bottle out of my hand. Without thinking, I slapped her. I flashed back to the time I cowered away from hitting Natalie for fear of being beaten to death and wondered if now my time had come. And then my friend Jerry said, "Ten points, dude!" and everyone started laughing.

She had made such a spectacle of herself that no one judged me for lashing out. But she was upset and started shouting, "I can't see! I'm blind!" Erin happened to be at the show, so she went to help Wendie. Wendie asked, "Who is this?" and Erin replied "It's Erin." Wendie punched Erin in the stomach and said, "You're the cause of all my problems!"

Wendie was convinced I was cheating on her with Erin, which wasn't the case. Erin and I had become friends after I apologized to her for the six-hour hell ride to Santa Barbara, but it was purely platonic. When I found out she liked to get tied up and whipped during sex, however, I mentally moved her into the "datable" column.

---

*I know that story has very little to do with the history of NOFX, I just love the idea of one of the Chili Peppers reading this book and finally learning what became of those outfits. Hi guys!

After Wendie and I broke up I ended up living in my van for four months. Some might consider this a hardship, but it was awesome. I would park in front of friends' houses, have dinner and drinks with them, and then lie in my van and write songs while listening to the rain hit the roof. I would go to a night class, have a few drinks and pass out, and then I'd wake up the next morning and already be at school. I loved the solitude of it. No one could bug me; it was just like that Descendents song.

It was the only time in my life when I lived completely alone. I always had roommates before that, and as school ended I moved in with the woman who I would eventually move from the "datable" column into the "marryable" column.

+   +   +

NOFX was still technically a band while I was in college, but Scott quit after our summer tour, and Melvin was still living in L.A., so we weren't practicing much. As my first semester was ending, Melvin called and said he found a drummer and a singer and taught them our songs. Without meeting either of them (without ever fucking practicing together once!) we went on a seven-date tour through Texas over winter break.

Our first time ever playing music together in the same room was at our first show in El Paso. The new singer, Dave Allen, stood completely still on stage. He didn't say a word between songs, and he couldn't keep the lyrics straight. Our new drummer, Scott Aldahl, was terrible, too. Combine that with zero practice and the fact that we sucked in the first place, and you can imagine how well we were received by the crowd.

We played New Year's Eve at a club called the Twilight Room in Dallas. We had played to a bunch of people at a skate park in Dallas on our summer tour, so the promoter figured we were a good draw. The truth was that at the skate park people were just there to skate and were doing their best to ignore us. So now, sounding worse than before, we were headlining New Year's Eve and ruining everyone's night. People booed, and Melvin got into a fight with some local skinhead. I think the skinhead threw something, or gave Melvin the finger (or maybe Melvin's girlfriend Chelsea started it, since she was along for the ride). But the guy Melvin socked had friends, and the show immediately turned into a full-on skinhead riot.

The owner of the club pulled out a shotgun and fired a round into the ceiling. Everyone scattered. We didn't finish our set. Happy New Year 1986!

Nothing went right on that tour. During one of the drives, I was sleeping in the back of the van when I awoke to some strange noise. A moment

Dave Allen.

later, a huge pickup truck smashed into us. The driver had fallen asleep at the wheel. The area of the van where I had been laying my head was completely crushed.

We were towed to a truck stop and had to sleep in the van until the next morning. It was so cold that the condensation from our breath formed sheets of ice on the van's ceiling. When we woke up, the ice was melting. It was raining *inside* our van. It was like a black cloud was literally over our heads.

When we got home I didn't even say goodbye to Dave, which I now sort of regret because it was the last time I'd see him alive. A few months after the tour, he rolled his pickup truck and crashed into a tree. His passenger got out and called an ambulance, but the steering wheel had slammed into Dave's body, causing severe internal injuries. He died at the hospital later that night.

22

Smelly

On my first night living independently from my parents, my roommate told me how he had strangled someone to death in the desert.

I was dating a girl named Gail. She was from the right side of the tracks and going to college at UC Santa Barbara. I was from the wrong side of the tracks and feigning interest in Santa Barbara City College so I would have an excuse to follow her out of L.A. after graduating high school. She moved into the dorms and I moved into a house with some random people I found in the classifieds.

I shared my room with a skinny blond guy named Jeff, and while we were settling into bed that first night we were talking—with the lights out—about how we both loved taking acid. I casually mentioned I used to deal drugs a bit in high school, and he casually mentioned he used to deal, too, and that one time someone ripped him off and he took revenge by beating the guy up, tossing him in his trunk, driving out to the middle of the desert, and strangling him to death with a rope while he and his friends took mushrooms. My blood ran cold. Who the fuck was I living with?

Jeff and I ended up hanging out quite a bit and became pretty good friends over the next few months. Nice guy.

College and I, however, were not a good fit. I left classes early or skipped them altogether. I had the best intentions of getting an education, but I just couldn't handle it.* When I wasn't in school I had an office job processing orders in some shipping and receiving department, but after about six months I had broken up with Gail, dropped out of school, and lost the job. I was back to selling acid and playing drums.

I met another punk in one of my classes and together we formed a band called Anti-Krieg with two of his ridiculously rich friends. Santa Barbara was a wealthy area, so half of the punk scene was comprised of kids from mega-rich families. Anti-Krieg's guitarist lived in a $6 million home perched on a cliff overlooking the ocean in a neighborhood called Hope Ranch, which is apparently one of the wealthiest areas in the state (Snoop Dogg currently has a house there). Adjusting for inflation and the California real

---

*In my forties, I was officially diagnosed with ADHD, and I'm pretty sure I have dyslexia. I lucked out finding a career that didn't require a college degree.

estate market it would probably be worth $20 or $30 million today. And then his family moved to an even more insane house with a koi pond that ran from the outside of the house under these huge glass walls into the house, where the pond and a swimming pool coexisted in this massive atrium area. It was the exact opposite of punk. But it wasn't that unusual in Santa Barbara.

Anti-Krieg built up a following fast. We got to a point where we could easily draw a few hundred people to a local show. Then the bassist got cancer and had to undergo chemotherapy,* and later the singer dissolved the group.

Just before Anti-Krieg broke up I ran into Melvin's ex-girlfriend Chelsea and Melvin's mom on State Street. Chelsea said I should call Eric because NOFX's singer had died, and their drummer had either quit or was about to get kicked out.

I made the call and I was back in NOFX. We jammed a bit, went into the studio to record our second EP, and hit the road that summer for my first U.S. tour.

Bumping into Melvin's mom and Chelsea that one afternoon was such a random, unexpected, and unlikely encounter, and yet without it I never would've ended up back in the band. At the time I was alone, with no band, no degree, and no job. I probably would've tried to make a go of it as a full-time drug dealer or ended up OD'ing or going to prison.

Or maybe I would've ended up strangled and buried in the desert.

---

*After Anti-Krieg broke up, he drove NOFX to shows in his van a few times. Once he was driving and a big clump of his hair fell out, blew out the open driver's side window, and then blew back into the van and landed on my lap.

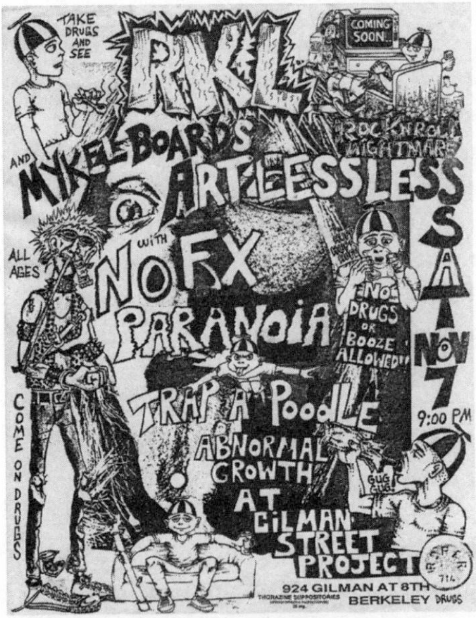

TAKE DRUGS AND SEE

COMING SOON!

RKL

AND MYKEL BOARD'S ARTLESSLESS

ROCK N ROLL NIGHTMARE

SAT NOV 7

9:00 PM

with NOFX

PARANOIA

NO DRUGS OR BOOZE ALLOWED!!

ALL AGES

TRAP A POODLE

ABNORMAL GROWTH

AT GILMAN STREET PROJECT

COME ON DRUGS

924 GILMAN AT 8TH

BERKELEY

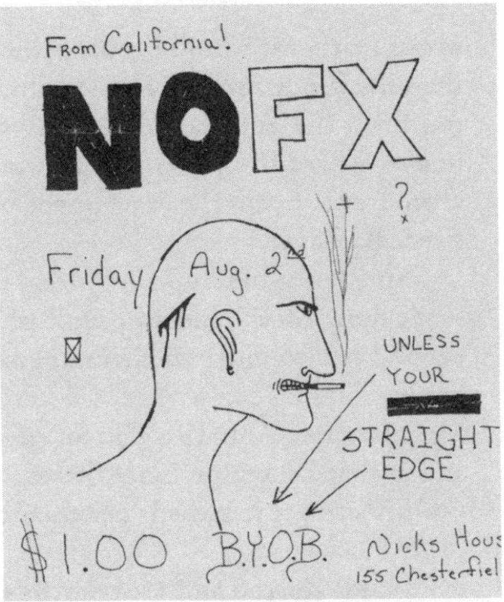

From California!

NOFX

Friday Aug. 2nd

UNLESS YOUR

STRAIGHT EDGE

$1.00 B.Y.O.B.

Nicks Hous 155 Chesterfiel

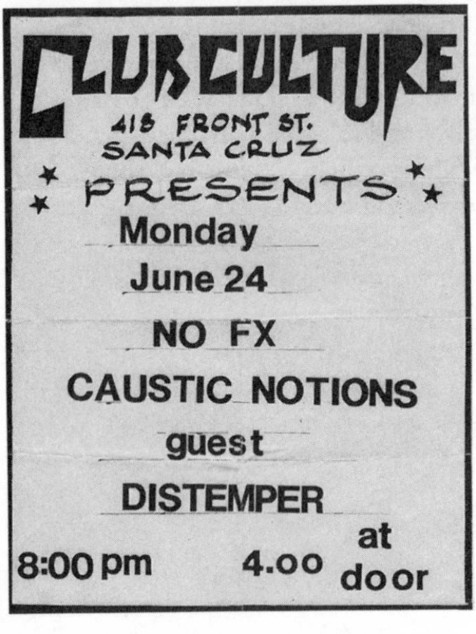

CLUB CULTURE

418 FRONT ST. SANTA CRUZ

★ ★ PRESENTS ★ ★

Monday

June 24

NO FX

CAUSTIC NOTIONS

guest

DISTEMPER

8:00 pm   4.00   at door

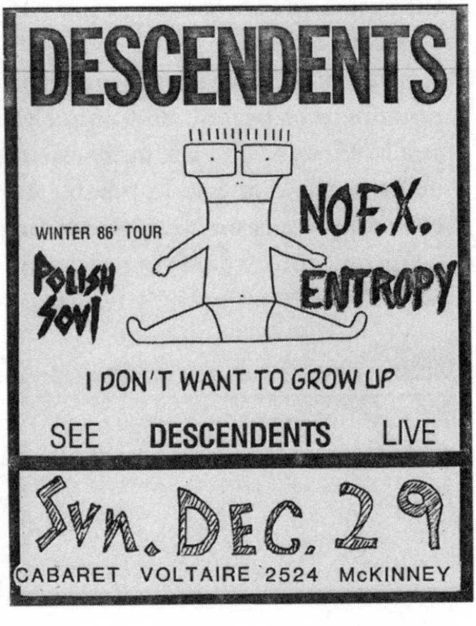

DESCENDENTS

WINTER 86' TOUR

POLISH SOUL

NO F.X.

ENTROPY

I DON'T WANT TO GROW UP

SEE DESCENDENTS LIVE

SUN. DEC. 29

CABARET VOLTAIRE 2524 McKINNEY

23

Melvin

The first time we played Detroit, four people paid a dollar each to see us and then left as soon as we started playing. When we played Detroit on our '86 tour with Smelly back on drums, four different people showed up to see us and actually stayed. But only because they were friends with the guy who booked the show: Scary Kerry.

At the end of the night Scary Kerry took us to his apartment, which was on the second floor above a pawn shop, surrounded by barbed wire, and accessorized with a grumpy bulldog and a shotgun propped against the back door. His a/c unit blew only the most tepid air, so we left the windows open to deal with the oppressive summer heat. Trucks were coming and going from the nearby industrial park all night, so the a/c unit sucked all the diesel fumes directly into his tiny living room.

When we arrived at the apartment, Scary Kerry made us a big pasta dinner. As we ate, he said, "Hey, you wanna see some crazy shit?"

He stuck a tape in his VCR and hit play. On his television screen there appeared a close-up of a man's face, looking up, mystified by some point of wonder just off screen. Then a woman's ass entered the frame and squeezed a huge log of shit into the protagonist's open mouth.

Dinner was over.

24

Mike

A friend of ours graffitied "NOFX" in huge letters on the side of our van before our '86 U.S. tour, and we spray painted squares on the tires so it looked like the van had square wheels. Did you know spray paint eats rubber? We didn't, until the second of four blowouts.

The graffiti also made us a cop magnet. We were pulled over and searched in Syracuse, New York, and the cop found a billy club we had stolen from a party somewhere. He said we were in possession of a deadly weapon, and one of us had to take the rap or he was going to arrest us all, so I took the fall.

I sat in a holding cell for eight hours, bored out of my fucking mind. I actually jerked off around 5 a.m. because I was alone with nothing else to do. I called my mom to ask for bail, but it was the middle of the night in California, so she just went back to sleep and waited until the morning to call a bondsman. Around 10 a.m., they transferred me to an actual jail, where I spent the afternoon playing spades with a table full of bikers (and winning handily I might add). I made bail around 5 p.m. and met up with the rest of the band, who had no idea when they might see me again. We had a show in Springfield, Massachusetts, with the band Subculture* that night, so we floored it the whole way there. It turned out to be the biggest show of the tour: Two hundred people showed up and Subculture sold 150 bucks' worth of merch!

We, however, showed up too late to play.

---

*When I was a DJ on my high school radio station, I was Mike Misfit. Later, one of my friends tried calling me "Chark" (because my last name is Burkett ... as in Briquette ... as in Charcoal ... "Chark"), but for some reason those nicknames never stuck. The first time we met Subculture on the road I was a scrawny kid, but the next time we saw them I had gained some weight, thanks to my unlimited college meal plan. I don't know if I'd call myself "fat" at 160 pounds, but one of the guys from Subculture started calling me "Fat Mike," and to this day everyone's confused by it.

25

Melvin

When NOFX started, I considered myself "straight edge." The L.A. punk scene was so fucked up and full of gangster drug addicts; the positive no drugs/no drinking message of the original straight edge movement resonated with me. And alcohol just made me sleepy, so it was easy to do without it. That didn't last long because beer is easier to come by than water on a punk tour, but it wasn't until my mid-twenties that I really took up booze as a hobby. Even then I was dissuaded a bit after spending a night puking in someone's garden somewhere on tour.

In the meantime, I was redefining "straight edge" to allow for open experimentation with any other drug that came my way. I smoked my friends' parents' weed as a kid, I took mushrooms in Ashland on tour, and when Chelsea's brother offered me a "sherm" outside the Olympic Auditorium one night I went for it.

It looked like a normal cigarette to me. I didn't know "sherm" meant that it had been dipped in liquid PCP. I wasn't a smoker, but it seemed like a good way to bond with my girlfriend's brother and his FFF gangster buddies, so after he took a hit I took one, too. The sherm went around the circle. Chelsea's brother and I both took our second hits, and when I turned back around to talk to him, he was on the ground, passed out. Then it hit me.

I must have collapsed, because people kept telling me to get to my feet. "There's cops over there—if they see you this fucked up they're gonna take you to jail!" The anxiety didn't help the spinning. Nor did the milk someone handed me. I drank it and puked it back up instantly and then ran for cover. I walked into a wall, fell on my ass, held my hands on my head, and curled up as small as I could to try and make myself invisible. Every time I opened my eyes I felt like I was on an out-of-control carousel that was actively trying to throw me off. And every time I tried to stand up I fell back down.

Mike found me, and I guess I blurted out some explanation of what had happened. He couldn't do much except sit with me and wait for it to pass, and like a good friend that's what he did.

Mike usually just focused on beer while I focused on hallucinogens. I dropped acid for the first time while he and I were at a Halloween party in the Valley. The Grim was playing and their drummer was dressed like Eddie Munster, but the acid convinced me it was the real Eddie Munster playing drums. After their set I spent the whole party tripping out on the shapes the moonlight was making in the ripples of the swimming pool and the shadows made by the leaves on the lawn. I got caught up in the idea that the shadows were just as real as the leaves themselves, and I was somehow able to flip a switch in my brain that would either allow me to only see the leaves or only see their shadows. Later, Mike got drunk enough to co-conspire with me to steal the police billy club that we kept in the NOFX van and which later earned him a night in jail.

Mike never messed with cocaine until he was in his thirties, but coke entered the picture for me right along with acid, PCP, and everything else. When I first met our temporary singer, Dave Allen, I went to hang out with him at a mutual friend's house and discovered they were running a moderately successful cocaine-dealing enterprise out of his friend's garage. A handful of punkers were cutting and mixing powder, weighing it on a scale, and packing it into bindles while listening to records. I offered to pitch in, and it became my job to fold the bindles. They never ordered me or paid me to do it, but hey, while I'm hanging out, why not donate some free labor to their drug racket?

Before I ever snorted any coke, Dave offered me a "coco puff," which is a cigarette that has been tamped down so the tobacco recedes inside the paper a bit and cocaine fills in the gap. It stood out from all the other drugs I'd done by offering a rush instead of a mellow or psychedelic high. It would be years until I tried coke again, but I chased the rush by seeking out any other "go-fast" drug I could find, which led me to speed.

I found a regular dealer who sold me cheap, black-and-red capsules that he called "bloody niggers." I would go to a punk show, snap one open, snort the contents, and slam dance all night long. It became my routine for a few months until one night I went home and couldn't sleep despite being overwhelmed with exhaustion. My legs cramped up, and I was covered in sweat as I watched the sun come up through my window.

After that I gave drugs a break for a while. Except for acid. And mushrooms. And lots and lots of weed. That still counts as "straight edge," right?

26

Mike

It took me years to figure out why my mom had a mirror on the ceiling over her bed. When I was twelve I watched TV in her room and thought, "Cool, I can see myself!" It finally clicked when I was staying at Caesars Palace in

Las Vegas in my twenties. "Oh, this is for watching yourself fuck! My mom had one of these. Ohhhhh . . . "*

My mom never remarried after my parents' divorce, but she had a French boyfriend for about eight years. He was the one who suggested they install the mirror, but I'm not sure if he or my mom should be credited for my first exposure to S&M porn.

Penthouse Variations is sort of like *Reader's Digest* for people into flogging and nipple clamps. It's mostly stories (supposedly submitted by readers) about kinky sex. I dug up a copy while snooping through my mom's belongings. Her copies of *Hustler* and *Cocks and Cunts* never did much for me, but the stories of bondage and submission in that issue of *Penthouse Variations* gave me my first boner. There was a story about a dominant wife who cross-dressed her husband and treated him like a slave, even allowing her friends to come over and rape him. Pretty intense stuff for a thirteen-year-old to read. But I must have jerked off to it like a hundred times.

I would forever associate female supremacy with eroticism. It shaped my sexuality and has always been a crucial component of all of my relationships. Natalie and I choked each other during sex, and she would scratch my back until it bled. Wendie turned the leather waders we stole from the Red Hot Chili Peppers into a bondage hood. And between the two there was Cindy.

Cindy was the host of the house party that Dylan, Melvin, and I played as a three-piece at the dawn of NOFX. I had no plans to make a move on her because Melvin had a crush on her, and I was already hitting on another girl that night. But Cindy walked up to me at the party and started making out with me, so I ended up with two girls and Melvin had none.

Melvin was bitter about that, but he kept it to himself. At least until one night at the Stardust Ballroom. Cindy and I were fucking in the parking lot between two parked cars. People kept walking by and looking at us, and Cindy was lying in a puddle of piss, so we decided to change locations. We crawled inside Melvin's station wagon, finished fucking, and passed out.

Melvin found us naked and asleep after the show.

"What the fuck are you doing?!"

He chased me in circles around the car. He was yelling, "You're gonna fuck the girl I have a crush on?" and I was yelling, "Don't hit me!"

After a few laps I couldn't help but laugh at the fact that he couldn't catch me. Then Melvin started laughing, too. I don't know if that same scene

---

*I have a mirror above my own bed now. My daughter Darla recently saw it and said, "This is so cool! You can wake up in the morning and see yourself!" And the circle goes 'round . . .

would've played out the same way with any other two people. But we left that show as friends.

Cindy and I only dated for a month, but that was the month when I first got my hands on some actual S&M equipment. Cindy's dad had been a CIA agent so their garage was full of cool old spy machines. One day we were digging through the lie detectors and code breakers (or whatever they were) and found a box of homemade leather sex toys. It wasn't the sleek, black S&M gear you see in sex shops; it was all tan leather with uneven stitching. Her dad had clearly taken some care to learn leather craft to fashion whips and body harnesses in his spare time.

We played with the whips but couldn't figure out how to fit into the body harness. The biggest mystery, however, was a butt plug with a hole through the middle and a length of plastic tubing running out of it. We figured it was some kind of crazy enema device, but we thought it would make a rad beer bong.

We took it into the kitchen, scrubbed it with soap, and attached a funnel to the end of the tube. As we poured in the first beer and sucked it out of the butt-plug end, Cindy's mom walked in.

"Where did you get that?"

"We found it in the garage."

Mortified, she turned around and left. I don't think I ever saw her again.

Sometime later we were driving around, and I got pulled over by a cop. Rightfully so: I was drunk from butt-plug-bonging. The cop looked in the back of the car and saw the plug. He picked it up.

"What is this?"

"What does it look like?"

Disgusted, he threw it down in the back seat.

"Get the fuck out of here."

When I started dating Erin, our first kinky experiment was on the road with NOFX. She and I borrowed the van one night for some private time after the show. We drove to an empty supermarket parking lot, and she tied me up and blindfolded me in the van, naked. She pulled out a whip, but just as things were getting good a police car pulled into the lot.

I couldn't see, I just heard her yell:

"Fuck!"

"What?"

"There's cops here!"

"FUUUCK!"

They banged on the window, and Erin opened the door to reveal what I'm sure was later a riveting conversation piece back at the station.

"Get the fuck out of here."

We retreated to the house where everyone was staying that night. Sadly, we never got to finish, and I ended up with two mosquito bites on my nuts.

Even at home it was tough to find privacy to explore. Erin and I moved in together right away and lived in a house on Page Street in San Francisco. At one point our roommates were away and we had the house to ourselves, so we really let loose. I was gagged, blindfolded, and tied up, spread eagle, on the bed. Erin left me there, helpless, while she went to take a shower. It was perfect. But then I heard a knock at the front door. And then I heard the door open. And then I heard someone walking up the stairs toward the bedroom.

"Hello? This is Alex, the landlord!" I would've happily responded had I not had a gag stuffed in my mouth. The door to the bedroom was wide open. The steps got closer, and then they stopped. I couldn't see anything with the blindfold on, but after a brief pause I heard footsteps quickly going down the stairs and out the door.

These days I'm very open about my sexuality, but at the time I was living in constant fear of being discovered as a fetishist. I was too embarrassed to walk into an adult bookstore to buy S&M porn. It wasn't until the late '80s that I was able to talk even a little about S&M with my band mates. After a tour date in Hamburg I bought some leather restraints and a ball gag from a local sex shop. When we were going through customs at the Amsterdam airport, an official pulled everything out of my bag.

I finally knew how Cindy's mom felt walking in on us with the butt-bong several years prior. I wanted to disappear. But the customs guy didn't seem fazed at all. It was Amsterdam—they probably see stuff like that all the time. Melvin and Smelly didn't seem to care either. They had probably picked up on my not-so-subtle lyrical references (for instance, naming an album *S&M Airlines*). That's when I realized I had nothing to be ashamed of. From then on I didn't bother to hide who I was or what I enjoyed. If I wanted to wear a leather hood made out of Hillel Slovak's pants while my girlfriend shoved a beer-bong butt plug up my ass in front of our landlord: so be it!

27

Smelly

I came up with a plan to murder my friend. I would suggest that we go get a drink or try to score some drugs and lure him into my car. I would take him up into the mountains to get high, and I would shoot him and leave him on the side of the road. It wouldn't be hard to get a gun—I knew enough sketchy people that it would only take a phone call. The authorities probably wouldn't investigate too closely. They'd just chalk it up as a gang thing.

It probably wasn't the most solid plan. But I needed to develop some sort of strategy, because I knew that, in the interest of survival, there might come a day when I would have to kill Raymond.

Raymond isn't his real name, because even though it's been years since I've seen him, the guy still petrifies me. And even though he's been in and out of prison for every violent crime imaginable, I don't want to accidentally implicate him in anything new and give him a reason to seek vengeance. For the sake of you and I both sleeping better at night, let's just say I made the rest of this chapter up.

◆   ◆   ◆

There was a corner in Santa Barbara where all the punks congregated for long afternoons of doing nothing. Every once in a while, this scary-looking dude would come by and people would scatter. He looked like a white version of Mike Tyson, with slicked-back hair and prison tattoos covering his arms, neck, and back. He didn't have to say a word or move a muscle: he automatically instilled a deep sense of fear in anyone who crossed his path. Everyone whispered behind his back, "That Raymond dude is fucking gnarly."

There were rumors around town that Raymond killed bums and winos for fun. I can't confirm that personally, but I never had trouble believing it. A mutual criminal friend told me about a time when he and Raymond kidnapped a guy who owed Raymond forty bucks. They tossed him in a trunk and were trying to decide what to do with him. Raymond said, "Fuck it, let's just kill him." My friend said, "Are you fucking kidding me? You're gonna go to prison for life over forty bucks?" Raymond didn't see the problem. Ultimately, they just pounded the guy senseless, took his shoes, and dropped him off in the middle of nowhere. But my friend capped the story off with, "Yeah, Raymond liked to kill people."

Once, my friend Lynn Strait (from the band Snot, and now deceased) walked into a party and Raymond bitch-slapped him in front of everyone for no reason. It was a domination thing in an animal-kingdom sort of way. Or more accurately, in a prison sort of way. He had spent seven of his late teenage years in a California Youth Authority detention center for beating up a cop. I'm sure it had an effect on his sense of social etiquette. Lynn once loaned Raymond his car and later asked if he could have it back. Raymond bitch-slapped him again and told him he'd give it back when he was ready to give it back.

He terrorized a city of punk rockers. And he was my best friend.

Once again I ran toward the thing that was supposed to scare me away. And once again I found myself compensating for my own insecurity by trying to prove I was a badass. I befriended Raymond because he was a badge I could wear and a counterculture I could explore.

I was working at a fabric store and I knew they kept a couple hundred bucks in the register overnight, so I told Raymond and we went down there with a couple of crowbars and tried to break in. The place was locked up tight, but we didn't want to go home without committing SOME sort of crime, so we climbed onto the roof of a nearby synagogue and broke in through an upstairs window. We found a safe but couldn't get into that either. We looked through drawers and desks, but there was nothing worth taking. All we ended up with was a gallon of ice cream, which we sat and ate together in the synagogue's kitchen. I risked jail for a gallon of ice cream. Such was my need for acceptance.

I became Raymond's sidekick and we tooled around Santa Barbara hassling his enemies, breaking and entering, and taking shit whether someone was home or not. I knew one punker kid who had a nice guitar, so we broke into his house and stole it along with a box of cassette tapes. I thought the guitar was a Les Paul, but it turned out to be a cheap copy so we smashed it. When I got home I went through the cassettes and found a NOFX demo. I was trying hard to be a sociopath like Raymond, but I still knew right from wrong. Seeing that tape turned my stomach with guilt. I choked it down.

Before I started hanging out with Raymond, the cholo gangsters who lived up the street never bothered me. Now they were driving by my house and mad-dogging me because Raymond's Mexican half brother was a shot caller with the Mexican Mafia, and now I was on their radar. It was no joke. I remember hanging out at Raymond's half brother's house, and he had guns stashed under the couch, behind the TV, in the flower pots . . . there was hardly a spot in the house where a gun was not in arm's reach.

Raymond and I lived on the Westside of Santa Barbara. One day we were hanging at a coffee shop with some friends when some Eastside cholos walked in. Raymond was up on his feet and in their faces, "What the fuck, puto? What the fuck you doing in our neighborhood?" The gang banter went back and forth, but the Eastsiders backed down and left. Then an hour later they came back with reinforcements.

It was 20 on 10. They rushed us and started swinging. Raymond went into Incredible Hulk mode and bashed back every attacker. I don't know if I was hit with a fist or a bat or what, but something got me in the gut and buckled me. I took a few kicks to my head while I was down, but the whole thing ended as quickly as it began. The Eastsiders had made their point— our group was laid out flat. I looked up. Raymond was the only one left standing. Raymond was always left standing. And usually hungry for more.

Honestly, though, most of the time he and I would just hang out and talk. I saw a gentle side to Raymond that no one else would've believed existed. We'd get high and talk about our aspirations, life, family, all that shit. He dropped his persona and offered private moments of real vulnerability. It was heartbreaking, in a way. Deep down . . . deep, deep down . . . nice guy.

But I still knew I needed a plan to murder him. Regardless of what goodness lay inside, he was still a volatile sociopath who could turn on me at any moment. Through Raymond, I started to associate with more criminal types, and I saw how they were totally cool one minute and callously beating the fuck out of someone the next. But with Raymond it wouldn't be as simple as a harsh beating or a stab wound. Once he locked onto a target, he got off on mentally torturing his victims. He harassed them and fucked with them nonstop. He held people hostage inside their own minds. It's one thing to beat someone up, take their money, and run. It's another to walk into someone's house, pick up their TV, and say, "What the fuck are you gonna do about it?" and walk out laughing. He was a predator who fed on fear.

There was a story going around about a kid who went along with Raymond on a "bum hunting" mission. Raymond allegedly killed a homeless guy in front of the kid and threatened to kill the kid if he talked. He was so relentless with his harassment that he never had to make good on his threats. The kid was so scared he killed himself before Raymond got a chance.

Thankfully, I never became one of Raymond's targets, but he did host one of the most frightening nights of my life. I went with Raymond to Oxnard to pick up his car from an acquaintance who had been repairing it. One of Raymond's friends gave us a ride to this ghetto housing project full of run-down tract homes, built within a labyrinth of cul-de-sacs. Raymond's car was waiting. But so were a dozen menacing cholos. We had been set up.

Raymond had pissed off someone, somehow, and it was time for payback. The cholos started in, "What the fuck, ese? What you gotta say now? You're in our fucking neighborhood." I don't know why they didn't kill us right there. If they were messing with Raymond, they had to know death was on the table, but miraculously they let us go. "We're taking your car, Holmes. What the fuck you gonna do about it? Fuck you! Walk back to Santa Barbara!" We walked out of the development and sat on a curb outside a gas station.

Raymond was steaming. He didn't like the taste of his own medicine. "Go back and see if they're still there. We'll steal the car." Classic no-win situation: look like a pussy in front of the guy I'd been trying so hard to impress, or confront a whole crew of pissed-off gangsters. I marched back into the development. Alone.

The cholos saw me approaching. One guy picked up a big-ass screwdriver, another grabbed a crowbar. "What the fuck you want, little kid? Fuck you, punk!" I don't know what I said; all my energy was focused on keeping the piss and shit inside my body. But I backed away, found Raymond, and told him what happened.

"Fuck that. Let's go in and get 'em."

Awesome. I'm going to die now. This time they saw us coming from much further away, and there was no more yelling or intimidation. They came at us, full speed. I turned around and ran, and Raymond was sensible enough to run with me. The cholos hopped into a pickup truck and gave chase.

We ducked into backyards and hopped fences to escape the maze of dead-end streets. But this was their turf and they knew every inch of it, so they were on our tail the whole time and they kept cornering us. We hid under cars and behind bushes and trash cans as we ran from yard to yard. They knew where we were going before we did. We found a broom handle somewhere and broke it in two, so each of us had a weapon, but we weren't kidding ourselves about how much that would help if we were caught.

For two straight hours it was a real-life version of *The Warriors*. I was the most scared I've ever been. We ended up in a yard that backed up to the freeway. The cholos must have thought we hopped the fence and ran up onto the freeway, because we saw them slowly driving up the on-ramp while we hid behind some bushes. We knew they couldn't turn around easily, so we bolted. We ran back to the gas station and there was a cop there. It was probably the happiest Raymond had ever been to see a police officer. We didn't go into detail, but we explained we needed a ride out of there. He must have known we were in the wrong neighborhood, because he dropped us off two exits down the freeway without too many questions. We hitchhiked to Carpinteria and walked another ten miles home to Santa Barbara.

A month or so later, Raymond showed up at my house, and it looked like someone had taken a cheese grater to half his face. I knew he had been down in Oxnard again, so I wondered if he had tangled with the cholos. He said he had jumped over a chain guarding a parking lot, hooked his foot on it, and fallen on the cement. It sounded like a reasonable explanation. If he had been beaten down he probably would've not only told me but also enlisted me to get revenge. All I know for sure is that he never got his car back.

* * *

If I hadn't rejoined NOFX and left for tour, I'm sure my friendship with Raymond would've eventually caught up to me. It certainly caught up to him: In 1989 he had the dubious distinction of being part of one of the first busloads of prisoners through the gates of Pelican Bay, the gnarliest prison in California and easily one of the top-ten gnarliest in the country.

Usually prisons are self-segregated by race: the Mexicans have their area, the blacks have theirs, etc. But since Pelican Bay was brand new, no one had claimed territory yet, so for the first few weeks it was just free-for-all race riots while the invisible lines were being drawn. And Raymond was right in the middle of it, probably standing tall while all the other criminals fell around him. Or maybe finally meeting his match.

What was it that finally landed him in jail? Rape. I lost touch with him before the arrest, so I'm fuzzy on the details, but from what I hear, he was in his twenties, she was fifteen, he said it was consensual, she said it wasn't. Supposedly, when the charges came out, a bunch of other girls came forward to say Raymond had raped them, too. After the judge handed down a sentence of twelve years, Raymond turned to his accusers and said, in open court, "When I get out of jail, I'm going to kill each and every one of you bitches."

He showed up to a NOFX show after he served his time, with some brand-new face tattoos and stab wounds. We caught up for a few minutes, but I haven't seen him since. He apparently pulled a gun on someone and went back to jail, then got out a few years later, and then went back in again for some crime that should've earned him his third strike and put him behind bars for life.

But it turns out the rape charges were filed before the three-strikes law went into effect in California. I just heard from a friend that he's out again.

Like I said: You'll sleep better if you believe I just made all this up.

28

Melvin

During one of our trips up to Idaho after Erik rejoined the band, I met an exotic, almond-eyed beauty named Iris. She had shoulder-length brown hair and the confidence and intelligence to match her looks. She had been to Europe and knew all about touring; she even spoke German. But she also had a German boyfriend, so I had to keep my hands to myself.

Chelsea and I had broken up, and I had moved to Santa Barbara and enrolled in psychology classes at City College. Smelly and I found a house to rent with some friends, which became the NOFX House. Normally a punk house shared by several dudes in their early twenties would generate stories of chaos and epic parties, but in truth it was a pretty mellow establishment. I was smoking way too much pot every day, so my roommates and I mostly sat around playing chess for four hours at a time. Someone would make a move and then we'd both sit there thinking about the next five moves we were going to make, and then, fifteen minutes later . . .

"Whose move is it?"

"I don't know, dude. I thought it was yours."

"Oh yeah, sorry."

Repeat.

Aside from a few house parties and building a skate ramp in the backyard, the only chaotic moment that stands out in my memory is one Christmas when we brought in a tree and couldn't figure out how to dispose of it afterward. We stuffed the whole thing up the fireplace and set it on fire. I don't know how we didn't burn down the house. We all stood on the front lawn, cheering as we watched flames leap from the top of the chimney.

Iris and I kept in touch and wrote letters back and forth for a while, and my patience finally paid off. When her relationship with the German guy ended she took a Greyhound down to Santa Barbara while I drove sixteen hours (each way) to Boise to pick up all her stuff and move her into the NOFX House.

Iris came along on the second nationwide NOFX tour, but she nearly didn't make it back. We played at the Metroplex in Atlanta, Georgia, and behind the club were several sets of tracks leading to a nearby train yard. Growing up in a city, I was more used to traffic than trains, so I was fascinated watching the freight cars come and go all afternoon. I decided to get a closer look at one train as it crawled slowly along its track, and Iris came with me. She had heard about people putting pennies on the tracks and the trains flattening them, so she placed one under the slow train's wheels.

We were on adjacent sets of tracks, waiting expectantly for this metal behemoth to flatten her penny, when we jumped at the ear-splitting sound of a train horn. We looked up to see a train coming toward us at top speed.

Everything went into slow motion. Iris tried to run off the tracks, back toward the club. My brain decided she didn't have enough time to clear the tracks, so I grabbed her arm and pulled her toward me, trapping us in the very narrow gap between the slow-moving train and the fast-moving one.

My brain knew that trains are meant to run next to each other but not into each other, so we'd somehow be "safe" in that little space. There wasn't enough time for me to explain this logic to Iris, of course, nor to tell my brain that we were still in horrible danger of being decapitated or dismembered should either of those trains have any stray metal parts hanging off of them, or should we lean too far in either direction.

Everything went back into fast motion as the highballing train barreled loudly past us, horn blaring and wind whipping. The gap was so tight we had to stand side by side, as if we were standing on the narrow window ledge of a tall building. I was frozen with fear, focusing only on using my mental powers to somehow physically shrink both of us down to a smaller size. Iris probably wanted to scream, but neither of us could even breathe.

I still don't know if I saved her life or endangered it further by pulling her back. When the train passed it revealed a pickup truck with an orange beacon light on the roof idling on the next track. A man stepped out of the truck and walked over to us.

"Was that you two on the tracks as the train passed?"

"Yeah . . . why?"

"I just got a radio call from the driver. He thought he hit you guys. I wasn't sure if I was coming to pick up bodies or what."

"No, we're okay."

You'd think he would've arrested us, or at least suggested we move off the tracks, but he just said, "All right," and drove off.

Iris recently told me she still has that flattened penny.

+ + +

As beautiful as the city of Santa Barbara is, my years living there were the darkest of my life. The small-town vibe of everyone knowing each other was offset by the "I don't give a fuck" hardcore surfer attitude. I was surrounded by rich kids getting wasted and crashing the new cars their parents had bought them. And after accidentally walking in on a girl shooting up in the bathroom at a house party I became keenly aware of the heroin scene lurking all around me. And of course there was Raymond.

He had a frightening reputation, and his family was somehow involved in the Mexican Mafia, but he was generally nice to me. Until one night at Eagle Billiards.

Raymond and I were shooting pool when he suddenly decided we were playing for pink slips. At the time he had a souped-up 1960s Buick and I had a beat-up Mustang, so I stood to gain more than he did, but I also knew there was no way I would ever drive away in his car. No one got the best of Raymond. I was either going to lose the game and lose my car, or win the game and get an ass-kicking. I tried to talk my way out of it. No dice. All I could do was play my best and hope a tornado hit the pool hall before it was over.

I held my breath after every shot. If my car and my ass hadn't been on the line I might've noticed the crowd gathering around us. I was a decent pool player, but so was Raymond. The game couldn't have been closer if it had been scripted. It came down to an empty table and a lonely 8 ball. Raymond took a shot and missed, to a chorus of "Oooooh!" from the crowd. He didn't leave me with an easy angle. My heart was racing and my hands were shaking as I drew back the cue. Raymond stared into me from the other side of the table, trying to throw my concentration.

I pocketed the 8 ball.

Raymond advanced on me. I dropped my cue and backed my way around the table, trying to play it cool.

"Forget about it, dude. I don't want your fucking car."

"Good, because I'm not giving it to you."

He broke off his pursuit. I thought I was in the clear, but from then on Raymond and I couldn't be in the same room without him vengefully glaring at me. It seemed like only a matter of time before I would become his next victim.

One night at a party Raymond started fucking with me. He said something about how I wasn't man enough to take his car, and then tried to slap me. I turned my head away and only caught his fingertips, but it was clear that Santa Barbara was no longer big enough for the both of us. After our next tour, I moved back to my parents' house in L.A.

The worst part about this dark era was that I dragged Iris into it. Long after we broke up she told me Raymond came over to the NOFX House one day while I was out. I don't know if he knew I wouldn't be home, but when Iris told him I wasn't there he forced himself inside and tried to rape her.

Thankfully, she was able to fight him off, struggling until Raymond got tired of her and left. Given that Raymond was later convicted of raping several other girls in town, I guess she got off lucky.

It might be unfair for me to blame myself for putting Iris in that situation just because I brought her to Santa Barbara and into that circle of friends, but I was crushed to hear about what she had been through. And I will always have to wonder if Raymond's attack might have been prevented if I had just taken his goddamned pink slip and the beating that came with it.

29

Mike

Iris wasn't able to fight Raymond off. That's just what she told Melvin. She told me the whole story, and you can imagine how horrible the reality was. She said she didn't want to tell Melvin what really happened because he would confront Raymond, and Raymond would kill him. She was probably right. I promised I wouldn't tell him, and I never did. Until now.

Sorry, Mel. Sorry, Iris.

30

Smelly

I injected cocaine the first time I ever tried it. Usually the progression is snorting, smoking, and then shooting, but, like everything else in my life, I did it backwards.

After I rejoined NOFX, Melvin and his new girlfriend, Iris, moved to Santa Barbara, and we rented an old California Craftsman house with a few other friends. It was a classic punk pad, with keggers and weird people and plenty of drugs in and out all the time.

Raymond came by one night with a syringe full of coke for himself, and I insisted on trying it. He shot me up, and it hit all my senses. It tasted like ether, it smelled like model glue, my ears whistled like a teakettle, and my brain clenched inside my skull. Then the adrenaline kicked in—I felt like the Millennium Falcon jumping to light speed.

And then it was over. I mean, I was still high, but the big roller coaster drop only lasts a few seconds, and then you want to go again. You *have* to go again. And again. And again and again and again . . .

I probably did six or seven shots that night. Probably within that hour. And that's nothing: Over the next year or so, there were nights when I would do two hundred shots in a row. Nights when I had no veins left and blood leaking out of my arms. Nights when I was crawling around the floor of my room, crying and scouring the carpet for pieces of white dust that might be injectable. Nights when I was panicking and stabbing myself with a needle, digging for veins, insisting that there must be a way to get another shot in me.

And cocaine wasn't even my biggest problem.

About a week or two after my first shot of coke, Raymond dropped by the NOFX House with some heroin. He needed a place to shoot up and I told him he could use our place as long as he got me high as well. He unwrapped this little black marble of earwax and then went to the bathroom. Not to shoot up but to throw up.

Heroin has a very particular smell to it. When you're a junkie going through withdrawals (or if you haven't done heroin in years) the smell can be a physical trigger. Nausea sets in hard and it makes you want to puke. To this day, I'll walk down the street and an odor will waft out of a shop that reminds me of the smell of heroin and my guts will churn. In fact, just picturing that little black marble in my head and thinking about that smell is enough that I feel sick right now.

Excuse me for a second.

✦ ✦ ✦

Raymond finished vomiting and cooked up a shot. As soon as he injected himself, he stabilized. He asked me if I really wanted some, and I said yes. After all, he made it look like so much fun . . .

Honestly, I didn't see what all the fuss was about. It was the opposite of shooting coke—less of a rush and more like slipping into a warm Jacuzzi. It hit me in the back of the knees, worked its way through my stomach, and went up to my head, which suddenly felt like it weighed 100 pounds. Every muscle in my body decompressed all at once as I drifted in and out of consciousness. It was pleasantly mellow, but I didn't see how anyone could crave the sensation all the time. And within an hour I was out in the driveway throwing up.

I didn't love it. I didn't hate it. I don't know why I even wanted to do it a second time. I could've easily walked away and never thought about it again. But my friend was always doing it so it was always around, and it was a nice tranquil high, so I gave it a few more tries. Within five months I was completely strung out and my life would never be the same.

As if all the vomiting hadn't been enough of a warning, I should've at least heeded Raymond's words when he first shot me up. I'll never forget them. There we were in the bathroom: I tied myself off, pretending like I knew what I was doing while he cooked up a shot for me. He found a vein and slid the needle under my skin. Just before he slammed down the plunger, he looked me dead in the eye and told me my future.

"Welcome to Hell."

On stage at the first Dr. Know show.

31

Dave

I was always a shy kid. I always felt self-conscious and out of place, even in my own home. My two older brothers were separated from me by more than half a decade in age, and they were both so good at baseball that they nearly went pro, while I couldn't get to first base with a GPS. When I was seven, my parents split up and my brothers both went to live with my dad while I ended up with my mom. I was more or less raised as an only child.

My friend Tommy Niemeyer* was like a surrogate brother. We grew up in Oxnard, California, together and discovered punk rock together when we found a flyer for a Stiff Little Fingers concert. It wasn't only my first punk show; it was the first time I'd ever seen a live band perform. We stood in back at first, but as people started pogoing and slamming we couldn't fight the urge to jump right into the middle of it all. From then on both of us dug deep into the punk racks at the local record store trying to chase the buzz.

Soon afterward, Tommy's family moved away from Oxnard. I was crushed, and I was isolated again. Being a punk in the early '80s was alien enough in big cities like L.A., but in a town like Oxnard—famous more for its Strawberry Festival than its music scene—it was social leprosy.

But I wasn't the only kid in the area getting bored of his Led Zeppelin albums. I was a regular at the Endless Wave skate park, where I met Mark and Bob from Agression (before they were in Agression) and Jaime and Gilbert Hernandez, who were publishing the now-classic comic book *Love and Rockets*. Jaime and Gilbert had a brother, Ismael, who was starting a band called Dr. Know with another new friend named Kyle Toucher.

I don't know if you can call six or seven guys a "scene," but it was something. And it meant that Ismael and Kyle didn't have a lot of options when it came to finding a second guitarist for Dr. Know, so they invited me to join. I had taken two guitar lessons and then quit, learning by ear instead while listening to my Circle Jerks and Black Flag records.

The only show I ever played with Dr. Know was outdoors at the Oak Grove Park in Camarillo. By that point, punks from nearby towns like Ventura and Port Hueneme had joined forces with the punks in Oxnard. Ismael dubbed our growing scene "Nardcore." We had fifty people at our little outdoor gig in the park, which was a pretty respectable turnout.

I, however, was shivering like a motherfucker. It didn't matter that the crowd was made up entirely of our friends; the stage fright was overpowering. I had already been using alcohol to abate my shyness and social anxiety, so of course I leaned on booze to calm my nerves at the show. Unfortunately, it worked. The show went smoothly, as far as I can remember (but after the amount I drank I don't remember much), and a destructive habit was born. I loved playing guitar, I loved the idea of being in a band, but after a lifetime of being ignored I found that alcohol was the only way I could deal with all those eyes suddenly staring into me.

---

*Who later went on to found the "splattercore" genre of metal with his band the Accüsed.

My tenure in Dr. Know only lasted a few months. I have a short attention span. If I hang out with the same people long enough I get bored and jump ship, no matter how good things are going. I started a band called M.I.A. and spent several months playing local shows and occasionally getting confused for a band from Vegas with the same name. When I got bored with that I joined a group called Ground Zero, recorded a 7-inch, and left after four months. Then I heard local legends Stalag 13 were looking for a new guitarist and joined them for a record-breaking year and a half. We played often and recorded a full-length album, but I got into one too many fights with Ron, the singer, because he was militantly straight edge, and I was militantly . . . not.

After that I was directionless. No band, no job, and living at my mom's. But before reality and depression had time to set in, I got a call from my friend Matt. He had a band called Rat Pack he wanted me to join, he had a job for me at a screen-printing place, and he had an apartment behind his dad's chiropractic office in Santa Barbara where I could stay. Things went well for a year or so. Rat Pack started as a punk band, then went metal for a while, and then I decided I was bored with metal and wanted to play punk again. Like I said: short attention span.

I walked into Fancy Music on State Street one day and saw an ad that read, "NOFX looking for punk rock guitar player." That's all it took. Every band I was ever in eventually hit an expiration date—Rat Pack's had just arrived.

32

Mike

You know that saying, "Be careful what you wish for, you just might get it"? We wished for a second guitarist who could play cool lead parts. We got Dave Casillas.

Dave was talented at guitar, but he was far more talented at getting wasted. When he wasn't forgetting the songs or falling off the stage, he'd spend five minutes between songs tuning his guitar (with the amp on) and somehow end up more out of tune than when he started. And he'd show up to practice or shows without pieces of his gear.

"Where's your distortion pedal, Dave?"

"I sold it for an 8 ball of coke."

An 8 ball, mind you, that Dave would do all by himself.*

When Eric Melvin is the most solid guitar player in your band, you're in trouble. But Dave was fun to be around, so it took us a while to accept how

---

*For the uninitiated, doing an 8 ball by yourself is like one person eating an extra-large pizza: it's not unthinkable, but it's meant to be shared.

bad he was on stage, just as it took us a while to notice Erik Sandin had become a heroin addict.

I would guess that at least a third of the Santa Barbara punk scene was on heroin at the time. In that little bubble it was somehow a socially acceptable drug. Strangely, heroin seemed to have the opposite effect on Erik than it did on most people. Instead of mellowing him out, it made him more energetic. He would go on to record *S&M Airlines*, *Ribbed*, *The Longest Line*, and *White Trash, Two Heebs and a Bean* as a junkie, and his drumming was always spot-on. The only thing that tipped us off to his problem was when dope sickness hit him on the road, and even that we didn't notice right away.

We did two long tours with Dave across the country and back, and Erik was sick just hours after we left L.A. We brushed it off as the flu because after a few days the drugs would be out of his system and he'd be back to normal. Dave was a much bigger issue.

We were at a house party after a show in Rhode Island when suddenly there was screaming and commotion. Dave was caught red-handed taking the wallet out of some girl's purse. We were supposed to stay there that night, but instead we were run out of town. We weren't able to get another show in Rhode Island for six or seven years.

When we got home from tour, we realized Dave had amassed quite a record collection along the way. It turned out he had been stealing from every house we stayed in. Records, money, medication . . . Rhode Island wasn't the only place where we were suddenly blacklisted.

During our first tour with Dave we also had the bright idea of trying to supplement our income by selling acid on the road. We bought two sheets of acid for fifty bucks apiece and sold half to a skinhead we knew named Dave Rosebro and his very large Mexican friend who had a huge slash over his eye like Omar from *The Wire*. The next day we were at the NOFX House and we got an answering-machine message:

"You gonna sell us bunk acid? You guys are fucking dead."

It felt like someone had popped a balloon in my chest. We got them on the phone and explained that we didn't know the acid was bad and we'd refund their money and, hey, we'll even give you a distortion box just to make it up to you. Thankfully, they accepted our offer and no blood was spilled. Except Dave Rosebro's when he later shot himself in the stomach with a rifle just because he wanted to know what it felt like. (He survived. We still see him around sometimes. Nice guy.)

Now we were out the money we paid for two useless sheets of paper plus a distortion box. We sold the rest of the fake acid on the road to try and break even, so in the end Dave wasn't the only one ripping people off.

In hindsight, we should've had Erik test the acid because, even though heroin and alcohol were his drugs of choice, he would do whatever drugs were the easiest to find. And acid was always easy to find. Most people don't realize that acid makes your farts smell worse than usual. Erik would destroy the van with his flatulence. It was an indescribable odor that was more of an evil entity than a smell. Combine that with his inhuman foot odor and that's where Erik got the nickname that would stick with him for the rest of his days: Smelly.

We were a van full of foul-smelling, drug-abusing thieves playing barely listenable music and selling fake drugs across America. It was the worst of times, it was the worst-er of times. And overall it was starting to wear a little thin.

33

Smelly

It was somewhere on the road to a show in Ashland, Oregon, when I realized Dave Casillas might become a problem. We left from San Francisco early in the morning, and he was still drunk from the night before, but he started pounding 40s the minute we got in the van. We stopped for lunch at a Burger King, and he couldn't manage to get the food in his mouth. We had to put his arms around our shoulders in order to walk him to and from the van. Mike and Melvin thought it was hilarious, but I was thinking, "We have a show tonight and he's not stopping. What the fuck are we gonna do?"

I voiced my concerns, and Dave said: "Don't worry! I'll sober up before the show!" And then he cracked open another 40.

Dave could barely stand up that night, let alone play guitar. This would prove to be a common occurrence on the rest of that summer's tour. Most people who drink at his level would simply pass out, but it seemed like Dave's body shut down before his brain did. He would be conscious, but his legs would be Jell-O. It was embarrassing when he would fall off the stage, but it was often even more embarrassing when he would remain on stage and attempt to play.

We brought our friend Juan on tour as our roadie, and when we arrived in Portland he got into an argument with Dave about his shitty playing. It got heated and Juan slugged Dave in the face. Dave grabbed his guitar and tried to swing it at Juan, but I intervened and broke up the fight. Dave was yelling, "You're going home, motherfucker!"

Juan was only guilty of articulating what the rest of us were feeling, but we couldn't keep him on the road with Dave, so we bought him a bus ticket home. I was bummed that we had to let him go. It wasn't Juan's fault that Dave's face always seemed to be asking for a punch. Hell, I punched him the night before: We were shooting coke after the Ashland show, and Dave claimed we had exhausted the supply, but I knew he still had some on him. I punched him in the face and laid him out. It was never too difficult to knock him off his feet. He drank so much that he did most of the work for you.

A few weeks before the tour we had a show booked in Ventura with RKL, and Dave was supposed to meet us for a ride to the gig. He was off shooting coke at some chick's house so we were waiting for him for over two hours, with no clue when or if he might ever show up. This was obviously in the pre–cell phone days, so there was no way to contact him or figure out where he was. We just sat and waited and stewed in our anger.

As fucked up on booze and drugs as I was at the time, I took the band and our shows seriously. Especially this particular show: RKL were our musical heroes, we worked hard to imitate their sound, and I had dedicated myself to learning how to thump my kick pedal as quickly as their drummer Bomber did. When Dave finally strolled up with that big, stupid smile on his face like he hadn't done anything wrong, I said, "Fucker!" and popped him.

After a couple weeks of drunkenly stumbling off stages across the country, we were staying at a house in North Carolina nestled next to a beautiful, quiet lake. We had a couple days off so we were drinking and swimming and enjoying the sunshine. There was a pier that led out from the shore into the lake and our host, Bo from Subculture, was very clear: "Don't dive to the right." He explained that the lake had been created by chopping down a bunch of trees in the valley and then flooding it with water, so there was a big stump hidden under the surface of the water to the right of the pier. We'd be fine if we jumped to the left, but he kept reminding us, "Don't dive to the right."

Sure enough, later that afternoon I was sitting near the shore when I heard a loud SMACK!!! Dave dove to the fucking right.

I didn't see him jump, but I turned and watched him emerge from the water, stumbling and deformed, like a swamp creature. His eyes were now farther apart, his nose was pushed to the side, and his skin had become an alien shade of gray. His face was split from the middle of his forehead, down the bridge of his nose, along the bottom of his eye to the middle of his cheek.

We got him to the hospital and they stuck over a hundred stitches in him overnight. When he got out he looked like fucking Frankenstein. I made some tactless joke like, "What's up, Scarface?" to lighten the mood. Everyone just stared at me, totally offended.

Thankfully he didn't lose his eye or any teeth, he was just grotesquely disfigured, so they let him out of the hospital, and we continued with our tour. The plan was to leave our van on the East Coast and fly to Holland to begin our first European tour. Dave had never been on a plane before; he drank so much wine to calm his nerves that the stewardess had to cut him off. One of the guys told one of the stewardesses it was Dave's first flight, so they made an announcement over the PA system: "Ladies and gentlemen, we have someone with us today who's never been on an airplane before. Sitting in seat 16F, we'd like to welcome our new flyer, Dave Casillas!"

Everybody turned around to see this slobbering, drunk punk rocker who looked like the victim of a recent axe murder with a hundred oozing stitches. I don't know who was more frightened—Dave, or every single other passenger on the plane.

After one of our shows in Europe, Dave and I were drinking tequila and at 3 a.m. we had the bright idea to wake the other guys up, yelling, "Woo! It's party tiiiiiiime!" Our tour manager, Dolph, palmed Dave's still-healing face and shoved him to the ground.

Dave's face was a symbol of all that frustrated us about our band. Even though Dave was the only one who couldn't stay on his feet, we were all drunks, we couldn't play well, our songs sucked, we had no sense of responsibility, and we were spinning our wheels trying to get somewhere with this ugly, scarred, stitched-together sound. Punching Dave was symbolically taking out our frustrations about ourselves, as much as it was literally taking out our frustrations about Dave. We were our own worst enemy, and somewhere along that European tour Mike started to crack.

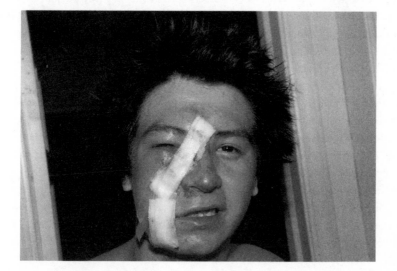

34

Dave

Those guys have vivid fucking imaginations! There's no way I was too drunk to eat a cheeseburger. And when I went to score coke before that RKL show I was gone for thirty minutes tops. (Not that I was keeping a close eye on my watch or anything.) And Sandin didn't punch me; he slapped me. I would've slapped him back, but his crazy friend Raymond was standing right behind him at the time, and I wasn't that stupid. And I definitely have no memory of selling my distortion pedal for drugs.

Then again, I do remember a guy coming up to me at one of our stops in Oregon, handing me a pipe, and offering me a "teaser." I had no idea what a teaser was, but it turned out to be a hit of crack. They call it a teaser because, sure enough, later that day I was begging Mike to front me some money to go buy more. I don't remember selling my distortion pedal to that dealer, but maybe I did.

Okay, yeah, that one is possible.

I tried coke for the first time at a house party in Santa Barbara and, as any coke addict will attest, it was a blast. We couldn't afford that shit down in Oxnard, so I rarely bought any for myself, but I would shoot it or snort it whenever it was available. And in Santa Barbara in the '80s, coke was very often available.

Booze and drugs seemed to be the perfect cure to my shyness and my crippling stage fright. And once we left for tour, every day was a party, and there was no authority figure around to say "stop." Alcoholism was an inevitability. I don't deny that I fell off stages. I admit that I regularly screwed up the songs. And okay, fine, I guess I could've been too drunk to eat that cheeseburger. I just have no memory of it either way.

I do remember tripping on acid one time in Ashland, though. Everyone was inside the house, and I was cowering in the van, totally freaked out. Sandin came out to check on me, and when he opened the van door I looked up and saw a fucking gorilla. I refused to leave the van and begged the gorilla to let me go to sleep. That Oregon monkey acid is bad news, man.

And they say Juan punched me in the face? No way. He pushed me and I swung my guitar at him, then they pulled us apart and I hid out in the van because I knew the guy could fight. The next day I made the band choose him or me, and they sent him home. But no one landed any punches. I mean, that one's on video—you can see it during the "Johnny Appleseed" section of the *Ten Years of Fuckin' Up* DVD.

(Okay, I just rewatched it and I guess he really did clock me good. Son of a bitch.)

There are a lot of videos from those days. I haven't seen them in years, but there's one from a night in Philadelphia featuring me interviewing people at the after-show house party, and you can see the light outside getting brighter as the sun comes up. I'm tickling Melvin's and Sandin's feet as they dangle from the van while they try to sleep, and the next thing you know, Mike is telling me it's time to leave for the next town. The nights drifted into days and back into nights, blurred by a constant flow of cheap beer.

I don't know how Mike was able to put up with all my shit. All I can say is he's an extremely patient person. He was at a payphone one night, trying to get directions to the next gig or whatever, and I was drunk, running around outside the van like a little kid at recess. For some reason there was a small brown-paper bag sitting near the phone booth that happened to be filled with soot. Why someone left a bag of soot near a phone booth I'll never know. Why I dumped the entire bag over Mike's head is just as much of a mystery. He looked like Elmer Fudd after Bugs had plugged up his gun barrel. He tried to grab the bag and throw it back at me, but he was playful, not pissed. If the roles were reversed, I would've been pissed. Soot doesn't come off that easily.

For all my antics, I wasn't the thief they describe, either. I stole only one record—a rare pressing of an X-Ray Spex album that Mike had mentioned was worth a good amount of money. Other than that the only thing I stole was an old Stalag 13 sticker that some kid had at his house. And a carton of cigarettes, which I guess was pretty dumb, since I was the only smoker in the band and the theft was easily traced back to me. But that was it. I definitely did not go through anyone's purse in Rhode Island.

At least, not that I remember. I mean, I guess I can sometimes be a thief when I'm drunk enough, so who knows?

I also don't remember anyone saying anything about "don't dive to the right." If they did say it, I wasn't around to hear it. Or maybe I just wasn't paying attention. I was drinking in the house with Bo from Subculture and saw everyone swimming out in the lake, so I ran out of the house and took off my shirt and shoes as I jogged to the dock. Why I chose to dive right instead of straight or left is yet another mystery, but I dove in headfirst.

Strangely, I didn't feel anything when my face hit the stump. I was just stunned and trying to figure out what had gone wrong. Someone said, "Dude, you hit the stump!" I touched my hand to my face and suddenly my hand was covered in blood.

"Oh my god! What are you talking about, a stump?" It was the first I'd heard of it.

The pain didn't set in until I was already at the hospital, but when it did it was intense. And it was followed shortly by a deep, unshakable depression. As if I needed two more big reasons to get blasted every day.

35

Mike

A German booking agent named Dolph set up a European tour for the Adolescents in the summer of 1988, and the Adolescents had to cancel, so Dolph needed an American band, ANY American band, to fill the dates. We had previously bugged Dolph to book us in Europe, but he never returned our calls. When he was completely out of options and facing financial loss, NOFX was better than nothing.

We left our van in Baltimore and flew to the Netherlands. Dolph had booked our first show in Rotterdam opening for a semi-popular industrial band called the Ex. We played in front of three hundred or so blank-faced Dutch goths and after the show, Dolph, with that classic German bluntness,

said, "I thought you guys were a lot better. I remember seeing you at Gilman Street and I thought you were good, but I must've been really drunk." Dave Casillas, who was currently drunk, got right in his face and said, "Fuck you! I think we're pretty good!" Dolph palmed Dave's freshly stitched face and shoved him across the room and we had to break them up. Only twenty-two more shows to go!

After our first show we had four days off in Amsterdam, where we stayed at a squat called Van Hall that was full of Italians who were there trying to avoid their country's mandatory military service. We drank and wandered the streets and ate pasta every night. Smelly only brought five dollars on the trip, which he spent on a single beer when we first arrived. But it's Europe: there's always plenty of beer to go around.

As is tradition in NOFX, however, things immediately went downhill. We were touring with a German punk band called Drowning Roses, so between the four of them, the four of us, our roadie Jerry, and Dolph, there were ten of us total stuffed into a standard van. And we had no trailer, so all of our gear and luggage rode inside with us: You couldn't put your feet down if you were sitting in back because the guitars and amps were in the way, so you had to sit in an upright fetal position. The drive from Rome to Munich was twenty-two hours.

I probably could've overlooked the discomfort if we had played any shows that went well, but Europeans didn't seem to enjoy us any more than Americans did. We were universally disliked. After a few shows we insisted that Drowning Roses perform as the headliners over us because it was clear they were better.

In Frankfurt, a feminist group protested the show because we had a song called "On the Rag." They turned the PA off after two songs and threw firecrackers and big, German beer bottles at us. One of the bottles nearly hit Melvin, so I picked it up and hurled it back into the crowd. Some huge dude jumped on stage to attack me, but Melvin shoved him into the drums and Smelly clobbered him with a bottle. Dolph got on the microphone and somehow calmed everyone down while we escaped backstage.

It finally started to sink in that maybe we were not a good band. It's one thing to brush off a bad crowd reaction or two, but once you've played a hundred cities across half a dozen countries, maybe the crowd isn't the problem. Why was I bothering with the fights and the thrown bottles and the general embarrassment of being a member of NOFX? We sucked so bad that we had become a danger to ourselves.

Operation Ivy put out their "Yellin' in My Ear" 7-inch around that time, and I loved it. I was vaguely acquainted with the guitarist, Lint, so I planned to return to the States and somehow convince him to let me be their roadie.

I would rather roadie for a good band than sing in a terrible one. It wasn't the most solid plan, but it was all I had.

When the tour was over we returned to Amsterdam to fly home. We emptied our bags and guitars out of the van, which was going to be picked up that night by Fugazi to use on their own first European tour. Of course, Ian MacKaye from Fugazi/Minor Threat was famous for coining the term "straight edge" and proudly declaring that he didn't use drugs or alcohol. Knowing that he'd be using our van for the next few weeks, we, in a blizzard of immaturity, intoxication, exhaustion, and frustration, poured a six-pack's worth of beer all over the inside of the van. It was petty revenge against an innocent target. It wasn't really about saying "fuck you" to Fugazi, it was just us saying "fuck you" to the tour and to everything that had been fucking us up for the past year or two.

The funny thing is we actually really liked Fugazi. This was in their early days when they were at their best. We opened for them that night, and I was thrilled to meet Ian backstage. "Hi, I'm Ian." I was barely holding back my giggles, thinking, "Of COURSE you're Ian!" He was super friendly and cool—the whole band was. They even let us use some of their gear on stage. So the guilt from our little prank settled in a bit earlier than it might have otherwise. I've spoken with Ian in the years since but he never mentioned the sticky, stinky van we left for them. Our apologies, guys.

That night we also met some members of another American band called the Yeastie Girlz. They asked me if I'd heard the new Bad Religion album, *Suffer*. They dropped the cassette into the stereo and basically changed my life over the course of the ensuing 26 minutes and 14 seconds.

It was the best thing I'd ever heard. It was a style of melodic punk rock that walked the perfect line between pop and hardcore. I listened to the tape ten times that night. I thought that if I tried, maybe I could come close to writing something almost as good. Maybe NOFX deserved another shot.

I abandoned my plan to be Operation Ivy's roadie. I had a new plan: stop sucking.

36

Smelly

Europe was like landing on an alien planet to me. I was baffled by the stringent political correctness, and I cracked up listening to people making all these strange sounds and using them as language. I snagged loose cobblestones to bring back to my friends as souvenirs as if they were moon rocks. We went to the Vatican, and I had never seen anything like it in my life. I don't consider myself a spiritual guy, but I was awestruck by its size and significance.

Just like that first station wagon tour of the Northwest, coming home from Europe felt like we had accomplished something real as a band. It didn't matter that no one liked us or that we ended up in physical fights with both our crowd and our tour manager. I considered the tour a success just by virtue of existing. We weren't looking at the band as a potential career by any stretch, but we had boldly gone where I had never for a moment expected us to go.

Not that the experience matured me in the least. I poured beer all over Fugazi's van interior along with everyone else, and I definitely earned the runner-up prize for childish drunken behavior next to Dave.

The night Dave and I woke everyone up at 3 a.m., Mike was livid. "You fuckers! I don't need this fucking shit! I'm going to fucking college! I have a fucking life! You're fucking embarrassing me—I'll quit this band right now, and it won't make any difference! Fuck you, you owe everybody a fucking apology!"

Thankfully, something turned him around by the time we got back to the States, and Mike decided to stick with NOFX.* But I was not done testing his patience by a long shot.

37

Melvin

We started calling Dave "Sal" because it was the name of Al Pacino's partner in *Dog Day Afternoon*. There's a scene in the movie where Pacino asks, "Is there any special country you wanna go to?"

Sal thinks for a moment and replies, "Wyoming." Pacino patiently explains that Wyoming is not a country.

Dave had never really traveled, so he was geographically clueless. When we landed in Europe, he asked, "Did we fly over an ocean to get here?" He caught shit for that one for the brief remainder of his time in the band.

Despite the setbacks and the thrown bottles, our first European tour was a beautiful moment in time. There are few things more magnificent than

---

*And these days *he's* the one keeping everyone up!

Amsterdam in mid-September. The canals, the bicycles, the architecture . . . we weren't jaded world travelers yet. We were wide-eyed twenty-somethings whose only responsibilities were to drink beer and play punk rock music. Back home we couldn't help but doubt whether we were making the right decisions by not doing more to prepare for our futures, but for those first few days in Europe we felt like all of our bad decisions were finally being rewarded.

It didn't even get me down too much when milky goo started dripping out of my dick after gulping down too much drinkable yogurt.* NOFX survived the long drives and the drunk fights between Dave and Dolph by adhering to our policy of just rolling with it.

The drummer from Drowning Roses didn't have the same philosophy. He let the road get to him, and he was always angry about something. I remember him being mad because he suspected one of us of using his stage towel.

"Zis towel smells like dick!"

We burst out laughing. We honestly hadn't touched his towel. His rage—especially when delivered via his German accent—was just hilarious to us.

"I know zis smell! Zis smells like dick!"

"Why do you know the smell of dick so well?"

The harder we laughed, the madder he got. He actually quit the tour halfway through, and Smelly pulled double duty, filling in for Drowning Roses for the rest of the shows. I can't say for sure if it was a purely altruistic move or if he had some residual guilt for wiping his dick on that dude's towel.

Some bands might have had the exact same experiences and come home feeling like failures. No one showed up, we lost money, our guitarist was a mess, and the guy who booked us would probably never work with us again. On paper, we were a disaster.

But we had a record out. We had been to Europe. And we were making friends, if not fans. We started from such a low place that by comparison we were on top of the world.

We would do better next time.

---

*Yeah, I know what you're thinking. But the doctor at the Amsterdam clinic assured me, in his best broken English, that it wasn't gonorrhea.

Recording Liberal Animation *at Westbeach Studios.*

38

Mike

I worked for a short time at McDonald's in high school. I also put in time at a couple of women's shoe stores (my dad hooked me up) and delivered pills for a local pharmacy. I delivered to the homes of Sammy Davis Jr. and Johnny Carson, but the only celebrity who ever answered her own door was Elizabeth Montgomery.* I wish I could tell you what they were all taking, but all the packages were coded.

I saved up enough money for my crappy bass rig, the tour van, and the recording of our first two 7-inches. I had enough left over to fund our first actual LP, *Liberal Animation*. It cost $675 total. We recorded and mixed the whole thing in three straight sixteen-hour days with Brett Gurewitz, the guitarist of Bad Religion and founder of Epitaph Records. He offered to put it out on his label, but I wanted NOFX to have its own label. That's what Bad Religion did, that's what Minor Threat did, that's what we were going to do.

Not only was I the only one in the band with any money, but I had fallen into a "leadership" role by default. Probably because I was the least fucked up. I didn't do drugs at the time, and I didn't drink nearly as heavily as the other guys, so I was the one handling all the stuff that required brainpower. I booked the tours, I dealt with the promoters, I loaded the van at the end of the night.† So I was the one who started the NOFX label: Colossal Wassail.

The first pressing of *Liberal Animation* was two thousand copies. We sold about twelve hundred over the course of our tours with Dave Casillas and our first trip to Europe (and lost another hundred or so when some Mexican gangsters grabbed a box full of them at a show in L.A.). I still have a few dozen sitting around somewhere. I should eBay them. Years later when we started to see some success I sold the album to Epitaph for about

---

*And she was one of the few who bothered to tip!

†Everyone would be wasted after the shows, so it always fell on me to play Tetris with our gear and fit it into the back of the van. My band mates would praise my van-loading skills: "Mike is the best at loading the van!" And I would ride that ego boost: "Yeah, I'm the best!" I realize now that they totally Tom Sawyer-ed me into loading the van while they went off to pick up girls.

50 grand (which I'm sure they've recouped by now). So overall it was a successful experiment in DIY record releasing.

Most importantly, it established our relationship with Brett Gurewitz. After hearing *Suffer* I knew we had to work with him again in order to somehow approximate the sound that Bad Religion had created.

First, though, we had to fire our guitarist.

39

Dave

Europe should've been the best time of my life. I should've been excited and happy for my first-ever trip out of the country, but I couldn't get into it. I don't know if it was the medication for my face or an overdue chemical shift in my brain or simply road fatigue. But by the time I got on that plane I just didn't give a fuck anymore. I couldn't have fun or change my bad mood no matter how hard I tried. I drank to deal with the depression, I drank to get myself on stage, I drank to fuel myself through the partying, and I drank because it was Europe and there was beer everywhere.

As we toured back through the States my depression never improved. In New Orleans we went into one of those tourist places that makes cheesy karaoke videos, and we filmed a music video for our song "Shut Up Already." Everyone in the video was hamming it up and mugging for the camera. I faded into the background and moped through the whole thing. Our friend and roadie DJ is in the video, looking like more of a band member than me.

Sure, there were still fun moments, like watching our roadie Jerry smear Ben-Gay on Sandin's balls while he was passed out. But I also kept getting severe headaches. Again, it's hard to pinpoint whether it was the booze, the depression, or my still-unhealed face, but halfway home I started saying, "I'm done with this shit" after every show. And meaning it.

Like every other band I'd been in, NOFX finally hit its expiration date. We played a victorious "welcome home" show in Santa Barbara after the tour, and a few days later I got the call from Mike telling me that everyone agreed I shouldn't be in the band anymore. It wasn't a three-against-one decision—it was unanimous.

◆ ◆ ◆

A few years later Mike called me up to invite me to a sold-out NOFX show at the Country Club in Reseda. The place held one thousand people. When I was on tour with them we were happy to draw twenty-five. I immediately thought, "Damn, I should've stuck it out!" But I never would've been able to hack it. I don't need extravagance or creature comforts. I can live in a fucking shack if it comes down to it. But I wasn't built for the road life. I love playing music, but I also love sleeping in my own bed.

I took the stage once more with NOFX at their three twenty-fifth anniversary shows in 2009. Sandin will tell you I was drunk at the San Diego show and still couldn't stay on my feet, but I only fell over at the very end, when I lost my balance after jumping up onto the monitor. But I rolled back up onto my feet and still managed to nail the leads. You'd think they'd give me a little credit.

But you know how it is with those guys. Vivid fucking imaginations.

40

Mike

Pam Shriver is a former pro tennis player who won a gold medal at the 1988 Seoul Olympics. While she was in Korea representing our nation, we snuck into the backyard of her mansion with some Baltimore punks and had a midnight pool party.

Before our first European tour, we ended up stuck in Baltimore for a few days after one of our shows was canceled. We bought a keg of beer and partied with the locals the whole time. They showed us around the city and took care of us, and we bonded with some of them enough to keep in touch to this day.

One Baltimore punk in particular served as an exceptional tour guide and party planner. His name was DJ, and he looked like a slightly smaller version of Smelly. They both had crazy dreadlocks and that excited/mischievous smile, and they both loved to get blitzed and cause trouble. His sense of humor and attitude completely meshed with ours. He kept an eye on our van while we were away in Europe, and when we returned to the states he hopped in with us and we drove him out to California. And that's where he stayed.

I don't know if remaining in Baltimore would've sent his life down a healthy, productive path, but moving to L.A. with NOFX definitely accomplished the opposite.

41

Smelly

DJ was only sixteen when we met him, but he was so goofy and hilarious that he fit in with all the twenty-something punks he was living with in Baltimore, and he fit in even better with NOFX. He pitched in as a roadie and everyone in the band loved him, but DJ and I grew closer to each other than anyone else. Which is why I feel bad for kind of ruining his life.

I guess in the end I can't blame myself entirely for DJ's willingness to shoot heroin, but I was the one who first stuck in the needle.

The first person I initiated into junkiedom was my friend Ming.* He was one of the older punk kids who went with me to my first show. We went to MacArthur Park one night to go to an underground club called the Scream, but it was closed for some reason. Two chicks pulled up, also looking for the club, so we chatted them up for a while. One of them seemed a little rough around the edges, so I asked if they knew where I could score some dope. They told me about a place nearby, so Ming gave me a ride to the Mexican neighborhood to get the drugs, and then a ride to the black neighborhood to get "outfits" (needles and other associated junkie tools). We drove up some side street and I shot up what turned out be really shitty Mexican junk. Ming was always open to new experiences, so when I asked him if he wanted to try it he said yes.

I cooked him up a shot and went to inject it in the top of his hand, but for some reason his blood coagulated in the needle and plugged it up. The standard procedure in such a case is to heat up the needle in order to liquefy the blood and clear the passage. Once the syringe was unclogged, I shot him up, but I didn't wipe the black residue from the flame off the needle, so Ming was left with a small, circular tattoo about the size of a BB pellet to commemorate his first fix.

---

*In the extras section of the *NOFX: Backstage Passport* DVD, Ming gives us a quick history lesson about Tiananmen Square.

It's still there. I cringe whenever I see it because I think about how I was partially responsible for his journey from being an aspiring artist going to college to being a substitute teacher who was shooting up between classes. Eventually I helped him get clean, but the drug took a lot from him during those years in between.

DJ was the only other junkie I ever mentored. Ming and I were shooting up in Ming's garage, and DJ wanted to be included. He put on a front like he had done heroin before but just forgot how to do it and needed a refresher course. He had just arrived in California; he was probably as eager to be accepted as I always was. I couldn't see that at the time, though. So I stuck in the needle and brought him down into the pit with me.

◆   ◆   ◆

My friend Johnny Sixpack started a gang called the Dog Patch Winos. Well, they weren't really a gang; they were more like a group of alcoholic misfits who liked to get as wasted as possible and wear matching jackets. I had been inducted before the tour, and DJ fit in with them immediately when he moved to California. They provided a modest network of people up and down the coast who could offer drugs and places to sleep. DJ and I became junkie hobos, couch surfing with friends and bouncing between crash pads in L.A. and San Francisco.

DJ was my junkie apprentice. Despite the fascination with heroin in our pop culture and the vast amounts of books and movies about the subject, there's so much more you learn when you actually start shooting up. I apprenticed under Raymond, but I earned my master's degree in Junkie Studies on my own, and now it was time to share my knowledge. I could teach a UCLA Extension course in that shit.

Lesson 1: Radar

If you're not a junkie, you may not realize that heroin is being bought, sold, and shot all around you. The need for junk gives you a sixth sense. When you walk or drive through a neighborhood where heroin is available, you know. You can spot a dealer from a mile away, and you can predict when he's going to make his handoff down to the second. You can look at two nearly identical drunk gutter punks and tell which one is holding. Other junkies can outwardly appear as Mexican gangsters or high-powered businessmen in perfectly pressed suits, but, either way, you see through the disguise.

And they see through yours, too. You'll walk down the same street you've walked down a thousand times, but now that you're a junkie some random sketchy dude will walk up and say, "Hey man, I'm holding, you want some?" It's a subconscious subculture. And later when you're trying desperately to get clean you'll still be acutely aware of every dealer, every user, and every speck of heroin within reach. For the rest of your life.

Lesson 2: Transport

So now you know where the dealers are, and you want to buy some drugs. You think it's going to be sexy and cool—you'll shake hands with someone and exchange a palmed wad of cash for a discreet little baggie, using a sleight-of-hand move that would make Penn & Teller jealous.

Well, yes, you hand over the cash very deftly, but they don't hand you a baggie. They pull a small, tied-off balloon out of their mouth, and you quickly take it and stick it inside your own cheek.

The concept is that if the cops stop either you or the dealer, you can quickly swallow the balloon and "retrieve" it later. Sure, it's gross that you're swapping spit with random scumbags, but this is probably the LEAST disgusting element of your future as a heroin addict, so you should try to get over it quickly.

Much more disgusting is what happens when you do have to swallow your stash. I bought four balloons (such was my tolerance at the time) from a dealer in Hollywood while hanging out with a girl I was dating. She didn't know I made the deal or that my cheeks were stuffed with heroin; we were just drunk and driving back to my mom's house where I'd been crashing while my folks were away.

I got pulled over. I was way too drunk to be driving, and I was ordered out of the car to perform a field sobriety test. As I was doing my best to walk a straight line and touch my fingers to my nose I gulped down all four balloons. And then I passed the fucking test! The girl I was with was probably confused about why I was so angry that I had just avoided a jail sentence.

I excused myself to the bathroom when we arrived at my mom's house and I stuck my fingers down my throat in order to throw up the balloons, but I couldn't get myself to puke, so I had to wait and let nature take its course.

The next day I went through my mom's cabinets and pulled out a spaghetti strainer. (I told you the spit-swapping wouldn't seem so bad after a while . . .) I put the strainer in the toilet and took a balloon-speckled dump. I went into the backyard and used the hose to melt away the poo while I panned for gold. After a full day of waiting to get high, watching my shit dissolve in that strainer was equivalent to being a kid on Christmas morning, running into the living room and seeing all those gleaming presents under the tree.

After I shot up, I washed off the strainer and put it back in the cabinet. It's probably still there. After all, when was the last time you replaced your spaghetti strainer?

Lesson 3: Funding

My circle of junkie friends had a racket going where we would steal high-end art books and sell them to some scummy guy we knew for 20 percent of the cover price. Snag a $200 book on architecture, make $40 cash. Enough to get high for the day. You'd walk into the store with a coat draped over your arm, shop around, and pile up the books that might be worth something, and then, on the way out, cover the pile with the coat and slip out the door. You could usually hit the same store several times, until one day you would walk in and they'd tell you to get the fuck out because they finally got wise.

DJ and I were hitting a store in the Valley that we had hit before. I had a car at the time, so I was the getaway driver and he was the thief. I parked at a gas station with easy access to an alley that would allow us a covert escape. While I was waiting for DJ, I got out to take a leak. I locked the car because we had probably a thousand bucks' worth of stolen books in the back. As I returned to the car after my pee break, I saw two big-ass dudes chasing DJ. They tackled him and started manhandling him. I grabbed my car's door handle: I had locked the keys inside.

The big dudes looked up at me while they roughed up DJ and could tell from our dreadlocks and matching Dog Patch Winos jackets that we were probably in cahoots. I ran down the alley, hid out for a couple hours, and watched the cops take DJ away. When the heat died down I borrowed a coat hanger from a nearby dry cleaner and retrieved my car. DJ ended up in county jail for thirty days. I kept stealing books and never got busted.

I guess the real lesson is that you shouldn't steal. But theft generally goes with the junkie territory, so you should at least try not to lock your keys in the car when you're the GODDAMNED GETAWAY DRIVER.

Lesson 4: Overdosing

My friend Jimmy Dread and I were shooting up at an apartment in San Francisco. I did my dope first, went to the bathroom, and came back to find Jimmy unconscious and not breathing. Everyone else in the apartment was too high to notice, so I dragged Jimmy to the shower and sprayed him with cold water. I guess current medical advice says you're not supposed to do that because it could send a person into shock, but that's what I was taught to do by other junkies. I assume you're not supposed to dump ice on a person's balls either, but I did that as well in my frantic attempt to wake him up.

He still wasn't breathing, so I called 911. Part of the junkie code is that if someone ODs you call the ambulance, wait until you hear the sirens, and then split. That way you're with them if they need you, but you also don't get busted. I could've gotten nailed for manslaughter if Jimmy died, since I was the one who copped the dope he was using. Best-case scenario I was getting arrested for possession. So I shouted at him and slapped him around until I heard sirens and then bailed.

Jimmy spent a few days in the hospital, but he lived.* I ended up with a pretty bad rep in the San Francisco music scene, though, because the rumors were that I left him for dead. No one gave me credit for calling 911, much less icing down his balls.

You start to grow numb to the news of friends OD'ing because you can't possibly keep up emotionally. Susan, one of my roommates from San Francisco, OD'd on Christmas morning and died in a Taco Bell bathroom. As soon as one of our other roommates found out, she grabbed all of Susan's stuff—her clothes, her bike, everything—and sold it all to buy dope. It sounds like a cold and ghoulish thing to do, but the truth is Susan probably would've done the same thing if it had been one of us.

Lesson 5: Social Stigma

If you've started shooting heroin in the first place, you're probably the type of person who already feels out of step with society, but heroin addiction will take you to an even lonelier place. It's not a party drug; it's something you do in dark alleys and bathroom stalls and places where you know no one's watching. Sure, you'll still spend time with your straight friends, but you'll spend more and more of your time with other junkies, or in pursuit of dope, or in pursuit of money to buy dope. It's a full-time job. But even if you manage your time effectively enough to hang out with your friends, your friends will stop wanting to hang out with you.

I moved into the basement of a party house in San Francisco, and a German girl named Suzy who I met on our European tour flew out and moved in with me. She OD'd the first night. I found her on the floor of the

---

*Although he's dead now.

bathroom and, just like Jimmy, threw her in the shower and smacked her around. Again: you're not supposed to throw an overdose victim in the shower. But you're also not supposed to let them stay asleep. If I hadn't been there to wake her up, she most likely would have died.

After clearing that little hurdle we just lived in our basement world of fucking and shooting up and shooting up and fucking. Mike and Erin moved into the house a month or so after I did and were so grossed out by our behavior that a couple weeks later Suzy and I came home and found all of our shit on the porch and the sidewalk. (Bringing my Dog Patch Wino friends over and having Johnny Sixpack and Bob Lush spray paint the kitchen walls probably didn't make me an ideal roommate, either.)

Without a place to live, Suzy and I went our separate ways. She tried to go straight but couldn't. She hanged herself six months later.*

Lesson 6: Dope Sickness

It's the fucking worst. You're nauseous. You're agitated. You shiver and sweat. Your muscles ache, especially the ones in your legs for some reason. And you can't sleep because your brain tortures you, whispering devilishly over and over again, "If you just had a little bit of dope you'd feel fine . . ."

The first time I was dope sick was when I was still living in Santa Barbara. I went home to visit my family for Christmas and didn't realize I was already an addict. I just thought I had the flu. And I didn't connect the dots when my "flu" went away the minute I got back to Santa Barbara and got some junk in my system.

I finally put two and two together on the next NOFX tour. I rarely scored on the road, so when I was hit with the same "flu" symptoms I slowly figured out the connection between the sickness and the distance from home.

I rode in the back of the van, shivering, sweating, cramping, and sleepless. DJ came out with us again, and I'm sure he was hurting just as bad. In the absence of heroin, the only way we could relax was by drinking to excess and then beyond. Our natural predilection for mischief coupled with our unbridled drinking and drug use gave birth to our new nickname:

The Moron Brothers.

---

*I've always carried a lot of guilt over Suzy's death, and it has only intensified in the years since I've become a parent. Even though I wasn't directly responsible for her habit or her living situation or her suicide, I've always been haunted by the idea that Suzy's mom put her on a plane to see me and never saw her daughter again.

42

Melvin

When I played the first NOFX 7-inch for my mom, I could tell she was struggling to think of something complimentary to say about it.

"Wow, I can really *hear* the guitar!"

She may as well have patted me on the head and hung our record cover on the fridge, but it was sweet that she cared enough to patronize me. As a fellow musician I think she wanted to encourage my artistic side. And she never really got a chance to travel when she was younger, so when we started touring she was happy for me to have the opportunity to go all over the States and Europe, even if it was in the back of a used dry-cleaning van.

But as the years went by she also saw me living in her house, broke, with no real commitment to school or any plan beyond continuing to make music she didn't understand. She wasn't off base at all for suggesting I join the army. She was just trying to help.

I decided to stick with the band for a little while longer and see where it took me. Then maybe I could go back and study psychology again, or maybe I'll look into architecture instead. Or maybe I'll just keep living the Hollywood life of going to bars and shows every night and occasionally hitting the road with my buddies. I was in my twenties, did I really need a plan?

But meanwhile I couldn't just lie around and be useless. My uncle was vice president at Fred Segal, and one night when he was over he offered me a job in the warehouse at their flagship Melrose Avenue store. I received and inventoried shipments, put price tags on $2,000 pairs of pants, took out the trash, stacked boxes, and did anything else the salespeople didn't want to do. I've always been a little OCD, so my stacks were straight, my work was done neatly, and I cleaned incessantly. I was a good employee. I probably could've worked my way up to warehouse manager if I had stuck with it.

One of my co-workers was a tall rocker dude named Skip who started a New York Dolls-ish band called New Improved God. They weren't part of the hardcore punk scene, but Skip and I got along, and I started hanging out with his friends. One of those friends was a long-haired metal fan named Steve Kidwiler, and we had two loves in common: pot and guitar. Steve and I were from different musical worlds, but we bonded quickly. He knew all the technical stuff about guitar that I had never bothered to learn, like diminished this and augmented that. And when I finally saw him jam one night I found that all that theory came packaged with undeniable skill and passion.

I played Steve the *Liberal Animation* album, and he offered me the same type of strained compliments my parents did. Punk wasn't his scene, but we needed a second guitarist, so I invited him to join NOFX. Luckily for us, he didn't have any better options.

Steve's first band, Tantrum.

43

Steve

I was ten years old when my mom took my brother and me to see Kiss at the Omaha Civic Auditorium during their *Love Gun* tour. I still have the ticket. And it remains unripped. While we were waiting outside before the show, the crowd was getting restless and shouting, "Open the fucking doors!" And then BOOM CRASH everyone funneled through the broken gates and we were caught in the mob like sand running through an hourglass. My mom tried to mask her fear. "Stay close to me!" Security couldn't stop the tidal wave of people, everyone pushed their way to the front, and ultimately my mom and I ended up with better seats than she had paid for. I got a photo with my Kodak 110 of a thumb-sized Gene Simmons blowing fire.

At the end of a miraculous night of makeup and drum solos and fake blood, my mom and I found a note on my mom's car that said my brother— who had wandered off with his friends—had gotten sick and called my dad to pick him up. We came home to find him in bed, resting up after a bout of reportedly ferocious vomiting. I relayed the awesomeness of the concert to him, and just as his jealousy was peaking I heard my mom on the phone in the other room: "Yes, Mr. Simmons's room, please."

She had correctly deduced that Kiss would be staying in one of two hotels in the Omaha area. She tried the Holiday Inn first and got lucky when she called the Hilton second. The next thing I knew my brother was on the phone with Gene Simmons. Gene extended his sympathies about my brother's illness and chatted with him for a minute, and then the phone was passed to me.

"So you came to the show tonight?"

"Yeah . . ."

"Uh-huh. Did you like it?"

"Yeah . . ."

"You don't sound very excited."

"Oh, no. Totally, man!"

My mom saw my deer-in-headlights look, gracefully took the phone, and thanked Gene for his time. The next day my mom went to the hotel's front desk to pick up a gift Gene had left for my brother: a personalized autograph on a piece of Hilton stationery.

That's when I decided I wanted to be a rock 'n' roller when I grew up.

◆   ◆   ◆

We were a military family so we bounced around a lot when I was a kid, but Omaha was where I saw Kiss, where I started playing drums and guitar, and where I bought my first record album: Olivia Newton-John, *If You Love Me Let Me Know*. I bought it mostly for the innocent-yet-sexy shag-haired beauty on the cover, but I was always open-minded about music, digging on everything from Nugent to Merle Haggard to Fifth Dimension to Chicago.

When my family moved to Merced, California, in the early '80s, I fell into a group of guys who introduced me to Ozzy and Maiden and early Motley Crüe. Some of the local skater kids played me the classic punk stuff—Sex Pistols, Dead Kennedys, Circle Jerks—and it was all right, but none of them had the guitar solos of Randy Rhoads or the drumming of Tommy Lee.

After short stints in a few other bands I started playing guitar in my very own rock group: Tantrum. We put on a couple well-attended DIY shows at a rented VFW hall and the Merced fairgrounds, and we sunk all our profits into recording a demo in a converted guesthouse studio, produced by a guy who normally recorded religious bands. (We nicknamed him "Kamikaze Ken" in the liner notes to cover for the conservative, suburbanite, glasses-wearing reality.) We sent it out and got a "we're very interested" letter from Time Coast (an indie label that released Ratt's first EP), but we never heard from them or any other labels again after that. And that summer at a keg party in the woods our drummer and bassist got in a fight over something that has since been completely forgotten about, and Tantrum ended ironically over the very thing it was named for.

I did a year and a half at Merced Junior College and then discovered an unaccredited, for-profit music school in Los Angeles called the Guitar Institute of Technology (currently known as Musicians Institute). GIT was a perfect excuse to get me out of Merced and maybe get another band going. My parents had some money saved up, and they figured that with credentials I could always get a gig as a guitar teacher, so they covered my tuition and wished me well.

My drummer friend Kenny and I found a junior one-bedroom apartment on Franklin and Whitley in the heart of Hollywood. Not too long after we moved in we were crossing the street on our block when a car came to a screeching halt next to us, quickly followed and boxed in by two LAPD cruisers. The cops shouted, "Get on the ground!" so we hit the deck and kept our noses to the asphalt until they apprehended their suspect.

Toto, I have a feeling we're not in Merced anymore . . .

Another day, I came home to find our front door ajar, Kenny on the couch with a look of pure fear on his face, and a guy who looked like a 'roided-out version of Billy Idol yelling something about how Kenny had stolen his rock. I assume he meant drugs, but he could've also meant a hunk of granite for all the sense he was making. Kenny hadn't stolen shit—the dude had just walked into the apartment as Kenny was about to leave for the day. I somehow reasoned with the guy: if we flipped the couch cushions and still couldn't find his rock, he would have to go. He agreed to the terms, but when we found nothing he demanded pieces of Kenny's drum kit as restitution. As he was gabbing I slowly folded up one of the cymbal stands in a way that allowed me to wield it as a potential weapon. "Now it's time for you to go." Thankfully, he listened.

The upside of living in L.A. in the late '80s was bearing witness to the restless music scene. Metal, punk, and alternative were blurring together. I would watch Guns N' Roses play at the Whisky on the Westside and Pigmy Love Circus play at the Scream downtown, and in between I would hang out at the Rainbow, hoping to catch a glimpse of Lemmy or Slash on their way to the VIP room.

The downside of living in L.A. was everything else. My time at GIT was trying, to say the least. You had guys from Bangladesh and Tibet who absolutely ripped on guitar but who were socially defunct, so there was little hope of forming a band with them. You had egotistical instructors trying to stamp out an assembly line of jazz-fusion players. And you had homeless street punks razzing you on Hollywood Boulevard as you made your way to and from class with your binder and gig bag.

It's hard to convey how unwanted you are as a guitarist in Los Angeles. Mosquitoes in Florida get a better reception from the public . . . and have better job prospects. After a year, the illusion that I was going to jump in a band and get signed to a major label had been thoroughly shattered. I was frustrated with school to the point of giving up, and I was commuting to and from Beverly Hills to work at a gas station for $4.75 an hour to pay my bills.*

My friend Kent had also migrated south from Merced and had been playing guitar in a band called New Improved God. They blended a throwback CBGB's punk sound with an alternative rock sensibility. The singer, Todd Godzilla, had half his head shaved and wore skintight jeans with a white dinner jacket on stage, and Skip, their bassist, was a 6-foot-2 version of Sid Vicious with long black hair down to his nipples.

Skip and I immediately hit it off. One evening I dropped by his apartment to ritualistically make a case of Budweiser disappear, and his roommate was at the kitchen table, rolling the first dreadlocks into the hair of a man named Eric Melvin.

Eric and I exchanged reptilian head nods and Skip mentioned Eric was in a band called NOFX that had just returned from a tour across the U.S. and Europe. I was impressed. I had never heard of them, but they had a record out and were touring Europe? They were living the dream!

---

*After a customer was robbed at gunpoint, I decided to close full serve every night after 8 p.m. When the owner found out, I rejoined the ranks of the Hollywood unemployed.

I hung out with Eric Melvin a few times and got along well with him (I mean, who doesn't?), and one night at Skip's, Eric mentioned they were kicking their guitarist out of the band for being too drunk. Skip was like a wingman trying to facilitate a hook-up: "Hey dude, why don't you join NOFX? Eric, why don't you get Steve here to play?" It put Eric and me in an awkward enough position that we agreed to meet up and listen to *Liberal Animation* together.

As we sat in my apartment and listened to the album, I thought, "How can I let this guy down easy?"

It was different from anything I had ever heard, I can say that much. The drumming caught my attention, but mostly I didn't feel like it was the right band for me, nor was I the right guy for their band.

But I really had nothing else going for me at the time. And there was a sense of urgency pushing me as I watched every Sunset Strip metal band go from the clubs to the major labels. Everyone was scratching lottery tickets and coming up a winner. I needed to start scratching a ticket of my own.

The reality, of course, is that that's not how it works. It's foolish to expect mainstream musical success in the first place, let alone to expect it to happen overnight. But Hollywood was, and always will be, full of fools. And I was one of them.

Melvin and I had a few beers and worked on some songs. I struggled with their unorthodox strum patterns—theirs was not a technique covered in the GIT curriculum—but I guess I faked it well enough because the next thing I knew I was in Melvin's Mustang, heading up the 2 Freeway to a guy named Ming's house where NOFX had a practice space set up in his toolshed.

I heard later they didn't like my long hair, my puffy-tongued high-tops, or my Randy Rhoads Kramer copy guitar, but there was no open animosity, or any impoliteness, at the audition. Erik Sandin's sickly, gaunt frame didn't register at the time as a symptom of drug addiction. I assumed he was on a Top Ramen diet like every other musician I knew. Fat Mike was one of the craziest bass players I had ever seen and one of the worst singers I had ever heard. We went through two songs and they gave me a copy of the demos they had cut for what would eventually be *S&M Airlines*.

I guess I was in?

EPITAPH 8201 SUNSET BLVD., SUITE 111
HOLLYWOOD, CA. 90028

NOFX

44

Mike

As the main songwriter and chief van loader for NOFX, it fell upon me to fire Dave Casillas. Smelly, Melvin, and I all agreed after Europe that he had to go. He didn't seem to care. We were NOFX in 1988. Who gives a shit?

We still liked the idea of a guitarist who could play rad leads and fill out our sound, and my new *Suffer*-inspired songs needed that dimension to them, so we started auditioning people. There was a guy from a Las Vegas band called Poor White Trash who came out to California to audition for us, and he was perfect. He played great and was fun to hang out with, so we said, "You're in!" He rolled up his sleeve to reveal a tattoo he had just gotten of the NOFX logo; such was his confidence in the outcome of his tryout.

And then he disappeared. We tried to contact him for two months before we gave up. We didn't hear from him again for more than five years. I'm not the guy who's going to say, "Don't do drugs," but I will say, "Don't do meth, kids: You could blow your chance to be in NOFX."

Eric Melvin brought in Steve Kidwiler, a friend of a friend from the L.A. metal scene. Eric had moved back to Hollywood, which had been completely taken over by hair rock. Steve had long hair, which I hated, and he was more into metal than punk, but he had loads of technical skill and was animated on stage.

Steve and I generally got along, but we also rubbed each other the wrong way. The most concrete example I can offer is when he wanted to thank God in the liner notes of one of our records. I didn't realize he was such a religious guy until then, and I'm a rather vocal atheist, so we ended up compromising: The liner notes had a list of all the thank yous, and we added a line that read, "Steve would like to thank God." It wasn't a big fight or anything, just an illustration of how he and I were from different worlds.

Despite the personality rift, we were able to put together our first listenable album, *S&M Airlines*. I consider that to be the first real NOFX album because, despite its flaws, it was a move to a melodic style of songwriting. It was a cross between D.I., RKL, and Bad Religion. It wasn't as good as any of them, but we were finally finding our sound.

Still, I have a hard time listening to it because my vocals are fucking terrible. Apparently I could write melodies, I just couldn't *sing* melodies. We recorded and mixed it in six days with Brett Gurewitz, and he brought in Greg Graffin from Bad Religion to record some vocal harmonies.

We signed to Epitaph in the hopes of getting the record out to more people, and we shot a video for the title track with a young filmmaker Brett had been working with. (We knew him at the time as the guitarist for a band called the Little Kings, but most people know him today as Oscar-winning director Gore Verbinski.)

Even though our video never saw airtime on MTV, and even though we were never featured on any commercial radio stations, *S&M Airlines* generated our first set of positive reviews and a gradual uptick in attendance at our shows. The record sold slow but steady: 2,500 copies in the first year . . . not bad! It was the first time we ever saw NOFX moving forward. The unthinkable was happening: people were liking us.

But since we had spent the previous five years sounding, performing, and behaving like shit, we had to rebuild our reputation from scratch. And that's hard to do when your drummer has a habit of pissing in people's silverware drawers.

The Moron Brothers.

45

Smelly

If you look closely at my toes, you'll see faded memories from a night in Milwaukee. I woke up on a hardwood floor as the newly risen sun baked me through the window. The normal hangover symptoms applied, but I didn't understand why my toes hurt. I sat up, and my eyes struggled to focus on the bloody mess at the tips of my feet. I wondered out loud what the fuck had happened, and DJ explained, "Yeah buddy, you tattooed yourself last night!"

On each toe was a letter:

T-I-T-S-N-B-O-O-Z-E

DJ and I had been using the phrase as our rallying cry: "Tits n' Booze!" But I had drawn the Z backwards, so my toes read, "Tits n' Boose."

Raymond taught me how to make a prison-style tattoo gun with a toothbrush, a ballpoint pen, a guitar string, and a motor from a Walkman. Thinking I was Mr. Fucking Rebel, I brought it on tour and scrawled deformed tattoos on any willing victims I could find. I was no artist—I have no idea why anyone would let me permanently etch their skin, but they did. One kid asked for the Samhain skull logo and when I was done it looked like a three-year-old had scribbled on him with a dried-out Sharpie. Helen Keller would've been able to create a more distinguishable version of that logo in her sleep. I tattooed a decent-looking spider on a girl's rib cage, but it was ruined when a nasty infection radiated out from it. I wasn't sterilizing the needle—it went from person to person, junkie to junkie. One of the guys from Subculture ended up with an ace of spades that got so gnarly and pus-riddled it made him look like patient zero for a new strain of smallpox. Who knows what diseases I was passing around? (Answer: Hepatitis C, most likely. But I'll get to that later.)

I can't fully blame alcohol and drugs for my behavior; it was probably a natural extension of my class-clown cries for acceptance and my love of all things anti-establishment. Every kid tests his or her boundaries when they first leave home. I just happened to leave home in a van full of punks with a homemade tattoo gun.

Booze was my fuel and DJ was my co-pilot. There was never a night on those early tours when we weren't wasted, and there was hardly a night when that didn't lead to some new level of mischief. We were *Jackass* before *Jackass* existed. If we were at a house party where the floors were slick with spilled beer, we went "human bowling": Spot a group of people standing around and talking, get a running start, and slide on our stomachs into them to see how many we could take out.

Jackass is funny when it's on TV, but not so much when it's in your kitchen. We filled people's ice trays with piss and slipped them back into the freezer. Or we just opened the silverware drawer and peed in there. One guy caught me peeing in his bathtub while scribbling the Dog Patch Winos logo on his bathroom wall with a fat Magic Marker. There was a perfectly fine toilet inches away, but I insisted on using the tub. He grabbed me by the back of my shirt and threw me on the ground, but when he was done pounding me I just laughed it off like a psychopath and partied on.

One night in Nebraska we put on a couple of lovely sundresses we found in someone's closet and tied a bunch of tampons to our dreadlocks. Then we dipped the tampons in ketchup because we're idiots. When the party ran out of beer, DJ and I volunteered to make a beer run. We were punks from California drunk-driving through Nebraska in drag, with bloody tampons in our hair. I turned to DJ and said, "Man, I don't want to go to jail looking like this," and at that exact fucking moment a set of red and blue spinning lights appeared in the rearview mirror.

I have no recollection of how I talked myself out of getting arrested and sold for a carton of cigarettes. I just remember the cop staring at me, saying, "Son . . . " and shaking his head in disapproval.

There was an art to our mischief. It doesn't take a lot of creativity to smash a TV or start a fight. We tried to use our imaginations. If I had to take a shit at someone's house, I would first stop in their bedroom and pull a pillowcase off one of their pillows. After shitting, I would turn the pillowcase inside out and wipe my ass with it, then I would turn it right-side-out again, put the pillow back inside, and return it to the bed. The source of the stench would be a mystery since there would be no skid marks on the outside of the pillowcase, and I would be two towns away before they ever figured it out.

Okay, so it was the imagination of a drooling twelve-year-old, but it was still imagination.

Once we were partying at a house where there happened to be a bag of plaster lying around, so when one of the guys at the party passed out, DJ and I put his leg in a cast. I mixed up the plaster with salt because I knew that would make it set faster. The guy had passed out with his legs crossed, so we took a bunch of fabric strips, dipped them in the plaster, and wrapped both of his legs together so he wouldn't be able to walk in the morning. It didn't set in time, though; he just woke up confused a few hours later, with a bunch of mushy paste and stiff cloth around his legs and torso. But again: it's the imagination that counts.

Occasionally the impish pranks were overshadowed by utter dickishness or frightening destructiveness. After making a mess of the plaster cast, I was running down the street high on acid, spray painting cars and jumping on them, and shouting, "Let's throw a barbecue!" just before throwing a barbecue grill through a plate-glass window. And then getting into a fight with an off-duty cop because he was trying to remove his daughter from my presence.

I don't know how I didn't get arrested—I would ask the other guys in the band for more details, but they were all hiding from me in the van at the time.

I never felt any pangs of guilt, regardless of how much destruction I caused. But the night after the off-duty cop incident my conscience started to catch up to me. We were staying with an art student who was extremely generous and sweet to us, and in return I took her brand-new Vespa and went wild in the driveway, taking it off jumps. I fucking wrecked the thing. But that's not the part I feel the most guilty about.

She told us we could have anything in the fridge except for two particular dishes: some sort of special pizza and some custom Jell-O mold she had created for her final project for art school. It was due the next day, and she needed it to graduate. What do you think was the first thing I fucking did when she went to bed? I wasn't being "punk," I was just being an asshole. I ate her art and betrayed her trust just because I could.

I woke up in the morning with her foot on my hair while she was screaming and cutting off my dreadlocks with a pair of scissors. If she had stabbed me in the neck with those scissors instead, no one would've blamed her.

✦ ✦ ✦

Strangely, DJ and I were able to get laid in the midst of all this. You would think girls would be turned off by a guy who accessorized his hair with ketchup-covered sanitary products, or who often rested his dick on people's shoulders until they noticed. But every night we were the out-of-towners, we had the spotlight on us, and we were brimming with unjustified, alcohol-infused confidence.

DJ and I had a contest to see who could nail more chicks. We kept a tally on the roof of the van and ended up tied at twelve at the end of that first summer tour. We would jokingly refer to ourselves as "the macho studs" and walk around house parties saying, "Macho studs! You're a macho stud? Hey, I'M a macho stud! Ladies, you need a macho stud? Because I'm a macho stud!" (Seriously, is it any wonder they started calling us the Moron Brothers?)

One night in Michigan our little comedy routine paid off. A girl from one of the bands we played with came up to us and said in her most seductive voice, "I wanna fuck the macho studs." Moments later I was on my back with my eyes closed while she rode on top of me. I sensed something to my left and opened my eyes to see a foot by my ear. I looked to the right, another foot. I looked up: DJ's ginger-haired balls were six inches over my forehead, rhythmically tapping against the girl's chin. "WHOA! DUDE! STOP!" We shifted positions and she was soon blowing me while DJ fucked her from behind. As soon as he entered her, I could see by his strained expression that his race had been run. He pulled his dick out and jerked off all over her back while staring at me cross-eyed. I shouted, "Dude, dude! DUDE!" and shielded myself from any friendly fire. I decided then that there are some things brothers shouldn't share.

Just like our pranks and mischief, my interactions with girls occasionally revealed my darker side. I boned a cute punk girl named Jenny in Nebraska. We passed out naked and drunk in the van, and at 8 a.m. I heard pounding on the window. "Jenny! Are you in there? Jenny? I can't believe you did this!" It was her boyfriend. She waited quietly with me until he split, and we ended up spending the rest of the day together.

We stayed in town the next night as well, and our hosts threw a party at their house. The boyfriend showed up. I don't know what he was thinking. I was with his girl on the other side of the room, and he was too meek to do anything about it other than stew on the couch. It's any guy's worst nightmare. But of course I made it worse.

At one point he muttered something along the lines of "I should kick your ass" under his breath when I was in earshot. In the middle of the party, I turned and loudly asked, "What, motherfucker?" He was silent, but I announced to everyone the insider information that Jenny had shared with me earlier: "Maybe if you knew how to fuck, your chick wouldn't be sucking my fucking cock and hanging out with me!" As if I hadn't humiliated him enough, I pressed on, this time challenging both his courage and manhood while mocking a physical feature about which he was probably already self-conscious: "As a matter of fact, you keep talking, I'm gonna take you outside, fuck your girlfriend, and make your nose even bigger!"

Yeah. I may as well have ripped off his balls and shoved them down his throat while I was at it.

Jenny should've realized that I was a piece of shit and walked away, but instead she followed us to our next several shows. She showed up and sang me some Broadway number about "our love is here and take me now before you regret it" or some nonsense. I told her repeatedly to go home and that I was not into her, but she followed us all the way to fucking Wisconsin before she gave up. We later immortalized her stalker behavior in a song on our *Ribbed* album.

The takeaway from all this is that booze and drugs make for some memorable nights, but they also make for some nights you wish you could forget. Also: If I ever get murdered, it was probably Jenny's boyfriend. Or maybe the Jell-O mold girl.

46

Steve

My first show with NOFX was at the Coconut Teaszer, a Hollywood dive that drew crowds by offering free beer and hot dogs to starving punks and metalheads on Wednesday nights. We were playing second on a bill with Wasted Youth, the Adolescents, Tender Fury, the Grim, and an unknown band from Seattle called Nirvana (who didn't bother to show).

I was awful.

I maybe got through "S&M Airlines" and one other song with some amount of competence, but beyond that I was a mess. But then I realized no one cared. Whenever someone from GIT played a show, the other students would all turn out to "support" their colleague, but they would usually just stand in the audience with their arms folded thinking, "I could've played that better." Not the punks. They were wasted and happy, and they seemed to like me. And the guys in the band didn't bat an eye at any of my mistakes.

Things moved fast those first few months. I had to learn the entire *S&M Airlines* album in three weeks and then it was straight into the studio.* My only previous recording experience had been with Tantrum and "Kamikaze Ken" in a converted guesthouse, and suddenly I'm in a real studio with Brett Gurewitz. I had just heard NOFX for the first time a month earlier, and there I was signing and initialing some piece of paper that said something or other about percentages and royalties that, to this day, I've never read.

---

*People later blamed me for bringing a metal influence to the *S&M Airlines* album, but all of the songs were written (and demoed) well before I joined!

We shot a video for "S&M Airlines" with then-unknown director Gore Verbinski that began with a live show at the Anti-Club. I dislocated my knee in the middle of the set (and consequently fell onto a bed of bottles and pint glasses left at my feet by all the people drinking near the stage). I had no medical insurance, so I never considered going to the hospital. I just wrapped my knee in an ACE bandage and went with the band out to Edwards Air Force Base the next day to continue the video shoot on one of the tarmacs. I couldn't move much with a jacked knee, so in the video Melvin is the one doing all the jumping (not that I could ever keep up with him anyway). All I could really do was a little Chuck Berry hop, which you can see Mike and Melvin doing with me in the video in either a show of solidarity or mockery—likely a bit of both.

For a low-budget punk rock music video, it was an ambitious shoot. I remember a moment when Gore duct-taped the camera to the end of a long PVC pipe and dangled it over the tarmac from his pickup truck as his friend drove at us at top speed. Gore pulled the camera up just before it collided with Fat Mike's grill to get a whipping overhead crane shot. Years later, when I was watching *Pirates of the Caribbean* with my son and Gore's name appeared on the screen, I laughed out loud and said, "I know that guy!"

◆   ◆   ◆

The word "tour" was the one that perked my ears up when I first got to know Eric Melvin. It was the mark of a real, working band and it meant adventure and excitement around every corner. But much like moving to Los Angeles, and much like attending music school, touring fell far short of my expectations.

For three and a half months we were trapped in a dry-cleaning delivery van with no rear seats, an odorous mattress flopped on a plywood platform above the gear, and a side door that opened only occasionally. We were surviving on a two-burgers-for-two-bucks meal deal at Burger King every day, and we were playing shows in backyards, often getting paid solely in beer. The days off were brutal when we were stuck in the middle of nowhere with nothing to do, and everywhere we went people kept saying, "You're not Dave," and treating me like (or addressing me as) Sammy Hagar (usually brought on by Fat Mike introducing me that way to the crowd).

Sleeping on floors and going without showers was tough at first, but I got used to it. And when we got a box full of the first pressing of *S&M Airlines* shipped to us on the road, it was a highlight not just of the tour but also of my young life. I had never been on a real record before. The feeling of validation sustained me for weeks.

But our tours lasted for months. And our tours also featured the Moron Brothers.

Do you know what a "pressed ham" is? It's when you're sleeping nose up and someone squats over you without any undergarments on and tries to touch your nose with their butthole. I once woke up to Erik Sandin mere millimeters away from completing such a mission on my face.

"Butterballs" was a game in which Sandin or DJ would wipe their fingers on their nut sack or asshole, approach an unsuspecting victim, and smear their stink on that person's nose. They'd say "butterballs" and expect you to guess where the smell came from: butt or balls? I don't care what kind of soap you use, that stench stays with you forever.

A "butt trumpet" begins when you stick a garden hose up your ass and load your colon with water. I remember watching Sandin prep himself just so, pull his pants up, and approach some poor guy at a backyard party sitting in a lawn chair. I've never felt so lucky to not be another person as when I watched Erik drop his pants, bend over, and evacuate his runny bowels into the guy's lap.

While the ass-related pranks were usually the vilest, some of the more subtle ones were more vicious. On one rare occasion I lucked into the shot-gun seat in the van. Sandin and DJ had somehow acquired a couple of spray bottles full of water. Every few seconds, as we crossed the endless desert of New Mexico, they would squirt the back of my head. It started as a minor annoyance, then a "Knock it off, you assholes!" and then it devolved into full-on Chinese water torture. Just when I thought they'd stopped for good: squirt squirt. It went on for hundreds of miles. Squirt squirt. I don't know where they were getting water to keep refilling the bottles, and I don't like thinking about the possibility that it wasn't even water after a while. Squirt squirt. What astonished me was that they never got to a point where they decided the joke was over. Never was there a moment of "Okay, he's had enough" or "Okay, this is getting boring." It went on endlessly, regardless of my reaction or lack thereof. I just leaned forward and stared at the dash-board, contemplating my life. Squirt squirt. Mike, of course, found it hilarious.

Partying in L.A. for me was about looking as cool as you could while shitfaced while looking for hot chicks to tell you how cool you looked while shitfaced. Partying on the road with Sandin was an entirely different (and rabid) animal. For one thing, the cuties in the punk scene at the time were few and far between, and for another there was no competing with Erik. He could charm the chrome off a bumper, even if he was blind drunk with tam-pons dangling from his hair. Before you noticed the cute girl over on the couch, Erik was already literally doing handstands to impress her. Minutes later they'd be off in the next room or out in the van or on the swing set of the local park. And using my towel as a sex rag.

At that point, all the girls I had been with were long-term girlfriends. Meanwhile, Erik and DJ had a competition to see who could hook up with the most girls during a tour. The prize was a cardboard crown from Burger King, and the motto was "quantity, not quality." They were tied 10–10 toward the end of the tour when Erik met a not-so-quality, hefty young woman in Albuquerque who was begging him to have sex with her. She followed him around all night and then followed our van to a 7-Eleven. He took her around the back and humped her in the dirt next to the dumpster after she agreed to buy him a bottle of Night Train. He returned to the van and announced with an equal mix of pride and shame: "Eleven."*

It's amazing what you can get used to. After enough time on tour, it was hardly a surprise to be asleep under a piano in someone's house and be woken up by the Moron Brothers bowling an empty pony keg at me. Since it apparently wasn't time to go to sleep yet, I stayed up and watched them put a fellow houseguest in an improvised body cast. I couldn't stop those guys from spraying me with a water bottle—do you think I could've stopped them from throwing a grill through a window, or jumping on a car and caving in its windshield the same night? Do you think I could've stopped them from devouring an art student's final project the next night? Or stopped them from further torturing that poor art student by using her camera to take pictures of themselves sticking her toothbrushes up their asses? (This was back in the days of film cameras; who knows how long she and her roommates used those brushes before developing the photos?)

A good night's sleep was something I stopped expecting early on. I remember one night we were supposed to stay at some place called the Vomit House. I had been in the band long enough to know that it probably wasn't called the Vomit House because it was full of flowers and feather beds. In fact, right as we pulled up, someone was vomiting off the balcony. Erin had flown in that night to visit Mike on tour, so they were going to get a hotel room for some private time, and I figured I could go with them and sleep in the van. We drove around for a couple hours, but ultimately they couldn't find a room. After some awkward glances I realized I was cockblocking them, so I took my sleeping bag and rolled it out under the van. When the vehicle above me stopped rocking back and forth, I finally drifted off but was woken up in the middle of a REM cycle by a flashlight and a cop shouting at me to come out. It's a bleak moment when you realize you would've been more comfortable at the Vomit House.

---

*DJ stayed an extra night in Vegas after the last night of the tour. He hooked up with one last girl and took the Greyhound back to L.A. in an attempt to make the competition a tie, but his final play was nullified upon review. Sandin won the crown. Although I hear the Albuquerque girl stalked Erik for a while, and he had to go by the alias "The Great Waldo Pepper" whenever he checked into a hotel in New Mexico from then on.

Through the lens of nostalgia some of these stories sound humorous, but when you're in the thick of it you're not laughing as hard. And things could go from ridiculous to scary at a moment's notice. Ridiculous: Erik and DJ spent the afternoon in New Orleans stealing gaudy tourist clothes from a souvenir shop. Scary: That night there was a huge brawl at our show, during which the power went off, the security guards got beat up, and they had to clear the place out. The owner let us stay and drink for free after everyone was gone. At one moment I reached over the bar to give myself a refill. I looked up to see the barrel of the owner's revolver level with my nose. "You can have all you want, but you'll ask for what you get." Point taken, brother.

One of the darkest nights, though, was when we played with D.O.A. in Minneapolis, and after the show Eric Melvin and I were talking to a NOFX fan backstage. The kid seemed a little socially awkward and out of place, so Melvin and I (always feeling a little awkward ourselves) invited him to party with us at the house where we were staying. I never saw him arrive at the party. I was exhausted (possibly from being up all night at some place like the Vomit House), so I passed out in the back of the van after a couple beers. I woke up to sirens and flashing lights speeding down the street. Cop cars and ambulances had gathered half a block away. We heard someone had shown up to the party, struck up a conversation with the wrong person's girlfriend or something, and gotten chased down and stomped by a bunch of skinheads. After investigating further, Melvin and I figured out it was the kid we had invited. The beating was so severe that he died from his injuries.*

None of this was happening the way I thought it was supposed to happen. Tour was supposed to be fun. Fights weren't supposed to break out. Guns weren't supposed to be drawn. Beer wasn't supposed to equal money. Drummers weren't supposed to destroy everything. People weren't supposed to die.

I was ready for adventure, and I was ready for a struggle, but I wasn't ready for this. And I wasn't ready for a junkie roommate, either.

---

*This was the inspiration for the song "Malachi Crunch." I was glad when Mike wrote it. The death of this anonymous punk kid probably barely made the local news, but hopefully the song allows him some form of immortality.

GOLDENVOICE

NOFX AT THE COCONUT TEASZER!! SUN FEB 19th
FREE BEER! FREE FOOD!

WASTED YOUTH

ADOLE-SCENTS

TENDER FURY

NIRVANA FROM SEATTLE

THE GRIM 8:30 pm

GET THERE EARLY

NOFX

ACID CLOWN

18 AND OVER AND THE KID

$1.00 OFF WITH THIS FLYER!
DOORS 8:00 pm
(8117 HOLLYWOOD CORNER OF SUNSET AND CRESCENT HEIGHTS)

1989

KESHA'S INN presents a SPLATTERFEST WITH:

The Accüsed

W/SPECIAL GUESTS:

Attitude Adjustment — WEST OAKLAND

NOFX — S.F.

PARANOIA — MARTINEZ

wed JUNE 22
$9 at the door $2 back in Food

KESHA'S INN: 2618 San Pablo Ave., Berkeley (415) 486-1257

EX-RUTHIES INN

THE WORD IS... CHANGE

TRAM 3 VAN HALL BUS 18
VAN HALLSTRAAT 625 AMSTERDAM

Fugazi
w/ IAN McKAYE from "MINOR THREAT"

ZONDAG OKTOBER 16
ZAAL OPEN 21.30
TOEGANG 8.

NOFX Los Angeles US SUBTERRANEAN KIDS

BOY EATS GIRL PRODUCTIONS PRESENTS

THE GRIM
SCARED X STRAIGHT
NOFX
ENTROPY

DOORS OPEN AT 8:00 PM

$5.00

SAT JAN 4

FLYER by DANNY... 85

2939 VANDERMEER
ELKS LODGE

ON LAS VEGAS BLVD. BETWEEN CIVIC CENTER & PECOS

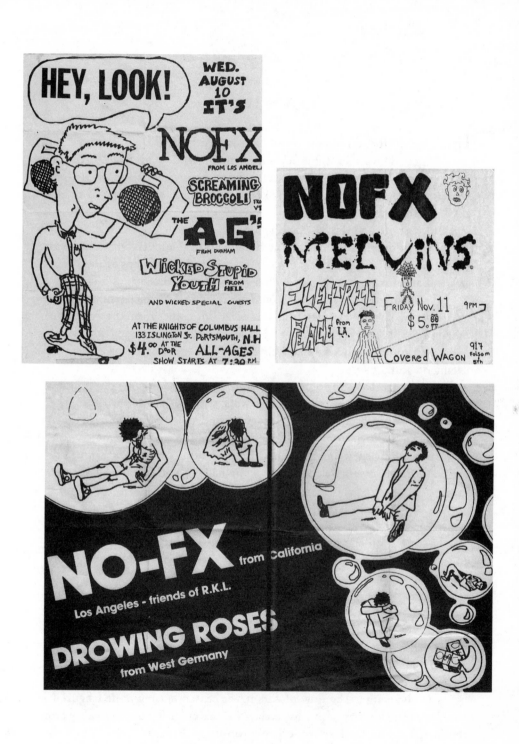

47

Melvin

I'll take credit for coining the term "Moron Brothers."

I forget when I said it, but it's a misremembered quote from the movie *Splash*. Eugene Levy is on a quest to prove the existence of a mermaid, and he has two idiot assistants. In one scene Tom Hanks asks Levy if there's anyone else around. Levy replies:

"No, just me and the Moron Twins."

It wasn't only the name that fit Smelly and DJ so well but the hint of exasperation in Levy's voice that so subtly captured the feelings of annoyance and embarrassment brought on by hanging out with those guys.

They inspired a song on our *Ribbed* album. Most people assume the lyrics are fictional, or an exaggeration, but every line comes from the exploits of Smelly and DJ. They'd get drunk and drugged out of their minds every single night and immediately channel their energy into creating chaos. Mostly by peeing on stuff.

I usually steered clear of their bullshit. Steve and I became pot buddies, so whenever we saw Smelly and DJ walk through a door with another twelve-pack of Milwaukee's Best, we left to find somewhere else to smoke.

They stole drugs from people's medicine cabinets, vomited on cue, and broke everything they touched. The Moron Brothers were a guaranteed disaster. Other disasters we could usually manage to avoid. Narrowly.

◆ ◆ ◆

We had yet another tire blowout while touring through the middle of the country somewhere, but instead of pulling over to the shoulder we pulled onto the median in the middle of the highway.

I forget where we were exactly, but we were close to a big city, so there were five lanes of cars whizzing by nonstop on either side of us. We needed to get to the shoulder to find a call box, but our gimpy van wasn't going to get us there. Someone needed to run across the road. I volunteered. Hell, I was an Eagle Scout . . . I could rescue us from this mess!

Squatting in the ready position like an Olympic sprinter, I waited for a break in the traffic. The flow of cars never ceased entirely, but I figured I could navigate my way across by letting the nearest cars pass and waiting for the furthest lane to clear while I was running—Frogger style. When the perfect pattern emerged, I took off.

I rolled my ankle and went down in the center lane.

Car horns blared and my friends went from cheering to desperately yelling, "Get up!" I was already up. My body had automatically popped back up off the ground, but my ankle was fucked. I hopped on one foot and dragged the other, trying to ignore the pain shooting through my leg and the cars growing larger in my peripheral vision.

I crossed the white finish line that marked the shoulder and slumped to the ground, out of breath. I painfully hobbled my way to a call box. We made the show that night just fine.

◆   ◆   ◆

We were leaving a bar in Buffalo at 2 a.m. (after drinking since 6 p.m.), and we were following our friend, Suicidal Steve, back to his house. Mike was driving and we had stuffed the van full of friends who wanted to party. Suicidal Steve went through a stale yellow light, and we got stuck at the red. No one was around except for one distant pair of headlights in the rearview. Mike gambled that those headlights didn't belong to a cop and turned left through the red light. He lost the gamble.

We emptied out of the van, and the cop lined us up on the curb.

"You guys been drinking?"

It was a rhetorical question. We were obviously blind drunk and clearly busted.

"No, officer. We're just leaving a show and going to a friend's house."

The cop went to open the side door of the van and all of us in unison explained, "It doesn't open." The door had been broken for a while; it would unlatch but it would only slide open a few inches. When the cop unlatched the door an avalanche of half-empty bottles and cans and a river of beer spilled out onto the street through the small opening.

We were too drunk to be scared. With all those open containers there was no possible way we weren't going to jail, so worrying wasn't going to help us. Mike was standing, and DJ was seated on the curb, so Mike chose that moment to let out a loud fart in DJ's face. Everyone cracked up. Except the cop. He spun around and asked, "What's so damn funny?"

"Sorry, sir. He just farted on my head."

We laughed even harder. The cop looked at our group and did some mental math about what the rest of his night was going to be like dealing with us.

"Get the fuck out of here."

When we got to Suicidal Steve's house, Suicidal Steve wasn't there. His roommate told us he had been arrested for drunk driving.

48

Steve

For all my complaining about him, Erik Sandin and I got along great when he was sober. By "sober" I mean when he wasn't drunk. He wouldn't be truly sober until a couple years after I left the band. But in the meantime we talked about dirt bikes and music, and I considered him a good friend.

I had no firsthand experience with junkies. I had seen and done my fair share of partying, but heroin was something for jazz greats and Lenny Bruce. When Erik was on tour it was the alcohol that fueled his worst behavior— he kept his smack use out of sight. I heard him puking one night but didn't know if it meant he had used good or bad shit. When we were back in L.A. we didn't hang out enough for me to notice it affecting his life. I was naïve about his addiction, and about the power of heroin itself.

One of my first lessons in dealing with junkies came after a NOFX show in Tijuana with Bad Religion and Big Drill Car. It was a crazy night, with kids jumping off third-story balconies into the crowd, some poor girl breaking her nose as a result, and me wriggling away from an unattractive but persistent groupie. After the show I let Erik and two of our other friends (who, I found out later, were also struggling with heroin addiction) crash at my place. I left my money from the show on the coffee table overnight. When I woke up it was gone. And later I also discovered a large gap in my record collection. I don't know which one of them stole my stuff, but I used to believe all three of them were good guys and good friends. Betrayal wasn't in their nature. That's what heroin does to people.

Sandin told me he was taking steps to get clean, so I agreed to let him stay at my place for a few weeks between tours. Early every morning, before I went to work, I got up and drove him out to the Valley to get methadone. And every night I listened to him scream in his sleep. I didn't understand methadone at the time. I didn't realize it was meant to kill the cravings; I thought he was getting high off the stuff. I felt like I was being duped, just like when my money and records were stolen. And then one day I found a burnt spoon behind my toilet.

We were leaving for tour, and we had to pick up Erik somewhere. I was in the van; Erik walked up with his new snare drum in his hand (another junkie had stolen and pawned his other one). I stuck my foot out and calmly planted it in Erik's chest.

"How many times did I tell you I didn't want that shit at my house?"

"What are you talking about?"

I explained that I'd found the spoon. He still didn't get it, or at least pretended not to. I spelled it out for him: neither that shit nor anyone using that shit was welcome at my pad. He didn't get mad or make a big deal out of it, he just changed the subject in order to deflect any real discussion of his problem: "You actually clean behind your toilet?"

49

Mike

When we went back to Europe after *S&M Airlines* came out, we were shocked by the response. In Germany we played a sold-out headlining gig to 350 fans who were slamming and singing along the whole time. Much better than being booed off the stage and pelted with bottles in Frankfurt two years earlier. Even though we were slowly gaining a following in the States, our shows never drew more than one hundred people. It was the first indication that we were on a better path.

We slept at the club, and the next morning around 10 a.m. Smelly discovered that they didn't lock the bar. He grabbed a bottle of Jägermeister, said, "This is MY breakfast!" and downed half the fucking thing before we even loaded into the van. He went from lucid to plowed in about ten minutes. Three hours later, we pulled into Amsterdam and everyone got out of the van. Smelly sat down on the curb, then slowly lay down, and then passed out.

He had laid his head in a pile of dog shit.

Strangely, Smelly was not the worst drunk on the trip. That honor belongs to our booking agent, Dave Pollack, who passed on our first European tour. After hearing our new album, he agreed to book us in Europe when Dolph politely declined the privilege of working with us again. Dave has booked every European NOFX tour since then, and he's become family. But he's the family member you hide from after his third glass of wine.

Dave has spent years training in the art of karate. Every morning, we would hear him in the hallway of the hotel doing an hour-long routine: "HA! HO! HA! HO!" And after the shows when he was wasted he would

Dave Pollack.

explain a dozen ways he could kick your ass, and then punch you for no reason. The man is over fifty years old as I write this, but if you are reading these words after midnight Berlin time, Dave Pollack is out there right now, wasted, putting someone in a slow-motion choke hold.

Still, he booked us a surprisingly successful tour (especially compared to the debacle from two years prior), and we actually flew home with a very small profit. It was the best-case scenario for NOFX at the time: not a total fiasco.

◆ ◆ ◆

Playing chess with Brett Gurewitz is no fun. Brett is too fucking smart, and he's read all the strategy books, so he always wins. I could beat him occasionally at speed chess, but I've only beaten him once at regular chess. I think. That could've been a dream, though.

While we were working our next album, *Ribbed*, Brett insisted we play chess at least twice a day during recording, and a full game between every mix. We had only ten days of studio time to finish the whole record; cumulatively we must have wasted at least two of those days at the chessboard. It was theoretically a way to blow off stress, but it just added to my frustration level.

When I recorded the vocals, I ran into the same old problem: I absolutely could not sing in key. I'd go over some of the same lines forty or fifty times and still end up with a not-that-great version. Brett thought a good way to mask my shitty singing was to layer on lots of vocal harmonies, but three-part vocal harmonies were a signature of Bad Religion's sound, and I didn't want to copy them so directly. Especially since people had already started comparing our bands after *S&M Airlines* came out.

I protested the harmonies, but Brett was convinced I would love the end result, so he would spend an hour or two working out the harmony parts and then play them for me. I would say I didn't like them, and he would fly off the handle about having wasted a big chunk of time.

And then he quit.

Thankfully he showed up the next day, and we pretended things were fine. But he kept suggesting ideas and working on parts that sounded like Bad Religion. At one point it boiled over, and we yelled in each other's faces.

"You're ruining my record!"

"You don't fucking listen to me! I know how to make you guys big! "

"You're making us sound like Bad Religion!"

"I'm the producer, I know what I'm talking about!"

It got ugly. My eyes teared up. I didn't want to argue with my friend and mentor, but I also didn't want to be written off as a Bad Religion clone. It made no sense to me to have grand, operatic harmonies in a goofy song about two drunk idiots with STDs. We butted heads about it. He quit again and walked out of the session. This time it was for real. He was done. Gone. Never coming back.

And then he showed up again the next morning like nothing had ever happened.

It was the worst recording experience I've ever had, but somehow Brett and I came out of it as friends. I remember finishing the final mix at 5 a.m. and going back to Brett's house to celebrate. We blasted the record at full volume. We were stoked. We knew we had made something great together, and we were proud of what we had accomplished. Every single argument had been buried and forgotten.

Within the first year, *Ribbed* sold ten thousand copies; four times as many as *S&M Airlines*. The crowds at our shows jumped by the same degree, and the reviewers talked significantly less shit.* Almost everyone points to *Ribbed* as the record that solidified the "NOFX sound," and they're right. *S&M Airlines* marked the moment when we knew what we wanted to sound like, but *Ribbed* actually sounded like what we wanted to sound like.

But everyone still said we sounded like Bad Religion.

50

Steve

All the group vocals for *Ribbed* were recorded with everyone's pants around their ankles. We had Pat Mack[†] and Mark Curry from the Dog Patch Winos in there with us, doing the doo-wop harmonies at the end of "New Boobs," and we needed some way to keep our minds busy so we wouldn't

---

*A fanzine called *Half Truth* (put out by Rich Wilkes, who went on to write the screenplays for *Billy Madison* and *Airheads*) somehow got Charles Bukowski to review the record—possibly due to the fact that our song "Green Corn" is based on Bukowski's movie, *Barfly*. He wrote, "Thanks for sending the cassette. My wife played it full blast, I said, 'Hey, hey, what the fuck?'"

[†] From the band Tex and the Horseheads.

psych ourselves out. I did the monologue part at the end of the song. Dave Smalley from All and DYS did the high-pitched crooning part, but he asked us not to credit him on the album because, I quote, "I don't want anybody to know." (He even made up a story about his whereabouts when he was on the phone with his wife.)

"New Boobs" was actually the most fun I would ever have in a recording studio. There's a pick slide in the song, which Mike did on my guitar with a credit card while I was playing. The vocal booth was covered in torn-out pages from porn magazines (knowing Brett Gurewitz it was most likely *Juggs*). And I smashed a guitar at the end of the song and ruined one of Brett's microphones in the process.

Brett had just bought a brand new mic that he claimed was worth $10,000. We were getting ready to do the guitar smashing take and he kept saying, "Whatever you do, don't hit my mic." We laid an old metal shelving unit on its back in the driveway for me to smash the guitar into. I wasn't even going to be swinging the guitar in the direction of the mic, let alone anywhere near it. "Whatever you do, don't hit my mic."

"Brett, I'm swinging the guitar way over here. I'm not an idiot."

Tape is rolling. I swing the guitar. It hits the corner of the shelving unit and shatters. A fist-sized chunk of wood ricochets back over my shoulder and hits the friggin' mic.

I kept smashing away. We got the take. Long after I'm gone, future generations will be able to hear the sound of me destroying Brett's $10,000 baby on wax, disc, or MP3. But for the rest of the recording session all I heard was "Dude, you hit my mic."*

◆ ◆ ◆

A couple months after we finished recording we were booked with Pennywise and Bad Religion at the El Portal Theater in North Hollywood, but only Pennywise played. We were wheeling our gear on stage when the fire marshal demanded that everyone in the crowd sit down. He was counting the number of attendees to see if the show was oversold, and it was. I was plugged in, tuned up, and pulling a guitar pick out of my pocket to play when the fire marshal walked over to me and said, "Quietly turn off your amp and roll it off the stage."

---

*More trivia: "Together on the Sand" is really just "Crazy Train" played jazz style. I never had much musical input when it came to songwriting, but when I got my window I threw in a healthy dose of Randy Rhoads.

I looked him straight in the eye and said, "Do not fucking shut down this show. Please." But his mind was made up.

The crowd tore the seats out of the floor, hurled bottles, and pulled down the velvet curtains on either side of the stage. I snuck out into the alley as police helicopters approached and circled overhead. I went around the front of the venue just in time to see the cops push a guy through a plate-glass door.

The shards tore his arm open all the way around. It looked like the goo that bursts out of one of those cans of Pillsbury biscuit dough when it pops open into a spiral. All the display windows along the front of the building, as well as the windows around the ticket booth and on every storefront for several blocks in each direction, were smashed by the crowd soon after that. Fire trucks showed up and blew people down the street with their hoses.

It was the end of December 1990. Another year with NOFX had come to a close.

51

Mike

Steve was mellower than Smelly or Dave (or the other Dave), but he was still, in my expert opinion, an alcoholic. He wouldn't black out or go crazy, he would just down a twelve-pack every night and sweat out a gallon of booze into the van seats as he slept. It was so gross. Once we stopped at a gas station after 2 a.m. and he went inside to get some beer because he needed it to fall asleep. In his haze, he didn't notice the word "root" over the word "beer" on the six-pack he purchased. He didn't sleep well that night.

We returned to Europe for the third time in the spring/summer of '91 and our crowds had gotten bigger. This time we were playing to 300 or 400 people every night, and we came home with almost $2,500 a piece in profit, which was completely unthinkable just a few years earlier. We saw the trajectory in front of us, and we were all stoked.

Except for Steve.

Steve saw us touring in a van, not a bus. Steve saw us sleeping in squats, not hotels. Steve saw us making 2,500 bucks per tour, not per show. From the perspective of other punk bands in the early '90s we were living the dream, but through the lens of the Hollywood rock 'n' roll world we were going nowhere. He started complaining about the shows and accommodations and pretty much anything else he could think of. We never had any big arguments, but it was obvious he was unhappy.

A week after we returned from Europe, he told me he didn't see us making a living as NOFX and he was leaving the band. He had a plan: He was going to join a band with his friend Skip—a guitar tech for Guns N' Roses—and they were going to play real rock 'n' roll and make real money.

I begged him to stay. He added so much to our sound, he was great on stage, and he wasn't a kleptomaniac. I knew replacing him would be tough. Especially since we had a U.S. tour booked only a few weeks later. I offered to guarantee him a set amount of money if he stayed on for the next tour, figuring the rest of us could take a hit until we reached the next level, or at least sold a few more records. He wasn't interested. Punk was a dead-end street. He needed to find a more lucrative genre of music.

Three months later, Nirvana's *Nevermind* came out.

If Steve had stayed in the band for one more year, he would have seen everything change, and he would probably still be in NOFX to this day. *Nevermind* was an extinction-level event in the music industry. L.A. hair metal was dead. Alternative, grunge, and punk took over. Even though NOFX wasn't on any record company's radar, curious kids flooded into record stores around the world to research Nirvana's punk influences, and some of them accidentally stumbled onto bands like ours. (It might have helped that our band name also started with "N.") The following years would turn out very well for NOFX.

Steve never did start that band with the Guns N' Roses dude. Years later he ended up in a country punk band called Speedbuggy for a while. He currently works as a tattoo artist in Merced, California, and does construction on the side.

We keep in touch every now and then. On more than one occasion he's said, only half-jokingly, "If you're ever looking for a guitar player, you know who to call!"

52

Steve

The myth has persisted for years that I left the band because I wanted to become a rock star. The truth is I left the band because I could no longer afford to be in it.

After my first European tour, I not only came home without having made a profit, but I also owed Mike $100. After my second European tour, I came home with $1,200,* which isn't such a bad deal after two months of seeing the world and getting fed every night. But in order to do the tour I had to quit the warehouse job Melvin had gotten me at Fred Segal, and it wasn't waiting for me when I returned. The other guys all had some form or another of family support (or were simply living on the street), but my parents were tapped out after GIT. *Ribbed* and *S&M Airlines* were selling well but were far from recouping. And the band still owed Mike money from the recording of earlier albums, and I assumed Dave's portion of that debt, so I wasn't exactly waiting beside my mailbox for a royalty check. When I had to sell one of my guitars to make rent I realized I was facing a serious decision about how much longer I could survive as a member of NOFX.

The tragic comedy of the second European tour made the decision for me. Halfway through, we hit a fucking deer. It was on a drive through the Alps, somewhere between Switzerland and France. I was asleep in the back of the van (lying on a mattress that had been bungee-corded to our speaker cabinets). I suddenly woke up in the front of the van, having been thrown over two rows of seats. Our driver, Herman the German, said, "I hit a Bambi!"

Herman (who earlier in the tour was sleeping in the van while one of the windows was smashed and our luggage was stolen) told us there were three deer in the road. He swerved to miss two but slammed into the third. The front end was wrecked and our radiator was destroyed. We were able to limp the van to a gas station, but of course it was closed because it was like four in the morning. Herman and I hiked back to the highway and found some police who called us a tow truck. We ended up renting a moving truck for the rest of the tour. We had a little more room, but I questioned how safe we were, sliding around in the back with all of our gear clumsily tied down and at risk of falling all over us. We also had to strap the back door open a bit so we could breathe, which allowed in all the exhaust fumes. When I said I wondered about "surviving" in NOFX, I meant it literally.

---

*I could have come home with more, but I was buying drinks, I got my first tattoo, and I got a terrible currency exchange rate at the airport. Plus our roadie, Timmy the Turtle, was pickpocketed somewhere along the way, and I ended up covering a lot of his meals and drinks for the rest of the trip, so that was a chunk of money I never saw again.

As the tour progressed I drank more heavily to keep my growing annoyance at bay. I ended up causing us to miss our first show in Ireland because our roadie Timmy the Turtle and I were chasing beers with shots of Southern Comfort in some London pub when we were supposed to be boarding our ferry. Melvin somehow found us and freaked out about how we'd gone missing. I figured we'd just catch the next ferry, but it doesn't work like that: you need advance tickets and customs clearances for the gear. Our driver drove south and somehow conned our van and gear onto a ferry along with a line of other vans that were part of Gloria Estefan's tour. The rest of us had to catch a separate boat a day later.

Sandin had been able to score dope with relative ease in London, but in Ireland he was cut off. After several days he completely fell apart. I never saw his heroin problem interfere with a show until one night in Ireland, when he couldn't get through a single song properly. I never watched Erik play drums before. I never had any need to look back and check on him because he always held it together. Now I was looking back in the middle of every song. He could barely stay seated on the drum stool, let alone play. It didn't go unnoticed by the crowd; half of them threw bottles and shouted, "Go back to America!"

I realized we would get a phone call one day with the news that Erik had OD'd. Then I realized we'd be lucky if we even got a phone call: Does the guy even carry a wallet half the time? He would disappear for days on tour—how long would he go missing before anyone realized something was wrong? He would just be another nameless bum swept away with the weekly garbage pickup. And then what would happen to NOFX?

The financial straits. The miserable drives. The dead deer. The black cloud of drug addiction. All of it on top of three years of Vomit Houses and Moron Brothers. It swirled in my head and it weighed on my back until it broke me at the last show of the tour in Bremen, Germany, with Bad Religion.

Erin and a few other girlfriends had flown out to meet the band during the tour. Our van was already cramped enough; now we were accommodating several hangers-on. After our Bremen sound check I had to solder something on my guitar, and when I finished I went to eat dinner with the band. They were all in this big restaurant booth and in front of them was a pile of scraps where all our food had been. The band and their girlfriends had eaten everything and left me with nothing. Mike apologetically offered me a plate of his half-eaten leftovers.

On most other days, maybe it wouldn't have been such a big deal, but with everything else on my mind I melted down. My guitar playing was paying for that food! Why were their girlfriends eating while I wasn't?! To add insult to injury, we were kicked out of our hotel that night because they saw us trying to sneak all the extra girlfriends into our room. I had to spend the night on the floor of Bad Religion's road crew's hotel room.

Bremen, Germany, would be my last show with NOFX.

It was actually one of our better performances. Kids were doing flips off the monitors, and some girls from the crowd sang "Together on the Sand" with me. One of Bad Religion's roadies shot a video of the whole show and showed it to us afterward. Other than our music videos, it was the first time I had seen myself on stage with NOFX. Video was rare back then—even when people shot our shows I never saw the tapes. This video captured us after three years of playing together, in a country far from home, with a happy and supportive crowd, at a moment when we were on our game musically yet still having fun. It was a touching time capsule that would always allow me to remember the good times with NOFX.

I loaned the tape to Eric Melvin. I never saw it again.

◆ ◆ ◆

I never made a definitive announcement that I was quitting, I just let it drunkenly slip out to Melvin at a party. He was crushed. We were close buddies, bonded over a thousand nights of sneaking off to smoke weed while avoiding the standard NOFX chaos. I was too chicken shit to tell Mike directly. I've never been good with confrontations, which is probably why I allowed so much friction to build up between the band and me in the first place.

I second-guessed myself heavily after I made the decision. "Did I do the right thing? Did I just blow my friendship with these guys forever?" I was relieved when I got a call from Mike inviting me to a Dodger game. We were able to sit down as friends and enjoy some hot dogs and beer; it was clear that NOFX was letting my departure roll off their backs, just like they did with everything else. I don't remember Mike trying to convince me to rejoin the band. If he did I probably dismissed it, not thinking he was serious. I just remember having a good time with a friend, and watching Daryl Strawberry hit two home runs and a grand slam.

Later, Mike would joke to people that the reason I quit was because I got hit by a foul ball and couldn't remember how to play the songs. It was one of many myths that have obscured the truth over the years. Other myths were that we were driven apart because of my religious views, or my supposed alcoholism, but the truth is we rarely talked about my Christianity, and I certainly wasn't drinking any more than Melvin or Sandin (or my predecessor, Dave*). I didn't need booze to fall asleep, but it definitely helped on the nights when I was sprawled out under a piano having pony kegs bowled my way. And the story about me buying root beer was just a bleary-eyed mistake in a dry county in the middle of the night that could've happened to anybody.

There were also myths about me leaving the band in pursuit of a money-making career in heavy metal. I ended up in a band with my friend Skip,† but it wasn't something we had planned while I was still in NOFX; we just played together because we were friends. Our songs never made it out of the living room.

I jammed with a band called Twister Naked for a while, and later I started a country/punk hybrid band called Speedbuggy, which was renamed Speedbuggy USA after we found out a band in Canada had already snagged the name. We toured a bit, and we opened for NOFX a few times, and it turned out my problem with NOFX wasn't necessarily NOFX—it was the life of a touring musician that didn't agree with me.

---

*Mike was the least heavy drinker of all of us, but that's not saying much. On that second European tour we went to a bar in the Reeperbahn area of Hamburg, and they had these tree stumps there for the purpose of playing "Hammerschlagen." Everyone gets a hammer and a nail (mix those two with booze and you know you're in for a good time), and the last guy to drive his nail all the way into the stump buys the next round. By the end of that night Mike was so tanked he was pissing in the middle of the street. We had called a cab to take us back to where we were staying, and when it pulled up Mike pissed all over the hood and bumper. We had to carry him up several flights of stairs, and in the morning I found him with his head submerged in the toilet. We dragged him into the breakfast room, where he lay in the corner while we ate, and then we carried him to the van afterward. He said he would never drink again. My understanding is that he has not adhered to that vow.

† People also claim that Skip was a roadie for Guns N' Roses or something, but again, false. He did work for a company that rented audio gear to some of the bigger bands at the time, though. I helped him deliver the twenty-four-track recorder to Metallica's studio when they were working on the Black Album. We were in there alone, so I moved all the mics on Lars's drum kit a millimeter or two. I wonder if they ever noticed. Or if I should demand a co-engineering credit on that record.

Speedbuggy went to Europe and the same old frustrations reared their ugly heads while enduring longer drives, smaller vans, and lower paydays than the tours with NOFX. I drank heavily just to get through it, and I recognized quickly that that wasn't healthy. Plus by that point I'd gotten married and had a one-year-old baby at home, so arguing with my fellow drunks while riding shoulder-to-shoulder in the middle of the night through Denmark to get to a show attended by five people wasn't where I really wanted to be. After one too many stupid arguments I vindictively ditched the band in the middle of a tour. Their driver filled in on guitar for the rest of the dates. I guess I'm more easily replaceable than I'd like to believe.

Even though they've had admirable success, I never felt like I missed the boat by leaving NOFX. It took at least two or three years before I saw my first royalty check, and it took another two or three years before I got one that was big enough to make me do a double take. There's no way I would've been able to hack it for that long, and banking on the idea that Sandin would clean up and that punk music would ever be popular enough to be profitable never would've seemed like a smart gamble.

But it's hard not to occasionally kick myself, knowing that if I'd stuck it out for one more album I could've tripled my income. I still get a check every now and then, but they don't come as often or as big as they used to.

Eighteen years after I quit I finally joined NOFX on stage again in 2009 at their twenty-fifth anniversary shows in San Francisco and L.A. I felt nothing but accepted and welcomed by the fans and especially by the guys in the band, who I'm lucky to still consider my friends. My wife finally got to see me play NOFX songs live, and I have to admit it was a rush being able to perform again. I got paid more in one night for the anniversary shows than I did on an entire tour in 1990. I tried to convince Mike to do an anniversary tour or just a few extra dates maybe on the East Coast, but I guess it wasn't meant to be.

But ultimately I believe there's a larger plan, and it's not Fat Mike's. I'm happy with my contribution to the band, and I'm appreciative of the fact that it made me some money and allowed me more travel than I ever would've undertaken on my own. I'm also happy with where I am today. With my music career mostly behind me I became a tattoo artist and eventually moved my growing family back to Merced. My kids enjoy making fun of me in old NOFX live videos on YouTube, and I've taught my son to play most of the songs from S&M Airlines and Ribbed on guitar. It's a good life. And every now and then I'll get a tattoo client who turns out to be a NOFX fan.

"Oh, dude! You played on Punk in Drublic?"

"A little before that."

"Oh, *White Trash, Two Heebs and a Bean?*"

"Before that."

"Oh . . ."

53

Smelly

The closest I've ever come to suicide was during our third European tour.

The deeper I got into my addiction, the more severe my dope sickness became when I couldn't score. My junkie radar helped me home in on users, and I'd follow them to figure out who the dealers were, and find dealers trusting enough to sell drugs to an unknown customer, but there were plenty of times when I came up dry. The sickness I felt during my first withdrawals at my parents' house for Christmas came back with a vengeance.

It was 6 a.m. somewhere in Northern Germany and I couldn't fucking sleep. We were staying in a shitty squat with no heat, so I was freezing, and my hard, lumpy bed was secluded from the rest of the band in a supply closet. It would've been hard enough to sleep in those conditions anyway, but the aches and nausea and illogical sweating made the experience unbearable.

It's the only time I seriously thought, "Okay. I could kill myself." It seemed like a reasonable course of action. Suffering through the night was not a possibility. Quitting heroin was clearly not a possibility. Death was on the table.

Instead, I took a shower. The warm water was comforting, but my mind was so foggy I forgot I didn't have a towel. The only thing I could do was put my clothes back on, which of course made them all wet. All I did was make everything worse.

Around 7 a.m. the shops opened, so I walked to a pharmacy, asked for their strongest sleeping pills, and downed the whole fucking box. It didn't put me to sleep, it just gave me these gnarly hallucinations. The world started swirling, and my brain started having conversations with itself that I was not involved in. It lasted for hours. When everyone else woke up, Dave Pollack asked me to go for a walk with him. I would hear him talking and ask, "What? What did you say?"

He would look at me confused and say, "Nothing."

Still dope sick. Exhausted. Covered in damp clothes. Having a lame acid trip. I think I passed out in pile of dog shit on that tour, but I was drinking so heavily that most of my memories have been blacked out.

Maybe I was dead already.

Courtney

I returned to L.A. after the tour, and DJ and I moved into a run-down 1920s-era Hollywood apartment occupied by my friends Anna and Dana (RIP*) and my drug dealer, Carlton. It was on the same block as the legendary Canterbury Apartments where the Go-Go's, the Germs, and a bunch of other first-wave L.A. punks used to live. Down the hall there lived a girl named Courtney Love.

Within thirty seconds I knew Courtney was a fucking nut. I don't remember exactly how we met, but I have a vivid image of her writhing around on her back on the floor of a bar and showing off her tits. She was never shy about her body; she worked as a stripper at an L.A. dive called Jumbo's Clown Room, so named because the owner used to work as a clown and had clown memorabilia on the shelves over the bar. These days Jumbo's is populated mostly by hipsters trying to be gritty, but back then it was full of sweaty Persian dudes in trench coats. It was the bottom of the barrel for L.A. strip clubs, providing temporary employment for junkies like Courtney.

Courtney was friends with Jennifer Finch from L7, who I was dating at the time. The three of us started hanging out and doing drugs together. We were like the Three Heroin-Using Amigos. Jennifer and Courtney made a game out of sleeping with each other's boyfriends. One night I called up Courtney because I wanted to get high, and she had a connection. We copped some dope and ended up back at her place. She won the game that night.

I called Steve from Courtney's apartment to talk about band business. Later, he played me back the message I left on his machine. I'm babbling on

---

*Dana's boyfriend was in a band called the L.A. Tourists. She was riding home with them from a show one night when their van ran off a cliff. Everyone in the car died except her. Fifteen years later, she came to see NOFX in Hollywood and on the way home she was killed by a drunk driver. She left a voicemail on Fat Mike's phone just before it happened, saying how great it was to see him and Erin at the show. They played the message at her funeral. And Mike memorialized her in a lyric in the song "Drop the World."

about practice schedules or whatever, but in the background you can hear Courtney say, "Bad boy . . . bad boy has diaper rash . . . bad boy better crawl over to mommy to get a spanking!"

And then you hear me sputter, "Uh . . . yeah, yeah, bye!" and hang up.

She was insane, but she was fun. She wanted me to be the drummer for her brand-new band, Hole. I said, "Fuck no!" I had been to her house and listened to her twang on her guitar a hundred times. She sucked. But as the years went on, her husband and her music made her famous, and her intense drug use became world-renowned.

But Courtney Love once told me that I was, and I quote, "the worst junkie she'd ever seen in her life."

She wasn't talking about my frequency of use or my tracked-up arms; she was referring to the fact that every time I saw her I'd be barfing. I would either be dope sick and puking from withdrawals or about to shoot up and puking in anticipation or just wasted drunk and puking the booze out of my system. If I hadn't eaten I would dry heave, or throw up bile or stomach acid. For a stretch of several years, I vomited several times a day, every day.

Let that sink in a bit: the worst junkie. That COURTNEY LOVE. Had ever seen.

Jay

Bob Lush was a Korean junkie who pimped out his girlfriend for drug money. He was ten years older than me, and you could see his homelessness on his face. But he was an awesome guy and a fellow Dog Patch Wino. After a night of drinking, he and I stumbled back to my Hollywood apartment, but before we could get to my door we somehow got separated, and Bob got lost in the building.

About a half hour later there was a knock at the door. I opened it to find Bob being propped up by this weirdo with long, straight black hair, a million piercings in one ear, a fringed, black-leather duster, and Ray Charles sunglasses (indoors, in the middle of the night). He looked like someone sent from the future to stop the computers from becoming self-aware.

Before he said a word, I assumed Bob had wrangled him up to party, because the apartment had gotten a reputation as a party pad. Anna and Dana had already given DJ and me a bunch of grief about our late-night rowdiness because they had regular jobs and, unlike us, needed sleep. I was sure we were on the verge of getting kicked out, so right away I copped an attitude and told the time-traveler, "Look, no one is fucking partying tonight. Get the fuck out of here."

"Fuck you, dude! I'm just bringing your fucking friend by!" He had found Bob wandering the hallways and was just helping him get home.

"Fuck you!" I responded.

Bob interjected, "Hey man . . . it's cool, it's cool. This is Jay, and he's cool."

It was my first time meeting our future drum tech and friend-for-life Jay Walker, and our first words to each other were "fuck you." We almost came to blows. But after a few more words I calmed down and they came inside.

It couldn't have been more than a couple minutes later that I had bonded with him so closely that I said, "Wanna see my strawberry farm?" and pulled down my pants to show him my herpes blisters.

I can't explain how we grew so close so quickly. Our personalities fit together so perfectly that I went from wanting to beat him up to laughing and showing him my dick almost instantly. And it's been love ever since.

Over the following months we became inseparable. Jay was normally a lone wolf, but I convinced him to join the Dog Patch Winos and we'd go out drinking every night. And every night I would get in a fistfight. I was 127 pounds, but I thought I was tough, and I knew I had Jay and the Winos behind me, so I would start trouble just for the fun of it. Like an asshole, I would get drunk, throw a sucker punch at some random person, and it would turn into a barnburner.

One night I was so shitfaced that I couldn't fucking see, which sucks when you're driving a car down Hollywood Boulevard. Jay guided me with his voice as I swerved down the road. We ended up climbing onto the roof of an apartment building and noticed a pool on the ground below. We talked about jumping from the roof into the pool but weren't sure if we would make it, so to test the theory I uprooted one of the TV antennas poking out of the roof and hurled it down to the pool. We wouldn't have made it. But no test is scientific unless the results have been repeated, so a dozen more antennas went crashing down to the pool deck that night, and a lot of people probably complained to their landlord about their suddenly poor TV reception.

Had those antennas not been there, I can guarantee you I would've tested the theory with my own body, and I would not be here today.

When we went our separate ways that night, Jay went to his apartment and started cooking a quesadilla, but he passed out on the floor while the stove was on and set the apartment on fire. He woke up in a cloud of smoke, but thankfully he was already low to the ground so he was able to crawl out without asphyxiating himself.

He needed a new place to live.

Quake

When you have hepatitis, your shit turns white and your piss turns brown. Jay and I moved into the closet of an apartment occupied by a chick named Melody and several of her hepatitis-ridden, junkie friends. The toilet was broken and clogged full of white shit and brown piss, so everyone would shit and piss in the bathtub and then turn on the water to wash it down the drain.

One day a new hepatitis-ridden junkie named Eric moved into the apartment. He sang for a band called the Stains, and he went by the nickname Earache, or Earthquake, or Quake for short. Quake was 6-foot-5, ten years older than us, and built like a fullback, with swastikas tattooed all over his body. He looked exactly like Rutger Hauer and always reminded me of Hauer's psycho drifter character in *The Hitcher*. He was handsome but scary; his eyes were piercing but soulless. He was a bona fide sociopath. When I first started going to punk shows, he was the guy everyone was scared of. Those who weren't smart enough to avoid eye contact with him learned a painful lesson. He would fucking squash people. And now he was living with us.

There were rumors about him killing people and making homemade Super 8 porn with Hollywood runaways, and stories about fourteen-year-old girls OD'ing at his house and dying. I heard a story about a time he offered some girls a ride home and then held them hostage and raped them. I would watch him shoot speed or heroin and then sit there and talk to the walls. He would be having an argument with Satan, and I would be cowering in my closet thinking, "Oh, fuck!"

But he was always really cool to me. Nice guy.*

He was another incarnation of Raymond: a violent, unpredictable, criminal drug addict. But guys like that are apparently drawn to me, so we

---

*Mike told me a story about Quake making a generous offer to drive him and his girlfriend Natalie home from Hollywood one night after a show. It was after 2 a.m. and the buses had stopped running, so they were about to take him up on it when Bill Bartell from the band White Flag stepped in and warned Mike that Quake was probably more interested in raping Natalie than seeing them safely home. Bill drove them home himself, and, after Mike learned more about the kind of guy Quake was, Bill earned himself a lifetime spot on the guest list for any NOFX show. (That spot has been free since September 2013, however. Rest in peace, Bill.)

became fast friends, even though he was one of the most frightening dudes in Hollywood.

Quake sometimes hung out with a tough-ass chick named Misfit who was part of the 18th Street gang. She did twelve years in prison for stabbing someone almost to death. But she was cool. Nice girl. One night we were all shooting dope, and Quake and Misfit ended up in the bathroom together. The noises they made sent shivers through my spine. It sounded like a violent rape. And I wasn't about to investigate or interfere, because one or both of them would've beaten and stabbed me regardless of what was actually going on. I just sat there thinking, "Quake is locked in the bathroom with Misfit. She's dead now." I processed that as a reality.

Misfit came around to hang out with Quake on several other occasions, so I can only assume it was either consensual rough sex, an ugly argument, or that she was so strung out on drugs it was worth hanging out with her rapist. Quake eventually got arrested for something and fled to Alaska. I'd get letters from him occasionally, written under a different name.

Around that time, I started shitting white. I had become a connoisseur of vomit, so I could tell that my latest bouts of puking were coming from a different source than usual. And the fever, yellowed eyes, and jaundiced skin were hints, too. I didn't bother going to a clinic; I knew it was only a matter of time before my roommates' hepatitis became my own. In an attempt to flush out my system I drank gallons and gallons of cranberry juice until my mouth blistered from the citric acid, and I snuck tablets of my roommates' medication. I didn't stop drinking or shooting dope, mind you, but somehow the symptoms slowly disappeared.

Quake wasn't as lucky. Years later when NOFX played in Alaska he came to the show and looked like a zombie. His hair was gray, he was bloated, and his legs were bright pink from his fucked up circulation. Soon after, the hepatitis killed him.

Misfit is dead now, too. I'm pretty sure she had AIDS, but I'm not sure if that's what killed her. It might've been an OD, or maybe murder. These were the type of people I was hanging out with.

The hepatitis is still in my system. I was officially diagnosed with Hep C in 1999. It's in remission now, but it could flare up at any time, and maybe even kill me. But all things considered, I'm fucking grateful. I was living with disease-carrying murderers, I was sharing dirty needles, I was using an infected homemade tattoo gun, and I was filling my body with the worst possible poisons. My friends were going to prison or dying from overdoses. Why was I the lucky one? When you live a junkie lifestyle, the chances are slim that you're going to make it out alive. I played Russian roulette so many times, and the worst thing to come out of it was Hepatitis C? I'll take it.

The absurdity of it all hits me every now and then. I'll be on stage, looking out at the crowd, and my mind will wander and wonder about the horror that might have been. Or I'll be surfing and looking out at the sun on the horizon and I'll think, "What a beautiful day . . ."

" . . . I shouldn't fucking be here."

Mark Curry

Jay Walker was a roadie for a Sacramento rock band called the Mimes. He moved down to L.A. with the band and was crashing with them (until he set their place on fire). Jay introduced me to a bunch of Sacramento musicians who would occasionally travel to L.A. for gigs. Among them was a charismatic drunk named Mark Curry.

Like Jay, Mark immediately fit in with the Dog Patch Winos and joined our nightly rampages through Hollywood. Drinking, fighting, chicks . . . mayhem. One night around 2 a.m. Mark showed up at our apartment with a broken hand after a fight, and we took him to Glendale Memorial Hospital. While Mark was being treated, I snuck around the hallways and stole everything that wasn't bolted down.

I took plasma bags and X-ray film. I ransacked supply closets and filled my pockets with totally useless stuff. I stole an electric cart and cruised through access ways and even stole a mattress. I stuffed it all into whoever's car we were driving. It had to be thousands of dollars' worth of shit. The only thing I kept was the mattress, because I needed it for the closet floor. Everything else got tossed or dumped somewhere. Utterly pointless destructive behavior.

At the time I was working for the *L.A. Weekly* newspaper as a runner for the art department. I would drive around town to various companies to pick up their advertising artwork or drop off proofs. It was a perfect job for copping dope: three hours' worth of work, eight hours to do it, and no supervisor over my shoulder. I would even steal books while I was out on runs.

A perk of the job was learning how to sneak into Universal Studios. One day I went there to pick something up and found an employee entrance that led into the theme-park area. So any time I had a delivery at Universal, I would grab DJ or another friend and we would spend the afternoon on the rides.

Once I was with Mark Curry and some other Winos at a show at the Universal Amphitheater, and afterwards I showed them a door that would allow us access to the park. They had an attraction called "The Miami Vice Action Spectacular," which was a live-action stunt show featuring explosions and Jet Skis. There was a part in the show where a stuntman jumped off a water tower onto a hidden airbag below. We snuck through the backstage entrance and took turns jumping into the airbag for a half hour and never got caught.

Mark was as much of a boozer and a partier as the rest of the Winos, but while we were all directionless losers, Mark was ridiculously fucking talented. When he picked up a guitar and started playing I was stunned. He played solo acoustic shows around L.A., and the music would just flow out of him. It was almost spooky how good he was.*

Aside from his solo shows, Mark performed in a funk rock band called Crystal Sphere. The members came down from Sacramento for meetings with record labels and Mark introduced them around. Among them was a doughy, goofy Mexican named Aaron Abeyta. He was a fashion disaster in a white T-shirt, suspenders, zoot suit pants, shiny shoes, and a stupid little fedora. I couldn't resist beating him up. I don't mean viciously; I mean like you do to a little brother. Every time Mark would bring him around, I would say, "Come here, you fat little beaner!" put him in a headlock, and punch him until I got bored.

Finally, I went to see Crystal Sphere play. They were like the Chili Peppers but with soul, and better. I mean: way better. As much as Mark's soulful voice took over the room, I was blown away by Aaron. This little goofball I had been drunkenly punching at every opportunity was an amazing guitarist and a damn good singer. Aaron had confidence, he had swagger . . . he was not the same person I had met off stage. I remember thinking, "Oh my fucking god. That fat little beaner is unbelievable."

I had no idea at the time how big a part Aaron would come to play in my life. He's a living, breathing example of how almost everything I have in this world is based on random chance. If Bob Lush hadn't stumbled into Jay, I wouldn't have met Mark, which means I wouldn't have met Aaron, which could've meant a completely different destiny for me. That first Crystal Sphere show was a life-changing moment, I just didn't know it yet.

So for the next couple years I just kept drinking shitty wine, shooting up, and beating on Aaron. But when Steve abruptly quit the band and Mike was auditioning guitarists, I said, "I got a guy."

---

*Years later, one of NOFX's most popular songs would be a punk version of Mark's song "Perfect Government."

Jack Attack—original lineup.

LARRY (DRUMS, VOCALS)   MARK (BASS, VOCALS)

AARON (GUITAR, VOCALS)   FERNANDO (KEYBOARDS, VOCALS)

54

Hefe

"Hold the bird, hold the bird!" my mom translated.

"What's going on?"

"She wants you to hold the bird."

A lady handed me an oversized chicken. She gave some urgent orders in Spanish, and my mom translated once more, "Hold on now!"

"Okay, I got it!"

I held the bird tight. My mom smiled. The chicken lady grabbed the bird's neck and suddenly WHACK!! She chopped its head off.

"AHHHHH!" I let it go and the body went flopping and flying all over the place, blood spurting everywhere. My mom laughed hysterically.

Another classic Abeyta family trip to Mexico.

Every year or so, my family would pile into the car and make the drive from Sacramento, California, to El Paso, Texas, to visit my grandparents. It's a twelve-hundred-mile trip, and when you're twelve it seems like it's twelve times longer. And a few times we drove an additional twelve hours to a small village just outside of Zacatecas, Mexico, to visit friends of my aunt.

Zacatecas was a small, dusty town like the kind you see in old westerns. Some kids might dream of living like a cowboy, but I realized quickly that it wasn't as glamorous as the movies made it out to be. We stayed in adobe huts with no plumbing. We bathed at the local swimming hole while the women did laundry in the same water. The toilet was an outhouse with a wooden bench inside that had a hole cut out of it. You did your business with the flies buzzing all around you and wiped your ass with old newspapers. It was especially unpleasant in there when my whole family came down with diarrhea from drinking the local water. The villagers had to ride a horse and carriage into town to bring back a doctor, who stuck a needle in my newsprint-covered butt.

And chicken wasn't our only meal. My mom pulled me outside one day, saying, "You have to come watch this," and we all gathered around as the men brought a cow into the center of the village and tied its legs together. One of the locals handed his oldest son a long knife like it was some sort of ceremony. The son approached the cow and opened its throat. The town celebrated as the cow kicked and mooed until it passed out. They boiled the blood on an open fire and gave it to all the young boys of the village. I guess it's supposed to help them become men. They offered it to me but I said, "Hell no."

It was even harder to watch them kill a pig on another occasion, because every morning I would walk past its pen, greet it with a friendly "Hey pig!" and toss it a handful of corn. Then one day there it was—strung up by its legs, squealing and fighting while they sliced it open. It made this horrible, desperate, high-pitched squeal like it knew it was going to die. When it stopped moving they used a blowtorch to burn off the hair and peel off the outer layer of its skin, then they fried the skin in oil in an enormous iron skillet. I was horrified by the whole process. But I have to admit: it tasted pretty good.

The trip wasn't all bad. I shot slingshots with my cousins while we watched the cattle graze, and I got to ride my first horse. They even had a movie night when some guys brought in a little 8mm projector and showed a Mexican cowboy flick. They served punch in little plastic sandwich bags with straws sticking out of them, and instead of popcorn we ate toasted pumpkin seeds served in cones of newspaper. It wasn't what I was used to, but it was fun.

Still, when I was older, I refused to go back. At sixteen, I was way too cool to be pooping into a wooden bench. But I did agree to return to El Paso after I was promised a day trip over the border to Juarez, where I would be rewarded with a handmade acoustic guitar. I had been playing guitar for a year or two by that point, and I was starting to get pretty good, but all I had was my brother's beat-up, cobweb-covered, off-brand electric guitar, and I wanted an instrument of my own.

I endured the car ride and the family time in El Paso and finally made it to the street market in Juarez. Dozens of guitars were hanging off racks and the guitar maker was sanding down the body of his latest creation. I picked a classic blonde off the rack, but when we got back to my grandparents' house I found that the tuning pegs were nearly impossible to turn.

When my grandfather saw the guitar, his eyes lit up. He tried to talk to me about it, but he didn't speak any English. My aunts translated and told me he wanted to play the guitar. I pointed out the problem with the tuning pegs, so he took me out to his workshop behind the house and oiled them for me. When we went back inside, he tuned the guitar and played a delicate, traditional Mexican song. I had no idea he knew how to play. It wasn't until we returned to Sacramento that my mom showed me a faded, black-and-white photo of him in his old band, holding an upright bass. It must have been a long time since he'd held an instrument, but he hadn't lost his chops.

When the last note of his song rang out, he handed me the guitar and looked at me expectantly. I took it from him and played the most impressive-sounding tune I knew: "Foolin'" by Def Leppard.

He let out an impressed laugh when I was done. The house was full of people chattering and talking over each other, but he and I managed to have this private moment together, bonding over music and communicating despite the language barrier.

My grandfather died before we were ever able to make another trip down to see him. Playing guitar with him was definitely the moment that bonded us, but I also remember him gathering the kids around and having my aunts translate as he told stories about riding with Pancho Villa during the Mexican Revolution.

I don't remember all the details so well, but Pancho Villa's men rode into my grandfather's village and told him to "ride with us or die." My mom told me about a time when she was a little girl—my grandfather took her to the site of the shootout that occurred when Villa's men took over the town. My grandfather ran his fingers over the bullet holes in the walls of one of the buildings in the town square and relived the battle.

My mom came from proud blood. She grew up in El Paso during an era when she wasn't allowed to sit in the front of the bus or drink from the same water fountains as white people. During her school days someone stole something from her classroom, so the teacher lined up all the Mexican kids and whacked them with a ruler while snarling about how they were all filthy and needed to be hosed down.

So when my mom got older she didn't take shit from anybody. One time my older sister came home from grammar school, crying about how some other girls had beaten her up. My mom went into the garage, grabbed a big-ass wrench, and said, "Let's go." They disappeared up the street. I was really young at the time and way too scared to ask for details when they came home later.

You didn't fuck with our family. Growing up in the ghetto of El Paso, family was all my mom had. If one of her brothers or sisters got fucked with, everyone else got their back. She had eight siblings—it was like having a built-in gang.

When my aunts were in their forties, three of them were living together in a house, and someone broke in through a window while they were sleeping. Instead of hiding under the bed or calling 911, they confronted the burglar with whatever weapons they could scrounge up from the kitchen. The burglar stood his ground, not afraid of three Mexican spinsters in nightgowns. One of them tried to grab him and BAM! He socked her in the face.

Big mistake.

My oldest aunt said, "You gonna fuck with my family?!" and stabbed him with a barbecue fork while my other aunt bonked him over the head with a frying pan. They swarmed him with fists, feet, and kitchen utensils, and he couldn't take them all on at once. He ended up begging for mercy as he climbed back out the window. My oldest aunt skewered his ass with the barbecue fork on his way out.

When I was a kid my mom was the disciplinarian of the household. The tradition of the belt was upheld in our house, and I was always incurring its wrath. A mailman stopped by our neighbor's house one afternoon and I ran into his truck and stole some mail-cart thing. The mailman saw me running away and knocked on our door. He and my mom found me hiding behind the garage and WHAP came the belt. "You never steal!" Whap! Whap! Whap!

The mailman's face went from anger to horror. "Oh my god! Please, this isn't necessary!" Whap! Whap! Whap! "Oh, I'm so sorry kid!" He was way more traumatized by the experience than I was.

In most families when the kid does something wrong, it's "Wait until your father gets home!" In our family it was "Oh thank god, dad's here to save my life!" My dad was a quiet guy. He must have experienced the same brutal racism growing up in El Paso, but I never heard any of his stories. His father got him a job on the railroads to keep him off the streets, and after my parents married and moved to Sacramento he landed a job as a mechanic at UPS. He worked his way up to chief mechanic for the local fleet and busted his ass to support our family, which included my parents, my older brother, my two older sisters, my younger sister, and me.

My mom's full-time job was her five kids, but when the summers rolled around she went to work picking tomatoes. She would leave the house at five in the morning when it was still dark outside, and she would sweat under the California summer sun until my dad picked her up after work. I remember going with him to pick her up and seeing the fields, the machinery, the big conveyor belt, and the look of utter exhaustion on my mom's face.

She wasn't doing it because we were broke; she was doing it to save up enough money so she could afford tuition at Sacramento State University. She earned a master's degree in social work and went on to found and direct a health clinic for low-income families.

And all of this while she was contending with diabetes.

I don't know how she made it through those long summers in the tomato fields when she had to take insulin shots every single day. The symptoms were sometimes so bad she'd pass out. She taught me what hard work and discipline really meant. She showed me that dreams become reality only after you've put in the time and poured out the sweat. If I wanted something out of this life, it wasn't going to be handed to me.

And what I wanted was to make it as a musician.

◆ ◆ ◆

My mom couldn't afford a babysitter or a nanny, and out of all five kids I was the biggest troublemaker. If she said, "Don't touch that," she could guarantee that I'd be touching it the minute she turned her back. I couldn't sit still, and Adderall hadn't been invented yet, so the only way my mom could keep me out of trouble was by playing records.

Our record player wasn't a dusty turntable in a forgotten corner of the house; it was housed in a massive, stately cabinet that ruled over the living room. I would be buzzing around the house at full speed, but when my mom put on a Gene Vincent record I would stop dead in my tracks and sit down to soak in the sound. Other parents used TV as a babysitter; my mom used music. She would be free to do the dishes or the laundry, safe in the knowledge that I was planted in front of the record player. But if she checked on me one second after the last track finished playing, something in the house would be broken or covered in sticky fingerprints.

Every song on every album would fascinate me, and my mom had broad, eclectic taste. Calypso, rock 'n' roll, classical, mariachi . . . I devoured them all.

In fourth grade, my classmates and I were ushered into the school cafeteria, where, one by one, we sat with a strange man and his strange machine. The machine emitted a tone, and we had to give a thumbs up or thumbs down depending on whether the sound was high or low. We listened to a series of boops and beeps in various frequencies, and it seemed like such a pointlessly easy task. But it turned out to be a test: the kids who could best differentiate between the tones were invited to join the school band. Having honed my ears after so many afternoons in front of the record player, I passed with flying colors.

The band teacher asked me which instrument I wanted to play, and I picked the trumpet because that's what I'd been hearing on my mom's mariachi albums. But the school didn't have any more trumpets left to loan out, and my parents couldn't afford to rent or buy one, so the teacher said I could play the flute instead.

I didn't join the band that year.

When I was in fifth grade my parents saved up enough to rent me a trumpet from Kline's Music on 47th Street, and before I even took my first lesson I was trying to play along with my mom's records. I learned fast, and by the time I entered junior high I was in the concert band. In high school I added marching band and jazz band to my résumé. I joined up with the elite Sacramento Freelancers drum and bugle corps for a summer and later went on to pursue trumpet all through college. So by the time I was sixteen and I unearthed that beat-up, cobweb-covered, off-brand electric guitar in the back of my brother's closet, I already had a well-developed ear and the ability to read music.

I wish I knew what brand of guitar it was. It vaguely resembled a Fender Jazzmaster, with sunburst coloring and three distinctive flat rocker switches. It was missing a string, so I took it over to Kline's.

"I need to buy a string."

"You mean 'strings.'"

"No, I just need one."

The clerk suggested I buy a whole pack of strings, which sounded like a scam to me. But once he replaced all the strings and cleaned and tuned the guitar I had to admit it sounded much better.

Again, before taking any lessons I sat down with the record player. I made marks on the neck of the guitar with different colors of crayon so I knew which notes to play in which order for which song. After a few tips from friends and a few lessons over at Kline's, I didn't need the crayons anymore.

◆　◆　◆

My friend Paul Peterson helped me learn a bit more about guitar, and I would jam with him and my friend John Cagney. We learned the first half of "Purple Haze" and the first half of "Dazed and Confused" and decided we were a band. We called ourselves Jack Attack. I think it was a rejected name that Paul's older brother's band hadn't bothered to use. None of us were named Jack. I think it was in reference to Jack Daniel's. An attack of Jack Daniel's.

Jack Attack only played one gig—an open house at our grammar school. It was one of those nights when the parents come in to visit the school and meet the teachers, and the principal had charitably agreed to let us provide the entertainment. From behind the curtain of the multi-purpose room we heard the principal give his welcome speech to the gathered parents and then conclude with "All right, now we're going to break and go to the class-rooms." Five or ten minutes went by and then, "All right everybody, and now we have Jack Attack." The curtains opened to an empty auditorium. The parents had moved on. Maybe seven or eight of our friends remained, waiting to see us. Pretty smooth move on the part of the principal.

We played the first half of "Purple Haze" and the first half of "Dazed and Confused" and jammed until we were tired and decided to stop. We played the whole set (if you can call it that) sitting in chairs with our heads down. That's how we practiced, so that's how we played! Our friends in the audience thought it was the best thing they'd ever seen, but unfortunately the Legend of Jack Attack faded away soon thereafter.

◆　◆　◆

Music was my main obsession, but comedy wasn't far behind. I would mem-orize Redd Foxx, Cheech and Chong, and Richard Pryor albums and per-form them with John Cagney and his brother Erick. I would watch cartoons with my brothers and sisters and imitate every character and act out every story line we had just seen. I would watch the Three Stooges and imitate all three of them talking to each other. Sometimes my siblings would laugh, and other times they would give me a bewildered look that seemed to show concern for my mental capacity. (Years later I would see that same look on Fat Mike's face while doing cartoon voices in the vocal booth at Westbeach Studios.)

In high school I grew close to a fellow class clown named Mark Curry. We had known each other since we were little, but it wasn't until we were teenagers that I realized he had just as vast a repertoire of cartoon voices as I did. I would start an Elmer Fudd scene and he would finish it. He could quote every Monty Python movie verbatim. We would go to the music store and study the clerks and customers and then go home and record skits about them. Between our mutual love of art, music, cartoons, and juvenile humor, we bonded fast. Wonder Twin powers: activate!

Mark and his friends were way better musicians than me, so they rightfully laughed in my face when I asked to jam with them. But I practiced so much that I caught up to them soon enough. We were called Crystal Sphere. We blended funk and rock and we were actually not that bad.

I worked nights at a metal fabrication shop for a year, grinding welds and sanding and painting metal doorframes for office buildings. It allowed me to afford a no-name-brand, candy-apple-red flying V guitar and a Yamaha G5 amp with a size-10 speaker at Kline's. Every night at the metal shop we would listen to the classic rock radio station, and I would focus on the guitar parts and visualize the notes. I would hear "Iron Man" and turn the main riff over and over in my head until I got home (close to midnight) and could figure it out on guitar. I would buy Van Halen albums and put them on the record player at 16 rpm instead of the traditional 33.3 so I could dissect the solos at a slower speed and perfect them. I was obsessed. I would play for hours every day. I put more time into guitar than anything else.

"Anything else," of course, included schoolwork. Toward the end of my senior year I was barely attending classes, and after earning nine days' worth of in-school suspension I dropped out just a few weeks shy of graduation.

Mr. Parker, the music teacher, called me at home and begged me to at least stick around for the last few concerts the jazz band had scheduled. Once I fulfilled my commitment and handed in my marching band uniform for the last time, Mr. Parker blew up at me for dropping out, shouting, "You'll never amount to anything! You're gonna be a bum!"

I shot back, "I'm gonna go to college, I'm gonna study music, I'm gonna make it as a musician!"

"You're never gonna make it!"

Nobody took me seriously when I said I wanted to pursue music. When friends and teachers in high school asked me what I wanted to be, I said I already knew and I was already doing it, and they all laughed.

They were right to be skeptical. If there's a kid out there reading this book and thinking about giving the finger to his or her high school diploma and trying to make it as a musician, I can tell you right now that it's a rough fucking road. It's a roll of the dice that almost never comes out the way you hope it does. There are brilliant guitarists with far more talent than me selling CDs on a subway platform right now.

But don't let anyone ever tell you that you can't do something. You can do whatever you put your mind to . . . as long as you're willing to pay for it with every ounce of sweat you've got.

Even then the success you find might not look like the success you imagined. But what the hell. Go for it.

55

Mike

We were packing up our equipment after a show at Gilman Street in Berkeley when suddenly someone came up from behind me and wiped his finger under my nose. I turned around and this creepy dude with long hair and sunglasses said, "You got frothed!"

Frothing is when you wipe your ass with your finger and then wipe that finger under someone's nose. It wasn't a particularly effective froth because I didn't really smell anything; it was mostly just confusing and annoying.

The finger belonged to a sleazy boozehound named Jay Walker.

Jay was a friend of Smelly's and part of an L.A. gang called the Dog Patch Winos. The Winos weren't a gang in the traditional L.A. sense of punching and stabbing; they were more of a merry band of drunks and junkies with adolescent senses of humor (e.g., frothing). While most gangs are all about pride, the Winos had none. While most gangs had harsh penalties for not having a cleanly sewn patch on one's outfit, the Winos would just safety pin their patches on. They weren't about starting trouble as much as they were about scoring drugs and living a total seedy, dirtball lifestyle.

I was never invited to be a Dog Patch Wino, and they were the only gang from which I was flattered to be excluded. They thought of me as a "college guy." I thought of them as "hopeless alcoholics." They were mostly homeless, but they congregated at a house on Fountain Avenue in Holly-wood. I hung out there once or twice but never felt welcome.

Jay Walker and his friend, Bob Lush,* needed a ride from Berkeley down to L.A., and Smelly offered them seats in my van. Thus Jay's gallant self-introduction.

We were driving along when Jay shouted from the back, "Pull over, we have to pee!"

I said I'd pull over at the next exit.

"No, we gotta pee now!" And then I heard two streams of piss hitting the side door of the van.

Zero pride also meant zero respect. Smelly brought a Wino named Johnny Sixpack over to my house once, and the next thing I knew he was spray painting swastikas on the walls of my kitchen. Or maybe it was just the DPW logo. Or both. I don't know. Does it matter? HE WAS SPRAY PAINTING MY KITCHEN!

I avoided the Dog Patch Winos as much as possible but still spent a significant amount of time with Jay at parties and shows. Unlike the rest of the Winos, he wasn't a total numbskull. We could have normal conversations, we could relate to each other, and he was pretty funny.

Over the next twenty years he would become a dear friend. And I would put him through more than enough to make up for all that pee in my van.

_____

*People often use the word "pimp" as a figure of speech, but when I describe Bob Lush as a pimp I mean it literally: he dated a hooker who would turn tricks so they could afford drugs. Bob drank so much that his liver was horribly damaged. One day he was fighting with his girlfriend and she threw him over a weight bench. It was apparently the last blow his organs could take. His liver burst and his life was barely saved by emergency surgery, which provided part of the lyrical inspiration for our song "Bob." The rest of the lyrics to that song are fictional (he wasn't a skinhead, he was a Korean with dreadlocks). It has become a crowd favorite, but I never found out what Bob thought of it. He OD'd before I got the chance.

56

Hefe

As I grew up and changed, so did the city of Sacramento. Gangs and the crack epidemic transformed the city in the '80s. The bars on everyone's windows went up so slowly I barely noticed the transition.

All my friends grew into teenage delinquents, and we all discovered booze, weed, and speed. We called our clique the Park Rats because we would hang out at Sky Park during the day and Garcia Bend Park near the river on weekend nights. The Garcia Bend parking lot was where things got sketchy. It was drinking, fights, and running from the cops every single weekend night.

But I tried to be one of the good guys. I earned the Order of the Arrow in Boy Scouts and was three merit badges short of making Eagle Scout before I quit. I studied Renbukai—a hybrid Japanese/Korean martial art—until my parents couldn't afford the lessons anymore. And for most of my junior year in high school I was a Guardian Angel.

The Guardian Angels were causing a major stir in the early '80s. Their founder, Curtis Sliwa, was all over the news as crime spiraled out of control around the country. Sliwa was a passionate guy, and the idea of a bunch of uniformed bad-asses taking to the streets seemed pretty cool to me, so when I caught a glimpse of a red Angels beret in a friend's backpack at school, I begged her to bring me to the next meeting of the Sacramento chapter.

I met the head of the chapter—a big black dude named CB. He interviewed me about my intentions right off the bat; the Angels were wary of people on power trips looking to cause trouble rather than prevent it. After he decided I was relatively mentally stable, he asked about my background and if I'd had any sort of fight training. I demonstrated a few Renbukai punches and kicks on a heavy punching bag and, feeling confident, offered to demonstrate a spinning back kick. I missed the bag and fell flat on my ass. He laughed at me, but they let me join.

Twice a week I showed up for push-ups, sit-ups, lap running, and sparring. A Kenpo Karate instructor taught us different moves, and about twenty of us would practice taking each other down. One day, a big, buff Green Beret came in to help with our training. CB introduced him to the group and then with a smile added, "aaaaaand Aaron. You're going to fight him."

We didn't have a lot of padding or safety gear, but we practiced "medium contact" and pulled our punches so we didn't hurt each other too badly.

Green Berets don't "do" medium contact.

The Angels all gathered around and I charged in with a kick. The Green Beret instinctively blocked it and POW—I got a left cross to the mouth and went sailing to the floor.

Everyone went "OOOOH!" Blood dripped from my lower lip. I gathered myself up and tried a few punches this time, but I didn't land any of them.

Bam bam bam! Kick to the gut. "OOOOOOH!" On the floor again.

No one could believe I stood up the third time, but I wanted one more try. Enough fucking around, it was time to pull out the big guns. I flew at him with a sidekick and the dude just jumped out of the way and BOOM, smacked me on the forehead.

"OOOOOOOOOOHHH!!!"

I felt like I had been whacked with a two-by-four. He had added a forehead lump the size of a silver dollar to my bloody lip, so I admitted defeat.

Later, as I was cleaning my wounds in the sink, the Green Beret came up to me.

"What's your name, kid?"

"Aaron."

"Erin . . . that was the name of my first love. You got a lotta heart, kid. You're all right."

And then he hugged me.

From then on he took me aside during the training sessions and worked with me personally. He taught me how to block and move better. His technique was some Special Forces combination of martial arts and American boxing. It was always an intense workout, and for six months he pounded me into fighting shape.

In order to graduate and join the street patrols, you had to fight three opponents at the same time—full contact. People got the shit beaten out of them. Women, too! Some tough chick would be fighting three guys; she'd take a full-force kick to the gut and stand back up for more. It was gnarly.

I knew what was in store for me, so I trained hard and mentally prepared myself for my graduation fight. But then Curtis Sliwa visited our chapter and saw everyone beating the shit out of each other with no pads or gloves and freaked out. So the 3-on-1 battle royales were canceled, and I joined the patrol after a mere observation of my kicking skills.

My first time patrolling was during the day, so I didn't think it would be too rough until CB decided we were going to walk through Oak Park. The neighborhood was one of the most dangerous in the city, and Oak Park itself was battleground territory for all of Sacramento's gangs. At the time it was mostly controlled by the Crips, who identified themselves by wearing blue. We walked through the park in our Guardian Angel uniforms. Which were bright red.

We didn't go unnoticed. Some gangsters saw us from across the park and we heard, "Whoa, whoa! What the fuck?!"

CB barked, "Everybody! Backs against the wall!" and whoosh! Our whole troop was lined up with our backs against the brick exterior of a nearby building, which would prevent us from being jumped from behind. There were about twenty of us and about the same number of gangsters. CB walked out to meet their leader. I was scared shitless and pretty sure we were all about to get shot.

CB introduced himself as the chapter leader of the Guardian Angels. The gang leader said, "I'm the funk lord."

There was a gang in Sacramento called the Funk Lords. These guys were all wearing blue, so I'm not sure if they were former Funk Lords, or if the Funk Lords had been absorbed by the Crips, or if they just happened to wear the same colors as the Crips, or if the guy was an actual Lord from the House of Funk.

Either way, he continued: "We don't need you people walking through our park."

"We're not trying to start trouble, we're just here to protect our community."

"We don't need no protection, we protect our own people!"

One of the other gang members peeled off from his group and walked down the line of Angels, getting in each person's face.

"Man, I'd fuck you up, man!" Then to the next guy, "Look at you with your funky little shoes, man!" Then to one of the girls, "What are you doing out here? You're a girl!"

Finally he came to me.

"You too cute, man. You too cute."

CB finished his chat with the funk lord and agreed that we would leave the park. He reached out to shake hands, but the funk lord just brushed CB's hand with the bandana hanging from his wrist.

"That's it? You're not gonna shake my hand?"

"That's it, my brother. Just touch and go."

We marched out of the park and I never saw any more action on any of my patrols. It was mostly just walking around the city and then back to headquarters. I remember patrolling in the pouring rain one night, getting soaked, and realizing I didn't want to spend my nights that way anymore.

I handed in my wings and beret. I had proven to myself I could hang with the Guardian Angels. It was time for me to hang on the other side of the law for a while.

◆   ◆   ◆

After dropping out of high school, my options for higher learning were limited, but I enrolled in music classes at Sacramento City College along with Mark Curry and every other dropout, reject, weirdo, punker, and ghetto-ass motherfucker who thought they were too cool for high school. Most of them would drop out a week after they started. I was just as much of a freak, but I took college seriously.

I enrolled in every music class they offered—jazz band, concert band, piano, music appreciation, music history and literature, and every voice class from opera to barbershop quartet. There was a point when I was taking three separate voice classes a day. I knew guitar couldn't be my only trick; the guys on MTV were all singing and playing at the same time, so I knew I had to step up. I took a full load of courses, learning about Vivaldi and Tchaikovsky and Bach and singing in Italian and French and working my way up from baritone to tenor while performing barbershop songs about mosquitoes.

Zing, zing! Zing, zang! Doo-wah, doo-wah, zing zing zing zing zang!

At night and between classes I put in hours at the local video store. The boss was a big-time speed dealer; he sold to me and I'd sell to my friends and fellow students. I also had a connection through a friend's older brother. We weighed the stuff at his house, stepped on it with powdered vitamin B, and portioned it out into little bags. It's not something I look back on with pride, but I have to admit I made slightly more than minimum wage.

I took speed for a while but wasn't a fan. It allowed me to stay up all night tweaking and jamming on guitar, but the whole time I'd be grinding my teeth and biting the inside of my cheeks. And the comedown made me feel like I'd been dragged behind a truck over a road made of sharp rocks. I'd shake and sweat, and my head and stomach would be angry at me. That shit was poison.*

Even with a full plate of school, work, and illegal activity, Crystal Sphere was still my main focus. Our first real gig was a battle of the bands at a club called the Oasis Ballroom. We did a couple of originals and covers of Billy Idol's "White Wedding" and Ratt's "Round and Round" and we came in second place. Although we suspected the voting system was rigged against us.

Our second gig was at a party at this guy Eric's house. In the middle of our set, a girl ran into the living room and shouted for us to stop playing.

"He's trying to drown her in the hot tub!"

---

*It's hard to relive some of these experiences because of the regret I still carry. The speed I was dealing destroyed people's lives. Their marriages were torn apart, they went to jail, they got shot. I cringe at the thought of my son or daughter picking up a copy of this book and learning about all the dumb stuff I did when I was younger. I really can't think of a more effective anti-drug message to pass down to them than just being honest: I tried drugs. They made me miserable. I stopped doing them. The best advice would be to cut out the first two steps.

Everyone ran outside to see Eric, our host, in the hot tub with his hands around his girlfriend's neck, yelling, "I'll kill you, bitch!" while her arms were flailing and splashing everywhere.

"I'll kill you, bitch" wasn't an uncommon exclamation in our circles. I remember hanging out at Garcia Bend and watching a guy grab his girlfriend's neck and slam her head into the hood of a car. When everyone around you is jacked up on speed you get used to that kind of insanity.

Someone pulled Eric out of the hot tub, an even bigger fight broke out, and the party was over. We packed up our gear.

Soon after, we played another party at my friend Jelly's house. This time we were in the backyard and the fight erupted inside. Middle of the set: BSHHHHHHH! Someone goes flying through a sliding glass door. Big fight, show over. But at least we got paid. Not in money, of course—Jelly* just handed us a sixteenth of crank, and I sold it for about 150 bucks.

We hardly ever got through a full set before a fight erupted. We'd stop and wait for the fight to finish, then start again, then stop and wait again, then play more . . . after a while it didn't faze us anymore.

We branched out and played bar and club gigs whenever we could and started getting paid in cash instead of crank. We even played a bonfire party for a bunch of skydivers at the Davis airport (they didn't pay much attention to us—we didn't connect with the skydiving demographic, I guess). We recorded songs for a 7-inch and celebrated its release with a packed show full of friends and family at a rented VFW hall on a stage we built ourselves. We felt like our band was really starting to grow. And I had a plan that was going to take Crystal Sphere to the next level.

A plan that would soon have me facing down the Secret Service and a fifteen-year federal prison sentence.

◆　◆　◆

Turns out that selling copies of your record to a bunch of your friends doesn't mean much when you try to convince a record store to stock your 7-inch. We pressed one thousand copies, and none of the stores wanted them, even the independents. We walked into a Sam Goody and asked them to carry our record, and they said they couldn't unless it came through a distributor. We said, "Well, fuck you then!" and walked out. We weren't very wise business people.

---

*Jelly later got shot for stealing someone's Harley. But I think he's still alive.

Mark Curry's uncle's roommate was an old black bluesman who not only taught me jazz chords and how to intonate a guitar but also offered up lessons about the ugly side of the music industry. He learned things the hard way back in the '60s and '70s. He claimed the only way to get a record on the radio was to give the DJs coke or cash. Which explained why we had been laughed out of every radio station in town.

I hatched a plan: I would take the five grand I had left from selling drugs and buy twenty-five grand in counterfeit bills. I would spread the cash around town and turn it into legit bills, and use the profits to pay off radio DJs to play our 7-inch.

What could possibly go wrong?

My cousin had a connection with a counterfeiter, and soon we had stacks of fake twenty-dollar bills filling the trunk of my car. We took the bills to liquor stores, used them to buy one-dollar lottery scratch-off tickets, and pocketed nineteen dollars in real currency. Plus we had a chance to win extra money on the side. Seriously: foolproof!

We took short three-dollar cab rides around the city, paid with 20s, kept the change. I had a plan to drive down to Disneyland and spread the bills around the park, but we never made it out of the Bay Area.

We stopped in Berkeley, and my cousin went to a flower shop while I went into a Carl's Jr. and ordered a burger. I handed the kid behind the counter a 20 and he called his manager over.

"We're gonna have to hold onto this."

"Why?"

"Well, we need to call the police."

"Can I still order my food?"

"Yeah, yeah, go ahead."

I played dumb and put in my order, but the minute the manager's back was turned I flew out the door. I ran and caught up with my cousin.

"We need to get out of here NOW. Give me your coat!"

I took off my trench coat and put my cousin's coat and glasses on. I had my hair in a ponytail, so I pulled out the rubber band and frizzed out my hair and hoped that I looked different enough from the description the Carl's Jr. employees were about to give the cops. I told my cousin we should split up so we took separate cabs back to where my car was parked.

We made it to the car without anyone following us, and my heart rate slowly returned to normal. As we were heading out of the city, my cousin asked to stop in People's Park to buy some weed. I protested, but he was stubborn, so we pulled over, walked up to some sketchy dude, and requested some drugs. We handed him a 20.

"This ain't real money."

Frustrated, we agreed to walk to a store, trade it in for real cash, and return. As we walked away, RRRRRT! Two UC Berkeley Campus Police cars screeched to a halt right in front of us. "FREEZE!"

The dealer took off running, the campus cops grabbed me, and my cousin bolted down an alley. One of the cars went after him; I got cuffed and tossed into the other car.

"Excuse me, sir, what's going on?"

"Shut up! You're under arrest."

"For what?"

"For participating in buying and selling drugs."

I didn't see my cousin get taken down, but as he was running he tossed all his counterfeit 20s under a car, which the campus cops retrieved. They searched me and found counterfeit cash in my pockets as well, so they knew they were onto something bigger than just a petty drug deal.

They took us to the station, read us our rights, and dropped us in separate holding cells. They interrogated us and kept asking where our car was.

"I don't have a car here, what are you talking about?"

"We need to put a sticker on your car so it doesn't get towed."

"We took the bus."

It was easy to run them around. One guy played Good Cop:

"We know you drove a car, we know you parked it here. Just cooperate with us."

I stonewalled him and then in came Bad Cop:

"What are you gonna do next, KILL THE PRESIDENT?! Do you know how SERIOUS this is?! You're gonna do HARD FEDERAL TIME!"

He kept repeating that phrase all night, "HARD FEDERAL TIME!" Then back to Good Cop:

"I'm doing all I can to help you here . . . "

They dragged me back and forth between my cell and the interrogation room (with the cuffs squeezed on so tight they cut off my circulation) for round after round of questioning. They dangled my keys in front of my face, and after a while they convinced me that my car really would be towed without a sticker, so I told them where it was, and they left me alone for a while. They searched the trunk and found 20 grand in leftover counterfeit cash, along with three bags of speed.

Then the Secret Service showed up.

Their routine was much more sophisticated. There wasn't any screaming or fake friendliness. Instead, they made me feel like I was sitting on a couch in a psychiatrist's office.

I never answered any question the same way twice. I made up fake stories about where we got the counterfeit bills, like "I found them in a garbage can," but of course they didn't buy any of it for a second. They asked me over and over again to sign papers that would allow them to search my car, but I kept refusing. They hounded me for hours. I was exhausted and hungry, and the campus cops and the Secret Service guys weren't too happy either.

One of the agents reached down and touched his belt between questions and later played me a tape of my statements contradicting each other. The odd thing was that my statements were clearly audible, but the questions from the agent were muffled and scrambled. This was some creepy *Enemy of the State* shit. But it was about to get creepier.

At one point, a new agent showed up and sat in the back corner of the interrogation room. He closed his eyes and rested his forehead on the fingertips of his right hand, as though he was in a state of deep concentration. The interrogation continued:

"Tell me, where did you get it from? What's the guy's name?"

I was too distracted by the guy in the corner to answer.

"Don't look at him. Don't look at him, look at me. Answer my question."

Another guy leaned over to the agent in the corner and whispered, "Did you get anything?"

"Nothing yet."

Maybe it was the lack of food in my stomach or the lack of blood flow past my cuffed wrists, maybe it was the pressure or exhaustion finally getting to me, but I became convinced the corner guy was trying to scan my brain for info.

I focused all my energy on running a Donald Duck cartoon on a loop in my head. Every time an agent asked me something, I'd just stare at the guy in the corner and think to myself, deliberately and distinctly, "Donald Duck. Quack quack. Donald Duck. Quack quack."

After a while, the man in the corner threw up his hands and said, "That's it. It's over."

The agents had a hushed discussion, and I overheard the corner man saying, "He knows what I'm doing."

They asked him, "Did you get anything?"

"All I got was a duck."

You don't have to believe it, because even I don't fucking believe it. I was tripping the fuck out. While the feds regrouped, they dumped me back in my cell. My cousin's voice came from the cell next to mine:

"What are you doing in there? Just tell 'em you want a lawyer!"

Duh.

As soon as I sat down for my next round of questioning, I said, "I just want to talk to a lawyer," three times, very clearly. That was it—the questions stopped.

They dumped us in county jail overnight. We slept on the floor of a hallway with a bunch of other inmates waiting to be processed and spent the next day in a cell with a dude openly shitting in the corner and a trustee with a mop yelling at us not to look him in the eye. Later they put us in a car and moved us to a holding cell at a federal facility in the middle of who knows where, filled with major drug traffickers and higher-end criminals. (The food was much better there, at least.)

I called my mom from a phone at some official's desk.

"Mom, I'm in jail in Berkeley for, uh . . . drugs."

"What?! What the hell?! Oh my god, where are you?!"

Click. The official disconnected us.

My parents somehow figured out where I was, hired a lawyer, and put up their house for a bail bond. We were released after a quick bail hearing and given a court date. On the way out they gave me back my backpack and wallet. The agents who had been hounding me all night were behind the desk eating pizza and snickering.

"Mmmm . . . this is great pizza, isn't this good pizza?"

"Yeah, this is good pizza!"

I didn't understand what kind of mind game they were playing until I looked inside my wallet: empty. I had bought them their lunch.

My parents picked me up outside the holding facility, and my mom screamed at me the whole way home. I barely processed any of it, though, because I still had HARD FEDERAL TIME hanging over my head.

I sat with the lawyer my parents hired and told him what happened. He made notes, occasionally shaking his head and chuckling to himself. And I didn't even tell him the part about Donald Duck. When we went to trial, I found out what was so funny.

There was no jury, just a judge. My cousin opted to go with a public defender. I thought he was crazy. This was the real deal: big bench for the judge, polished wood railings, heavy desks for the prosecution and defense . . . federal fucking court.

My lawyer cross-examined the campus cop who made the arrest.

"How long have you been a campus police officer?"

The cop proudly answered, "Five years."

"And in those five years, how many arrests have you made?"

The cop proudly answered, "I have made 126 arrests."

"Wow. That's pretty good. And out of those 126 arrests, how many resulted in convictions?"

The cop's pride evaporated while he sputtered and searched for an answer. My lawyer answered for him:

"I guess we can go ahead and say twenty-seven now, right?"

He made the cop look incompetent, and he paraded out my sparkling high marks in all my college courses to show I wasn't a thug. But none of that should've really mattered when you're talking about a trunk full of drugs and counterfeit cash.

My lawyer pointed out that my rights were not read to me until I got to the police station, and he asked the cop about dangling my keys in my face and asking about my car.

The cop lied, "I never shook the keys in his face."

"Did you ever *show* him the keys?"

"I never shook the keys in front of his face."

"Did you ask him where his car was parked?"

"Yes . . . because we had to put a sticker on it because it was gonna get towed."

The judge facepalmed hard. She didn't say a word—her facial expression said it all: "You fucking morons."

The cops claimed they found my car, saw a fake 20 on the seat, and used that as probable cause to search the trunk. By arresting me without reading me my rights and then taking possession of my keys they had fucked up the chain of evidence. Since they had my keys, the fake bills from my pocket, and access to the car, they easily could've planted that 20 on the seat (which is exactly what they did, because we never would've left a twenty-dollar bill, real or fake, lying on the front seat of our car in Berkeley). All the stuff they found in the trunk was now inadmissible as evidence.

The judge turned to the campus cop: "I just need to clarify something. Why were you following them?"

"Well, they were dressed kind of nice . . . "

"What do you mean?"

"Well, usually people that hang out in that park aren't dressed nice. They had nice clothes on, and their hair was combed . . . "

"I dress nice. What if I was walking through the park and my hair was combed and you harassed me?"

"Well, uhhh . . . "

"I'm done with you. Get out of here."

She berated the cops for screwing up the whole arrest and then looked down at my cousin and me like we were disobedient pets. She was furious, but she couldn't punish us. "You two are very lucky. I don't know what the hell you were doing, or what the hell you were up to, but consider yourselves lucky."

She slammed down her gavel: "Case dismissed."

She had just handed me my life back. I didn't take the lesson lightly—I was legitimately scared straight. I vowed never to do anything illegal again for the rest of my life.

My parents made me pay for the lawyer bills and court fees, which sucked up all the profit I had made from the counterfeit cash and my past drug deals, so I ended up right back where I started: with one thousand Crystal Sphere 7-inches.

I still have some at my parents' house. I'll give you one if you want.

57

Melvin

I went over to the Dog Patch Wino house with my girlfriend once. It was early in the day, so everyone was still passed out. It was like walking into a crime scene: bodies strewn all over the floor, furniture in awkward positions, and it smelled like piss and stale beer.

We were talking to Smelly when my girlfriend suddenly yelped, "Hey!" I asked her what happened and she explained that one of the limp bodies had reached up and grabbed her ass. She couldn't tell who it was because they were all practically on top of each other. They were all giggling, but they pretended to be asleep.

The Winos were raunchy, trashy, fucked up dudes, but they weren't so bad. And if it weren't for the Winos we never would've met Aaron Abeyta.

My girlfriend's friend Rob had just moved to L.A. from Omaha. He wanted to audition for our open guitarist slot, so I set him up with Mike. A few days later we walked into Mike's apartment, and Mike invited him to sit down on his couch and play an unplugged electric guitar.

"Where's the amp?"

"Let's just try this first."

Rob assumed he'd be jamming at full volume in a practice space with NOFX, so he was a bit thrown, but he did okay. Aaron's audition was scheduled right after his, so Rob and I hung around to watch. As soon as he started playing we both knew Rob was beat.

58

Hefe

I opened the door to my parents' house and there was a young, skinny kid with dreadlocks there to pick up Mark Curry and give him a ride to San Francisco. Mark took some luggage and a bunch of our 7-inches, intent on getting them into some San Francisco record stores. He came back three or four days later completely hammered. He had vomit in his beard, and his luggage was drenched in beer. He didn't sell any of the 7-inches. He and his new friends had apparently been using them as Frisbees.

The kid with the dreadlocks was named DJ, and Mark's new friends were called the Dog Patch Winos. Whatever happened during those few days in San Francisco, it changed Mark forever. A business-savvy, college-minded, goal-oriented musician walked out of my parents' house that day. A Dog Patch Wino came back. He wanted to drink all the time, every day. We were trying to get a DBA set up, stir up interest from labels, work on songs, whatever, and he was constantly distracted by the thought of getting another beer.

Mark, Larry (our drummer), and I decided to move down to L.A. and take Crystal Sphere more seriously. We had already taken several trips down to play shows at the Coconut Teaszer, and on one of those trips I briefly met Erik "Smelly" Sandin, another skinny punk with dreadlocks who barely paid attention to me after saying hello. Around the same time I met Jay Walker, who confused me by wearing sunglasses at night and indoors, but I later found out they were prescription glasses he wore because he couldn't afford to repair his normal ones.

We found a cheap one-bedroom in the Lynwood Apartments in the dead center of Hollywood. I moved in with Doug (our friend and roadie), but Mark and Larry couldn't move down for a couple weeks, so in the meantime we let Jay Walker crash with us. In exchange for our hospitality he showed us how to survive in Hollywood.

Jay and the Winos had the city locked down. They were all homeless, but they never spent a night on the street or went a day without booze. Despite their raggedy appearance (and associated smells) they picked up girls at clubs, went home with them, used their showers, and borrowed their cars. They bounced from one girl's house to another, never overstaying their welcome, slowly working their way through the roster and eventually back to the top of the batting order. Some of them were young rich chicks looking to piss off daddy; some were recently divorced cougars trying to feel young again. Either way, Jay would rack up charges on their credit cards and ride around town in their Mercedes.

Food was never a problem. Jay knew a bouncer or a bartender or an unsecured back door at every bar and club in town, and he would get us all in for free on whichever night they were offering free grub. Exposure 54 had a free barbecue night. The Coconut Teaszer offered free hot dogs that we smuggled home in plastic bags lining our pockets (our freezer was full of them). The Acapulco restaurant offered a full Mexican buffet as long as you were drinking, so we would order water, grab a toothpick and an olive from the bar, and offer up the illusion of a cocktail while grazing until we were stuffed.

If I needed extra rent money, I'd buy sodas at the grocery store, toss them in a cooler, and walk up and down Santa Monica beach selling them for a buck apiece. I could profit 60 or 70 bucks in a couple hours. And when we needed extra money to party we'd panhandle. Jay bounced around to all the tourist spots and flew signs that read "Take A Photo With A Punk Rocker" or "Jokes For A Quarter." I usually just hung out by Mann's Chinese Theater and tried to target the German tourists, who were always the most generous. All the Winos pooled their money at the end of the day (although I'm sure they all kept some for themselves), and we'd buy a keg of beer to celebrate.

Like most newcomers to Hollywood I signed up to be a background extra in movies and TV shows. Of course, being a Mexican I was always cast as a criminal. Every time I'd show up on set they would hand me a bandana. I was in the background of some show featuring Barbara Eden where I was being booked in a police station, and I was in an episode of *Beverly Hills, 90210* where Brandon Walsh goes to a dance party with his Mexican girlfriend from the ghetto. My most prominent role was in a Lifetime mini-series called *Love, Lies and Murder*, in which I played a prison inmate and was directed to walk directly toward the camera.

I tried my best to get more camera time during other shoots, but usually I'd just end up pissing off the directors. During the Barbara Eden shoot I broke free of the cop who was booking me and escaped, which completely distracted from the scene and which got me totally chewed out. When I was filming a scene for *Stop! Or My Mom Will Shoot* at LAX that involved Sylvester Stallone running through the airport, I realized that if I walked a bit faster I would be in the shot when Stallone passed me. They kept yelling "CUT!" and the assistant director kept starting me from further back. I walked faster each time, but I don't think I made it into the final edit.

Working as an extra usually meant long, tedious hours of standing around, so, just like when I was a kid, if I was left unsupervised I would find trouble. My friend Gumdrop Lou (the guy who hooked up Crystal Sphere with that sweet skydiving gig) and I were on the Universal Studios lot doing background work on *City Slickers*. In the opening scene, Billy Crystal, Daniel Stern, and Bruno Kirby are running with the bulls in Pamplona, so there were hundreds of extras lining the fake Spanish streets, all wearing the same traditional white outfits. At one point I looked around and thought, "Wow, there are so many extras here, and we're all dressed the same. I bet they wouldn't notice if we split."

So we did. We snuck onto a bunch of rides in the Universal Studios theme park, including the tram ride that takes tourists through the studio backlot. One of the more popular stops on the ride is the moment when the "Red Sea" parts and the tram drives through it. When the water parted, we jumped out of the tram and ran in the opposite direction as the sea closed behind us. "Hey! Security!!"

Security guards came out of nowhere. They were on our heels, but we made it back to the set of *City Slickers* and mixed in with the crowd like nothing was going on. Security arrived and pointed us out to one of the ADs.

"Those two, right there!"

"What are you talking about? They've been here all day long."

We played dumb, and as the security guards looked out over the sea of similarly dressed extras, they even doubted their own eyes for a minute.

We tempted fate further on the set of the TV show *Gabriel's Fire*. Gumdrop Lou and I hopped into an unattended golf cart and cruised through the Warner Brothers lot in Burbank, waving hello to people and getting confused waves back. We puttered right past the security office and waved hello without being questioned, so we got bolder. We walked onto other sets and pretended like we belonged there. Finally, we walked into one of the production offices, and someone said, "Hey! You two, come here!"

"Uh, bye! We gotta go work!"

We hopped in our cart and zipped off—zzzzzzzzew . . . but not before we heard the crackle of a walkie-talkie and the word "Security!"

Another golf cart appeared and chased us through the Warners backlot like we were in the finale of *Pee-wee's Big Adventure*, but yet again we were able to run back into the crowd of extras and escape getting fired.

All while earning a steady, legitimate paycheck.

◆ ◆ ◆

Our apartment was bursting at the seams with Dog Patch Winos crashing in every corner, and Crystal Sphere needed space to practice, so a bunch of us pitched in to rent a house on Fountain Avenue. Our friend Lip from the band Lip and the Smoochers slept under the pool table, two girls lived in the back bedroom, Mark Curry slept on the floor of the practice room between all the equipment, and our friend Phil set up a room in the crawl space.* We probably had eight or nine permanent residents and dozens of other people partying and crashing for days at a time.

It was everything you would expect from a degenerate rock 'n' roll party house: people breaking shit, people kicking holes in the walls and smashing windows, loud all-night parties and impromptu wrestling matches, constant drinking and bong hits . . . The girls would bring home random dudes from the bars, and neighborhood rivalries would spark fistfights. Once Lip was woken up by a fight between two strangers so he crawled out from under the pool table to shut them up and got belted in the mouth and knocked back down to the floor. In his own house!

The girls also owned two little pit bulls that pissed and shat everywhere. You'd wake up in the morning and end up soaking your socks by stepping in one of their puddles. Then again, it could've been puddles of human piss just as easily because Smelly and DJ would come over and pee on the random people passed out on the floor. Hard to say if either was preferable to step-ping in the vomit that was spread around the carpet every morning.

No one was openly shooting heroin at the Fountain house, but a dealer named Carlton lived around the corner, and people went over to his place to shoot up instead. One day, out of curiosity, I knocked on the door and walked in. It was a dark, grimy place with lighters, spoons, and a coffee mug full of needles on the kitchen counter. Carlton was preparing to inject a shot between his toes. A bunch of people I knew were hanging out and getting high; guys who would hang out at our house, guys from the Coconut Teaszer, people I never would've suspected. "Whoa, you too?" It seemed like every single person I had met in Hollywood was secretly doing heroin. I was happier when I didn't know about any of it. I never went back to Carlton's again.

I moved out of the Fountain house not long after I moved in. Unlike the Winos, I actually had shit to do during the day that required me to wake up before the sun went back down.

I picked up classes at Los Angeles Community College from where I left off in Sacramento. Plus I took a day job at Ticketmaster, selling tickets

---

*Somehow he was able to convince girls to go down there with him. If I were a girl, I would've assumed he was luring me to my death . . . that's how horror movies start!

(mostly for New Kids on the Block) over the phone. I parlayed that into a gig at Los Angeles Children's Hospital as a lab assistant by hinting to the woman interviewing me that I could score her Rolling Stones tickets. Once I had the job she couldn't fire me for not being anywhere near able to get her free tickets, but they had no problem firing me for being grossly incompetent and unqualified.

I was supposed to prep bacterial cultures but I told the lab guys I had never done it before, so they walked me through the process while secretly wondering how I got hired. I would answer the phone, and doctors would request test results that I had no idea how to get for them, so I would pawn the call off on someone else, or run to the bathroom and ask someone to take care of it for me. They would tell me to spin blood or urine in the centrifuge machine, but I didn't know how it worked so I would just sit there and stare at the samples for half an hour. They'd come back and ask, "Did you spin those samples?"

"No."

And they'd freak out because the doctors upstairs were waiting on important test results. They fired me in less than two weeks.

Crystal Sphere, meanwhile, was gigging around L.A. and finally getting some attention. We had to rebuild our fan base out of nothing, but our live shows—which featured clown wigs, oversized novelty sunglasses, and other comic props that would've gotten us kicked off *The Gong Show*—were earning us fans beyond the usual Dog Patch Wino crew that always showed up to support.

We hired a local promoter named Desi Benjamin to be our manager, and he showcased us to A&R guys from a bunch of labels.* They all passed, but success still seemed inevitable. Mark's songwriting was too good to be ignored.

And it wasn't ignored: Mark got signed to Virgin Records. As a solo artist.

The rest of us were bummed that Virgin didn't sign our whole band, but we were happy for Mark. He had a hard life, and he deserved every bit of success that his talent earned him. He tried his best to sell Crystal Sphere to the label, but none of us expected him to turn down his solo deal just to slum it with us. And Mark didn't forget us: when he got his first advance check he filled our cupboards with groceries and our cars with gas, and he bought me a reissued 1962 Fender Strat. We remained close friends, and we visited him while he put together his demo in a zillion-dollar-per-hour

---

*He pops up in *The Decline of Western Civilization Part II: The Metal Years*, credited as "18 Year Old Concert Promoter."

recording studio with top-notch musicians, female backup singers, and Grammy-winning producer Ed Cherney (who produced Eric Clapton and Bob Dylan, among others).

Then we went back to selling sodas on the beach and stepping over piles of vomit every morning. Music was never a guaranteed career path—as everyone we had ever met was fond of reminding us—but we felt like we were in a band that really had a shot, and it had just disappeared before our eyes. Mark tried to at least get the label to allow us to be his backing band on the road, but they weren't interested. We were left to fend for ourselves.

A couple weeks after Mark signed, I got a call from Smelly. His band, NOFX, needed a new guitar player. I had no other irons in the fire, so I figured "what the hell?" He came over to my apartment and played me the *Ribbed* album.

The guitar sounded awful, the singer sounded worse. It wasn't music, it was a sloppy blur of sound. But I didn't have many options, so I asked Smelly which songs I should learn for the audition. As he was scanning the track listing with his finger, he nodded out.

I thought, "Man, he sure is thinking for a long time," but then I realized what was going on.

"Erik. Hey. Sandin. Sandin!"

He snapped awake and continued his sentence right where he left off, as though he'd been conscious the whole time, "and you should probably learn this song. Maybe this one . . . " And then he nodded out again.

What the hell was I about to get myself into?

59

Mike

When I was auditioning people to replace Steve, I had them play songs from *Ribbed* in my living room on an electric guitar that wasn't plugged in. It caught people off guard. They expected to jam with the whole band, or at least have some distortion to cover up the rough edges of their playing, but now that the band was finally starting to sound good I had developed what some musicians might call "standards."

Joe Rimicci from Jughead's Revenge aced the audition, and I actually offered him the slot, but then his father got sick and he said he couldn't tour with us because he had to stay home and run the bar his family owned. This turned out to be not the smartest career decision—the bar eventually went under anyway.

Smelly recommended his friend Aaron Abeyta, who was in a funk-punk-fusion band called Crystal Sphere. He came to the audition dressed like a cholo, which I thought was cool because he looked like a Suicidal. This was purely a coincidence: he didn't know anything about punk. He just liked the cholo look.

Not only did Aaron nail all the parts, but he also said he played trumpet, and we happened to have a song featuring a trumpet on *Ribbed*, so I figured that might come in handy in the future.

I told him he was in. The only problem was his name. My girlfriend's name was Erin. I wasn't about to deal with the constant annoyance of saying, "No, I said Aaron, not Erin!" so I suggested a Mexican-sounding name, like "El Jefe."

I don't speak Spanish, so I didn't realize that the "h" sound is usually spelled with a "j." You would think Aaron would know that, having been raised by Mexicans, but it turns out he speaks less Spanish than my daughter did at age six after hanging around with the nanny all day.

And so, from that moment forward, Aaron Abeyta would be known to the world as "El Hefe."

60

Hefe

I should probably officially confess:

I am not a punk.

I went to see TSOL once, but I was far more familiar with mariachi and barbershop than I was with the bands that influenced NOFX. It was a struggle to distinguish the rhythm patterns on *Ribbed*, and it took me a while to figure out how the hell they were strumming. I studied blues and jazz. Even the metal songs I knew were based on stuff we'd covered in my junior college music classes. I had to unlearn everything about proper guitar technique in order to play punk.

Through the Winos, I met a lot of guys from the L.A. punk scene, like Scotty from Verbal Abuse and Greg Hetson from Bad Religion (although at the time he introduced himself as Greg Hetson from the Circle Jerks), but it was never a big deal to me because I didn't listen to any of their bands. I

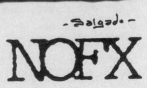

EPITAPH

6201 SUNSET BOULEVARD
SUITE 111 HOLLYWOOD
CALIFORNIA 90028

was briefly introduced to Fat Mike once, but the name NOFX carried less weight for me than the Circle Jerks, so I didn't pay him much mind. I just said, "He looks like Peter Brady!"

He knew I was busting his balls, so he just sneered and said, "Fuck you." I'm sure he doesn't remember that. Certainly neither of us mentioned it months later when I was sitting in his apartment for my audition.

Mike insisted I play the songs for him on an electric guitar with no amp, which I thought was totally weird, but which was actually really smart of him. Aside from the NOFX songs I had learned, I showed off a few jazz and blues riffs that seemed to impress him, and I sang a bit so he could check out my voice. I think what cinched the whole thing was when I nailed the little riff at the end of the song "El Lay." Mike said none of the other candidates could pull that one off quite right. It was no challenge for me: it was a rip-off of a riff by the Steve Miller Band.

I was in right away, even though I wasn't sure I wanted to be. Mike's only reservation was that my name, Aaron, was too close to his girlfriend's name, Erin, so they'd have to call me something else.

"How about we call you 'El Hefe'?"

"Whatever."

I guess this was really happening.

"We leave on tour in three days."

Wait, what?

◆ ◆ ◆

I told the Dog Patch Winos I had joined NOFX, and none of them believed me. Jay Walker told everyone I was full of shit. NOFX had offered him a job as a roadie, and he hadn't heard anything about me joining. And everyone knew I wasn't a punk and would be totally out of place in the band, so everyone thought I was joking.

I showed up on the day we were supposed to leave for tour, and there was Jay.

He laughed and said, "Wow. This is going to be interesting . . . "

◆ ◆ ◆

We only had two rehearsals and a van ride to Berkeley for me to work on the songs before my first show. I was freaked.

Mike kept saying, "Don't worry about it."

"Dude, I can't do this, there's no way."

"Yes you can."

We'd run through a song in the van. I would fuck it up, and Mike would say, "It doesn't matter. Trust me. It's punk rock."

What kind of insane mentality is that? How could I not care? For my whole life, all I had done was care! I strived for perfection every time I picked up an instrument! All those lessons, all those college classes, all those hours of practice, all those rehearsals and gigs with Crystal Sphere—all of it had been leading up to stepping onto a stage where no one actually cared whether I even hit the right note?

Gilman Street wasn't exactly the Sacramento Sports Arena, but it was the biggest crowd I'd played for yet. Crystal Sphere's biggest show was for 150 friends at our record release party, but the crowd at Gilman was at least double that. No one in the band had explained the size of their draw—I flew in blind. And to top it off, at the last minute Mike decided we'd open the set with "Together on the Sand," which I sing and play without any backing from the rest of the band. I walked out on stage wearing Florsheim dress shoes, a long chain wallet, and a fedora, looking as out of place as I felt. Mike introduced me as the new guitarist and, mercifully, the crowd cheered.

With Crystal Sphere I would jump around a bit on stage, but the faster music of NOFX and all my nervous energy had me bouncing all over the place. I fed off the crowd and tried to match the energy of the rest of the band. And just as I started to get comfortable, a Dog Patch Wino named Redhead Max hocked a huge green loogie onto my chest.

I grabbed the mic and demanded to know who was spitting on me, and I threatened to kick his or her ass. A security guy on the side of the stage wearing a hockey mask leaned over and said, "That means they like you, dude!" I still had much to learn about this strange world of punk rock . . .

Other lessons came hard and fast. After the Gilman show we had an all-night drive to Salt Lake City, so the guys popped various tapes into the tape deck and schooled me on all the punk rock I should've been listening to all these years. Most of it was unlistenable; why couldn't any of these bands record their music in a decent studio?

When we finished playing at Gilman, kids asked me for photos and interviews for their fanzines. The ego boost of modest fame was a new experience. After the Salt Lake City show a kid was interviewing me and asked what my influences were. I said, "I really like Parliament. Led Zeppelin is cool . . ." Mike told me I couldn't say stuff like that without getting crucified by the punks. I learned to answer "the Descendents," because they were the only punk band NOFX had played for me that I could actually stomach.

The guys had already been poking fun at me in rehearsals, saying I looked like Miguel from the movie *The Bad News Bears*. On stage in Salt Lake, Mike told the crowd I was actually in the movie, and a myth was born.

Mike kept saying it on stage, and when people asked me about it I rolled with it. I thought the jig was up when we played Santa Barbara on a different tour way later and Brandon Cruz from Dr. Know called me out on it. He was a child actor and was actually IN *The Bad News Bears* as the pitcher for the rival team, so he told everyone I was lying. So I tried to come clean. I admitted it wasn't me, but then people said, "You're just saying that because you don't want us to know!" and the myth lived on. In a bizarre twist, George Gonzalez, the actor who DID play Miguel, published a website about his acting work, and on his résumé page he claimed to be the guitarist for NOFX. No wonder people still ask me about it.

Mike mocked me endlessly on stage for our first few shows. I still felt like a fish out of water, so I just took it at first. But after five or six shows I fired back at one of his insults with, "You know, Mike, I could take your face, roll it in some dough, and make gorilla cookies." The band burst into laughter, probably more due to the fact that I had finally grown some balls than from the joke itself.

Mike said, "I don't have a gorilla face. Melvin looks more like a gorilla than I do!" And the crowd loved it.

After a few more exchanges like that during the tour, Mike's wheels started turning. We talked about ways to pick on each other on stage, and how we could gang up on Melvin, too. Our stage banter naturally turned into the Three Stooges give-and-take that we eventually became known for.

Having never been on a real tour, I didn't know what to expect. It was exciting being in new towns and having keg parties every night. I was used to watching Smelly's Moron Brothers routine at the Fountain house, but on the road he was streaking down streets and peeing on cats.* Jay Walker macked on every girl in sight. In Nebraska there were only like ten people at the show, and the promoter had gone to see the Red Hot Chili Peppers across town. Somewhere along the way someone gave us a ton of expired chocolate bars they had rescued from a factory dumpster, and we subsisted on them until our stomachs couldn't take it anymore. We played ABC No Rio in New York and while everyone went to eat I stayed in the van and kept an eye on the gear. Sure enough, seconds after they left someone tried

---

*Seriously, a cat! I was in the bathroom with him at some girl's house when a cat came in and sat next to the toilet. He was peeing into the toilet, and without any hesitation he turned and purposely soaked the cat in piss. The cat angrily meowed and shot out the door. When we left the bathroom we saw the owner stroking and cuddling the cat. "Oh, little Fluffy. Little Fluffy has been out in the rain! Oh, poor kitty . . ." She didn't understand why we were laughing our asses off.

to break in. It was a cargo van with no windows; I could hear the thieves whispering outside, and I was scared shitless. The lock button popped up. I reached over and pushed it back down.

"It's still locked, man!"

"I just opened it!"

It popped up again. I pushed it back down. This went on a couple more times.

"I think someone's in there, man!" and then footsteps running away.

That was my first trip to New York City. I had never seen huge sky-scrapers before. I had never felt Florida humidity before. I had never been outside of California, El Paso, or Mexico. When we rode into Salt Lake I woke up, looked out the van window, and started shouting, "Snow! We're in the snow, everybody!" They all laughed at me; I had never seen salt flats before.

And speaking of rude awakenings: hygiene. NOFX had no problem sleeping in the van or on floors or going days without bathing. I thought the idea of not showering every day was insane, but it proved to be a challenge when we were moving around so much and staying at houses with showers that were dirtier than us. I would dab on English Leather cologne to mask my body odor and add product to my hair to maintain my pompadour, and I would drown in ridicule from Mike and Smelly. We never had time to do laundry, so I would rinse my tighty-whiteys in the sink and hang them to dry inside the van during the next day's ride. Smelly would turn his head and get tangled in my skid marks, and soon I was being shouted at by the whole band to dry my clothes somewhere else.

After a while I gave in. I was exhausted from traveling and playing every day, and I was tired of being laughed at by my band mates. I stopped show-ering, I threw away my cologne, I let my hair get messed up . . .

The metamorphosis was complete. I had become one of them.

✦   ✦   ✦

At the end of that first tour, Mike handed me $2,200. I couldn't believe it. I was making 400 bucks a month at the time—this was enough for me to live off of for a long while. For the first time in my life it looked like I could ac-tually make a living playing music.

I think it was a revelation for the rest of the band, too. Toward the end of the tour Mike said, "I think we have enough money to afford a hotel," and no one could believe it. They were so happy to be crammed into a single room at some fleabag off the freeway because they had been so used to the crusty lifestyle.

When I got home, Mark Curry was auditioning people to be in his touring band. He wanted to use the Crystal Sphere guys, but the label insisted we all submit to a formal audition process. I was the only one who made it through.

Touring with Mark and being backed by Virgin Records was a night-and-day change from the world of NOFX. Instead of sweating junkie burglars in a cargo van, our stop in New York City had us staying in a fancy hotel and getting wined and dined by the label reps. And I didn't get spit on once during the entire trip.

When I returned from Mark's tour, I immediately went back out on the road with NOFX to Europe and it was the same disgusting drunkenness I had seen on the road in the States times ten. We rode in a cargo van for hours on end, sitting on a lumpy layer of luggage to play for a bunch of grunting, drunk, bearded Vikings squatting in buildings with no power or heat. In the Christiania district of Copenhagen, some girl passed out on the sidewalk, and I watched some gross, fat shithead pull his cock out and stick it in her mouth. I ran inside to tell everyone what was going on, and it turned into some stupid drunken brawl. Plus Smelly got the clap so to combat it he was downing tetracycline. But not tablets prescribed by a doctor—he was eating the stuff you get from the pet store to kill the bacteria in your fish tank. As if his acid and heroin farts weren't bad enough, the tetracycline gave his farts this unholy moldy fish tank smell that nearly suffocated us all.

And then back on the road with Mark . . . opening for Keith Richards . . . showering every night . . . wearing clean underwear . . .

I was running myself ragged with the constant traveling. I couldn't keep both bands going forever. There was already a schedule clash where I had to leave one of Mark's tours a week early to tour with NOFX. Mike finally asked which band I was going to choose. He was bummed at the prospect of losing another guitarist, especially since our stage banter had become so comfortable and our shows were getting bigger all the time.

I had a long talk with the other guys in Mark's band. They had no idea why I was conflicted. They all would've chosen NOFX.

Sure, we were traveling in comfort and style with Mark, but at the end of the tour we were still just hired guns. I not only made less money at the end of Mark's tours, but I could be replaced at any time, and I didn't own any of the music or any shares of the merchandise. NOFX was offering me a full quarter of everything: I would be their partner. I felt guilty about abandoning Mark, but the other guys pointed out that he was the one who took a solo deal, and that I needed to look out for myself.

I called Mike and Mark and told them my decision. And I wondered if I was making the worst mistake of my life.

Mark toured for a while, opened for bands like Lenny Kravitz and INXS, and was featured on MTV as a "Buzz Clip." Then EMI bought out Virgin Records. Virgin had big plans to promote Mark's second album, but those plans fizzled after the merger, and the album flopped. When his contract was up, EMI didn't re-sign him.

Mark and I are still friends. He lives in Indiana and still releases music independently. We send each other tracks over the internet and help each other out with projects from time to time.

But I think I made the right decision. From the moment I returned from my first tour with NOFX, I never had to work a day job again.

61

Smelly

A year or two before Hefe's first show, we played Gilman, and after the show Johnny Sixpack and I got blitzed and somehow ended up wandering through a nasty part of Oakland. It was one of the worst neighborhoods I'd ever seen, with abandoned houses lining the streets. We were the only white guys for miles, and Johnny had a swastika painted on the back of his Dog Patch Wino vest.

As if we didn't stick out enough already, Johnny found a pair of ski boots on the sidewalk and put them on, so every step he made was announced with a loud Ka-KLUNK, Ka-KLUNK, Ka-KLUNK. We happened upon a dark corner bar, and Johnny brazenly entered. A bar full of black guys turned to stare at the two dumbest-looking white freaks in all of Northern California. You could practically hear the sound effect of a needle scratching off a record. A loud, high-pitched voice cut through the awkward silence: "Damn! Look at them crackas!"

If I learned anything from Johnny, it's that in a situation like that you just have to own it with your attitude, so I asked, "What's a guy have to do to get a beer around here?" And we walked over to the bar.

Ka-KLUNK, Ka-KLUNK, Ka-KLUNK, Ka-KLUNK...

We sat there and finished at least one beer before someone came up and said, "You know, son, this might not be the wisest place for y'all to be drinking." We finished one more beer before heeding his advice.

Later we ended up in some squat, and I was throwing up as always. I passed out, but every time I woke up I would puke. The next day, Johnny told me he was flirting with some chick and kept saying, "Watch this, I can make my friend throw up anytime I want. Hey! Wake up!"

I would stir, slur out "What?" and puke every time. I don't know if it helped him get laid or not.

✦   ✦   ✦

During the *Liberal Animation* years we'd have maybe 30 people at our shows. After *S&M Airlines* we drew 130. After *Ribbed* it was more like 230. It hit me that we may actually be going somewhere with this.

We played a gig with SNFU one night and got paid maybe 150 bucks, while SNFU took in about 500. Mike crunched the numbers and said, "If we can make 500 bucks a show, we can do this for a living." I humored him, but despite the increased album sales and show attendance I still thought he was nuts.

When Hefe joined NOFX, our Gilman draw was usually only about 80 or 100 people (who probably would've been there whether we were playing or not). But when we pulled up to Gilman for Hefe's first show there was a big sign outside that read "SOLD OUT."

We were shocked. My moment of celebration was brief, however, because I had just spent six hours in a van to get from L.A. to Berkeley and I needed to get high. I went to the McDonald's around the corner and locked myself in the bathroom to shoot up. I fixed up a shot but dropped the needle on the floor. It fell straight down and the tip hit the tile. The very end of the needle, the tiny sharp point that's supposed to pierce your skin, was blunted and curled back into a "U" shape.

"Oh fuck oh fuck oh fuck oh fuck oh fuck!"

I forced it into my skin. I jammed and jabbed and finally—"poof"—my arm ruptured. Blood everywhere. But I got the heroin into my system. Out of a needle that had just been dropped on the floor of a McDonald's men's room.

We played well that night, and Hefe spazzed out on stage and won over the fans with his antics and guitar playing. But I mostly remember Bob Lush (who had hitched a ride with us) crawling on stage in a drunken stupor and passing out with his head inside my kick drum. I didn't have a front head on the drum, so he just laid his head down on the pillow I kept inside it to muffle the sound. Mike and Hefe had to keep jumping over him while they played.

I celebrated our first sold-out Gilman show by stealing someone's van. DJ and I decided we needed a box of wine, so we hopped in the first thing with wheels and drunkenly tore down the streets of Berkeley. We didn't realize some kid was sleeping in the back. He woke up to us riding up on the sidewalks, hitting trash cans, hanging out the door, and climbing onto the hood. He screamed in terror, but we refused to let him out.

I vaguely remember getting out of the van and kicking the passenger door in. I'm not sure if I stopped on my own or if DJ or the kid in the back somehow stopped me. All I know is that DJ and I (and our hostage) are lucky to be alive.

I slept it off on the ride back to L.A. the next day. Bob Lush was sleeping next to me, and at one point he turned and draped his arm over me. In his dry, raspy, half-asleep voice, he purred, "Come on, baby, let's fuck."

"Bob, it's me, Erik. Fucking knock it off."

"Well fuck you then, bitch." He rolled over and passed back out.

62

Melvin

We stopped in Sacramento and met the extended cast of Hefe's family just as we were about to set out on our first U.S. tour with our new guitarist. It was the only time I met his mother. She was sweet and hospitable and made us all feel right at home. The only thing a little off-putting was the cataract that had clouded out one of her eyes. That, and her psychic visions of the future.

She grabbed Smelly's wrists. "Mijo, come here. Give me your hands." She hovered her hands around his. "You have been in a dark place for a long time. But there is light at the end of the tunnel. Why are you blocking me?"

Smelly pulled away. He tried to act casual, but we could tell she had gotten to him.

Later, while we were chatting about the upcoming tour, she interrupted and told us, "Stay away from glass, there's going to be broken glass. And there's going to be a fight or a riot, but you will be all right if you stick together." Then she looked at us gravely:

"Be careful around the airport."

Confused, we explained we weren't flying anywhere during the tour, we'd be in a van the whole time.

She replied, "Just be careful around airports."

After we left the house, Hefe said his mom always had a sixth sense about things. She just knew stuff. We asked him what she was talking about when she brought up the airport—he had no idea.

A few days later we were at a house party and Hefe was sitting on a couch near a door with several panes of glass in it. As he stood up, a fight broke out and someone threw someone else into the door. The panes of glass shattered all over the seat Hefe had just vacated. Okay . . . stay away from glass—pretty freaky. But at least we had gotten past the big fight his mom had predicted.

Toward the end of the tour we were standing outside the venue in Albuquerque because it was packed to the gills. We heard the openers stop playing, and the guitarist came outside wearing what looked like a red shirt but was really a white shirt covered in blood. He said, "I'm so bummed I'm going to miss you guys."

Nazi skinheads had infested the Albuquerque scene, and apparently one of them had jumped on stage and stabbed this guy while they were in the middle of playing. Everyone flooded out of the club, and a huge brawl erupted. The Nazi who stabbed the guitarist leapt into his car, which was swarmed by the local punks. Big Ed, this fucking enormous Native American dude who had helped set up the show, jumped up and down on the car's roof, caving it in and trapping the skinheads inside.*

We didn't see what happened after that because we all retreated to the van to keep from getting sucked into the fighting or arrested by the dozens of cops that showed up. Smelly and Hefe were yelling, "Stick together!" as they remembered Hefe's mom's advice.

Broken glass and the occasional big brawl weren't such strange occurrences on a punk tour. If those two predictions were the only ones Hefe's mom had made, I might've blown them off as coincidences. But the warning about the airport is the one that freaked us out the most.

Sometime in between the broken glass at the beginning of the tour and the riot at the end of the tour we were driving from Utah to Colorado, cutting through Wyoming. I was sleeping in the back of the van when I felt it slow down and heard Jay, who was driving, say, "Oh shit, there's dogs."

I had smoked a bunch of weed the night before in Salt Lake City, and the people we stayed with gave me a quarter ounce for the road. When I heard "dogs" I popped up and clawed through my bag to find the contraband.

Jay slowed to a stop at the roadblock and a friendly Wyoming state patrol officer said they were checking vehicles to make sure the lights work for highway safety. He stood back and called for Jay to turn on the brights and

---

*We actually stayed at Big Ed's house a few times over the years and his mom always made us fresh tortillas and scrambled eggs for breakfast. Nice guy.

turn signals, and for a moment I thought maybe we were in the clear. Then one of the dogs launched into a barking fit.

The cop's demeanor darkened and he demanded Jay pull the van off to the side. I opened the bag of weed—immediately filling the entire vehicle with the unmistakable stench of skunk bud—and stuffed the entire quarter ounce into my mouth.

A quarter ounce of pot is about the size of a candy bar, which would be a hard enough thing to choke down in one gulp, but this wasn't a smooth, chocolate-y, nougat-y treat; it was a sticky, bristly block of stem-filled sativa. I had no saliva left after the first few chews, but I desperately kept at it.

I stuffed the empty plastic bag back into my pack as the troopers pulled open the van's sliding side door. "Everybody out!" I held my head down, dangling my hair over my face to mask my hard-working jaw. "You, too!" I pretended to fumble with my shoelaces to buy me a few extra seconds while everyone else piled out.

I stood on the side of the road, chew, chew, chewing, while the cops and dogs searched the van. I still hadn't swallowed the last of the weed when the dog found my backpack and the cops asked whose it was. I raised my hand and tried to look innocent.

They found the empty plastic bag, but there was still a tiny pinch of weed left in the corner. They found my pipe, too. The trooper held the baggie aloft with a wide grin and declared, "El busto!"

Fuck. Did he seriously just say "El busto"? Are we in the middle of a Cheech and Chong movie right now?

A guy with a beard, dark sunglasses, and a baseball cap that read "DEA" took me aside while the troopers made the rest of the band unload all of our gear and luggage. He threatened me with a trafficking charge. I swore up and down that the baggie was just remnants from the night before. I explained that the pipe wasn't even mine, and we were just a band on tour.

The DEA guy knew we weren't totally innocent, but he also knew we weren't international smugglers. The cops all had a pow-wow and decided to let me post bail on the spot if I handed them $400. Since jail and a trial was my only other option, I borrowed the cash from the band fund, and we drove off.

Yeah, "post bail." I probably could've fought the whole thing and claimed it was an illegal search, and they probably knew that, but we both knew that flying back to Wyoming and hiring a lawyer would've cost me way more than $400. I guess I bought lunch and beers for the Wyoming State Troopers that afternoon.

As we drove away, the pot I swallowed finally hit me. The entire van and everyone in it was vibrating. I felt like I was floating, but not in a good way. And then we saw the sign for the very next exit after the roadblock:

Rock Springs Airport.

Hefe's mom had called it. If only her divining powers could have warned me about the next day, when I would expel a horrific, green, skunk-bud-odored shit.

63

Mike

My dad was less than 5 feet tall when he graduated high school. He grew a few more inches when he reached college, but I can only imagine that his height might have been part of why he always seemed to have something to prove. Part of it might have also been that he grew up surrounded by the competitive atmosphere of Hollywood—my grandfather, James S. Burkett, produced all of the *Charlie Chan* movies in the '40s and left a legacy to live up to. And part of it might have been a weak relationship with his own parents, considering he once stopped talking to my grandmother completely for more than two years.

I don't know why my dad was the way he was, because we never became close enough to talk about things on that level. I don't think he consciously woke up one day and decided to be distant and neglectful; I think he just had a problem with any serious emotional interaction. He didn't know how to deal with fatherhood. And he certainly didn't know how to make sense of his son's interest in punk.

Back when my mom's tactic of sending me to therapy to dissuade me from pursuing punk failed, my dad came up with a plan of his own. When I was sixteen, he asked me to join him on a business trip to Italy, followed by a week of vacation in Israel. Despite our strained relationship, it sounded like fun. So I went. It was not fun.

That's not entirely true. There were some good moments. But it started off as a drag. We were in Florence for five days, and my dad had shoe-related business meetings every day. One afternoon I actually went to lunch with him and Kenneth Cole. Nice guy. But, like with my dad, we had very little in common.

My dad was embarrassed that I went to lunch with Kenneth Cole wearing a stained, torn-up T-shirt. "Didn't you bring any *nice* clothes?" Most of the time we spent together was punctuated by bickering. When he found out from a hotel employee that I had slept until noon, he berated me for wasting time. "You're in Italy! Do something, walk around!"

To get him off my back I went to see the statue of David and all that, but as a sixteen-year-old punk I couldn't have given less of a shit about any of it. Most of my time there was spent alone in my hotel room, jerking off three times a day and watching Italian TV.

Luckily, I brought an issue of *Maximum Rocknroll* with me. The magazine always had scene reports from all over the world, and someone named Stephano Bettini had written in from Florence. His address was in there, so I went and knocked on his door.

"Hi, I'm a punk rocker from California."

"Come in!"

We listened to records, and I made tapes of some Italian hardcore he had. He was in a band called I Refuse It, which happened to be playing that night with another band called Putrid Fever, so of course I said I'd be there.

Then, as I was walking back to my hotel, I took a wrong turn and got lost in a maze of alleyways. I spotted a bright red head of hair and realized it was my ex-girlfriend, Cindy (the one with the butt-plug beer bong). I walked up and, as casually as possible, said, "Hi." She freaked out over the coincidence. She was only there for one day on some class field trip thing. I never would've crossed paths with her had I not found that address in *Maximum Rocknroll* and then gotten completely lost. Another piece of evidence for my theory that mole men with magnets are somehow controlling my destiny.

We met up later that night to go to the hardcore show. It was in some basement rehearsal space in some ancient building. There were forty or so people there, slamming and dogpiling and going off. Cindy and I got drunk, rode back to my hotel room on the backs of a couple motorcycles, and had sex one last time.

So the trip wasn't all bad. And I have to admit I was impressed by the Vatican when we passed through Rome. And after that we went to Israel and floated in the Dead Sea and water-skied in the Red Sea.

In between all of it, though, were slices of time with my dad that were nothing but awkward. We had some pleasant dinner conversations, but we argued more than we agreed, and the trip meant to bring us closer together just underscored how distant we truly were.

On the last day we went to a kibbutz, which is like a traditional Israeli farming collective. We toured the grounds and saw how everything worked and ate dinner with the family who lived there. After dinner, my dad took me aside and explained the whole reason for this trip.

He wanted to leave me on the kibbutz.

He and my mom thought I was going downhill. They hated that I was getting into punk and thought six months on a farm in the Holy Land would help steer me right somehow. I don't know where this Jew-wakening came from—we were Jewish by heritage but never religious at home. We never celebrated holidays, I was never Bar Mitzvahed, we never went to synagogue. I guess he figured Israel was far enough removed from L.A. that I would eventually work my rebellion out of my system.

Of course, I threw a fit. No high school kid wants to ditch all of his friends. NOFX had just started four months earlier, and I was trying to make something of it. No fucking way was I going to live on a kibbutz in Israel. He did his best to sell the idea, but I wasn't budging so he eventually backed off.

I have to give credit to both of my parents for generally being reasonable people. They would concede an argument if I made good enough points. I rarely found myself in a "because I said so" situation.

When I wanted to start Fat Wreck Chords in the early '90s and make a real go of having my own record label, I asked my dad to co-sign a bank loan for $20,000. I had done the math: *S&M Airlines* had sold 10,000 copies on Epitaph by that point, so I only needed to sell 5,000 copies of our new EP, *The Longest Line*, in order to recoup the loan.

My dad said he would co-sign, but only for $14,000. I was offended. I wasn't starting a lemonade stand. I was being conservative with my sales estimates, and I knew what I was doing. And here he was trying to teach me some lesson ten years too late.

Instead of co-signing, he offered to loan me the full $20,000 out of his own pocket. That probably sounds like a thoughtful, fatherly gesture, but he explained that he didn't want to ruin his credit by co-signing a bank loan I might default on.

He may not have had faith in me, but he did loan me the money. And when *The Longest Line* recouped, and I offered to repay the loan in full, he told me not to worry about it. It's funny: If I had been broke I'm sure he would've held the debt over my head forever, but because I was actually making money it was suddenly no big deal.

He wasn't the kind of dad who took me to baseball games. He didn't have the slightest clue how to relate to me. And he tried to dump me on a kibbutz. But I'm sure I could've had a worse father.

64

Smelly

Free tip: If you're buying a junkie a store-bought gift for Christmas or their birthday, you may as well hand them heroin, because they're just going to return or sell the present for drug money anyway.

I was at the Glendale Galleria returning a comforter my mom bought me, but for some reason the security tag was never removed so the alarm went off when I walked into the store. Some mall cops grabbed me. I tried to explain that I was bringing the comforter in, not taking it out, but I looked exactly like what I was: a fucked up punk junkie, so they took me to mall jail.

Eventually they verified I was telling the truth, but they had already called the real cops and given them my name. I had a bunch of outstanding warrants for stupid misdemeanors and parking tickets, so since I was already in custody I was transferred to a holding station and held on $700 bail.

I called my parents and asked them to bail me out. The jail was only five minutes from their house, but they very matter-of-factly explained they wouldn't be coming to get me. They had bailed me out for similar stuff a couple of times before, but they saw how fast I was descending, and they were going to try tough love this time.

My dad, ironically, was more affected by it than I was. He had a moment of clarity, realizing that his son was in jail, and it was his example that had likely steered him there. He quit drinking—cold turkey—that same day, and hasn't had a drink since.

Meanwhile, I was laughing it up in a dormitory full of like-minded troublemakers. Jail wasn't that big of a deal; it was just horribly boring. Luckily Raymond had explained jailhouse etiquette to me, so I knew I should stick with the white guys and keep out of other people's business. But the vibe wasn't as heavy as I'd expected. Everyone was hanging out and trading stories and laughing it up.

For all the lessons Raymond imparted to me, he never mentioned you're not supposed to rip epic farts in a cell. Being the goof-off I am, I did just that and waited for everyone to laugh. But in jail farting isn't funny, it's disrespectful. Some older cholo guy got in my face and made it clear that I had fucked up. The mood in the room went from casual fun to seriously tense. Our respective racial groups took us to neutral corners, and I avoided getting murdered once again.

Later on the cops took our shoes and herded our group into the drunk tank, a big padded room with a drain in the middle of the floor for piss. I remember a skinny black guy heckling the cops with his hyperactive Chris Tucker voice and once again I was back to enjoying jail. But after twelve hours, as they lined us up to go to county, they pulled me out of line and said, "Okay, you're gone."

Out of everyone in the room, mine was the only name they called. The bus to county was already idling outside. I was probably facing a couple weeks in county jail, which is, by all accounts from my friends, a much harsher experience than joking around with Chris Tucker, but I was released on my own recognizance and given a court date. I ended up borrowing money from Epitaph Records to pay off my fines and working it off later. My dad may have been sobered by the experience, but my own moment of clarity had been postponed.

◆ ◆ ◆

My drug dealer, Carlton, was living in a house around the corner from the studio where we were recording *The Longest Line*. Recording had become a struggle. Previously I would knock out full albums in a couple days; now it was taking me a full day just to get through a single song. During a break one day I excused myself to go get some "lunch" and went to Carlton's.

The front door was open, but Carlton wasn't home. A girl named Justine was there instead. I knew Carlton kept his stash in a little lock box, so I hatched a plot with her to rip off Carlton. I picked the lock on the box and we split the four balloons of heroin he had inside. Carlton was shooting up a hundred balloons' worth of junk per day at the time. There was no way he would notice four missing balloons. Justine and I shot up and swore each other to secrecy, and I went back to the studio feeling somewhat refreshed.

The next day I returned to Carlton's and he greeted me with a punch in the face. Justine had ratted me out (I assume for the promise of more dope). Scrawny as I was, I still probably had 20 pounds on Carlton. His body had been so weakened from drugs that he literally lost a tooth while eating pancakes, and his arms were covered in gnarly bruises and pus-filled abscesses. I decked him. I had just ripped off the guy, and now I was beating him up. Justine pulled me off him and Carlton pulled out a knife, so I figured that was probably a good time to leave.

Carlton was more than just a dealer; he was a friend. We regularly partied together in Hollywood, and wherever he lived I was always welcome to crash. I had alienated my family, I was hiding from my band mates, my friends were all homeless or dead, and now even the junkie of all junkies didn't want me around.* I had been kicked out of my parents' house on Christmas morning a few years earlier after a fight with my dad, and they made it pretty clear that I shouldn't come around to their place when they refused to bail me out of jail. I drove to their house but knew I couldn't go inside. I tried sleeping in my car, but the loneliness of it was just too much to bear, so I went to my friend's mom's house. She had a garage with a spare room in the back, so I broke in and spent the night there.

The next morning I heard my friend's mom rustling around, so I hid in the shower to avoid getting caught. When she left, I stole 80 cents in change that was lying on the counter, because it was 80 cents more than I had in my pocket at the time. I added the guilt from the theft to the loneliness of the night and the endless depression and self-pity that had taken hold long ago, and drove back to my parents' house.

I was going to rip them off. It was the last line left to cross, and I was ready to cross it.

Your mind whispers to you when you're a junkie. Twenty-four hours a day, your addiction begs to be fed. You may know that going clean would be what's best, but the addiction won't let you listen to yourself. It's the craziest, gnarliest obsession and drive you could ever possibly feel. That's why people sell their bodies and their children to get high. It's torture and prison and slavery, and you cannot escape. That little dude in your head will just keep whispering forever, "Let's get high . . . let's get high . . . let's get high . . . " The more you ignore him, the louder he gets, until you can't ignore him anymore.

I listened to the voice enough to borrow money from my parents based on a lie, but I vowed never to steal from them. I watched my fellow junkies rip off their families and it seemed like the worst crime a person could commit. But it was inevitable that my ever-dwindling ethics would soon be tested.

I knew my mom and dad were both at work for the day. I opened the garage door and saw the turntable that my dad and I had used to spin all those classic albums. I saw the stereo speakers that had cradled me and nurtured my love of music.

I loaded them into the car.

My mind started to shut down. The struggle between my conscience and the voice was pulling me apart. I stood there for who knows how long as the

---

*Carlton, like so many of my friends from that era, is dead now. But it wasn't the junk that got him; it was testicular cancer. He beat the odds, and they beat him at the same time.

dope kept chanting, "Go pawn it. Go pawn it. Go pawn it." But my conscience knew I had arrived at a place I said I'd never go. I was so desperately
alone and trapped I could hardly take it. If I didn't listen to the voice it
would have its revenge with dope sickness and endless mental torture. If I
pawned my dad's stereo, there was no turning back. It was defeat. It was
oblivion . . .

    . . . it was a moment of clarity. I put the stereo back and drove away.

65

Hefe

In one of my first fanzine interviews I was again stumped by the question of
which punk bands I liked, so I said, "I really like that band Niratta."

"You mean Nirvana?"

"Yeah, that's it."

Nevermind came out soon after I joined NOFX, and we bumped it on
the tape deck in the van all across the country. We were in awe that a sound
like theirs could succeed in the mainstream.

"Do you realize what this means?" I said. "The door is open now! All we
have to do is make a record where the guitars and vocals are in tune and we
could get big!"

Mike laughed off my suggestion. "That will never happen. I'm just being
realistic, dude."

I insisted it could, so when we went in to record *The Longest Line* I did
my best to help us sound like professionals.

NOFX had never intonated their guitars before. Mike would complain,
"My bass is just always out of tune a lot. There's nothing you can do to fix
that." I wrenched his neck into place and hallelujah: it stayed in tune. I
showed him and Melvin how intonation works, and we got the guitar takes
we needed.

Mike's voice was an entirely different challenge. I sat in the booth while
he was in the studio singing the title track and pointed out when he was
sharp and when he was flat, putting all those years of vocal training to the
test. It was a ten-hour process that left both of us frustrated. In the end, I
worked with the producer to comp Mike's vocal take together, sometimes
one word—or even one syllable—at a time, and Mike was amazed that we
had created the illusion that he could sing.

When we recorded "Kill All the White Man" I busted out my old trumpet from my high school jazz band days. I had brought it on my first tour with NOFX and messed around with it on stage between songs or at house parties between drinks. Mike got a kick out of it and wanted to incorporate it into our sound. It paid off: "Kill All the White Man" became a minor radio hit.

. . . in Germany. But it still counts!

66

Smelly

Jay Walker was one of the few Dog Patch Winos with a bank account, so he let DJ use his account to deposit and cash welfare checks. One day while I was away on tour, Jay went to withdraw some cash and found his account empty. When he protested to the bank, they showed him surveillance footage from the camera over their ATM, and there was DJ, draining the account.

It was probably only 50 or 60 bucks, but it was a knife in the back of a fellow Wino, and that kind of betrayal was not tolerated.

Under the pretense of heading to an out-of-the-way party, Jay, Mark Curry, and some other Winos coaxed DJ into a car and drove him up the winding roads into the Hollywood hills. DJ figured something was up when the car didn't stop at any liquor stores on the way, but he was a small guy squeezed between two of the largest dudes in the DPW crew. He asked where they were going and they kept their friendly faces on the whole time, telling him not to worry, there would be a party coming up.

They pulled DJ out of the car in some desolate spot, methodically broke two of his fingers, beat the fuck out of him, and left him for dead. He had to hike a mile or so back down the hill and crawl up to someone's house to ask for help. He spent a week in the hospital. He was no longer a Dog Patch Wino.

DJ was shattered inside, and I don't mean the broken ribs. He was a sensitive kid, and he had finally found a city and a scene where he felt like he belonged. Now he was cast out and alone. He wandered out of L.A. and down his own lonely road of desperate junkiedom. He wasn't seen or heard from again for years.

DJ wasn't a bad person; he was just a junkie. Good people don't rip off their friends, junkies do. For a while I had been telling myself I wasn't a bad person, either. "This isn't me. I don't want to be a slave to this drug. This isn't who I was intended to be."

But it was becoming harder for me to ignore the truth. I wasn't a good person; I was a junkie. The struggle put my emotions through the wringer. I would be watching TV, and I'd see a commercial featuring a fictitious happy family holding hands and smiling at the promise of a new day, and I would break down into tears. My mind would spin together a monologue of self-pity:

"What has my life become? I can't get out of this prison. I want to be like those people, but instead I'm this fucking person. I'm a good person! But I can't get off these drugs!"

It would happen daily. It didn't have to be a sappy commercial, either. I'd break down watching the Olympics or sob uncontrollably while watching *Little House on the Prairie*.

"Look at these people living their lives. That's what I wanted. I don't want to live this way! But I don't know how to get out of it. This is how I'm going to die—alone and strung out."

My body was losing patience with me, too. After a night of drinking with the Winos, I came home and prepped my regular bedtime shot. Normally, I kept a "wake-up" handy (a little bit of heroin set aside so you can conquer the inevitable dope sickness you feel first thing in the morning), but in my drunken state I thought, "fuck it," and added my wake-up to my normal dose. I squeezed the plunger halfway down and blacked out.

I woke up eight hours later, lying on the floor, with the rig still in my arm. I had overdosed. My body had shut down. The syringe was half full of blood. I can't explain why I didn't die. By all rights, my story should end right here.

It wasn't until years later that I appreciated how close I came to the grave. At the time, I was just angry. My blood had coagulated in the syringe and made the half dose that was left all thick and gooey. I wasn't relieved that I had made it through the night alive. I was pissed that I wasted half a shot.

❖   ❖   ❖

We toured Europe in support of *The Longest Line*, and yet again I was dope sick as the sun came up after another sleepless night. We were at some shitty hotel in Frankfurt and I knew there was a train station nearby (in Europe, the sketchies always hang out by the train stations). I went down to our van and pulled out the briefcase with all our tour money in it. I took out forty bucks.

Even after all these years, I never told anyone in the band about that. To this day, I owe the band forty dollars. This is my confession. Mike, Melvin, Hefe: I promise to pay you guys back.

I walked the streets until I found two Turkish dudes who had also evidently been up all night. In broken English, we negotiated for some heroin. One guy took off. I didn't give him the money—I was at least smart about that. But then the police showed up.

I figured we were going to jail, but they just hassled us for twenty minutes and let us go. We met up with the missing Turk, and he handed me the baggie I'd been dying for. I asked the guys where I could score needles. They pointed in some nonspecific direction and split.

I followed their points down a road into a subway tunnel and walked into *Night of the Living Dead*. There were seven or eight homeless crackheads tweaked out of their minds, scattered and leaning against the walls of this small, dank tunnel. They seriously looked like fucking zombies, with unearthly pasty skin and white goo dribbling from their mouths. They were the gnarliest crackheads I had ever seen, but I was already in motion toward a fix. I tapped a guy with frizzy red hair and did my best to pronounce the German word for "syringe."

They all turned and came at me. They wanted to mug me, but they were so fucked up they could only stumble and meekly grab for my clothes. I pulled away and took off running. Two of them kept chasing me for a while until I lost them.

I got back to my hotel room and thought, "Fuck it, I'm just going to snort this stuff." After suffering through a night of dope sickness, nearly being arrested, and fighting off zombies, I was done fucking around.

But when I opened the baggie I wasn't greeted by that familiar sweet smell. I dipped my finger into the powder inside and inspected it closely for the first time.

They had sold me a baggie full of breadcrumbs.

✦　✦　✦

There were fonder memories from that tour, too. With bigger crowds came bigger paydays, and after a show one night, Dave Pollack came to us and announced we had just, for the first time in our lives, made $10,000 in a single night. We were in a bar and we bought drinks for the house. I got up on the bar, turned my pockets inside out, pulled my dick out, and did what I like to call "the Elephant Dance."* We did tequila shots and marveled at how we had somehow bullshitted our way into 10 grand.

Later that night we were walking to the van and I grabbed Hefe and said, "Come here, you fat little beaner!" and beat him up like always. We were rolling around in the street when the cops pulled up and shined their lights on us. It was the second time on the tour that I avoided German jail.† By the end of the tour I had physically kicked heroin, but as soon as I was home I copped. We made $10,000 apiece in profit for the tour, so I took my stack of mixed foreign currency to an exchange place downtown and chipped off 60 or 70 bucks at a time every day. I probably didn't want to exchange it all at once because I figured if I had a stack of cash I would use it for dope, but I ended up burning through half of it anyway, so all I did was fuck myself over with the change fees.

Ten thousand dollars was more money than I'd ever made or had ever planned to make. And half of it went right into my arm.

---

*DJ and I employed a lot of penis/testicle-related performance pieces, including "Batman" (in which I stretched out my scrotum skin between my fingers and flapped the edges like a bat), "The Trampoline" (in which I stretched out my scrotum skin and bounced my wiener off it), "Alien Space Eggs" (in which I rested my balls on a flashlight and shined the light through the translucent scrotum skin), and "The Flower" (which was always the showstopper: I "planted the seed" by grabbing the base of my dick and using the other hand to poke the top of the penis, inverting it. Then I "buried the seed" by pulling my nut sack over the inverted penis. Then I "watered the seed" by spitting on it. And then I let go of my nuts and told the audience to "watch the majestical flower grow" as the penis slowly and naturally de-inverted itself.). Try them at home!

†On the same tour, Jay drank a ton of Jäger after eating a ton of peanuts and puked up peanut butter, and I took a shit in the sink of a hotel lobby bathroom because Dave Pollack was occupying the stall. Good times.

From left: Kent, Limo, Jay, and Chris Shiflett.

67

Mike

In 1992, Fat Wreck Chords (which Erin and I were running out of the living room of our apartment) released *The Longest Line* and signed Lagwagon for their debut album. That same year, Erin and I got married and NOFX hired a spazzy Canadian named Kent as our sound guy. (He's still our sound guy to this day, but over time we've also added Manager/Booking Agent/Golf Partner/Grill Master to his title.)

1992 was also the year when I was shocked to discover that NOFX had made $10,000 in profit after our European tour. Each! Every tour up to that point had gotten steadily better, but it seemed like we had just skipped a step or two. Once the celebrating subsided, though, I realized this money came with a curse attached.

Back in 1988, Smelly moved into the basement of the house that Erin and I were sharing with six other people. He and his girlfriend at the time locked themselves down there for weeks at a time to just fuck and shoot up. Our roommates couldn't take it after a while, and I couldn't defend his behavior. When Erin and I were out one afternoon, they dumped all his stuff on the porch. His habit since then had only gotten worse.

Still, I couldn't really justify telling him to stop doing drugs. He never missed a rehearsal. He played perfectly on the records. He never fucked up a show (except for one time in Ireland). He always put the band first. Melvin and Steve would smoke pot and forget parts of the songs—that was a problem. Dave Casillas sold his gear for coke money—that was a problem. Everyone in the band did one drug or another (except for me, of course). Just because Smelly's drug of choice was less socially acceptable than everyone else's didn't mean I had a right to tell him how to live. He did his job, and he did it well.

Smelly's habit could subsist at a minor level on petty book theft, a meager income from the band, and a part-time gig at the *L.A. Weekly*, but if you hand a junkie 10 grand he's going to get seriously fucked up. Like *Basketball Diaries* fucked up. And there would be no turning back.

When we returned from Europe we were rehearsing in preparation of our next album, and I took Smelly aside and told him he needed to quit doing heroin. I told him we didn't want to kick him out, but if he didn't go to rehab we would get Bomber from RKL to play drums on the new album. He didn't resist. He knew he was in over his head, and he didn't like the vision he saw of his future. It was one thing to be humiliated by not having his photo on our first 7-inch; it was another to be replaced for a recording session now that we had come so far. The band was the one thing he took seriously. His eyes welled up at the idea of losing it. My eyes welled up at the idea of losing him.

He was crashing on a friend's floor at the time, so he went into the closet to get his bag, and he handed me a bunch of needles and a bit of heroin. "Okay. Let's do this. Take it." I was honored that he had put his trust in me and relieved to see he was truly dedicated to getting clean.

Two minutes later he said, "Wait," and pulled out the remaining needle and heroin he was holding back.

68

Smelly

Mike said, "It's either drugs or the band. It's your choice." I knew he wasn't bluffing. The band had pushed me to get clean in the past, but I could hear in Mike's voice that they were really ready to let me go this time.

No one wants to be a junkie or an alcoholic, but a lot of junkies and alcoholics don't respond well to interventions. They deflect or deny or try to dodge blame. But I immediately said, "Okay." I had no argument to possibly offer. I was fucking miserable. My friends were dying. My family had shut me out. Every time I thought I had hit bottom I kept sinking lower. The only thing I had left was NOFX. It was my last foothold in reality. It was the only thing that made me happy or gave me any sense of pride. Without it, I had no identity. No soul. I would be lost and anonymous. I would die homeless, cold, and alone.

I was crashing in a friend's closet in San Francisco when Mike confronted me and demanded I surrender all my drugs, needles, and outfits. I had two balloons in my pocket. I pulled them out and gave Mike one, but I palmed the other. When he wasn't looking, I popped it in my mouth and held it under my tongue.

We had a long talk. We both cried. It was one of the heaviest moments of my life. But the minute he walked out the door the junkie voice kicked back in: "He's not going to drive around with heroin and needles. He's going to throw it away somewhere nearby. Go find it . . . go find it . . . go find it . . ." I dove into every dumpster for blocks. I never found my stuff. But I got a syringe from somewhere and shot up half the balloon I had left. Mike insisted I stay at his place for the rest of the practice sessions so he could keep an eye on me. I carefully apportioned out the small bit of heroin left over and shot it up behind Mike's back over the next few days.

As soon as I arrived in L.A. to record *White Trash, Two Heebs and a Bean*, I went to a methadone clinic and started treatment. I called my mom and told her I was finally ready to get clean, and she was relieved and supportive. In between takes at the studio I rolled around L.A. with her and Hefe, shopping for rehabs. The first "doctor" I saw was an "addiction specialist" named Dr. Tom, who handed me a mountain of Valiums, Klonopins, and an illegal semi-synthetic opioid called Buprenex that you shoot up to mitigate opiate withdrawal symptoms (but which is highly addictive on its own). Here I was trying to run away from drugs and he was pushing them on me harder than any dealer.

We visited a bunch of other rehab places, but they all seemed so clinical and cold. I felt like I was shopping for my own insane asylum. Most of the nicer places had a huge wait list to get in, or they chose patients with insurance first. All I had was $5,000 left over from our successful European tour, which was never going to be enough to let me jump the line.

Dr. Tom's Valiums and Klonopins kept me afloat enough to finish recording *White Trash*. The band members raised their eyebrows when they saw me popping pills, but I convinced them it was special medication to help me kick. I was still getting high, but I had found a loophole: a doctor prescribed it, so it's totally cool if I inject Buprenex into my stomach a couple times a day. It's more than likely that if I had kept up that kind of behavior and relied on quacks like Dr. Tom to handle my sobriety I never would've made it. But on the last day of recording I got a call from a guy named Buddy Arnold. Of all the lucky breaks I'd had in my life, his phone call may have been the luckiest.

Brett Gurewitz wasn't producing our record, but we were recording in his studio so he'd come by to hang out, and I told him about my mission to go sober. Brett had already been down that road, so he made some phone calls on my behalf (without me even asking him to do so). It was because of his efforts that I got the call from Buddy, who introduced himself as the founder of a group called MAP, the Musicians' Assistance Program. Buddy was a jazz saxophonist from back in the day who had played with people like Buddy Rich and Tommy Dorsey, but after his own struggle with addiction and a couple stints in jail he left music and founded MAP to help other musicians with their substance abuse problems. He knew I was looking for placement at a rehab center and said, "I have a place for you, but you have to go right now. You have to get there by tomorrow morning."

I had literally just finished the last day of our recording session and I had nowhere else to go. I'd never met Buddy before in my life, but he pulled a bunch of strings on my behalf to get me a spot in a rehab facility. If he had called me a week earlier I would've blown him off because Mike hadn't given me my ultimatum yet and we would've been in the middle of recording. If he had called me a week later I may have already been kicked out of the band. I hate to sound like a fucking hippie, but it really seemed like the universe was trying to tell me something.

◆   ◆   ◆

The rehab facility was called the Ranch, and it was about two hours outside of L.A. in the middle of a town called Desert Hot Springs. After checking out all the rehabs in L.A., I expected to see lab coats and clipboards and easily moppable tile floors, but since Desert Hot Springs was known as a spa resort destination I thought I might also be walking into massage tables and Jacuzzis and make-your-own omelet stations. The Ranch was neither.

My friend Lynn Strait had been sober for a year at that point and wanted to help me through the process, so he picked me up and drove me out to the desert. We exited the freeway in the middle of nowhere and crawled up this long, gravel driveway to find three plain, prefab buildings. One contained a small office and a cafeteria, the other two were barracks: one for kicking, the other for treatment and meetings. There was nothing else around for miles. I had forty bucks in my pocket—if I had been in any city in America, I would've left and copped dope somewhere. But we were deep into the desert, at least a 10-mile walk in the California August heat from anything close to resembling civilization. I wasn't going anywhere.

As we drove up that long driveway, I made a promise to myself. I was going to finish this, no matter what it took. My whole life I'd never followed through on anything. I was a procrastinator. I was a goof-off. But this time I was sticking to the plan. It was a two-month program, and I was going to do whatever I was told. Even if I ended up getting high again the second I left, I would at least know I did what I was supposed to do. I would at least know I kept my word to myself.

They searched me for contraband, checked my vitals, and put me in a small room with two twin beds and a roommate named Mike. I was scared at first. All these dudes were walking around who were clearly straight out of prison. With my long dreadlocks and gaunt frame I felt as out of place as I looked.

The first week was detox. No meds, just white-knuckling. People were having seizures, people were throwing up on themselves . . . the Buprenex and the methadone had helped me work most of the junk out of my system, but I still spent a few nights of that first week being unable to sleep and puking.

Once you've detoxed, you're on a schedule. At 5:30 a.m. someone pounds on your door for a wake-up call. At 6 a.m. there's a morning meeting and meditation: "Today we're gonna work on this or that, Be grateful you're here, it could be worse," some prayers, etc. You watch the sun come up over the desert and then take a half-mile walk to get the blood flowing, followed by breakfast. After that, an hour and a half of intense physical labor. Pulling weeds, moving piles of rocks, raking the gravel driveway. Why did we have to move rocks? Don't ask why. Sometimes you have a job and you just do it.

The hard labor was surprisingly my favorite part of the day. Even though it was early in the morning and 100 degrees outside and ultimately pointless, it was a good time for reflection. My mind would just travel. It helped me feel clear.

For a week you'd be the rock-moving guy. For a week you'd be on kitchen crew. For a week you'd be the toilet cleaner. Whatever it was, you just did it and didn't ask questions. You weren't better than this. You've been on your own, and what have you been doing? Shooting dope. So maybe it's time to listen to what somebody else has to say and fucking humble yourself. It wasn't Betty Ford bullshit. It wasn't Hollywood celebutantes on probation. It was raw to the core.

At 10 a.m. there was therapy. People talked about their parents and their issues and the roots of their addiction. When the therapist turned to me and asked how I was, I'd say, "Fine." He'd ask what was going on with me that day, I'd say, "Nothing. Everything's fine." I wasn't trying to be defiant; I just didn't have enough perspective to recognize my own issues.

"Okay, so you're telling me you've been shooting dope for eight years, running around homeless, and everything's fine?"

The therapist took me aside one day and said, "Look, dude. You're so fucked up that you don't even know it. You've balled up your emotions and stuffed everything so far down, you can't face them. You're not going to make it."

I was surrounded by paroled criminals and people with drug issues that stretched farther back than my own, but it turned out that, emotionally speaking, I was just as fucked up as any of them. It would be years before I could really work through the issues I had with my own self worth and my need for acceptance and my relationship with my father, but I did my best to at least get the ball rolling in those 10 a.m. group therapy sessions. I had made a promise to myself to try, after all.

After therapy, there were classes; different topics each day about what drugs do to your body and brain. Then lunch. Then more readings and more classes and more therapies and dinner at 5 p.m. and free time from 8:30 to 10 and then lights out. It was regimented, the same exact schedule, day in, day out.

Every now and then they broke up the monotony (and rewarded our good behavior) with a softball game at a park, or a trip to see a movie. Once they took us to a theater to see *Encino Man* with Pauly Shore—easily the worst-reviewed movie of 1992. On any other day I would have preferred a bullet to the brain, but after weeks of being broken down both physically and emotionally it was the most fucking awesome and hilarious movie ever.

Within the first week after detox I could feel myself changing. I wanted so much to shed my past that I made a decision to cut off the dreads that had literally been dragged through the shit with me. We were in one of our afternoon meetings, and I made my mind up. The meeting couldn't end fast enough. I kept repeating, "Gonna cut these fuckers off, gonna cut these fuckers off . . ." in my head. The second the meeting ended I grabbed a pair of scissors, went to my room, and started chopping. I didn't want to give myself a second to reconsider. It needed to get done. With every handful I hacked off, I felt my head getting lighter. I was shaking, but I was cleansing myself of all the shit that had been weighing me down. I was a lizard shedding its skin and starting life over.

When I was done I looked like a cancer victim. It was uneven and clumpy, but I evened it out with some clippers and the transformation was complete.* I left behind the image of the punk rock party guy, and I felt free. I actually felt fucking free.

When I checked into the Ranch they weighed me in at 127 pounds. When I left I was 165. It's still skinny for someone who's 6-foot-1, but it's a far more healthy weight. My skin had also gone from a greenish gray to a mixture of tanned and burned from all the yard work. Combined with the buzz cut, I left rehab a completely different human being.

On the last night before someone is discharged, everyone sits in a circle and takes turns saying goodbye and good luck. I still keep in touch with some of the people I met. Mike, my roommate, was easily my closest friend inside. Not only did we share tight quarters but also similar attitudes and senses of humor. At the end of a brutal day we would lie in bed and laugh out loud to release the tension. We'd fart and laugh and fart some more and laugh even harder. We leaned on each other more than anyone else in those barracks and have remained close to this day. I would miss farting next to Mike. It was a tearful goodbye.

As a contrast I always butted heads with a guy named Ron who whined constantly and questioned the whole process. He would agitate me on purpose until I threatened to beat his ass, then he'd run to one of the counselors and tattle on me for threatening him, and I'd get called into the principal's office. After everyone in the discharge circle said his piece, I said my own goodbye to each person, and I called Ron out. I told him he needed to keep his fucking mouth shut and listen for once in his life. I didn't have all the answers, but neither did he, and the worst thing you can be in a place like that is a fucking know-it-all. I don't know if my words had any impact, but

---

*I kept the dreads in a grocery bag. I still have them somewhere. They're a symbol and a reminder. And they probably smell awful.

later when I was packing up I snuck into the common room and peed in the Gatorade bottle he was storing in the fridge. I was a new man, but I was still a Moron Brother.

The final goodbye of the night was from a stereotypically sassy and effeminate gay guy we had nicknamed Silly Billy. I have to imagine he strategically placed himself in the circle for comedic effect because after two dozen heartfelt farewells Billy opened his speech with, "Hold on to your tits, honey, I have something to say to you!" All the seriousness was sucked out of the room. "I've been watching you walk around this place . . . mmm mmm MMM mmm!" He snapped his fingers in the air for punctuation. "If you EVER decide to come to me, I will . . . " He gave me a look that communicated all manner of steamy sexual congress. My face turned beet red, and we all cracked the fuck up. It was even funnier than *Encino Man*.

✦   ✦   ✦

As scared as I was when I entered rehab, I was twice as scared when it came time to leave. What was waiting for me on the other side? I could follow through on two months of work, but what about following through on every single day for the rest of my life? How do you change twenty-seven years of behavior in sixty days and remain on the right track? The counselors had done their best to prepare me for the transition back to the real world, but I didn't want to leave. But I couldn't stay.

In nearby Palm Springs, there's a cable car that runs to the top of a mountain. Tourists ride up the sheer mountain face to a lush national forest at the top. The front porch of our barracks faced the mountain, and every night, for two straight months, I stared at the little light on that cable car as it went all the way up and all the way down and all the way up and back again off in the distance. When my friend Dera picked me up in the morning to take me home, the first thing I needed to do was ride that fucking cable car.

She happily drove me to the base of the mountain. We bought our tickets, and up we went. The cable car lifted us from the 100-degree desert Hell to a cool pine forest with a majestic view of the world below. We spent a couple hours up there, soaking in the beauty of it all.

I had kept my fucking promise.

69

Hefe

Before the intervention, Mike tasked me with keeping an eye on Smelly's habit, since I was tied in with the Dog Patch Wino crew. Smelly thought he was hiding it so well, but when he'd be locked in a closet saying, "Hefe, don't come in here," I had a pretty good guess as to why.

I never said anything about Smelly's drug use because it never interfered with the band. And I felt like I would be betraying him by giving him an ultimatum. Smelly was the guy who got me into the band, and now less than a year and a half later I'm going to threaten to kick him out? Besides, at times it was entertaining. I remember walking around San Francisco with him and we passed this mega-fancy restaurant filled with people in suits and little black dresses. Smelly said, "Watch this," leaned up against the huge front window, and sprayed vomit all over it while looking one of the diners dead in the eye.

Thankfully Mike took care of the intervention, and after *White Trash, Two Heebs and a Bean* was in the can,* Smelly found a spot in some rehab place out in the desert and disappeared down the road to recovery.

Two months later, my friend Doug came by my apartment. Some big guy with a buzz cut came in with him and said, "Hey, how's it going?"

I said, "Oh, hi," and turned away. I felt like I had met this person before, but couldn't quite place where.

"Hey stupid! What, you don't say hi to your friend?"

---

*Some album trivia: Mike incorporated my trumpet skills into several songs on *White Trash*, but for the complicated run at the end of "Straight Edge," I just made trumpet sounds with my mouth. I loaned my vocal talents to the song "Johnny Appleseed," which is about Smelly's pursuit of female company on the road. One night before recording I was staying at Mike's apartment in the Mission District of San Francisco and there was some drunk Mexican dude outside yelling at no one. We could hear him through Mike's window: "Fuck with Marvin? Fuck with Marvin?! He's down for the cause! Down for the cause, Holmes!" Like teenagers at a sleepover, I started imitating the guy and cracking Mike up as we lay there in the dark. That's where my improvised cholo-speak between the verses of "Johnny Appleseed" comes from: "Hey man why you always talking shit about Johnny anyway? He's down for the cause, Holmes!"

I stared right at him. Still couldn't make the connection. And then . . .
"Oh shit, no way!"

I had never known what a healthy Smelly looked like. It was like someone had taken a mangy, starving street dog and groomed him for the kennel
club. Or like that scene in *Indiana Jones and the Last Crusade* when the guy
drinks from the wrong grail, but in reverse.

His personality had changed, too. He was focused on keeping his shit
together, but he was also easily stressed out. On tour he would point someone out to me and say, "That guy is about to cop dope. He's waiting for his
dealer. There's his dealer right now." Sure enough, I'd look over and there
was the handoff. I considered myself street smart, but I wasn't nearly as
hyper aware as Smelly.

"Somebody just copped dope in front of my face. I gotta get the fuck out
of here." And I'd go with him to find somewhere else to be. He still had a
long journey ahead of him.

70

Smelly

In the winter of 1989, long before I pushed my parents to their limits, I
talked them into buying me a plane ticket to Costa Rica. I had remained
friends with my ex-girlfriend, Gail (the one I followed to Santa Barbara),
and she told me she was going to Costa Rica with her brothers. I was living
in the closet at Hepatitis Junction at the time, so she took pity on me and
invited me to join them.

Flights to Costa Rica back then weren't as regular as they are now, so I
landed at the San Jose airport four days before Gail and her brothers with a
surfboard, a bunch of acid, and twenty bucks in my pocket. It was the middle of the night, and I didn't speak a word of Spanish, so I just hopped on
the bus labeled "El Centro" and hoped it would take me to the center of
something.

Costa Rica is gorgeous, but San Jose, the capital, is a total shithole. I
stepped off the bus and wandered the streets, hoping to see something that
said "El Hotel." I was jonesing hard after the long flight, so I enabled my
junkie radar to scope out track marks on the arms of passersby. I acquired
no targets. It was going to be a long four days.

As I was walking, a fourteen-year-old black kid with a Jamaican accent spotted me and asked me what I needed. I asked about a hotel, and he was excited to help me. "Oh mon, come on! I show you! Let me carry your bags!" I assumed he might rip me off, so I carried my own stuff, but he took me to a hotel that only charged four bucks a night, and as soon as I checked in some guy gave me some weed for free. Stoked! The kid's name was Chongo (yes, seriously), and he said he'd be back at 10 a.m. to hang out.

He showed me around the city for the next couple days, and I took him with me to greet Gail and her brothers at the airport when they arrived. They thought it was hilarious that I had only been there a few days and had already befriended a local jungle boy. "Friend" might be a strong word, though: I later discovered he had stolen my camera.

The other thing Gail and her brothers noticed right away was that I looked like a fucking corpse. I had spent four days going through heroin withdrawal and drinking heavily every night. Gail's brothers were just like her: studious, college-and-career-minded people who were as far removed as you could get from the world of Raymond, Quake, and the Moron Brothers. We had a blast traveling around, surfing, riding in buses with chickens, and checking out the jungle, but they couldn't believe how hard I was drinking. Gail poked fun at me for being so drunk all the time, especially the night that I only stopped drinking because I lost the coordination required to get the bottle to my lips. I spent every night in a bar, and I spent more than a few days the same way. Gail and her brothers would go check out some volcano; I would opt to sit and drink.

Despite missing out on some sites, I fell in love with Costa Rica. Everything felt raw and real. The empty beaches, the wild jungles, the barely noticeable villages . . . I learned the difference between loneliness and solitude.

One late night in Tamarindo, I took some of the acid I brought with me and paddled my surfboard across a river to a secluded beach. I walked along the beach for a couple miles, aided only by the moonlight. I was enjoying the solitude. And I was frying my balls off.

I came across a stretch of sand where a group of leatherback sea turtles were spread out and laying their eggs. It was the most beautiful thing my acid-riddled brain had ever seen. I became a turtle Lamaze coach. I fixated on one of the mothers and sat with her for like four hours, showering her with support. "It's okay, buddy . . . just let 'em go!" She was grunting, and mucus was trickling from her eyes. "Just let 'em go and you'll be free, and your babies will have the whole world in front of them!"

Hours later, mom finished burying her eggs and exhaustedly dragged herself back into the ocean. I was nearly crying with joy. Then a figure appeared on the beach: a poacher with a stick and a very serious hunting knife. He was poking the sand, looking for soft spots, and scooping up eggs wherever he found them. I went from overjoyed to totally bummed. I was watching life and death, beauty and ugliness, all at once. I felt like I was experiencing something significant, seeing some grandiose metaphor that summed up my life.

I walked back down the beach and paddled my surfboard back across the river to our hotel. I was excited to tell everyone about my bonding experience with the turtles, but what fascinated the locals the most was the fact that I had paddled my surfboard across the Tamarindo River in the first place.

The river, apparently, is swarming with enormous alligators. So much so that they currently run tours of the river specifically to show off just how many alligators call it home. No one could believe that some gringo idiot paddled safely across a river of certain death and disfigurement and then, after seeing what lay on the other side, paddled all the way back without being torn to shreds.

If I was searching for a metaphor to perfectly sum up my life, that was fucking it.

◆   ◆   ◆

After my post-rehab cable car ride, Dera dropped me off at Brett Gurewitz's studio in L.A., where my mom was waiting to pick me up. I walked into the lobby and said, "Hi."

My mom looked up from her magazine, said "Hello," and went back to reading.

She didn't know I had put on weight and cut my hair. Five seconds later she looked up again, completely shocked that she didn't recognize her own son. She said, "Oh my god!" as she jumped up to hug me.

I bought a used pickup truck with the $2,500 I had left in my bank account after paying for rehab, moved in with my parents, and started going to Alcoholics Anonymous and Narcotics Anonymous meetings. I didn't like them at first. I was expecting an atmosphere of support and camaraderie, but AA meetings in Hollywood were filled with people trying to pull chicks and hand off their screenplays. There were soap opera actors bitching about how their agent didn't get them a Pepsi commercial while I was struggling to stay off heroin. You're supposed to mentor other recovering addicts and be available, but everybody seemed to be in it for themselves. Thankfully a friend brought me to a meeting in Long Beach a year later where there were punkers and bikers and people I could relate to. Some of the people I met at that first meeting are dear friends of mine to this day. I moved to Long Beach a week later and stayed for good.

The first time I saw Fat Mike after rehab he really pissed me off. We had two shows lined up at the Whisky, with Green Day as our opening act. I showed up to band practice early because I hadn't played drums in over two months. When Mike arrived, he walked in with a six-pack of beer and held one up to me in celebration.

"Yeah dude! What's up?"

I offered back a sarcastic, "Wow, bro. Thank you. I appreciate that." I knew I couldn't control other people and I was going to be around booze and drugs from time to time and I would have to learn to deal with it. But I still thought to myself, "That is so fucking rude." One of my best friends, who knew what I was going through, showed up with booze and had zero respect or consideration for my situation.

My nerves were raw at the time. I felt like an infant trying to make sense of the big, scary world.* I was nervous about people expecting me to party. I was nervous about remembering how to play our songs. I hadn't drummed clean in years. I needed a supportive, calm, sober environment, but I knew I wasn't going to find that on the road with NOFX. Yet the only reason I had cleaned up in the first place was so I wouldn't lose NOFX. Rehab was a victory, but the war wasn't over.

◆   ◆   ◆

When I was in San Francisco before my intervention, I got a call from a photographer who was freelancing for *Rolling Stone*.

"Are you still doing drugs?"

"No. I don't know what the hell you're talking about."

---

*Or like Brendan Fraser's caveman character in the 1992 classic *Encino Man*.

"If there's some money in it for you . . . are you still doing drugs?"

"Now we're talking."

Rolling Stone was doing a piece on heroin in the music industry, and the photographer had been hired to get a picture of a junkie shooting up, so a mutual friend put him in touch. He flew to San Francisco, gave me $350 out of his pocket to buy drugs and rented a hotel room for the night to shoot me shooting. I ended up with a good supply of dope from him. In fact, the balloon I surrendered to Mike was probably purchased for that *Rolling Stone* photo shoot.

During the photo session, I explained clearly and repeatedly: don't show my face. I don't know who was responsible, but guess whose fucking face was shown plain as day with a needle in his arm in the September 17, 1992 issue of *Rolling Stone*? And guess whose mom happened to purchase that very same issue during a routine trip to the grocery store?

I had asked one of the staff at the Ranch to pick me up a copy of the magazine when it came out, and when I saw myself in that photo it dropped me into a dark void. There I was, trying to change my life and move into the future, and I was still staring down my past. Dreadlocks and all.

I was angry. I made impotent threats to sue. But I talked myself down. I made my choices; I had to be responsible for my own actions. I can't blame everyone around me. I sucked it up.

But when my sister called and told me my mom had seen the photo, it stung. Responsibility for my actions meant accepting the guilt of hurting those who loved me, even when I was already struggling under the massive effort of getting my shit together.

When I arrived at the Whisky for my first sober show, Billie Joe from Green Day seemed a bit jumpy. We caught up for a while, and he breathed a sigh of relief when he found out I had gone sober. He confessed he was scared to play the show with us. Confused, I asked him why.

It turned out that when I stole that van and drunkenly smashed my way through the streets of Berkeley, Billie was my back-seat hostage.

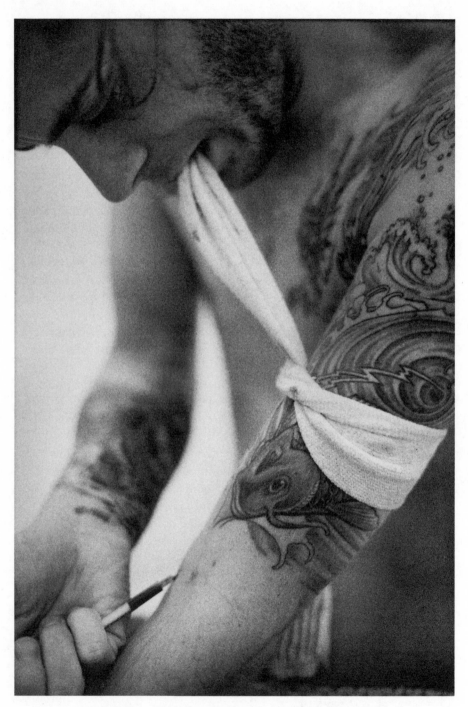

Originally published in Rolling Stone, *September 1992.*

71

Mike

Los Angeles has played host to nearly all of punk rock's most famous riots, and I'm proud to say I was at no less than five of the classics.

January 1983: TSOL and Social Distortion at S.I.R. Studios in Hollywood

The cops were outside, trying to shut down the show. Jack Grisham from TSOL said, "Everyone sit down! They can't make us all leave if we're all sitting!" So we all sat. It was a powerful moment of passive resistance, and Jack was right: the cops had no idea what to do. Then TSOL launched into "Abolish Government" and everyone jumped back up. The crowd started slamming and the billy clubs started flying.

I was at the show with Floyd, the guitarist from False Alarm. His mom often drove us to shows and waited around to drive us home afterwards. Being short, scrawny sixteen-year-olds we were somehow able to evade the police, who were focusing on bigger game. We squeezed out a back door, jumped into Floyd's mom's van, and sped off.

February 1983: The Exploited, Youth Brigade, and Suicidal Tendencies at Mendiola's Ballroom in Huntington Park

Youth Brigade was playing when the cops came in and started swinging. My friends and I ran out the back door and there were a dozen or so cops waiting there, whacking kids with billy clubs as they funneled past. I was in the middle of everyone so, again, I dodged the clubs. And when we ran outside I was ahead of everyone, so when the cops sprayed Mace I was out of range, while my friends were temporarily blinded.

Thankfully we weren't far from Floyd's mom's van.

June 1983: Dead Kennedys at the Longshoremen's Hall in Wilmington

The Longshoremen's Hall wasn't built for live music, so the sound was awful, and I'm pretty sure they oversold the venue because it was uncomfortably packed. My friends and I went outside because we needed a break while Dead Kennedys were still on stage. When we went out, the cops went in.

We watched the battle erupt from the safety of Floyd's mom's van.

December 1990: Bad Religion, NOFX, and Pennywise at the El Portal Theater in North Hollywood

A band called Pennywise had recently signed to Epitaph Records, so Brett put them on a show opening for us and Bad Religion. The venue was oversold, the fire marshal declared the show unsafe, and the cops came in.

We walked on stage and, just after I said, "Hi, we're NOFX!" they cut the power. The cops chased everyone out as the crowd tore up the seats and smashed every pane of glass in sight.

No idea what Floyd's mom was up to that night.

May 1993: NOFX, the Vandals, and Pennywise at the Patriotic Hall in Downtown Los Angeles

We were backstage during another oversold show when the head of security came in with a bloodstain the size of a dinner plate on the side of his shirt. He had been stabbed. If the head of security couldn't keep himself secure, there didn't seem to be much hope for the rest of us.

Pennywise didn't care. They went on and got the best crowd response of the night. We didn't want to seem like pussies, so we played, too. We finished our set this time, but it was mayhem outside the venue after the show ended.

We hid backstage until the crowd dispersed. When we went outside one of the only cars left in the parking lot had been set on fire and was now simply a smoldering mess of melted plastic and blackened steel.

Warren from the Vandals stared at it and said, "That's my car."

Again, I can't help but feel like there's an inner-core-dwelling race of mole people magnetically pulling the knives, billy clubs, and Mace out of my path and pushing me toward an odds-defyingly happy life. I didn't avoid the beat-downs and stabbings and arson because I was smarter or worked harder or lived more virtuously than anyone else. I didn't form a band that people liked because I was a musical prodigy with all the right influences and a devotion to proper technique. And I have no idea how everyone in my band avoided jail and death long enough for us to find each other and stay together. How else can I explain it other than benevolent mole men?

◆ ◆ ◆

The riot in '93 seemed to signify a tuning point for NOFX. Smelly was sober. Fat Wreck Chords was doing well enough that Erin and I hired a third employee. NOFX's new album, *White Trash, Two Heebs and a Bean*, was a departure from our Bad Religion copycat sound and is now considered one of our best records. Somehow, we had made it past the cops, the gangsters, the drug addicts, and the general death and destruction that were always waiting in the wings.

When we went to Europe that summer, we found ourselves, for the first time, booked on major festivals in front of thousands of people alongside big-name rock acts. Our very first was the Bizarre Festival in Germany with Sonic Youth, Porno for Pyros, Helmet, and New Order. Hole was also on the bill, but they were playing before us. Courtney Love and Smelly had dated a bit, and she was pissed that his band was billed higher than hers, so when we started playing the first song of our set (the newly released "Sticking in My Eye"), she jumped on stage and started whacking Smelly on the head with a drum stick, derailing our performance in front of fifteen thousand people.

The mole people are kind, but they also have a sense of humor.

72

Melvin

I don't remember the stabbed security guard or the cars on fire or the broken glass at the Patriotic Hall riot because I was backstage, partying with the guys from Pennywise and the Vandals. Someone came in to tell us about the riot, and Warren from the Vandals clicked into the character of a hyped-up football coach, offering us an intense halftime strategy speech.

For some reason, there was a chalkboard in one of the dressing rooms. Warren grabbed a piece of chalk and frantically scribbled a bunch of arbitrary lines and shapes on the board.

"Alright guys! Here's what we're gonna do!"

We all laughed as he called out instructions for our "team." He told us how we were supposed to run and tackle and block and guard, and then he dramatically wrapped it up by dropping his pants and flopping his dick onto a table.

"And after we're done with all that, we're gonna give it to 'em like THIS!"

With all his might, he slammed his fist onto his cock.

Everyone watching winced in pain, and before we could emotionally recover, Warren had punched his dick at least two or three more times. Then he shouted "LET'S GO!" and ran out of the room.

Any other memory I may have had from that night has since taken a back seat to that one.

73

Smelly

I was sitting in Timmy the Turtle's van with some other people when the Patriotic Hall riot broke out. People were fighting left and right, and the cops came in to do battle. Our friend Paul ran up to the van with blood streaking down the side of his face, saying he had been jumped and needed a place to hide. We were stuck in the van watching the pandemonium all around us.

I had driven my pickup truck, which I had bought with my last remaining dollars, to the show. A cop took cover behind it to shield himself from kids throwing rocks. I watched helplessly as rocks and bricks bounced off my car 50 yards away.

That truck wasn't much, but it was all I had, so I held my keys in my outstretched hand and walked slowly up to the cop.

"Dude, that's my car. I gotta move that car."

"GET DOWN!"

He pulled his gun on me. I couldn't blame him for not wanting to give up his one piece of protection when he was outnumbered thirty to one by brick-wielding punks, so I slowly backed away. But then I saw two kids pushing a dumpster across the parking lot, intent on ramming my truck. I wasn't backing down for them.

I ran toward the kids and BOOM, connected my fist with one of their jaws. The kid went down, and the dumpster went off course. As the kid tried to get up, I kicked him in the face. His teeth exploded out of his head. He looked up at me, bloody and completely confused.

He whimpered, "Why?" as he tried to compute what had just happened.

"That's my fucking car!"

His friends came up to rescue him, but my adrenaline was off the charts. "WHO ELSE FUCKING WANTS SOME?!"

They turned and ran as if I were Godzilla. Warren from the Vandals had parked his brand-new car right near mine, but I couldn't stick around to protect it from the crowd. I ran back to Timmy's van to wait out the riot and drove my truck out of there as soon as I had a chance.

◆ ◆ ◆

The first year or so out of rehab I got in a lot of fights. To say I was on edge would be a vast understatement. I was experiencing every emotion, all at once, all the time, and it was, for the first time, completely undiluted. I was learning how to be human, and being human fucking sucks.

I would boil over at the drop of a hat. One night I was at Raji's nightclub, and some guy was picking on some other guy, so I picked a fight with the bully. One night at a Lagwagon show, two jock dudes were bumping into people, and I sucker punched one and wrestled the other to the ground. A half hour later I found them and apologized.

The scariest moment was at a NOFX/Lagwagon show in Bakersfield. This muscle-bound dude started shit with me backstage. He wouldn't let me get by him, and he was talking shit and yelling at me. It was a domination thing, Raymond and Quake style, and judging by the prison tattoos, he probably came from the same world. I would've let it go entirely, but a few songs into our set I got blasted from behind as the guy ran through my drum set, demolished it, and did a stage dive.

I saw red. The musclehead was floating on top of the crowd, so I did my own stage dive and landed on top of him. I pulled him to the ground and beat his fucking ass. I was on my feet, he was on the ground getting punched and kicked. Hefe and some of the crew jumped into the crowd with me, and security dragged the guy out.

When the hall cleared at the end of the night, I saw the dude walk back in with his shirt off, looking for me. The way I see it, if someone is going to hit me, I should probably hit him first. It's just good strategy. I didn't run or shy away, even though the guy had obviously been putting in a lot of time on a prison weight bench. He could've had a knife or a gun or a group of homeboys ready to swarm me, but I had a big, heavy pair of channel locks that I used to tighten my drum hardware. I put them in my back pocket and walked across the venue floor to meet my new friend.

He said, "What's up, fucker?!" The channel locks connected to the base of his temple above his ear and proceeded down his cheek and across his jaw.

It wasn't a "crack!" or a "pow!" it was a "thud"—like hitting a fucking water-melon. His brain shut off as he spun and collapsed to the floor.

I leaned over and whispered in his ear: "You wanna fuck with me, dude?"

The people remaining in the hall didn't know any of the backstory, they just saw me assault this guy with a hunk of metal and watched him drop.

"That's fucked up! What'd you hit him for?"

"Fuck you! I'll fucking hit you, too! You don't know who this is!"

I had blood all over my hands. The musclehead was unconscious and his face was completely caved in. His friend dragged him outside. I told the crew, "I gotta get out of here." I left my drums behind and hauled ass to our hotel. They covered for me because they knew I was either going to jail or getting jumped by whoever else this guy had with him.

I could've killed him. A half inch in one direction or another, or a slightly different angle on the swing and it would've been over for both of us. I would've had a tough time convincing a judge it was self-defense when all those witnesses had watched me walk up and clock the guy with no provocation.

I needed to learn control.

About ten years later, a guy came up to me after a show in San Luis Obispo.

"Hey, what's up, man? Remember Bakersfield? That was me."

My heart sank. Oh fuck.

He smiled. "I just wanted to say, bro . . . respect. You fucked me up, dude. You busted everything in my fucking face. I've been in and out of the pen since then, but I just wanted to tell you, respect. And man, it's cool."

Another fucking alligator in the river.

◆ ◆ ◆

The only time NOFX ever toured as an opening band was a two-week run with Fishbone, and we were stoked when they turned out to be super cool guys. One night in Florida I finagled a female fan into the back lounge of our tour bus, and she graciously treated me to a blowjob. Upon completion, she walked out of the bus, and Angelo from Fishbone was outside. He had been scamming on the same girl earlier in the night, so he grabbed her and they started making out right away. I yelled, "Dude, dude, dude! Stop, stop, stop!" He asked what was up and I quietly explained that she had just fin-ished blowing me moments before. He was puzzled for a second, but then shrugged and said, "Well, at least I know ya!" and returned to his makeout session.

Almost all of my memories from the tour are fond ones. Like when we were working out the parts to a new song called "Don't Call Me White" at sound check, and the Fishbone guys started making fun of us and singing their own version called "Don't Call Me Dwight." But one bittersweet moment sticks with me the most.

Everyone was drunk and partying in the lounge of the tour bus, except for me. I developed a routine of going to bed early and generally avoiding the after-show parties so I wouldn't be tempted to drink. I was lying in my bunk and could hear everyone else having a good time, and they started having a discussion about me. They said how proud they were of me for staying sober and, in very heartfelt terms, how happy they were for me. I was flattered and deeply touched, but almost instantly I became depressed. I wanted to be out there with my buddies, having fun and talking until the late hours. But I couldn't put myself in a situation that might risk the very thing they were praising me for. I was listening to them bond as friends, and I felt like my bond with them was fading.

In the early days of NOFX, when Mike and I both lived in San Francisco, we drove to L.A. together in his car for band practices. We blasted music for the first half of the trip, and then we would stop for gas and pick up a twelve-pack of beer. For the second half of the trip we talked and drank (and showed up to practice wasted). Whatever our personality differences were, each car trip made us closer. Now it felt like those types of moments were buried in the past.

As I listened to my friends say how much they loved me, I was alone and separated from them in a way that may never be bridged. It threw me back to my childhood, when I was desperate to belong, when I craved acceptance. I had finally found my place in this world as a member of NOFX, and I had finally been accepted by a small group of true friends, but now I didn't belong with them, either. It's a struggle that continues, on some levels, to this day. In order to remain a part of my best friends' lives, I have to isolate myself from the type of moments that forged our bonds in the first place and that they continue to share without me.

Loneliness is part of the price of my sobriety. But it at least felt good to know I was loved, and I'm lucky to have such supportive people around me. I never told them that I overheard their conversation. But thanks, guys.

74

Mike

The worst night's sleep I ever got was in an abandoned building in Osaka, Japan.

A San Francisco band called All You Can Eat helped us book our first Japanese tour in January 1994. We didn't apply for work visas or anything, we just flew in with our instruments, sleeping bags, and eight overstuffed duffel bags full of T-shirts. In Japan, bands don't tour in vans or buses; they tour in trains. So we would take a bullet train from one town to the next, then board a local subway, and then walk with all our luggage and gear (sometimes a mile or more) to the gig. All You Can Eat had been to Japan before, so we followed their lead blindly. We never thought of asking, "Hey, can we just take a cab from the train station?"

After finally getting a small taste of the comfort provided by hotels and tour buses in the United States and Europe, we were back to sleeping on floors. The one night we actually paid for a hostel it was just an 8-by-8-foot room with thin sleeping mats and no bathroom or sink. In Osaka, someone involved with the show offered us a place to stay in a big apartment building. He took us up to the tenth floor and opened the door to a vast, freezing, empty room with hardwood floors and spray paint all over the walls.

"What is this place?"

"It's a Yakuza safe house."

"What does that say on the wall?"

"It says 'Get the fuck out, you don't belong here.'"

Then he added, "If anyone comes in the middle of the night, run." And walked out.

I can't imagine anyone else in the band or crew slept any better than I did. A bunch of fans followed us to the building and stayed with us, but none of them had sleeping bags or anything. They just curled up in upright fetal positions, trying to keep in as much body heat as possible to defy the frigid temperature. Aside from my sleeping bag, I also had a blanket. I suppose I could've offered it to one of the fans . . . but I was really cold.

Despite the hardships, Japan was good to us. We had three hundred people at each show and came home having made a profit. And sleeping on hardwood floors and taking subways to shows was a valuable lesson in humility.

It was a timely lesson, too, because two weeks after we returned home, Green Day released their major-label debut, *Dookie*, and once again, everything changed.

75

Hefe

I'm a picky eater. I always lost weight on our European tours because I wouldn't eat their weird vegan stews or horse-cock sandwiches. Until our later tours when I realized there was a McDonald's on every corner, I would be on an involuntary juice fast for weeks at a time, supplemented by bread and cheese if I was lucky. So if you've ever eaten fermented soybeans before, you know I had to be pretty wasted to try that shit on our first Japan tour.

I got shitfaced every night in Japan because it was considered an insult not to drink with the promoters after the shows. There was a local band called the Garlic Boys who convinced me not only to eat the waxy-sticky-dead-rat-carcass-tasting-vomit-smelling fermented soybeans, but also to stand up and shout Japanese phrases to other noodle bar patrons, which I later learned were things like "eat my shit you pussies." Roughly translated.

Other than a horrible night's sleep at an abandoned Yakuza safe house, my most vivid memory of our first Japan tour was being startled by a scream coming from a bathroom and Jay Walker stumbling out of it with his pants around his ankles. He had been unpleasantly surprised by the bidet feature of the fancy Japanese toilet. The rest of us spent the evening experimenting with the sensation of a water jet on our butt cracks.

76

Smelly

After a twelve-hour flight and an hour and a half on a train, I just wanted to go lay down and relax, but our hosts in Japan insisted on taking us out on the town. For eight more hours we went from bar to bar, restaurant to restaurant, carrying our luggage and gear. I was grumpy as fuck.

I left everyone in one of the bars and took a walk around the corner to get some peace and quiet. I leaned up against a long brick wall and about thirty seconds later, two big, tattooed Japanese dudes walked up and leaned on the wall right next to me, one on each side. There was easily a hundred feet of wall for them to occupy, but they bookended me instead. They didn't say a word, and neither did I.

Feeling creeped out, I started walking, and they both fell into line right on my heels. I continued back toward the bar, and they followed me like a little human choo-choo train. Once I re-entered the bar, they disappeared.

I told one of the locals what happened and he pointed to my arms. It was the dead of winter, but I had walked out of the bar in a T-shirt. "That's Yakuza," he said. "They don't want you there because of the tattoos." Tattoos were uncommon in Japan at the time. The only people who had them were gangsters. I don't know who they thought I was or why they acted so strange or where the fuck they appeared from, but it was a fittingly odd welcome to this completely alien country.

Japan made me feel illiterate and helpless. In Europe I could at least make sense of the signs and figure out, "Okay, I have to go to 'Haffen-strasse,'" but in Japan I couldn't make out the alphabet. And unlike in Europe very few people spoke English.

But I found other ways to communicate. One night in a noodle house after the show, I spit out some food onto my plate, and one of the locals involved with the show ate it in order to get a laugh from his friends and appall the American.

He had no idea who he was dealing with.

Through sign language and pointing I got him to spit out a piece of his own food, and I matched his stunt. It escalated into a friendly gross-out contest, with each of us smiling and spitting into each other's mouths. Having matched each other again, he filled up half a glass with gooey, stringy loogies, and I downed it with a smile to the shocked laughter and applause of his friends. I took the glass and commanded myself to vomit up his loogies, his spit, his re-gurgitated food, and half of my bowl of noodles into it. I pushed the glass across the table to him and he officially surrendered. The crowd cheered my victory and we were bonded without ever saying a word to each other. And as a show of good faith, I guzzled down the glass of vomit myself.

Our nation's honor had been defended. You're welcome, America.

77

Mike

My lawyer and good friend Stacy Fass called me and said Hollywood Records wanted to meet with me. I had learned from musician friends in similar situations that it was always worth taking the meeting because you usually got a free dinner out of it. I had hoped we'd get courted by Maverick

Records so we could get a naked Polaroid of Madonna like she had sent to Rancid, but apparently dinner with Hollywood Records was all we were worth.

Between courses, they made their pitch. I told them we were happy with Epitaph. They said, "Well, that's fine if you want to play second fiddle to Rancid and the Offspring for the rest of your career. But we'll make you our number one priority."

The come-on went from backhanded flattery to promises: "If you want to take your band to the next level, we'll do that for you." And then they busted out the classic douchebag technique of subtly undermining my self-esteem by pointing out they could get us better press than we had gotten ourselves, and maybe they could finally get our videos played on MTV.

It made me feel like shit. I thought we had built up something special, and here these guys were telling me we were nothing. We were running behind the pack and missing our moment to make something of ourselves. We were blowing it.

◆ ◆ ◆

By the time 1994 rolled around, Bad Religion had left Brett Gurewitz and Epitaph behind and signed to Atlantic Records. They were on the radio and the charts, and by the end of the year they released *Stranger Than Fiction*, which ultimately went gold.

In February of '94, Green Day (who were on tour opening for Bad Religion at the time) released *Dookie*, and the punk scene went fucking apeshit. The album charted all over the world, won a Grammy, and has since been certified diamond (a feat achieved by only about a hundred or so albums in history). On April 8, 1994, the Offspring released *Smash*, which was the first Epitaph release to not only go gold but six times platinum, and which became known as the best-selling independent album of all time.*

In the '80s, punks were like the Freemasons or Skull and Bones. We had our own club, our own rituals. We could identify each other in public and, as far as straight society was concerned, we spoke a coded language. Punk allowed us to wear an outcast label as a badge of pride instead of a mark of shame. But suddenly our secret language was being decoded by the major labels. Our rituals were laid bare in the press. And the doors to our secret clubhouse were kicked open by MTV.

We were flooded by interview requests. At first it seemed flattering, but we were rarely asked anything substantial about NOFX. Every single interviewer asked us more about what we thought of Green Day and the

---

*Also on April 8, 1994, Kurt Cobain was found dead in his home.

Offspring. They didn't know who we were: their editors just threw them at us with no research because they heard our name somewhere and had column inches to fill.

So I started lying. If they weren't going to entertain me by asking different questions, I would entertain myself by providing different answers to the same questions. But some interviewers just wrote their own answers. When one Swedish magazine printed a completely fabricated quote from me that said, "We hate our fans," I gave up. Why do interviews in the first place? When I was a kid I heard the Descendents on Rodney on the Roq at 11 p.m. and fell in love. They weren't on the station's normal rotation, they weren't on magazine covers, they weren't on MTV. The fun was in the discovery. I wanted our fans to discover us the same way. We made a conscious choice to stop talking to the press, and I didn't answer another dumb interview question for the next seven years.

We had made music videos and tried to get them on MTV with zero success. Their alternative music show, *120 Minutes*, played Bad Religion's videos and invited them to do in-studio performances, but they didn't air us once. When we were about to release *Punk in Drublic* in July of '94, we made a video for the song "Leave It Alone."* This time, MTV came to us instead of the other way around.

And we suddenly wondered why we ever cared in the first place.

We had been watching all our friends' bands try to catch the wave of punk popularity, and it seemed so desperate. When Bad Religion signed to a major, I remember Greg Graffin telling me, "We're just gonna see how far we can take this." I never asked myself how far we were going to take NOFX. Financially, I was happy as long as I never had to work another day job. We didn't need MTV to take us to the next level: we had built ourselves up slowly and steadily on our own terms. We never needed them before. We didn't need them now. We told Epitaph to politely decline MTV's request for the video (which surprised both Epitaph and MTV), and we stopped making music videos for the next twelve years.

In July of '96 we played a huge show at the Olympic Velodrome, which was the arena where they held the cycling events for the 1984 Olympics. An MTV rep chatted me up backstage and casually suggested that if NOFX gave MTV a video, then the latest music video from No Use For A Name (the biggest Fat Wreck Chords band at the time) "might have a longer life."

---

*In which you'll notice me wearing a huge leg brace and not moving around much . . . but more about that later.

It was very artfully put, but it was extortion, plain and simple. The repercussions of not playing ball were made perfectly clear.

We didn't give them a video. No Use's video disappeared from MTV (even though their record was charting and in serious rotation on commercial radio). And I realized I didn't want to deal with corporate fucks like that ever again.

✦ ✦ ✦

So there I was at dinner with Hollywood Records having my ego strategically deflated and promises of superstardom dangled in front of me. It was strange how the tables had turned. When our band was a disastrous failure, we believed we were great. Now that we were actually good, Hollywood Records had convinced me we were a disastrous failure.

I asked them what they could offer us that Epitaph couldn't. They said more distribution. I said we were already in every record store I'd ever been to. They said they'd get our videos on MTV. I said we weren't making videos anymore. They said they could get us more press. I said we weren't doing any more press. They didn't understand why I didn't want any of the things they were offering—the things that most bands would sell their souls to get. And I left the dinner questioning every decision I had ever made.

The next day I couldn't believe I questioned myself for a minute. The decisions we made got us to where we were, and we were happy where we were. They couldn't offer us a single thing that would make our band bigger, let alone better. The whole experience left a bad taste in my mouth, and I told my lawyer not to tell me about any more major-label offers.

While we ultimately decided to stay on Epitaph, the band and I discussed the idea of signing to a major very seriously over the next several months. In retrospect, not signing was obviously the right decision, but at the time it wasn't the easiest stance to take. Everyone was signing. Everyone was hanging gold records on their walls. I saw Rancid on *Saturday Night Live*, and I have to admit I was jealous. I grew up watching that show. Fear played on that show. NOFX on *SNL*? It would've been a fabulous disaster.

But then I saw Rancid on the cover of *Spin* and was really glad I didn't have to sit through an interview and a photo shoot to whore myself out in their magazine. I saw Bad Religion doing radio festivals and was really glad we weren't slaves to radio programmers. (When you're on a major, you have to fly around the country at your own expense, playing radio festivals for free so the stations will keep playing your songs. You are every radio station's bitch.)

And for every Green Day, there was a Jawbreaker: a band that signed, got dropped, and lost all their fans and credibility. For every Offspring there was a Samiam; for every Rancid there was a Seaweed. I was self-aware enough to recognize I was no Billie Joe Armstrong. I'm too much of an ass-hole, and I seem to have a problem singing in key. My voice is too whiny, and I wasn't about to start writing love songs about taking a girl home and making her dessert. Most of our songs don't even have choruses.

The bands that signed (and the ones that continue to jump from success-ful indie careers to not-so-successful dalliances with the majors) let their egos drive their decisions. Bands want fame and accolades; they don't think about making a living over the long term. They want big cash now and they want to play stadiums. But when you fall from a major, you fall hard. You can't play a stadium and then play a 500-seater. It's humiliating. But if you play a 1,000-seater and then go down to a 500-seater no one really notices. (And going downhill has always been part of my plan.)

By the time this book goes to print, major labels will most likely be as irrelevant as . . . well . . . printed books, but all anyone has ever heard from bands is how major labels screwed them. You would think everyone would've eventually caught on, but for some reason everyone's ego allows them to think, "Oh, it'll be different with us. We'll be their number one priority." The truth is the majors don't really screw you. In almost all cases they have every intention of trying to make your band big. They give you a shot (and if you kiss the right asses, maybe two shots). But if you don't con-nect with the public, they stop doing business with you and move on to the next band. Regardless of what they say over that first expensive, candlelit dinner, you are a product. You are getting into bed with a corporation. You are not an artist. You are an employee.

I really do believe in the DIY ethic. I know that sounds like a fucking line, but it's the truth. We were the biggest punk band at the time that didn't sign to a major, so we were in a unique position, but we never looked back, and we never had to kiss anyone's ass. Epitaph never told us what to do, and they gave us everything we ever wanted. Once we officially made the decision not to sign, it seemed like it had been the obvious choice all along.

It never charted and it took eight years, but *Punk in Drublic* eventually went gold, selling more than 500,000 copies in the United States (and more than a million worldwide) without any help from radio, mainstream press, or MTV.* From there we were able to build a career where we never had to answer to anybody. And I bet those shitheads from Hollywood Records don't even have jobs anymore.

---

*And, you know, it had some good songs on it, too.

78

Melvin

I was seduced by the pitch from Hollywood Records. I sat next to Mike while the execs blew smoke up our asses and told us about radio play and movie soundtracks, and it sounded like we were poised to break through to major status. Then Mike would poke holes in everything they said, and when he rephrased everything, it didn't sound quite so good.

If I had been calling the shots, I may not have jumped across the table to grab a pen at that first dinner, but I likely would've bought what they were selling eventually. Thankfully my band mates turned out to be more immune to bullshit than I was. Even Hefe, who came from the mainstream music world, understood that a sudden surge of popularity wasn't always a good thing. Mike's best illustration was pointing out all those bands on MTV that had a big video one summer and were completely forgotten about one summer later. He rightfully feared that we could become one of those bands. Slowly, the stars faded from my eyes.

I never felt any significant pangs of envy or regret over our decision to stay independent—it's probably the main reason we're still standing after all these years. The only thing that hurt was watching the rise of Blink-182. Not because I have any problem with those guys (in fact we consider them bros), but because they were the only mainstream punk band that seemed like they were directly ripping us off. We were always the "joking" band. Rancid, Green Day, and the Offspring all had their own personae. We cornered the market on lowbrow humor. The funny songs. The Mike/Hefe stage banter. I don't know if it was conscious plagiarism or just our influence on them, but watching Blink-182 copy our style and get hugely popular with it was the only thing I resented.

In fairness, their sound is more polished. And they're younger and more attractive than us. If we weren't going to exploit our sound on a major, someone else was bound to—it was just a matter of time. But when they offered us a million dollars to open for them on one of their tours, it felt satisfying to turn it down. Our pride probably has a price . . . they just haven't hit it yet.

◆ ◆ ◆

As our popularity continued to surge in the mid-'90s we toured constantly. We branched out into new territories, like Eastern Europe and Scandinavia. We set foot on new continents like Asia, Australia, and South America. The years became a blur because we were road dogs, constantly on the move. As a result, our live show was the tightest it had ever been, but it suffered after a while because burnout set in without us even recognizing it.

Did we just fuck up a song we've played fifty times in a row on this tour alone? I'd talk to Hefe after a show, and we'd realize that at one point or another we both had zoned out on stage and drifted into autopilot, thinking about home, and the simple pleasure of sitting on our own couches.

We weren't unappreciative of what we had; we were just numb from so many dressing rooms, stages, hotels, buses, and planes. I lashed out by trashing dressing rooms, usually by instigating one-man food fights. One night in Germany I hurled a bottle of red wine across the room just to watch it smash open. I wasn't drunk—it was very matter-of-fact destruction. Maybe this will be interesting. Maybe this will break the loop we're stuck in. But other than a splatter stain on two walls and the ceiling, everything was still the same afterward.

Dave Pollack turned to me and said, "You know you're going to have to pay for that, right?" I sheepishly apologized. It cost me $500 to have the room repainted. We had a band meeting to discuss our conduct in dressing rooms and the senseless messes we were leaving in our wake. I later realized there was no "we" about it: The meeting was addressed to the group to prevent embarrassing me, but I was the only one whose behavior needed addressing.

79

Smelly

I have to admit I was a little jealous when I stayed up late and saw Green Day's "Longview" video premiere on MTV's *120 Minutes*. And I was a lot jealous when "Basket Case" started getting played soon thereafter. Jealous isn't exactly the right word—I was happy for them. But I envied the fact that they had written such amazing songs. For a while it wasn't fashionable to admit you liked Green Day, but when *Dookie* came out—before it became a spitting target for the punker-than-thou crowd—we were all blown away by how good it was.

Nirvana had lit the fuse, but Green Day was the explosion. When the music industry doors opened to NOFX after Green Day's success, it was a confusing, strange time. Friends we had shared stages and floors and vans with, friends we had done drugs with and made fun of, and friends we had almost accidentally killed in drunk-driving incidents, were getting rich and famous. Or were at least getting free meals out of guys in suits.

Thankfully we had enough sense to realize, even back then, that we weren't a commercial act. The only one of us who can actually play or sing well is Hefe, and none of us are good looking (especially ape face). The chorus of every Offspring song was a catchphrase; our most popular song, "Linoleum," doesn't HAVE a chorus. If we tried to play the role of a major label band, it would've come off as fake. Our old fans would've abandoned us, and the new audience we would've been courting would've seen right through us.

Drawing that line in the sand gave us more credibility than we had expected. People took music, especially punk music, very personally back then, and we found ourselves immune to the bitter backlash felt by the bands that signed. Instead of going from sold-out stadiums to empty dive bars we went from 1,500-seat clubs to 1,500-seat clubs.

Whether we had ended up in front of chanting stadium crowds (we never would have) or playing on a street corner for spare change (far more likely), I would've considered every day a gift. Majors vs. Indies is a good problem to have. Without the band I probably would've ended up a plumber. Or dead. Regardless of which direction we took, we were winning as long as we were NOFX.

80

Hefe

Man, I joined NOFX at the exact right time. Every tour since my first one did better and better, and after *White Trash* came out I was making almost $100,000 per year. I was living the life of a doctor or a lawyer, but without having to wear a suit.

And then I got my first advance check for *Punk in Drublic*: $240,000. Fuck being a doctor!

Our financial success came so gradually that at first we didn't really process it, but *Punk in Drublic* was undeniably a new level. We headlined at the Hollywood Palladium, and the crowd was wrapped around the block when we pulled up. All of us had our noses pressed up against the windows of the bus as we stared in disbelief at four thousand kids wearing NOFX T-shirts.

The same scene repeated itself over the course of the next year all over the United States and Europe. Every show was sold out, and we started sharing festival stages with huge mainstream acts: Beck, Neil Young, Smashing Pumpkins, Radiohead, Bob Dylan, Foo Fighters . . . I hung out with Chris Cornell from Soundgarden and Shannon Hoon from Blind

Melon* all day at one fest, and I shook hands with Tori Amos backstage at another. (No one else in NOFX gave a shit about her music, but I hugely respect her musicianship and vocal abilities.)

When Christmas 1995 came around, my family had no idea what hit them. I have a big family, so everybody usually draws names out of a hat and buys a gift for one person, but I bought gifts for everyone. I took my dad out and bought him an enormous TV, an entertainment center, and a surround-sound speaker system, and I loaded up a van full of presents for my brother, sisters, in-laws, and everyone's kids. I handed out thousands of dollars' worth of Christmas cheer. I was the Mexican Santa Claus.

I bought a house and I married my girlfriend. I was successful beyond anything I had ever envisioned when I first marked up my brother's guitar neck with a crayon. But we had gone about it in the weirdest way. We were playing the same festivals and venues as all these MTV-groomed major-label acts; the only difference was that we weren't on a major label or MTV.

When Mike sat us all down to discuss the crazy offers we were getting, his point of view was that we had little to gain and everything to lose. I played devil's advocate and wondered aloud if we were missing the boat that Green Day, Rancid, and the Offspring hopped on, but ultimately I voted along with everyone to stay independent.

I saw the ugly side of major labels while working with Mark Curry. Maybe we could've made a few more bucks, maybe we could've opened for Keith Richards, maybe we would've stayed in nicer hotels. But we had freedom. I didn't know anything about punk labels before I joined NOFX, but I saw the difference right away. We didn't have to dance for the suits or take orders from anyone. We did whatever we wanted, and we were still somehow making the same amount of money as the people who had to scrape and bow before their labels. It was an easy choice: empty promises or being free.

And sure enough, the backlash from the punks came down on everyone who signed to a major or submitted to MTV. Rancid's tour bus got spray painted and pelted with bottles by angry punks while we held our heads high.

Then again, Rancid went platinum, and we only went gold. So did Offspring. And Green Day ended up playing stadiums. Blink-182 headlined the Reading Festival over us in 2010 and made like half a million bucks . . .

My god . . .

WHAT DID WE DO???

————

*This was only a month or two before Shannon was found dead of an overdose in his tour bus. The day I spent with him he was proudly talking about how he was clean and sober. Really a shame—he was a cool guy.

My first wedding.

Me and Tori Amos.

81

Smelly

In junior high I was hanging out at a friend's house when he produced a .22 rifle and, for shits and giggles, put it to my head. He quickly moved the barrel and fired it into a tree outside his window. With my ears still ringing, he put the warm barrel back against my skull.

A gun's trigger has to travel less than half an inch before firing. So I think it's fair to say I came within half an inch of having my brains blown out that day. My friend and I didn't hang out much after that.

Almost twenty years later, NOFX played in Prague. Around 2 a.m., after the show, we were walking near the Old Town Square, guided by our friend Carol. Two guys walking in the opposite direction suddenly bulldozed their way through our group. I heard Hefe yell from behind me, "Jay! We're getting jumped!"

I instinctively grabbed one of those huge table umbrellas from a nearby sidewalk café. I wasn't really thinking clearly; I just didn't want to get jumped. As I struggled with my unwise choice of weapon, one of the guys walked straight up to me, pulled out a revolver, stuck it in my chest, and cocked back the hammer. I dropped the umbrella.

When I heard the click of the hammer a strange calm came over me. It wasn't panic; it was an acceptance of my fate. Everything went quiet and moved in slow motion. My brain was very practical about it, thinking, "I'm going to get shot in Prague," without a hint of fear or anxiety. "Okay. This is it."

I stood there for a few seconds, but nothing happened. I took a step back and then turned around. I felt the gun in my back. My brain came to a new, equally calm conclusion, "Okay, this guy is a cop. I'm going to jail in Prague."

Carol said calmly, "Just walk," and we all took her advice. My pace grew quicker, and the pressure of the gun against my back subsided. After a few seconds we all took off running and went around the block. When we turned to see if the guys were following us, they were gone.

No matter how well my band was doing, no matter how well I stuck to the right track, no matter how safe and secure I felt about my future, I knew we were always, at any given moment, just a half inch away from losing everything.

82

Melvin

Even though I grew up contending with the gangsters and skinheads and junkies of the L.A. punk scene, and even though NOFX has since traveled to some of the sketchiest parts of the third world in defiance of State Department travel advisories, one of the most memorable times I was jumped was in Amsterdam. You never know where you're going to find trouble, but you certainly don't expect to find it in a city where the scummiest lowlife on the street still has straight teeth and a nicely pressed button-down shirt.

The Netherlands had either just beaten Ireland or just lost to Brazil in the World Cup; so everyone was out and everyone was drunk. Limo (our monitor man, keyboardist, and occasional muscle) and I were walking through town with our girlfriends. It was getting late, and our walk took us beyond the more heavily trafficked canals toward the less well-lit ones. Ahead was a group of eight guys, hanging out on the street in a circle, chattering loudly.

A man on a bicycle cut through the group, and for a moment he seemed to stop and converse with them before continuing along toward us. As the bicyclist passed us he said, "Make another way." I thought he was asking us to move to the side of the road so he could get by, but in retrospect he was probably telling us to change our direction and avoid what lay ahead.

The laughter of the eight Dutch guys grew louder as we approached. They were clearly drunk, but again, how afraid could I be of such nicely pressed button-down shirts?

As we crossed their path, an arm jutted out inches in front of my face as one of the Dutch guys pointed to one of the others in his posse. I pulled my girlfriend back and gingerly pushed the guy's arm out of the way. We walked on and were about 15 feet away when Limo's girlfriend said, "They're coming up behind us."

We turned around and the guys broke into a run, closing the distance before I had time to react. One guy grabbed my shoulders and spat a bunch of Dutch at me while laughing maniacally. Someone translated: "He says he's going to throw you in the canal!"

My Tang Soo Do training from age ten kicked in as I threw his arms off my shoulders, grabbed his nicely pressed button-down shirt, pulled it down around his arms (popping all the buttons), and pushed him away. Another guy kicked Limo from behind. I found out later that one of the guys had said to Limo's girlfriend, "We're going to rape you." Limo turned and punched one of them—I don't know if it was the kicker or the potential rapist. I shouted, "Run!" as I pulled away from another guy trying to grab me.

The four of us skittered awkwardly down the cobblestone streets with the Dutch guys in pursuit. Limo tripped and fell along the way and ended up with some gnarly bruising. Everything was closed so there was no shelter to be had, but at the next corner we found a restaurant that still had a light on and a few tables outside. I snatched an empty pint glass off one of the tables and hucked it at our attackers. Before it had time to miss its target I had already grabbed another glass and smashed it on the side of a table to create a weapon. A man in an apron came out of the restaurant and wailed sadly: "My glasses!"

The Dutch guys caught up and one of them picked up a table to hold it like a shield, and we faced off like DIY gladiators. One of the girls yelled, "They're attacking us! Please let us in!" The guy in the apron shuffled us through the door and stayed outside to try and calm the situation down while we caught our breath. He came inside after a while and explained, "Soccer hooligans, you know. It's World Cup. Just stay here. I told them I was going to call the police."

We thanked him, and after a while the well-dressed hooligans wandered off. We hung out in the restaurant a little longer to make sure we were in the clear and to give the adrenaline some time to subside. I was ready to kill somebody. I was going to slit someone's throat with that broken glass. It forever made me more paranoid about what can happen when you're just walking down the street. These fucking wasted, stupid people with their fucking soccer bullshit. Of all the places in the world, how did things get so fucked up along the canals of Amsterdam?

The man in the apron told us, "He was mad because you tore his shirt."

83

Smelly

I got a letter in the mail from the Baltimore County Department of Corrections. The return address was Erik Sandin.

The letter inside was from DJ. He had been arrested for heroin possession and sentenced to eighteen months in prison. He knew my parents' address and had somehow convinced the authorities that he was me. So now, because of DJ, I have a prison record. I made him call a lawyer and clear it up years later, but according to the computers his fingerprints are still on file with my name as his alias. So if he ever ends up with another warrant out for his arrest, so will I.

Getting a letter from myself in prison was one of the many haunting reminders of the fate I'd narrowly avoided.

Courtney Love and I had drifted apart long before I went to rehab, but in 1993 we were reunited at the Bizarre Festival in Germany. It was the first major festival NOFX ever played. We were scheduled to go on early in the day, but we were still looking out at a crowd of about fifteen thousand people. We opened with "Sticking in my Eye," which begins with a soft bass intro and then kicks into high gear when the drums come in.

As I was about to bring my sticks down onto the crash cymbals and officially mark the biggest moment of our career, someone started whacking me in the head. It fucked up my timing and trainwrecked the song. I turned to discover Courtney, spazzing out on my drum riser, excited to see her old friend.

We caught up after the set and she sarcastically whined about how Hole had played earlier in the day than us. Pearl Jam was huge at the time, and she said, "I can't believe I'm fucking opening up for you guys. Pearl Jam opened for us once."

I held up my index finger and smiled, "Once."

Both of our lives had changed drastically since we first met. I had gotten clean; she had gotten married. We were both on top of the world. But when we saw each other a couple years later, things had changed drastically again.

Hole had gotten huge, and at another European festival we were indeed opening for Courtney. Her husband's suicide and her addiction (along with the ensuing arrests and tabloid coverage) had left her a vacant shell of a person. I found her backstage, surrounded by handlers with a cigarette dangling out of her mouth. Forget spazzing out on a drum riser; she could barely stand up to hug me when I said hi.

She called to one of her entourage to bring her child over, "Give me my baby! Frances, come here, give your mother a hug. Momma loves you." She looked like some cross between *Mommie Dearest* and Mr. Burns. She hugged the kid for a minute and then handed her back off to a nanny and returned to smoking and staring into space through half-closed eyes.

It broke my heart. She had everything and nothing at the same time. I felt sad for her, and I felt worse for her little girl. Courtney and I weren't the closest, but she was my friend. She was the one who used to make fun of me for being such a bad junkie. Now she was another ghost, reminding me of what could've been.

I said, "Hey Courtney, I just want to tell you that I love you, and if you ever need anything I'm here for you. You don't have to be like this." I knew it would go in one ear and out the other, or just bounce off her forehead. But I had to say it.

She muttered some sort of semi-conscious thanks, and I told her she'd be in my thoughts. That was the last time we spoke.

84

Hefe

All the festivals we played in 1995 were milestones, but the milestone we were most excited for was the Reading Festival in England. Not only was it going to be our biggest audience and payday to that point, but it also had prestige. The history of the festival stretches all the way back to the '60s and has been headlined by pretty much every major rock act ever. It took a long time for Mike and Dave Pollack to negotiate a place for NOFX on Reading's main stage, and we earned it on our own terms.

The day before we were supposed to play, we had to cancel.

We were backstage at the Pukkelpop Festival in Belgium when Courtney Love staggered through the catering tent with her entourage. Every head was turned as we watched her minders prevent her from physically falling over. Smelly went over to talk to her since they had been friends back in the day. The rest of us just sat there, stunned by the tragic scene.

The thing about a train wreck is that you can't help but watch. When Courtney took the stage, I was on the side in the wings. Jay and Smelly were down in front by the barricade. I decided to join them so I could get a better view.

Festival stages are huge—this one was easily 10 or 15 feet tall, maybe higher. As I climbed down, my wedding ring got caught on a loose nail. I tried to drop to the ground and the skin on my finger gave way as if it were a banana peel. If one of the security guys below hadn't caught my ass, my finger would've popped right off. The ring snapped off the nail and I hit the ground. I looked at my hand and saw a clump of red and purple ground beef staring back at me.

Security rushed me to the medical tent and an EMT poked and prodded at my hand. He only spoke Belgian-ese or whatever, so someone had to translate for me: "We're going to have to cut your finger off."

The EMT pinched what was left of my finger and there was apparently no sign of blood reaching the fingertip, so I boarded an ambulance and spent the whole ride to the hospital thinking they would have to amputate part of my fret hand. Everything I had worked for my whole life was dangling by a few exposed tendons.

At the hospital I asked the doctor if I was really going to lose my finger. He laughed and said, "No, who told you that?" He gave me a shot to numb the pain, cut away the peeled flesh, and wrapped my finger with a cartoonish amount of gauze. I had some healing to do, but my hand remained whole, and I breathed the biggest sigh of relief in my life.

Mike was pissed. We lost a ton of money pulling out of Reading at the last minute. We went to the festival anyway since we had to get to England for our flights home, and we joined Pennywise on stage for a version of "Kill All the White Man." But that was all the NOFX the Reading crowd would see for the next seven years.

It could've been the last time any NOFX fans saw El Hefe play guitar ever. I choose not to think about it too often.

85

Mike

There was a time when I was the least alcoholic member of NOFX. I never understood how the guys in my band could drink all day and night and be fine the next day. Once or twice a week I drank until 4 or 5 in the morning, but I felt so destroyed the next day (and sometimes even the day after that) that I could hardly operate. Then I discovered a little miracle called Vicodin.

When we were opening for Fishbone at the Palladium in 1994, I jumped in the air, and when I landed I bent my knee in the exact opposite direction knees are supposed to go. I finished the set in excruciating pain, with my leg up on the monitor.

I had torn my ACL, which was bad enough, but after surgery, instead of letting my knee heal properly, I dragged it on tour through Europe for six weeks. When I came home I couldn't bend my leg, and they had to slice me back open and put me in a machine that moved my leg in a slow bike-pedaling motion, nonstop, twenty-four hours a day, for a week. I cured the pain (and the boredom of sitting alone in a hospital room with no cable) by popping ten Vicodins a day. I got so high I apparently gave someone at Fat Wreck Chords a raise from my hospital bed and had no memory of it after I was discharged.

Neither the machine clamped on my leg nor the catheter in my cock bothered me, thanks to my new friend, Vicodin. After my knee healed, my new friend and I explored our relationship further. We went to shows together, we went snowboarding together, we had sex together. Not only did it help me take a harder beating in the bedroom, but I found I could get the same buzz with less booze and wake up without a hangover.

The concoction served me well and provided consequence-free good times . . . for a while.

86

Smelly

I woke up in Italy one morning, and when I moved my neck, it popped. I felt like I had been paralyzed. I managed to grab the phone and get a doctor to my room, and it turned out I had pinched a nerve. Not a big deal, except for the fact that the doctor prescribed me muscle relaxers.

In rehab they explained that, yes, sometimes you will need to take medicine. You need to find the discipline to take it as directed and strictly follow the doctor's orders. But there I was, alone in a hotel room, holding my potential relapse in my hand.

It's like handing a little kid a big glass jar full of M&Ms and saying, "You can have one M&M now, and you can have another one in four hours. You can't have a handful, you can't have one every few minutes, but we're going to leave you alone, staring at the jar." In theory, the kid can obey orders. But those four-hour stretches between M&Ms are going to be brutal.

It was a test I didn't want to take. I was in that bed staring at those M&Ms for four days straight. When I took one as prescribed, that old feeling came back. And the angel and devil on my shoulders were soon locked in heated battle.

I stayed true. But the tests kept coming. In Germany, we played some outdoor show in the middle of nowhere. Our bus was parked on a dead-end street that may as well have been called Heroin Alley. No one else could see it, but my junkie radar was going crazy. There were dealers up and down the street, people shooting up in the bushes nearby, people hiding dope under our fucking bus in between buys . . . I wondered, "Why couldn't we have played here two years ago?!"

Also around that time, Mike became very fond of pills. He was brazen about popping them in front of me and was always conversationally cataloging his intake from the night before to anyone who would listen. I don't think anyone can really relate to being an ex-junkie unless they're actually an ex-junkie, so I don't think Mike understood how much stress he was putting on me. In the band's mind, sobriety was as simple as "don't get high." I knew I couldn't control others, and that I had to find my own ways to cope with uncomfortable situations, but when people boarded the bus to sell and trade pills right in front of my face I had to draw a line.

I asked Mike to keep the drugs out of my sight, and he listened—to an extent. Our sound guy, Kent, had been promoted to manager, so I asked him to talk to the band on my behalf because I hated being the killjoy ruining everyone's fun. The band tried to be polite, but they weren't obligated to go sober along with me. Inevitably there were moments when I was surrounded by booze and pills and temptation.

I never floundered. I never relapsed. But the stress and the resentment from test after test slowly built up.

By '96 Mike's pill use was impacting our shows. We toured Italy with the Vandals, and he called the crowd spics and wetbacks from the stage. He was trying to be sarcastic and edgy, but the pills and wine fucked up the tone and delivery so the crowd was just bummed, and so was I. Too often he was blurring the line between being a funny drunk and a belligerent dick. I pulled him aside after a show and said, "You can't insult people like that—it's not fucking cool." I don't remember his response. I just know it didn't solve anything.

I tried to explain to him that he was on the road to becoming an addict, but he politely brushed off my warnings. He just kept popping Valiums and Vicodins like he was a kid with a big jar of M&Ms.

87

Mike

The mid- to late '90s were very good to us. Erin and I bought a condo and operated Fat Wreck Chords out of an upstairs office while storing the stock in our garage. Thanks to the sudden popularity of punk, all the early Fat signees—Lagwagon, Propagandhi, No Use For A Name, Strung Out, Face to Face, Good Riddance—sold tens of thousands of records right out of the gate. By '96 we bought a house, moved the label into its own offices in downtown San Francisco, and used our new garage for an S&M dungeon.

Recording I Heard They Suck Live.

Most bands have that moment where they sign a crazy record deal or their single tops the charts, and suddenly they're bathing in money and they don't know how to handle it. But NOFX and Fat Wreck Chords just did slightly better year after year until one day we looked around and realized that we owned houses and belonged to neighborhood associations.

In '95, Fat Wreck released NOFX's first live album, *I Heard They Suck Live*. We recorded it at the Roxy in L.A. They wanted to charge us $1,500 to use the club's name on the album, but that seemed expensive, so we figured we'd just wait twenty years and mention it casually in our book instead.

Even though *Punk in Drublic* sold more copies, *I Heard They Suck Live* was our first album to enter the *Billboard* 200 (#198, but it still counts) and was the biggest record on Fat at the time. And even though most of our fans hated our next record, *Heavy Petting Zoo*, it still hit the charts and peaked at #63. It has the distinction of being our biggest selling record out of the gate with the worst reviews since *Liberal Animation*.

What *Heavy Petting Zoo* lacked in hits it made up for with the album artwork, which featured a farm hand finger-fucking a sheep on the CD and cassette versions and 69-ing a sheep on the vinyl version. At least one record store in France was shut down for hanging up the promotional posters. In Germany there was some court order that prevented stores from

We meet a lot of Ho's on tour.

displaying the album because apparently pornographic images of bestiality are illegal over there. (Weird porn illegal in Germany? Since when?!) You're not a real punk band until a government entity censors your album cover, I suppose.

Meanwhile, the neighborhood association noticed that we had removed one of our garage doors to make our S&M dungeon, and they shut us down because it was against code to do so. When we moved to a nicer house in a new neighborhood we built one in a secret room inside the house instead.

88

Hefe

In 1996, I was living in McKinleyville, a barely noticeable dot on the map five hours north of San Francisco. It was quiet and beautiful and extremely cheap. With the release of *Heavy Petting Zoo* I literally had more money than I knew what to do with, so I decided to fulfill one of my lifelong dreams and open Hefe's Nightclub.

Mike tried to talk me out of it. He wasn't snide or condescending; he seemed genuinely worried that I was going to lose money. He was especially concerned with my idea of buying a building to house the club, so I compromised and said I'd rent instead. Mike said, "Okay, that's better. You're still going to lose money—you just won't lose as much."

I hate to give him the satisfaction of admitting this—but he was right.

I found a building in nearby Eureka, which only had a population of about fifty thousand people, but which was the perfect halfway stop for bands on tour between Oregon and San Francisco. We hosted every genre of music—the calendar was as eclectic as my mom's old record collection. I tooled around town with jazz great Maynard Ferguson in my '47 Chevy, I took the Sugarhill Gang out to eat at Denny's, and I drank a very satisfying beer at my very own bar while watching Foghat play "Slow Ride" at my very own night club.

I used to play Foghat songs with John Cagney when I was first learning guitar, and now here they were at a club I had built from my career as a guitarist. I had come a long way since Jack Attack.

But while my head was in the clouds, everyone in the whole place was ripping me off. Security guards were letting friends in for free and drinking on the job. Promoters were skimming from the door. The sound guy even stole the fucking knobs off the mixing board!

At one point I was getting an estimate for security cameras, and the salesman pointed out that the sink behind the bar was full of pennies. He explained that one of my employees was running an old scam: pour a drink, but don't run it through the register—just collect the cash and toss a penny in the sink. At the end of the night, count up the pennies, figure out how much cash never went on the books, pocket that amount, and the receipts would still all match up.

Shows would be packed, with lines of people around the block, and I still wasn't making any money. I was being threatened with a lawsuit from some asshole who claimed he was beaten up by security. I caught his private investigator outside the club, shooting photos from his car. Another nightclub owner in town had cameras aimed at my building and called the cops on us any time he saw anything he could interpret as a problem. The same guy circulated a petition to get us closed down and was also tight with someone from the Alcoholic Beverage Control Board, so I constantly had the ABC up my ass. They eventually found some underage girl who snuck in with a fake ID, and we found ourselves fighting just to keep our liquor license.

It was easy for things to spin out of control because I was always away on tour. I established a hip-hop dance night once a week, which is a tough thing to get going; you have to promote like hell and be consistent about it so word of mouth can grow. Some of the staff members hated hip-hop, so when I was away they just wouldn't open the club that night. They'd sit at the bar and drink with their friends, or book bands I hadn't authorized, while all that promotional work was flushed down the toilet. I would've made a change in management, but in a town like Eureka there weren't a lot of options. I would put out an ad looking for someone to manage a nightclub and I would get the guy who managed the local Denny's.

Karma has a way of coming around, though. Suicidal Tendencies played the club one night while I was on the road and I got a call from Mike Muir's younger brother, who said the manager was trying to take a percentage of their merch sales. But I had a policy of never charging bands for merch. And according to Mike Muir's brother the manager had denied them everything on their rider, offering them some pizza instead. I probably could've defused the situation, but I'd had it with everyone trying to screw me over. I told Mike's brother that it sounded like they were being ripped off.

There are a handful of bands out there you really don't want to fuck with. One of them is Suicidal Tendencies. I heard later that Mike Muir picked the manager up by his throat and had him pinned against the wall. The manager cried out for security, but they took their time before politely asking Mike to put the manager down at his earliest convenience.

One of the only success stories to come out of Hefe's Nightclub was the weekly gay dance night. One of the local radio DJs was gay so he helped promote it, and I went to the campus of the nearby College of the Redwoods and told their Gay Straight Alliance about it. In a small town like Eureka there aren't a lot of options for gay nightlife, so people took notice. The local news even came down to do a report about it.

Fat Mike joked a few times: "So Hefe, it was your dream to open a gay nightclub?" But I'm loud and proud about it. It wasn't just some dance night—it was a safe haven for a lot of people who were otherwise surrounded by Redneck Country. People would pull me aside at the club and say with deep sincerity, "Thank you for doing this for us."

One day I walked into my bank and my usual teller said, "Hey, I want to thank you so much for what you're doing. We don't really have much out here. Thanks for your support." On his desk was a picture of him with his wife and kids. I don't know if they were beards, or if the picture was fake, or what. I just knew our club was allowing him to be himself in a town where he otherwise had to hide.

Despite the pats on the back from the gay community, I was over being a club owner by the end of the first year. The only problem was I had signed a two-year lease, so I kept the nightmare going, losing money left and right the whole time.

When the lease was finally up, the staff had a huge farewell party. The next morning I found that they had discharged the fire hydrants all over the place. There was trash everywhere, things had been stolen; it was exactly the wreck I should've expected. I sold everything I could—the sound system, the lights, the walk-in cooler—and tried to offset my losses with every tax deduction I could possibly take. When all was said and done, I lost somewhere in the neighborhood of $150,000.

To Mike's credit, he never once said, "I told you so." But he did, in fact, tell me so.

89

Melvin

There came to be a little voice in my head, always whispering, "You don't deserve to make this much money." I don't know where it came from, but as my lifestyle noticeably changed, the voice nestled in for a long stay.

I was happy. I was living a musician's dream: money in the bank, another tour always coming up, and everything on our own terms. But for some reason I felt compelled to give away the cash that wouldn't stop filling my pockets. I would go to bars and leave outrageous tips. I had a roommate living with me, rent-free. And when a friend of a friend was trying to unload his failing coffee shop, I bought it from him.

Mike tried to talk me out of it. But I didn't see how it could fail. The shop occupied a couple of storefronts on Melrose Avenue, about a block and a half down from Fred Segal. It was a cool space. People came in and ordered coffee. Didn't seem so complicated . . .

By the time the ink was dry on the lease, I realized why Mike had been so pessimistic and why the previous owners were so desperate to escape. Nothing was up to code: They had illegally taken down a wall between the storefronts; the health inspector demanded we replace the edges of all the tile so we could mop properly; we needed an extra toilet due to our seating capacity; the refrigerators were missing gaskets; I had to break my lease and cut a hole in the roof to install a bigger hood over the oven for fire safety . . .

Every time the health inspector or the fire marshal or the landlord came by, I ended up spending a few grand just to keep the place on its feet. Equipment and construction cost me well over fifty thousand within the first few months. But soon enough Spun Melvin's was open for business.

Spun Melvin's.

In order to get around the problem of the illegal missing wall, I sectioned off part of the café, built a stage, and called it a performance space so it was technically a separate business. My vision was to have some cool acoustic shows there, but most nights were floppers. The most memorable was when Fishbone frontman Angelo Moore came in to do a spoken-word performance. He spouted lines of improvised gibberish, punctuated by discordant saxophone solos. I think there were eighteen people there. I gave him eighty bucks.

I originally thought the place would run itself, but I was wrong. I hired my friend Derek to be the manager, and I hired my rent-free roommate Sean to be the chef. They weren't entirely unqualified for their jobs, but if I had been their asshole boss instead of their bro maybe I would've told Derek to charge more for the sandwiches so we could turn a profit, or maybe I would've told Sean to use fewer eggs in his omelets so we could keep costs down. And there were little things, like noticing a burnt-out lightbulb in the shop before leaving for tour and then coming home six weeks later to see that it still hadn't been replaced. I never wanted to call out my friends on their shortcomings, and even if I wanted to I lacked the communication skills necessary to do it. I don't know why I couldn't ask them to change a simple lightbulb. (Or why I didn't just change it myself.)

If I had thought about it for five minutes before making the purchase, maybe I would've realized I had no idea how to run a café in the first place. Let alone how to run a café while being away on tour for months at a time. For three years—the full term of my lease—I poured two or three thousand dollars into the place each month just to keep the doors open and meet the payroll. But on top of that was the emotional cost. The moment I woke up each morning, the weight of what I had to deal with at the coffee shop would hit me like a sledgehammer. Anxiety built in the pit of my stomach. And again my inability to communicate made things worse as I bottled up all the tension and swallowed the stress every night. Just five minutes of thinking could've saved me three years of mental anguish.

When it came time to renew the lease I ran like a rat fleeing a sinking ship. I was on the road when I called Derek and told him to sell all the equipment and close the place down. And of course that didn't go smoothly, either. The equipment sold for way less than it was worth, and the landlord discovered the hole we cut into the ceiling and kept my security deposit. It was bummer after bummer, but by the time I was home from tour it was all over. I never set foot in the shop again. I've tried my best to avoid mentally calculating how much money I lost, but I probably sunk over $180,000 into Spun Melvin's over the course of three years.

It was a comedy of errors, but not a very funny comedy of errors. An expensive comedy of errors. And an expensive lesson about being more vocal and direct. As I looked back on the whole experience, I realized keeping my problems to myself was at least half the burden. It ultimately allowed me to evolve and become more direct, because I knew I couldn't afford to go down in flames like that again.

90

Smelly

Among the vast piles of strawberry baskets and magnifying glasses in my grandmother's garage was an old motorcycle. If there was anything that symbolized freedom, rebellion, and counterculture—and offered the thrill of dangerously high speeds—it was that iconic, rusty machine.

At age twelve, I wasn't supposed to mess with it, but I figured out how to get it started and rode it to a nearby dirt lot where the local kids rode their BMX bikes. I tore through the lot like a tornado, with every eye fixed on me and every jaw on the floor. It was love at first ride.

I was even more obsessed with motorcycles than I was with music. I borrowed, bought, and stole motorcycle magazines and devoured them, cover to cover. I stared at the pictures and transported myself onto the track along with each rider. It was another form of escape that constantly occupied my thoughts.

I can't fault my parents for not having much money, but I was pretty bitter about the fact that when my younger sister wanted to explore acting they were happy to pay for acting classes and dance classes and head shots. Meanwhile, I was sweeping up at a factory to save up for a motorbike. When I was fourteen, though, I finally made enough to buy a disassembled motorbike through the classifieds, and my dad agreed to help me put it together.

It could've been the greatest father/son bonding moment of all time. It doesn't get more America than that: building a motorcycle with dad. And it started off great. The bike had magnesium hubs, so my dad showed me a little science experiment. He scraped some of the magnesium off, put it into a small pile, and lit it on fire. Magnesium burns with a bright, hot, gnarly flame, so when he lit the pile it went BGGGGHHH and I went, "Whoaaaaa!" Now that was a nice moment.

But the fun died out as fast as the flame. From there on, building the bike was torture. "What the fuck are you doing? Get over here! Pay attention!"

When NOFX started to make money, I not only bought my own top-of-the-line, fully assembled motorbike, I started my own fucking motocross team.

Today, when people think of motocross, they think of crazy stunts, loud music, and scantily clad female fans. But in the early '90s that wasn't the case. If you were into skateboarding or snowboarding, you could buy VHS tapes of dudes getting radical, but if you were into motocross the videos were super square and cheesy. The sport was controlled by corporate bike manufacturers, so they highlighted their best clean-cut, milk-drinking riders and focused entirely on racing, never on freestyle tricks.

The motocross riders I hung out with were lunatics. They kind of had to be to buzz around dirt tracks at top speed with a guarantee of more broken limbs than financial reward. Jordan Burns, the drummer from Strung Out, was a fellow moto fan, so he and I decided to make motocross videos that truly showed the lifestyle of the sport. We filmed parties, fights, strippers, and—most importantly—gnarly bike stunts, and set it to punk music to show people what the sport was really about.

And that's where the modern image of freestyle motocross came from: our videos. We enlisted Jordan's friend, Kurt Haller, who had worked on a few snowboard videos in the past, to help us shoot and edit everything, and we put out a video called *Moto XXX*. It sold like wildfire, thirty-five thousand copies in the first six months. We made a small (and unexpected) fortune. Within the same year, Fox Racing put out a video called *Terrafirma*, and Fleshwound Films put out a video called *Crusty Demons of Dirt*. They shared a similar vibe and focus, and the whole sport changed almost overnight. It went from Walt Disney to Larry Flynt.

We took the money we made from our first video (and five sequels) and founded the Moto XXX racing team. We advertised the videos through the team and the team through the videos. We sunk 250 grand into a semi trailer with our logo on it and started entering Supercross races.

The American Motorcyclist Association—the governing body that ran all the major national races—hated our guts. Our guys were in the pit next to Team Honda, blaring punk music and surrounded by girls in bikini tops and dudes covered in tattoos. I'm sure the AMA was pressured by all the major teams to squash us because we always seemed to end up hidden in the back of the pit, and we were fined constantly. We handed out hundreds of stickers, and they got plastered all over racing stadiums, so we were fined for "damaging stadium property." Right next to our sticker would be a Suzuki sticker, but I never heard about Suzuki incurring any fines . . .

One of our first sponsored riders was an up-and-coming teenager named Brian Deegan.* In 1997, we entered him in the AMA Supercross Championships at the L.A. Coliseum. It was only our team's second major race, but in front of forty-six thousand stunned spectators Brian took first fucking place. As he flew over the final jump to cross the finish line, he let go of his bike and let it sail through the air, and he made motocross history.

---

*He would later go on to form the Metal Mulisha, a notorious motocross team that took the Moto XXX philosophy to the next level.

The crowd went apeshit. It was as if the Bad News Bears had just beaten the New York Yankees. No one could believe an independent team of obnoxious punks had beaten the multibillion-dollar Japanese corporate machine. One of the astonished announcers on ESPN wondered aloud, "Can you win a race and not be on the bike at the finish line?"

His fellow announcer answered, "Well . . . he just did!"

The AMA awarded Brian a $2,500 purse for his victory and then fined him $1,000 for his "hazardous" ghost ride. It didn't matter: Brian's career took off and Moto XXX couldn't be ignored after that. The videos kept selling, the victories piled up, and Moto XXX became infamous in the motocross scene (and an ever-growing thorn in the AMA's side).

Over the next decade we grew so much we could afford to pay some of our riders 150 grand a year. Jordan, Kurt, and I never made any profit because every dollar we made went back into expenses and employees and traveling and promotion. It cost about half a million bucks a year just to keep the team running, and we were never able to hook a big enough sponsor to relieve the burden. And as videos became more widely available on the internet, our VHS and DVD sales ground to a halt. When the economy finally took a huge shit in 2008 it spelled the end. The few sponsors we had pulled out, and we couldn't afford to put the team on the road. We had to walk away.

But for fourteen years we hung in with the corporate teams, and we kicked their asses. And we remain the most successful privateer team in history in terms of results and longevity. We traveled and raced and had the time of our lives. And it became a much healthier outlet for me than drugs, drinking, or knocking out random skinheads. I still ride and race to this day.

Recently I was in a Starbucks and I noticed a woman with a Moto XXX sticker on her laptop. I couldn't help but smile with pride. It's a phenomenon that has spread further than my herpes.

Jordan Burns, me, and Kurt Haller.

91

Hefe

My daughter Kalyn was born in the middle of my nightclub madness, and between NOFX's touring schedule and the stress of the club I could hardly enjoy my first couple years of fatherhood. The one place I could let loose was on this new thing called the Warped Tour.

There was something about the Warped Tour's summer camp vibe that brought out the troublemaker in everyone. I had the same let's-see-if-I-can-get-away-with-this attitude that I did when I was doing movie extra work with Gumdrop Lou, or when I was bouncing off the walls as a young kid.

Those first few Warped Tours all blend together. We had a half hour set during the day, a barbecue at night, and twenty-three hours of time to kill in between, so, depending on the tour, I paired up with Fletcher from Pennywise, or Lars from Rancid, or Tre from Green Day, or Brody from the Distillers, and searched for trouble.

Brody and I shot bottle rockets into one of the production buildings where everyone had their computers and tour paperwork set up.* Tre had a paintball gun and we sniped other bands' buses. My impersonation skills came in handy when I got a hold of a walkie-talkie and pretended to be Dicky from the Mighty Mighty Bosstones:

"This is Dicky from the Bosstones, can you send some Vaseline and tissues over to my bus? And don't tell my wife, okay?"

The girls in the production office thought it was hilarious; Dicky not so much. I guess he heard the broadcast over someone else's walkie, because his voice came crackling back:

"Who the fuck is that? That's not me!"

Before Kevin Lyman (the Warped Tour founder/organizer) was able to confiscate my walkie, I played plenty of other games to entertain the production girls.

"Can we get some security assistance over at the NOFX bus, we have a serious problem."

"Who is this?"

"This is Bob Backslide, I'm new in production."

---

*Some lady came running out of the office and caught Brody, but I got away. To Brody's credit, she didn't rat me out as the mastermind.

Warped Tour, 1996.

"I'm at the NOFX bus—I don't see anything going on. What are you talking about?"

"Oh, now it's over by the Pennywise bus."

I ran the security guy from bus to bus until he came to the production office and busted me.

"Dammit, Hefe!"

"Oh, hey. You got my fax."

The production girls later made me a special laminate with the name Bob Backslide on it.

Usually it was just harmless fun, but I've always had a problem with knowing where to draw the line. One night, Fletcher and I commandeered a bunch of hot dog vending carts, pushed them into a pile topped by some cardboard boxes, doused them with lighter fluid, and set them ablaze. We had no end goal; it was just the most possible trouble we could get into at the moment. I have no idea how it was eventually extinguished or if Kevin Lyman ever knew that I was responsible for the fire.

I stepped up the destruction one night in Kansas with Lars (or was it Tre?), when we tossed a bunch of smoke bombs into a porta potty and peer-pressured one of the stagehands into using his forklift to drop the porta potty into the nearby river. We cheered as the potty dropped into the water and floated off into the distance, spewing plumes of smoke out of the open door.

Kevin Lyman woke up to a $10,000 fine for the environmental damage we had caused (not to mention the replacement cost of the porta potty). The stagehand was sent home. I would've copped to it if I knew he was going to get fired, but he was gone before I had a chance. Then again, maybe Kevin knew it was us, and his hands were tied because he knew he couldn't kick his two biggest headliners off the tour.

Either way, Kevin: sorry for all the trouble I caused on your tour. And you should drop by sometime. I've got some amazing pictures of a porta potty gently making its way down the Kansas River . . .

92

Melvin

I was taking a peaceful dump one morning on the Warped Tour when I noticed some movement through the gap in the door of the porta potty. A moment later the whole thing started shaking, and I felt it lift off the ground.

I tried to open the door, but the porta potty had been loaded onto a forklift from the front, so the door was pinned closed. I pushed and struggled and managed to get the door open about an inch.

"HEY! HEYYYYYYYY!"

The noise from the forklift drowned out my shouts. I screamed louder and pounded on the door as I imagined myself getting dropped and covered in shit, piss, and toxic blue chemicals.

Finally, I felt the forklift lower the porta potty to the ground. I burst through the door and saw one of the production guys we had been hanging out with.

"Dude! What the fuck?!"

"Melvin, I'm sorry! I thought nobody was in there."

The guy was fired and sent home the next day, but not because I told anybody what happened. Apparently he got drunk that same night and dumped one of the porta potties into the river. At least I hadn't been trapped inside that one.

93

Mike

A hundred and fifteen degrees is hot no matter where you are, but it seems even hotter in Houston, Texas. The organizers of the '98 Warped Tour decided to move the show to an indoor venue, which was an old shed where they normally sold cattle or something. It was shaded, but it sounded like the bands were playing inside a huge tin can. I was tempted to cancel because we knew the fans would not get their money's worth, but Kevin Lyman begged us not to.

The legend goes that we took the stage, played our set, and then, by way of apologizing for the shitty sound, threw our guarantee—5 grand in cash—out to the audience in singles. The truth is that our guarantee was actually 12 grand; we just told the crowd it was 5. And the other truth is that we only threw out $2,500 in bills.

Warped Tour was a blast for us nearly every year we played, but '98 is the year I'll remember the most. Bad Religion and Rancid were on the bill, and we were all friends, so we hung out every day, and we had our own private battles of the bands to see who got the best crowd reactions. At the time we were, in my opinion, three of the best active punk bands, so we set the bar high for each other, and we all turned in some of our best performances. Brian Baker from Bad Religion watched us play every single day. He had his own reserved seat on a speaker on the side of the stage. I'll never forget him telling me, "I can watch you guys every day—it's always a different show." It was an honor.

I mean, Chris from Anti-Flag watched us every day, too, but, you know . . . who cares?

94

Melvin

On the '98 Warped Tour I met a girl who I'll call "Abby Froman" from a ska band I'll call "the Sausage Kings." She had bright red hair, and I had bright blue hair, so when we started dating everyone thought we were the cutest couple they ever did see. I don't remember how we met—the whole summer was a blur of booze, drugs, and barbecues—but I remember the attraction was instant and by the second week of the tour we were an "item."

It was a perfect summer of playing and partying, and with the endorphins of new love (and possibly some residual ecstasy) running through my system my heart ran away with my head. We were driving a rental car along a country road in North Carolina on a day off, on our way to meet up with Abby's family. On an impulse, I pulled over and said, "Will you marry me?"

I don't know why I said it. I have a romantic side that doesn't process reality sometimes. I just thought, "It would be so great if we got engaged right now," and for whatever reason no other part of my brain tried to stop me, or point out that we'd been dating only a couple weeks and maybe I should take a minute to think about this decision. I always wanted to find a nice girl to spend my life with. Why not Abby? And I also wanted to be this amazing person who brought happiness to her life, and it seemed like this would do it.

It worked. She said yes.

We hugged and kissed and got back on the road to her aunt's house. And a little while later my brain woke up and asked, "What the fuck did you just do?"

We went to the New York diamond district, with its mazes of steel doors and bulletproof glass, and I bought her a ring with five kite-shaped diamonds (mounted together to form a star) from a very serious-looking Orthodox Jew. Despite making small steps toward being a more open, communicative person, it was easier for me to have fun and play along rather than explain that I had rushed into this. My mind was so afraid of allowing itself to doubt my decision that it would've been easier for me to steal from one of those diamond merchants than to simply sit down with Abby and talk about how I felt.

Abby moved into my house in L.A. and, predictably, things soon went south. We had barely known each other for a month and a half, and most of that time was spent on the road. If we'd had time to get to know each other without any pressure, maybe things would've developed, but with the cloud of the engagement over me I was hypersensitive to the smallest irritation. If she said anything negative my brain spun it into, "Why is she so negative all the time? I can't be around someone so negative. She is negatively impacting my life." And over time it allowed me to build up the false justification I needed to break up with her.

No matter what she did or said, I internally framed it as a reason why I should get out of the relationship. She opened up to me about issues from her childhood, and instead of being supportive I told myself it was a red flag that might mean trouble down the road. I was acting like a coward.

Actually, a coward would have just started a fight and found an excuse to break up. What I did was worse. When I finally tried to end it she said she didn't want to break up, so I suggested she just move out for a while and we could rebuild things slowly and naturally. It wasn't a bad idea; it might have even worked if I'd had any intention of following through with it. But instead I just stopped calling her.

I couldn't be more ashamed about how I treated her. I heard she wore the ring for a long time after it was over. Aside from a couple of emails I haven't seen or spoken to her since we broke up, but my dad friended her on Facebook a while back. He even went to her house for a Passover Seder. I'm hoping that counts as a small sign of forgiveness.

•   •   •

Lexi knew everyone in the Albuquerque punk scene, but then again it was a pretty small scene. We met in the early days of NOFX, and I saw her every time we traveled through New Mexico, but we were always just friends. Some time after I broke up with Abby, Lexi visited L.A., and I met up with her at a friend's party. Despite Puck from MTV's *The Real World* trying to cockblock me, Lexi and I went home together and a two-year relationship began.

A previous girlfriend had gotten me into E when we were partaking in the early '90s rave scene, and I discovered Klonopins soon after, but Lexi and I became mostly partial to cocaine. She worked as a cocktail waitress at a Hollywood strip club, and she would bring home coke for us. The place closed at 2 a.m., so she usually didn't make it home until 3. Sometimes I'd meet her at the club and we'd do lines before she left work. Then we started buying bindles here and there. As our use became more habitual, it made sense to buy in bulk.

My dealer wasn't the kind of guy you could call at midnight to meet you somewhere and sell you an 8 ball. He had a $400 minimum order, and he didn't work after dark. He didn't look like a drug dealer; he was an average white guy in a polo shirt with a boring haircut. But his stuff was the best in town. He believed in his product, too. I remember him showing off how flaky one of his batches was. I nodded, pretending to be impressed, but I didn't need a sales pitch.

I didn't throw many huge parties—the coke was mostly for me, Lexi, and the occasional friend who would stop by.* And once Mike started doing coke, he and I teamed up to buy a few baseball-sized bricks of it to take on the Warped Tour. It became our "thing." Everyone on the tour knew which bus had the blow. And soon it got to a point where, if we were on someone else's bus, they'd automatically put out a line for us without us asking for it.

---

*I met the guys from Weezer in Japan and partied with them on the Warped Tour. Their bassist at the time, Mikey Welsh, called me to hang out when we were in L.A., and we did blow all night and then did it again a night or two later. Then a month or two later Weezer put out a press release saying their bassist had left the band and checked into a psychiatric hospital. He'd had a mental breakdown, partially due to drug use. I felt a little guilty for contributing to his downfall but wondered if I maybe also gave him the push he needed to get clean. Either way, they found him dead in a Chicago hotel room in 2011. Suspected drug overdose leading to a heart attack. Rest in peace, Mikey.

In retrospect it seems excessive, but at the time we felt like we had some cool little secret, like we were in the Bad Boys Club.

For a guy who had a problem with communication, cocaine seemed like the perfect medicine. For years I would smoke weed and fade into the background of every party, or I would sit with a beer while conversations were carried by others. Cocaine turned me from a listener into a talker. And when people learn you have several hundred dollars' worth of powder in your possession, you make a lot of new friends.

I never saw a downside to the drug until one night in New York City when Mike, Erin, and some friends of ours rented a limo for a night of partying, and I broke into a sweat after inhaling a fat line in the back seat. I was shaking, and someone asked if I was okay. My heart was slamming against my rib cage, and sweat cascaded down my forehead into my eyes.

It was a frightening moment. But not frightening enough to stop me from doing more blow later that night.

It was one thing to do coke on tour or at a party, but most of the time I just did it at my house. I would stay up until 5 a.m. on a Tuesday, passing a mirror back and forth with a friend, thinking we were talking about everything while we were really talking about nothing. We were doing the coke because the coke was there, not because we were particularly enjoying it. As the next year went by, I didn't like the way it made me feel anymore. I would wake up with a hangover, even if I hadn't done any for a few days. And waking up just in time to watch the sun go down stopped being the mark of a good party and started becoming depressing.

I still had everything that had made me so happy a few years prior, but now I felt empty and unfulfilled. I used to enjoy being active and going to the gym; now I couldn't motivate myself to get off the couch unless it was to head to a bar. I grew bitter, and instead of blaming the drugs, I blamed Lexi. It was an ugly, complicated breakup because she had moved into my house and our lives were intertwined on every level—all the way down to our cell phone plans. And after breaking up with her I was still passing the mirror every night and still depressed and hungover all the time. I had a series of flings and one-night stands, which may sound glamorous to some guys, but it was less about sex and more about some sad search for validation.

It wasn't until the birth of my first son years later that drugs faded from my life. In the meantime I had found a substance that finally made me chatty, but it still couldn't get me to truly communicate. Least of all with myself.

95

Mike

The biggest mistake most singers make when they start a side project is that they still sing. No one wants to hear that—they may as well just listen to the original band. So when Joey from Lagwagon and I started discussing the idea of a punk cover band, we knew neither of us should be on vocals.

Spike Slauson worked in the warehouse at Fat Wreck Chords and sang AC/DC covers in a bar band on the side. He was our second choice. The concept of the band was going to be a group of musician friends local to San Francisco (NOFX and Lagwagon both had members spread out in a bunch of different cities) who could play random gigs for fun or as an excuse to party. Marty from Bracket was the first choice, but then I realized he didn't drink. Spike was in.

Me First and the Gimme Gimmes started in 1995 and has so far refused to stop, despite being told via his lawyer that Glenn Frey hated our version of "Desperado" and being booed by thirty-two thousand people during our version of "Stairway to Heaven" at a Pittsburgh Pirates game.

The Gimmes can also be credited/blamed for introducing me to cocaine at age thirty-one.

At an after-show party in Berlin on the Gimmes' first European tour in 1999, everyone was sitting around a big table doing coke and peer-pressuring me about it like they were stars of an *Afterschool Special*. The dealer who had brought the drugs sprinkled some coke in my beer, so I drank that and it gave the beer some extra "zing." I spent the evening doing lines in the bathroom with our guitarist, Chris Shiflett. I was hooked. I mean, not hooked like addicted, hooked like when someone tries Starbucks for the first time. (Incidentally, I have since, on occasion, added cocaine to my lattes, and I strongly feel that Starbucks should redefine "Colombian roast.")

The truth about cocaine is that it's not that great. It's just that doing cocaine is better than not doing it. Like with pills, coke was a tool for me to counterbalance my drunkenness. But of course, the downside is that it turns you into the most interesting person in the world . . . to yourself.

Ecstasy, on the other hand, is a fucking blast. Your whole body feels tingly. It makes everything better. It releases serotonin and dopamine and puts you in a state of euphoria. I wish I had some right now. But I'm trying to take it less often because it takes a few days for your serotonin levels to normalize after you use it, and it supposedly makes holes in your brain. Still: kinda worth it.

Ray Harvey, our booking agent in Australia, handed me my first hit of ecstasy in the spring of 2000 after a festival show NOFX played with Pennywise. The festival was on some remote farm in a town called Torquay, so the only place to party after our set was at the post-show rave. About an hour after I dosed, Fletcher looked at me and said, "Your pupils just got huge!" An electronic group called Sonic Animation was on stage, and they featured two colorful, fuzzy, costumed characters that looked like the unholy love children of Cookie Monster and the Pillsbury Doughboy. The ecstasy turned those fuzzy idiots into the funniest things we'd ever seen. We were all shouting at them, "Blue Character! I love you! Fuck you, Yellow Character! You're no Blue Character! Blue Characterrrrrr!"

We went all night and into the next morning, when we had an hour-and-a-half van ride to the airport. Kent had done so much ecstasy that he ceased making sense. He wouldn't shut up, but he also wouldn't form complete sentences. Or even complete words. "Oh, this one time I was ghrbldblblghghaghabldaghhhh . . ." We shouted at him to shut up, but he went on and on for the full van ride.

In the summer of 2000 we headlined an eight-band bill in front of twelve thousand people at a huge outdoor show in London—our biggest headlining show at that point. We had played festivals before, but this was our show and our crowd. It was a landmark moment for us, and we had everything to prove. So of course I convinced Hefe and Melvin to do ecstasy with me before we played.

None of us had ever performed on ecstasy. It was a way to challenge ourselves and a way to say "fuck you" to The Way Things Are Supposed To Be. We talked a lot on stage, but that wasn't unusual for us. And it got sloppy toward the end (especially when Melvin had to play his accordion), but again, not unusual. Overall we pulled it off, and cocaine and ecstasy became part of my touring arsenal.

Over the years I had to give up Vicodin before shows because it would dry up my vocal cords and fuck up my voice, and I learned that doing coke before a show left me wanting more in the middle of the set. But I found a formula that worked for me: Valium with four vodka drinks before a show to loosen up, two or three vodka drinks during the show to have some fun, a line of coke during the encore to even out the drunkenness, and then some coke or ecstasy after the show to fuel the party for a few more hours.

The concoction served me well and provided consequence-free good times . . . for a while.

96

Smelly

There are three shows in the history of NOFX that will always stand out in my mind. The first is when we played Reno on our first summer tour and three hundred people slammed to our music for the first time. The second was the Bizarre Festival, when Courtney slapped me in the head and we played to our first festival crowd. And the third is when we headlined in London to more than ten thousand people on Three Mills Island. I remember the lights, the sea of heads, the tsunami of crowd noise . . . I didn't even get pissed when Mike admitted to me on stage that he, Hefe, and Melvin were on ecstasy.

As cynical and sarcastic as we are, and as nonchalant about our success as we can be, we were proud of ourselves that night. We're not the kind of band that high-fives or group hugs after our shows, but we all hugged that night when we walked off stage.

◆　◆　◆

A year and a half later we returned to the UK to play a festival called Gig on the Green in Glasgow, Scotland. Early in the day, Rugly, our guitar tech, came into the production office and told me and Kent a story about how one of the local crew guys was drunkenly bugging him and Jay for a free T-shirt. When Rugly told the guy off, he spat on Rugly and took a swing, so Jay clocked the guy in the face. They weren't sure if it was Jay's punch or Rugly's follow-up or the fact that the guy's head smacked into a parked car as he dropped, but he ended up unconscious with a broken jaw.

Later, Jay was unloading some merch from the back of a box truck with Frida (our European merch salesman) when the broken-jaw guy entered the truck with two of his friends: a tall, tough guy who looked like a human tree trunk and a squat, bulky dude who looked like a haggis with eyes. Tree Trunk grabbed Jay and bounced him off the walls of the truck like a rag doll. Broken Jaw came at Jay with a broken bottle, but Frida intercepted him and tangled him up. Jay broke free from Tree Trunk and Frida yelled, "Run for it!" Jay ran down the ramp out of the truck. Haggis tried to follow him but tripped on the ramp and ate shit. Jay escaped backstage and told me the story. I don't know how Frida managed to get out of there.

It turned out that Broken Jaw and his buddies were part of some local biker gang, and soon there were rumors circulating backstage that our band was due for payback. We had to walk a few hundred yards down a dirt road to get from the dressing room to the stage, so we asked some of the cops working security to escort us when it was time for our set. They refused. They knew who was after us, and they didn't want any part of what might be coming our way.

We started our long walk. Jay and Limo were carrying crates with bottles of water and booze for the stage. As we got to the ramp that led to the stage, Broken Jaw and Tree Trunk came out of nowhere, along with ten of their friends. Jay dropped his crate and got into a fighting stance, Limo hockey-checked Tree Trunk to the ground. Broken Jaw grabbed a bottle from Jay's crate and hurled it at Jay. It narrowly missed Jay's head and smashed on the side of a truck next to us. A dozen Scottish hooligans were yelling and grabbing at us; I pulled one of them off Jay as Jay went tumbling to the dirt. Jay scrambled under a semi trailer, disappeared into the crowd, and made his way back to the bus to hide. The rest of us made it to the stage, and security kept the gang dudes away from us.

We played our set while these thugs waited for us in the wings. One of them was brandishing a screwdriver and yelling, "I'm gonna fucking stab you in the fucking heart!" They kept giving us the universal sign for "I'm going to cut your throat." In the middle of the show, the power was cut. The threats and sign language continued. The power came back on. The power went back out. Repeat. We somehow made it through the tensest set of our lives.

There was a police paddy wagon waiting for us by the stage to escort us back to our tour bus. Mike, Erin, Hefe, and Melvin jumped in and bailed, but I refused to leave the crew behind. I remember thinking, "Those fucking pussies," as I handed out pieces of my drum hardware to the crew so we could defend ourselves.

The paddy wagon never returned. The crew and I took turns watching each other's backs and loading the gear into a truck that was backed up to the stage. By the time we were done most of the biker dudes had dispersed. We walked back down that long dirt road, and the remaining bikers threw garbage, bottles, and insults at us for a while, but we made it back to our tour bus unbloodied.

The bikers went from bus to bus looking for us, and our driver met them outside and convinced them we were on some other bus. When they were gone he came on board and said, "All right, I fixed it for you, but we have to get out of here." None of us relaxed until well after we crossed the border into England.

We'll go back to almost any part of the UK on any given day. But 2002 was the last show NOFX will ever play in Scotland.

97

Mike

My friend Jim Cherry called me from a pay phone one night and told me he had a gun to his head.

"The last thing I want to say is thank you so much for everything you've given me. If it wasn't for you, I'd still be laying carpet."

Jim was the original bassist for Strung Out (one of the first bands signed to Fat Wreck Chords), but he was voted out of the band in 1999 and never fully recovered from the heartbreak. To mask his depression he developed a fifty-Vicodin-a-day drug habit. The pills had run out, and that's what brought on his phone call.

I told him not to do it. He was in L.A. and I was in San Francisco. I said, "If you really do appreciate what I've done for you, let me come down and try to help you."

"You'll come down here? You'd do that for me?"

"Of course."

I was on a plane at six o'clock that morning. I picked him up, we ate, and I drove him to the same rehab facility where Smelly had gotten clean. Smelly pulled some strings to get him admitted, and I footed the bill since Jim couldn't afford it on his own.

After three months, Jim emerged clean and sober. He dove back into songwriting for his new band, Zero Down. He was happy and appreciative of all the good things he had in his life.

Less than six months later, Jim died in his sleep of a congenital heart defect unrelated to his drug use. When your time is up, it's up.

I cared about Jim, but I didn't cry when I heard the news, just like I didn't cry when I heard about the numerous suicides, overdoses, fatal car wrecks, or other premature deaths of a number of friends before and after Jim. It's not that I wasn't saddened by their deaths, and it's not that I've never broken down into tears over the loss of someone close to me, but I do wonder if I have a problem with empathy. I care and I love and I feel. But I've got a disconnect inside me that sometimes keeps my heavier emotions at bay.

My only theory about where that disconnect comes from is my BMX bike. When I was ten, someone stole my Huffy from behind my mom's apartment, even though I had chained it to the railing. My dad was pissed, but he replaced it with a brand-new Diamondback. A month later, someone snapped my lock off the bike rack at school and stole the Diamondback, too.

My dad lost his shit. He yelled at me and berated me and blamed me for the bike being stolen, even though I had properly locked it up. I cried, of course. I was just a kid, and I couldn't make sense of why it was all my fault. Even apologizing to my dad didn't seem to make things right.

When I calmed down a few hours later, I made a conscious decision: I was going to stop caring about things. Caring about things only caused me stress and tears. My dad cared about things and it turned him into a dick. If I could teach myself to let go of the natural attachment to material possessions, I could avoid ever feeling so helpless and upset ever again. I became an accidental Buddhist.

That philosophy has stuck with me and has shaped the ethos of NOFX. I don't play fancy guitars. I drive an Econoline van. Stuff isn't important to me. I spend the money I make on good food and good times with friends. I'm not saying I haven't treated myself to a few nice things; I just don't let myself get bummed out when those things break or go missing. It can be a very emotionally healthy way to live.

Except for one drawback. In my quest to stop caring about things, I seem to have allowed myself to care less about people. I built an emotional wall inside myself at age ten, and I didn't have any way of knowing where that wall should begin or end. It has protected me from a lot of pain, but in my attempt to care less I worry that I've taught myself not to care enough.

I think it was right after our first European tour with Dave Casillas when my roommate Brian told me he had just tried to hang himself. I was making potatoes and beans in the kitchen when he walked in with a gash above his eye.

"I tried to hang myself just now."

"What are you talking about?"

"I tried to hang myself with this whip. It broke."

He held up an old bullwhip and explained how he had ended up falling and banging his head against the dresser.

Like my ex-girlfriend Wendie, Brian was a bike messenger. And, like Wendie, he suffered a head injury on the job that had fucked his brain up. He said strange things all the time that had no relation to the current conversation.

"You shouldn't do that," was all I could think to say. At the time I didn't know how to handle a situation like that. Do I call the cops? Do I have him committed? I talked it over with Erin, and we couldn't come up with any decent answers. Thankfully, the next day he seemed normal again, so we naïvely hoped it was just one of his characteristic post-brain-injury non-sequiturs.

The next night, everyone in the house was getting ready to go out to a party when we heard Brian's ex-girlfriend scream.

She had broken up with him and moved out of the house very recently (because he had become unbearably depressed and unhappy since the bike accident), but she was going to join us at the party. Brian was in his room, listening to the first Damned album and drinking Jägermeister, and she went to check on him. When we heard her scream we all went rushing in to discover Brian hanging from a transom with a noose fashioned out of a co-axial cable.

I lifted Brian up and our roadie/roommate Jerry untied the cable to get him down. Brian let out a "Huhhhhh" so we thought he might still be alive, but it was just air escaping his lungs. I checked his pulse and checked for breathing. He was gone.

His face looked like it had been dipped in red paint because all the blood that rushed to his head gushed out of the cut he had made over his eye the previous night. Snot and pus oozed from his nose and mouth, and the smell of his evacuated bowels filled the room. We called 911, and some paramedics arrived about ten minutes later. Relatively speaking it was a fast response time, but take a moment right now to imagine someone you know lying on the floor, recently asphyxiated, in a slowly growing pool of blood, pus, and shit while several girls shriek and cry uncontrollably. Now hold that image for ten straight minutes.

After the coroner took his body away we all went to the party. We weren't being callous; we just couldn't bear to sit around the house because it was suddenly such a heavy and depressing place. When we came back, Jerry's girlfriend and her speed-freak friends rifled through Brian's things and took his leather jacket and records. Erin, Jerry, and I couldn't believe they were doing it, but before his parents moved all his stuff out I did take one of his RKL records.*

We tried to clean the blood out of the carpet before his parents arrived a couple days later, but we didn't do a great job. They just stood there looking at the stain, crying. I didn't tell them about my conversation with Brian in the kitchen. Partially because it wouldn't have helped their grief in any way. Partially because of my own sense of guilt.

While most people would've been emotionally scarred by the experience of cutting their roommate's body down from a noose, the disconnect I developed at age ten allowed me to move on without letting it sink in too deep.

---

*Brian's girlfriend later went on to marry the singer of RKL. I don't know if that counts as a coincidence, but it's a little weird, right?

But maybe that's not a good thing. Two of my housemates had to go into therapy after Brian's death—that's the price you pay for caring. But maybe caring is worth the price.

I don't think about Brian much. I was much closer to Jim, but I can't say that I get misty-eyed when I think of him, either. It wouldn't be until the birth of my daughter that the walls inside me started to crack. And it wouldn't be until the death of another dear friend that they would be completely shattered.

98

Hefe

I was young and naïve when I first got married, so it's no surprise that it ended in divorce within a couple years. After the split I cut loose for a year or two, but I interrupted my rebound with another doomed engagement to a woman named Nicole. We moved in together way too fast, and we got engaged way too faster. Maybe if I had taken my time I would've looked deeper into her eyes.

You don't need a urine sample to determine what type of drugs someone is using—you just need to look into their eyes. Bloodshot? Probably weed. Huge, dilated pupils? Coke or LSD. When someone is on heroin or opiates, all their muscles relax, including the ones in their eyes, so the pupils shrink down to these tiny little pinholes. I had seen those eyes on Smelly and Carlton and so many of the Dog Patch Winos at the Fountain house. Now I was seeing them on my fiancée.

Nicole was sick all the time, but I chalked it up to legitimate illness. She disappeared randomly and didn't show up when she was supposed to, but I chalked it up to flakiness. But when I noticed her eyes it all fell into place. The sickness was sometimes a result of heroin withdrawal and sometimes just an excuse to go to the hospital to score morphine. The disappearances were due to meetings with dealers and fellow users who were grinding up and snorting OxyContin.

And of course she was always short on cash. Every day there was another story, like "I crashed into some guy's car in this parking lot." I'd offer to make out a check, and she'd come up with a flimsy reason for me to write it in her name instead of writing it out to the owner of the phantom dented car.

I caught Nicole in lie after lie and confronted her about her pinned pupils, but she never admitted to anything until one day—with her mother by her side for support—she confessed it all. Her mom kept a cool head and said, "I understand if you don't want to be with my daughter anymore. It's up to you. Just give us the word and we will take her out of here and she'll be out of your life."

I tried to do the honorable thing. We were engaged, after all. I said I'd stick with her and try to help her through her recovery. I upheld my end. She didn't uphold hers. She lied about going to counseling appointments; I'd find out she hadn't been there in weeks. She came home high and made up more excuses about why she needed money. I finally signed her into an inpatient rehab clinic because she couldn't stay clean. When I dropped her off, it was over. I didn't tell her that at the time (she had enough to deal with), but I knew I wouldn't be picking her up when she got out.

◆ ◆ ◆

I first noticed Jen when the robots behind MySpace.com suggested that she and I should connect online due to our mutual cyber friends. When I clicked on her profile, not only did I discover a sexy blonde that I wouldn't mind meeting, but I noticed that her profile photo had some sort of animation and would flip from picture to picture, and I wanted to know how it was done. I kept sending her messages, but she wouldn't give me the time of day. But I was persistent, and after a month or so I got her phone number.

We met up the next time NOFX had a gig in L.A. (she lived in nearby Valencia) and hung out at a bar after the show. I ended up changing my flight home and spending five extra days with her. Then she flew up to Humboldt County, and we spent another week together, and we bounced back and forth like that for a while.

We traded immature jokes, drank beer, and watched the sun come up from my hot tub. We couldn't get enough of each other, but she was reluctant to let me call her my girlfriend. It was hard to blame her: a guy in a band, with an ex-wife and kid, who lived 600 miles away? Not exactly the image of a guy looking to commit.

I showed her I was committed by offering her a promise ring, and she finally agreed to give us a try. Over the next few months we got to know each other more intimately. I watched her connect with my daughter, and I saw what a life together might look like. Before NOFX left for that summer's Warped Tour I took her to Clam Beach, dropped to one knee, and presented an engagement ring. She said yes.

At the end of the summer, Jen flew out to our Warped date in North Carolina to surprise me for my birthday. She decorated our bus with streamers and balloons and brought out 20 pounds of my favorite tri-tip on ice, which Kent grilled to perfection that night. No woman had ever done anything like that for me before. My past relationships always imploded the minute things got serious, but with Jen things kept getting better.

About six weeks later, when Jen was on tour with me in Rio de Janeiro, she started feeling nauseous. We thought it might be from the long flight or a bad piece of meat from dinner, but when the nausea persisted she took a pregnancy test in our hotel room. The instructions were in Portuguese, but the results were clear. We stood on our hotel balcony, looked out at the ocean, and held each other while both silently thinking, "Oh shit . . . "

Jen and I were both petrified at the thought of explaining the situation to her religious parents, especially her dad—a retired police officer trained in the use of firearms. I thought about disappearing into the streets of Rio, changing my name to Roberto, and making my way by selling bananas to tourists. But her folks were overjoyed to find out they were going to be grandparents, and I turned away from the banana-selling life. We had to change our wedding plans and elope in Vegas before she gave birth, but after our son Jaden was born we had a proper ceremony in Malibu with Jay Walker serving as our officiant.

The guys in the band still love to make fun of me for meeting my wife on MySpace, but the truth is our relationship is the most stable and fulfilling I've ever experienced. And when Jaden's teacher tells us that our son has been making fart noises in class, I'm glad I have someone in my life who can explain why I shouldn't be giggling.

99

Mike

I didn't like George W. Bush from the very beginning. I didn't like that he, as governor of Texas, callously oversaw the execution of 152 inmates (several of whom have since been proven innocent or had serious doubts raised about their guilt). I didn't like the way his dad ran the country, I didn't like his party's platform, and I didn't like how he stole the 2000 election. I suspected he would fuck up the country pretty bad if he were in office, and by 2002 my suspicions had been soundly confirmed. The USA PATRIOT Act, stem-cell research restrictions, anti-abortion measures, pulling out of the Kyoto Protocol, tax cuts for the rich that plunged us into a record deficit . . . he was every progressive's worst nightmare. And he hadn't even invaded Iraq yet.

We played several shows in Florida in 2002, and I thought back to the 2000 election and how everything had supposedly hinged on just a few hundred votes. We had played Florida in 2000 as well, performing to at least two thousand people each night. I couldn't help but think that if I had used my public platform to encourage people to vote for Gore, maybe I could've swung the election the other way. Or at least made it harder for Bush to steal it.

Let me be clear: Both political parties in the United States suck, and our democracy is a joke. But while Bush was busy executing people, Gore was focused on climate change. I'm not sure I would have approved of every single thing Gore would've done as president, but I'm sure our world would be a better place if he'd been elected. There is a fucking difference.

So I started a website, PunkVoter.com, with the stated goal of removing George Bush from office in the 2004 election. Everyone at Fat Wreck Chords pulled double duty to get the site up and running. We provided info about voter registration and reported on every terrible decision made by the Bush administration. We weren't Rock the Vote with a polite, nonpartisan agenda of increasing voter turnout. Our agenda was clear: FUCK GEORGE BUSH.

Our political director Scott Goodstein (who would later go on to serve in a prominent role for the Obama campaign) got me invited to an event in New York where celebrities, activists, and representatives from various groups like mine gathered to discuss how John Kerry could defeat Bush. Scott introduced me around and explained PunkVoter to people. I was wearing a powder-blue leisure suit and had dyed, spiked hair, so I stood out among the crowd (by design). I pressed the flesh with people like Russell Simmons and Michael Moore, and I talked to Harold Ickes (Clinton's deputy chief of staff) for almost an hour.

Scott also set up meetings with wealthy record company people in an attempt to get some donations for PunkVoter, but stepping back into that world made the bile rise in my throat. I didn't want to go out and beg for money. I already had money. I wanted to use the tools at our disposal. We had bands, we had stages, we had a record label, we had media access. We were going to do things differently. Instead of financial donations, I called in every favor I could from every notable band I knew and was able to put together a two-volume compilation album titled *Rock Against Bush*.

We did get a handful of very generous monetary donations—Billy from Faith No More and Noodles from the Offspring kicked in 10 grand apiece—but it was way easier to get bands to donate a song than cash. We got songs (some of them previously unreleased) from bands like Green Day, Rancid, the Foo Fighters, Sum 41, Dropkick Murphys, Ministry, Social Distortion, and No Doubt. Almost every single band we approached said yes.*

It was so fucking inspiring to see people rallying around a cause and shedding the apathy that had plagued previous elections. It felt like we were really doing something positive and instigating tangible, grassroots change. And then, of course, came the backlash.

I wrote political lyrics from the beginning (even our first 7-inch had political themes), but the serious songs tended to get overshadowed by our songs about refusing to shower or having sex with obese women. I was flooded with emails and internet comments telling me to stay out of politics. Every day it was "Shut up!" or "What do you know?" or "You're drunk."

But among all the negativity there were tons of supportive emails and touching moments of optimism that kept me going. I got an email from a kid who worked at KFC who had been inspired by our website to register all

---

*Blink-182 and the Vandals said no. Good Charlotte agreed to give us a song, but they refused to do a PunkVoter photo shoot for a magazine because their manager was worried it would hurt their image.

his co-workers to vote. I sat on a plane next to some Republican business-man for a short flight somewhere, and after ninety minutes I had convinced him that George Bush was a bad person. We had a civil, polite conversation, and I spouted facts and figures he wasn't aware of, and by the end of the flight he said he wouldn't be voting for Bush again. Slowly but surely we were reaching people.

We raised over $1 million, which we used to take out partisan magazine ads and put up partisan billboards in the swing state of Ohio. It turned out to be enough to score myself an invite to a campaign brunch in San Fran-cisco, where I got to meet John Kerry himself. I gave him a *Rock Against Bush* CD, and he seemed stoked. He said he would listen to it on the plane en route to his next campaign stop. Maybe he was bullshitting, but I'd like to think he at least listened to Bad Religion's "Let Them Eat War."

After eight years of not doing a single interview, I finally had a reason to talk to the press again. I did something like sixty interviews and media ap-pearances leading up to the election. I still didn't care about advertising our band, but advertising PunkVoter seemed worthwhile. I always thought about that businessman I met on that plane: If I could convince one person on a short flight, I could convince a hell of a lot more people on a radio show.

Through the spring, NOFX toured in support of PunkVoter, playing in front of more than fifty thousand people. We brought Jello Biafra on the road with us to give political speeches before each performance, and we reg-istered thousands of kids to vote every night.* But mass media was able to reach 10 or 20 or 100 times as many people in one small interview segment than we were able to reach in months of touring, so along the way we stopped at every radio station that would have us, and I did my best to pro-mote the cause.

NOFX broke its print silence in the April 2004 issue of *Alternative Press*, which was a big enough deal to earn us the cover. The previous year the Dixie Chicks had insulted George Bush on stage, and their fans went apeshit. The Chicks fanned the fires of the controversy by appearing naked on the cover of *Entertainment Weekly*, so we parodied their photo shoot for

---

*We also brought Scott Ritter (a former Republican, a U.S. Marine, and one of the U.N. Weapons Inspectors who criticized the Bush administration for its rhetoric about WMDs) on the road to speak to the crowds. I remember playing craps with him and Jello Biafra one night in Vegas and him telling us these crazy stories about how he had been fired for speaking out, and how the government was trying to discredit him. Coincidentally, a sealed conviction for a misdemeanor sex crime was somehow made public in 2003. (We also lost money at the tables that night . . . not sure if I can blame Bush for that one, though.)

our *AP* cover as a show of solidarity with them and as a middle finger to the punks who were turning against us. We stripped down and stared into the camera as seriously as possible while strategically covering up our cocks and nipples. I think it resulted in Blockbuster refusing to stock the issue or something. *AP* was probably excited to have our first exclusive interview after so many years, but it should've been obvious that putting a naked, middle-aged punk band on the cover of their magazine really wasn't going to help their sales.

I was nervous every time I had to represent PunkVoter in public because everyone was constantly trying to attack me. I knew if I misspoke or didn't have my facts straight my comments would be dissected and I would be called a liar and the message would get lost. I was weighed down by more responsibility for PunkVoter than I ever was for NOFX.

Howard Stern was pretty cool during my interview on his show, even though I wasn't at my most articulate due to the sun not being up yet. He had Michael Graves (the guy who sang for the Misfits in the late '90s) call in to represent the punk rock Republican viewpoint, and I was worried that I wasn't in any condition to effectively debate, but Howard tore him a new asshole without needing much of my help.

Dennis Miller, however, was still proudly toeing the Republican Party line. I was invited to be on his short-lived talk show along with Amy Goodman from *Democracy Now!* and Eric Schlosser, the author of *Fast Food Nation*. I couldn't sleep for a week beforehand. I had done very little TV in the past, and I had never publicly debated someone as smart (and smug) as Dennis Miller before.

Miller's people gave me a list of fifteen points Dennis wanted to talk about, so I researched each topic exhaustively and hammered out some talking points in my head and tried to anticipate Dennis's counterpoints so I could offer some counter-counterpoints. I was anxious, but I was ready.

Dennis didn't ask me about one fucking thing on the list. Amy Goodman went out first, and she's a fucking genius, so she destroyed Dennis. Eric Schlosser went out and destroyed him a second time. I went on third, and the first thing Dennis said was, "I find Bush to be more of a punk than Kerry." He made the case that Bush was more "real" than Kerry and then asked, "Why would you wanna Punk Against Bush when he's your peeps?" I was thrown. On any normal day, with a couple drinks and some diazepam in me, I would've had a sarcastic, witty retort locked and loaded. But this wasn't on the list! I froze and said something about John Kerry being a snowboarder and being in a band, which made him kind of punk rock.

In my mind, I thought, "This is how it's going to be. He just got his ass kicked twice on the air, and he's going to take it out on me now."

Dennis kept changing the subject, and I never really got to say the things I wanted to, and it was over before I knew it. I returned to the green room and met up with Vanessa, the PR person for Fat Wreck Chords, who was by my side at most of these interviews and appearances. She reassured me that I had done well and said that one of Dennis's producers was next to her backstage and that he was actually backing me over Dennis when I was speaking. I watched the episode later and gave myself a B-. I hung tough, but I could've done better.

When NOFX was booked on *Late Night with Conan O'Brien* we were only going to play music, and I didn't have to sweat about a debate. But I wanted to be sure we could make a political statement with our performance, even if I wasn't going to be joking about Abu Ghraib on Conan's couch.

We would be playing the song "Franco Un-American" from our new album, *The War on Errorism*. The song isn't specifically about Bush, but in the course of performing it live on the PunkVoter tour, I had changed the lyrics of the bridge to "We all know George Bush is an imbecile / He loves Dick but he hates homosexuals." It was an obvious play on the first name of Vice President Dick Cheney, but I thought some uptight network standards and practices people might not appreciate my clever turn of phrase. I made sure to specifically ask the censors about it and readily offered to change the words because I'd rather sing a different line than be bleeped. But they insisted the lyrics were acceptable.

The motherbleepers bleeped me. And not only that, they bleeped the word "from" in the line "I eat no breath mints 'cause they're from dehooved horses." That one remains a mystery.

We all wore anti-Bush shirts, and we had a flag with a picture of Bush's face painted like a clown draped over our keyboard. And the second line of our bridge, "We're sick and tired of the embarrassment / The whole world wants us to get a better president," was delivered intact, so we made as broad a statement as we possibly could with our two and a half minutes of air time. After we finished, Conan shook our hands and went to commercial, joking to the camera, "NOFX, playing next week at the Republican National Convention!"

Networks never let late-night shows take a defined political stance because they'll alienate their viewers with different beliefs, so I think we caused a bit of turmoil behind the scenes. The show's booker, Debbie Wunder, was a friend of ours, and months later she told us there was a joke going around the show's offices about bands that wouldn't be invited back on the show. People would say, "Oh yeah, we'll have them back right after NOFX plays here again."

On Election Night I had a party at my house with a bunch of friends and all the people from Fat who had sacrificed so much to make PunkVoter successful.* I had two shot glasses full of pills ready for distribution, depending on which way the results went: Valium in case of a loss, ecstasy in case of a victory. When they called Ohio for Bush, a few people took the Valium, but most of us just took the ecstasy anyway. We hugged and congratulated each other for all our hard work. We were teary-eyed, not so much because we were sad about losing, but because we were proud of ourselves for putting so much effort into something we believed in. It was a sad night, but it was also kind of nice.

But the next day was definitely depressing. Not only had the reality of another term of Bush sunk in, but all of PunkVoter's enemies took to the internet and piled on the schadenfreude. People couldn't wait to tell me how I'd wasted my time and didn't change a fucking thing and that I should've kept my big Jew nose out of politics. At subsequent Warped Tours kids would say as much to me in person. And then, to add injury to the insults, I got hit with a $300,000 tax bill on the money we raised. We spent every penny of the million we had raised on putting out ads and sustaining the campaign, but because we were a partisan organization supporting a specific candidate we weren't tax exempt the way Rock the Vote and other nonpartisan nonprofits are. Even the IRS was giving us shit.

I have zero regrets. As hectic and stressful as it was, that year and a half was probably my most important contribution to society and my most meaningful civil service. Sure, Bush stayed in office. But we turned shitloads of people on to politics who may have remained apathetic for the rest of their lives. And we registered tens of thousands of people to vote. The youth vote in 2004 was up by about 4.3 million votes from 2000, and John Kerry won the youth vote by 10 percent over Bush (compared to Gore winning the youth vote by only 2 percent). And in 2006, when the Democrats finally took back the House and the Senate, the youth vote was even higher. PunkVoter can't take credit for all of that, of course, but we were certainly a spoke in the wheel. We worked hard and combined our efforts with those who were like-minded, and together we pushed for the changes we wanted to see and ultimately made things better.

That's kind of the whole point of democracy, right?

---

*I invited Jello Biafra, but he didn't show. After the party I checked my phone and had four missed calls and a message from him asking, "What's your address? I'm on Glover, where's your house?" So I'm pretty sure Jello Biafra spent Election Night 2004 just circling my block.

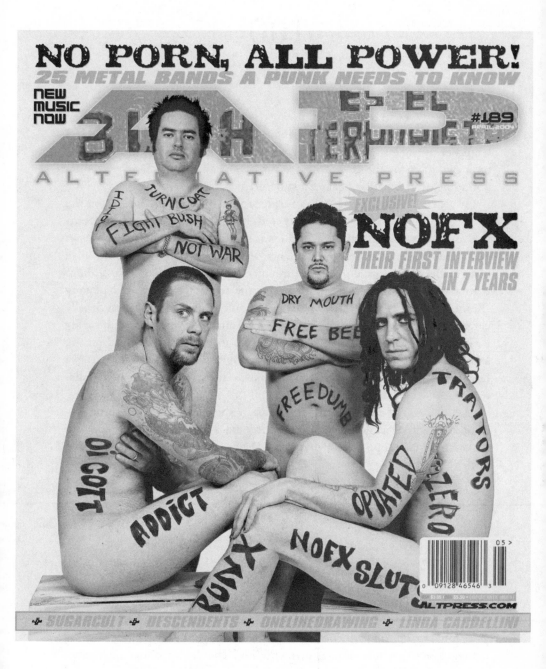

100

Melvin

We played Conan on a day off during the same Warped Tour when Mike and I were flush with cocaine baseballs. I stayed sober for two days so I would be at my best for the taping, but I had been using so heavily that it took two days for the comedown to hit me. I had a nasty hangover and a pounding headache that peaked just before we performed.

It was freezing in the studio in order to balance out the heat from the lights, so I was shaking because I was cold, I was shaking because I was coming down off weeks of partying, and I was shaking because I was nervous as hell about playing our first performance on network TV. I was on the edge of an anxiety attack when Conan announced us. I asked Mike for a Valium before we went on, but it didn't have time to kick in. I started playing "Franco Un-American" way too fast, but I didn't realize it, so when Smelly came in I thought he was dragging the tempo and I felt like we were blowing it. I tried to focus my uncontrollable nerves into jumping around on the small risers that functioned as a stage, but every time I landed there was a huge BANG, as if I weighed a thousand pounds. You can hear it—distinctly—on the video.

I didn't notice the cameras or Conan or the audience or anything else until it was all over. I'd love to get another crack at playing on his show to make up for our sloppy performance, but from what I hear we're not invited back.

101

Mike

I was never all that driven to have a kid, but Duncan from Snuff told me it was a kind of love I could never otherwise understand. He said you can love your family, you can love your wife, you can love your friends, but nothing comes close to the love of your own children. That love sounded like something I wouldn't want to miss, and when I finally experienced it I discovered that Duncan was telling the absolute truth.

Of course he neglected to mention that a deep, profound love was only part of the equation. There's also a deep, profound panic when a dog bites your child's skull. And a deep, profound disgust when you first have to scoop the shit out of her vagina during a diaper change. And he definitely didn't mention the deep, profound amount of vomiting. On your clothes. On your bed. Directly into your spouse's mouth. But I still have to say it's worth it.

My daughter Darla was born in 2004 and was named after my favorite character from *The Little Rascals*. When we first brought her home she would only sleep on my chest, which is an indescribable experience. As she's grown I've had countless unforgettable moments of joy that I couldn't have otherwise achieved. All those drunken nights on tour take a back seat to the smile on Darla's face when—after four mutually frustrating days of me trying to teach her—she finally learned how to ride a bike.

Growing up with an absentee dad made me very conscious of the value of quality time. Even though I'm away on tour for a good chunk of the year, I call and video chat from the road whenever possible. And when I'm home it's "Daddy Darla Time." I never just plop her in front of the TV; we do shit together. We go on hikes, and she fearlessly picks up banana slugs and salamanders. I never thought I'd make a sober trip to Las Vegas, but one day there I was: trying to fit fifteen stuffed animals she won at the midway games in Circus Circus into the overhead compartment on our flight home.

People who work normal jobs probably spend a few hours with their kid each night before bedtime, but when I'm not touring I'm around my daughter for full days for long stretches of time. So if you do the math I probably come out ahead on quality time. And I'm more fun than normal parents. I've got blue hair and tattoos. Darla's friends ask me why I wear nail polish and I tell them, "Because I'm a rock star and I do whatever I want!" When Darla's school had a career day, the kids didn't care much about the dad who worked in software, or the dad who designed medical supplies. But the kids ate it up when I showed up with a guitar and played a song I had written for them called "I Don't Wanna Go to School." There's a photo from that day of Darla looking up at me as I'm playing, and the look of pride in her eyes absolutely kills me every time I see it.

She has brought balance to my life. Part of the reason Erin and I wanted to have a kid in the first place was because we realized we had maybe been taking our drinking and drug use a bit too far. Coke wasn't just something I did on tour anymore, or something we saved for big holiday parties; we were doing it on random nights at home, or after having dinner with friends.

When I'm around Darla, I don't want to be wasted. I don't even want to be hungover. I want to be present. I want to experience the moment and create all the memories I possibly can. So as much as I may party on the road

or with friends, being around Darla forces me to sober up and fly straight for as much time as I'm with her.

But in the beginning I hadn't exactly figured that part out yet.

Erin was sober the whole time she was pregnant and for at least a year afterwards, and I was sober whenever I was around her because it didn't make sense for me to get fucked up if she wasn't going to party with me. But I got bored. I like doing drugs. And Erin developed some health problems and had some surgeries and started taking painkillers, so during Darla's early years our communication stopped and our drug use and arguing increased.

Our problems began long before Darla, back when Fat Wreck Chords started becoming successful. Money can turn you into a dick. You expect things to go your way, and when they don't you can throw money at them until they do. The more money we had, the shorter our patience became. And we weren't just living together, we were working together every day, so we clashed over the business as well as the personal. Eventually we started driving to work in separate cars.

Money and work and drug use were just the tip of the iceberg. It became obvious to everyone around us that our marriage was in trouble, but we had been together for so long we couldn't imagine being apart. Darla was the perfect distraction to keep us from dealing with the real issues that were developing. As was the phone call telling me my father had died.

◆ ◆ ◆

Epitaph owed me $360,000 between my performance advance and mechanical advance for our *So Long and Thanks for All the Shoes* album. I asked them to combine both advances into one check so I could show it to my dad.

Why the hell would I do that? I thought I didn't care whether my father was proud of me, but here I was going out of my way to prove something to him. I don't know why it mattered. Showing him the check was supposed to be me giving him the finger. But maybe I was just a son looking for his dad's approval.

He was impressed by the check. He thought it was fake at first. After he saw me becoming financially successful he opened up a little. Mostly, though, we would just talk about things like his investments in the stock market, and he would offer business-related advice. We kept in touch over the years, and we never had any sort of falling out, but we were never close. And it wasn't that he didn't try, it was that the act of him trying was always painfully awkward and unnatural. Once I went to visit him when he was living in Palm Springs, and he showed up at the airport with a NOFX shirt,

spiked bracelets, and dyed orange hair. He brought a copy of the local newspaper, which, per his request, had run a small story on one of the back pages
about Fat Mike from NOFX coming to Palm Springs for a visit. I could tell
he cared, but I didn't know how to react to a weird gesture like that, and he
didn't know how to communicate in any other way.

Once or twice a year I flew down to meet him for a round of golf in Palm
Springs, but once I invited him to come up to play golf at Pebble Beach. He
was well aware of the fact that there's an eight-month wait to get a tee time
there: it's a golfing mecca—I thought it would be a treat for both of us. He
just said, "Oh, no thanks," without even thinking about it. That hurt like
crazy. He didn't mind me coming to visit, but, just like when I was a kid, he
had no real interest in going out of his way to spend time with me. The gap
between us never closed.

For years, my dad had stress-related asthma attacks. He would go to the
hospital and they'd medicate him and the attacks would cease for a while,
then they'd start up again and he'd repeat the cycle. In all that time, they
never noticed he also had diabetes. The symptom that finally gave it away
was dementia. He would tell a funny story and then tell the same exact story
again ten minutes later. And then again ten minutes later. And then again
ten minutes later. By the time the doctors figured it out, there was nothing
they could do.

He got worse as the years passed, and his friends slowly stopped hanging
out with him because his repetitiveness and forgetfulness became uncomfortable. One day his wife called me and said, "He's really sick, you should
come down." I flew to his house, where he had been hooked up to machines
and was struggling to survive. His memory was nearly gone, but he remembered I was his son. The doctors said he only had a few months left, so I
thanked him for being my dad and told him I loved him.

He said, "I don't know if I was that good of a father."

I told him, "You were fine."

I didn't want to let him off the hook completely, but I didn't want to
burden him with how resentful I was toward him either. I was raised not to
lie. But he deserved to go peacefully.

He didn't go peacefully. He survived for a long while after that, and every week I would get a call. He would have no memory of our previous
conversation, and he would say the same thing:

"I don't know if I was that good of a father."

And I had to repeat my farewells and my stock response, "You were
fine."

It always wrecked me. I cried and got angry every time. I eventually told
his wife to stop calling me. It was too depressing to keep living out the final

conversation with my dad over and over again. It wasn't doing either of us any good. She persisted, but I told her, "He wasn't a good father to me. He wouldn't have told you this, but he barely ever wanted to see me. I'm not going to see him just because he's sick."

She finally said, "I understand."

She called me a few months later to tell me my dad had fallen in the shower and hurt himself. She called a few days after that to let me know he had died.

NOFX was in the middle of the 2006 Warped Tour at the time, so flying home for the funeral would have meant a series of canceled shows. Most of my dad's friends were from out of town, so we decided to hold off on the funeral for a few weeks to allow everyone to make travel arrangements. Warped Tour was swinging through Fresno in July. If I had to miss playing one city for the funeral, I was at least happy to have an excuse to skip that one.

I drank and did coke all night before the funeral. Our tour bus dropped me off in front of the synagogue, and I stumbled out wearing a disheveled suit after maybe an hour's sleep. My half-sister, Jennifer, greeted me, probably wondering why I looked like a drunker version of John Belushi. She had grown up similarly distant from our father, but she and I had kept in touch over the years. We watched all of our dad's friends get up and give speeches about how great a guy he was, how generous he was, how good of a friend he was, and we were both in tears. Our dad's friends thought we were crying because we missed our father. The truth is we were crying because we never knew the guy they were all talking about.

I didn't want to speak at the funeral. Erin had suggested I prepare something because I had no idea how the day was going to go. I planned to say that I loved my dad and I wish I knew him better, but that was all I could think of that would be honest and kind. At the end of the service his wife implored me to say something, but I resisted at first. The rabbi presiding over the funeral had said in his speech, "Paul was a father and a great golfer," so when I finally gave in to my dad's wife's request to speak, I got up and said, "First of all, my dad was a shitty golfer." It got a mild laugh from his friends. I followed it up as planned: "I loved my dad. I wish I knew him better." And I returned to my seat.

Darla was barely two years old when my father died. I brought her out to Palm Springs to meet him once, but she has no memory of him now, and the dementia likely erased any memory he had of her.

At the end of it all, I didn't know my dad any better than Darla did.

102

Smelly

Mike kept his head relatively (relatively . . .) clear during the PunkVoter days because he knew his politics were under the microscope, and he wanted to stay sharp. And during Erin's pregnancy and Darla's early years he held it together pretty well.

The problem may have been that he was holding it together so much at home that he needed a release, so he partied to a self-abusive extent when we started touring again.

Throughout our cross-country tour with the Loved Ones in early 2006, Mike was always saying, "There's no more Darby Crash, there's no more Sid Vicious." He somehow felt obligated to take up the banner of the Punk Rock Wastoid and take his drinking and drug use to the next level. I don't know if he was using that as an excuse for his declining behavior, or if he was trying to design a new image for himself, but he wasn't the Fun Party Drunk anymore—he was becoming a wreck.

I've always known that Mike was unpredictable. Before every show, ever since that very first performance at the Cathay, part of me wonders, "Okay, what are we going to get tonight?" because some nights Mike is a diamond and some nights he's a lump of coal. Depending on his mood and his substance intake, he may blabber on and angrily alienate the crowd and kill the flow, or he may land every joke and nail every song and leave everyone wanting more.

On that Loved Ones tour, it was coal almost every night. He screwed up the songs, ran off to the side of the stage to talk to friends in the middle of the set, and wasn't funny. Part of being punk is that you're not supposed to give a shit. Well, I give a shit. I want to be known as a tight, funny, good band, not a drunk, sloppy, careless band. I felt like Mike was trying to sabotage the shows on purpose. He was trying to make some sort of "There's no more G.G. Allin" point, but really he was just undoing everything we had worked so hard to accomplish.

And do you know why there's no more Darby Crash, Sid Vicious, or G.G. Allin, by the way? Because all those motherfuckers are dead, that's why.

The bullshit built up as the tour went on, and the inevitable reckoning came in Washington, DC. During the show, Mike put out two lines of coke on his amp, and he and Melvin snorted them right in front of me.

Up to that point, I had tolerated their drug use with relatively little complaining, but snorting a line of coke right on stage felt like a slap in the face. It was stupid rock-star ego bullshit: "Look at me! I'm doing coke!" And for all of our cheeky lyrics and "adult" sensibility, there is a fine line of responsibility that is definitely crossed when you're doing cocaine in front of a mostly young, impressionable crowd.* But mainly I felt completely disrespected. I had been respecting their party space for over a decade, and they couldn't wait two more songs and take their drugs out of my sight?

I walked out of the club to go to our hotel the second our set was over. I was ready to explode. My anger had been building not only since the beginning of that tour but since August of 1992. Ever since I got out of rehab I had worked hard to manage my emotions and keep myself in check, and I was being tested every night we played. Those guys couldn't give a fuck about my sobriety or what I had to go through every night on tour just to keep myself from punching the walls. After more than twenty years together, I was ready to quit NOFX. Fuck Mike. Fuck Melvin. Fuck all of it. I was a ball of volcanic rage.

As I walked out of the club, a fan saw me and said, "You fucking sucked."

It wasn't a friendly jab. He honestly felt ripped off, and he was completely justified in his opinion. But he picked the wrong moment to express it.

"What'd you say, motherfucker?" I didn't want to go to the hotel anymore, I wanted to beat this kid into the ground. He was going to bear the brunt of all my hostility, and it was going to be biblical.

"You guys fucking sucked. I'm pissed. Fuck you guys."

"I'm fucking pissed, too, dude! You want me to show you how pissed I am?"

I got within 10 feet of the kid when my friend Shawn jumped between us and held me back. Thank god he did, because attacking that kid would've been the worst mistake ever. Who could blame him for calling us out on our shitty show? Why was I willing to punch a guy I totally agreed with?

---

*Yeah, maybe I sound like a grown-up talking about "protecting the children," but the way I see it, if we feel enough of a responsibility to tell people how to vote we should probably feel just as much of a responsibility to be real with them about drug abuse. And I've seen enough friends die to know just how fucking impressionable kids can be. Mike always contends that drugs are fine in moderation as long as you don't stray into addiction, but I can tell you firsthand that addiction is not a choice.

My brain snapped back into reasonable mode, and I continued down the road to our hotel. I stewed about it all night. I called friends for advice and had arguments with Mike and Melvin in my head. On a piece of Holiday Inn stationery, I wrote a letter mainly directed at Mike, recounting the history of our friendship. We used to sit and talk for hours. We had things in common. But everything had changed. I felt like we had grown so far apart that mutual respect was no longer a priority for him, and that fucking hurt. I wrote that I loved Mike and Melvin, and that I loved the band, but if they couldn't offer me the same respect I had been affording them, then the band would be jeopardizing my sobriety and I couldn't stay.

When I got on the bus the next day, I didn't talk to anyone. I was still fuming, so I just rode from DC to Atlantic City in my bunk, wondering if this tour would turn out to be my last. The friends I called from my hotel room had advised me not to make any decisions while I was still upset.

In Atlantic City, I called a band meeting and read everyone my letter. Mike apologized right away. Then he included the word "but . . . " and I stopped him.

"I don't wanna hear it. I've been hearing excuses for a long time." He clammed up.

I actually got more of a pushback from Melvin, who said something like, "Dude, you were just looking to get mad at us. You were trying to see what we were doing."

"You're on the stage that I'm on! I'm not trying to see what you're doing, you're doing coke right in front of me!"

They both quickly realized how far I must have been pushed to sit and write a letter and insist on my first-ever band meeting after all that time. I handed Mike the letter, and he and Melvin both apologized again. We ended the meeting amicably and met up with a photographer for a scheduled shoot. The pictures taken that day tell the whole story. The other guys are all together, posing and mugging for the camera; I'm off to the side, buried inside my own head.

We didn't talk much that night or the next day. We played a show in New York City and barely made eye contact on stage, in the dressing room, or on the bus. I knew Mike and Mel were sorry, but I was still pissed and hurt. The meeting had made things awkward, so I wasn't sure if the guys were avoiding me because they were upset or if they were just giving me space to cool down, but we were all on edge.

Then came Worcester, Massachusetts.

Mike was drinking with some local punk kids at a bar across from the club before the show, and he downed his usual Valiums backstage. When we got on stage he was hammered, and by the middle of the set he had lost all coordination. We were playing "The Brews," one of our easier tunes, and instead of playing B, E, F#, he belly-flopped off the front of the stage into the barricade.

Fifteen years earlier we had kicked Dave Casillas out of the band for getting too drunk and falling off stages. And he was just the guitar player, not the guy who was supposed to be steering the whole ship.

The next day we held an intervention, and I wasn't the one who organized it. We had all watched Mike get worse over the course of the tour. We were not only concerned for his well-being but also generally embarrassed to be around him. The band was sick of playing sloppy, awful shows, and the crew was sick of mopping Mike off the floor at the end of the night.

Unlike the meeting a few days earlier, Mike deflected the complaints this time. "There's no more G.G., there's no more Darby Crash—punk is about excess!" We stood firm, and I told him he wasn't G.G. Allin. He needed to be himself. Ever the Great Rationalizer, he offered a compromise. He wouldn't stop drinking, but he would stop taking Valium. That was the pact we made in order to move forward.

He broke that pact at the next night's show. He adjusted his promise, saying he would still take Valium, but only a half instead of two wholes. It wasn't long before that pact was broken, too. In Mike's defense, the shows did improve after that meeting. He was still mixing too much booze with his pills, but Worcester was thankfully an isolated incident.

That summer we brought two buses on the Warped Tour: one for me and one for Mike. I don't know what he did on his bus all summer; I was just happy to be removed from it. And around the same time we established a "party" room and a "sober" room in every backstage area so I could hang out and be quiet and boring and Mike could do drugs and get weird (and also be boring).

Mike has never fucked up as bad as he did on that tour, but I still think he has some issues with substance abuse that need to be fully resolved and that may cause serious problems for him down the line. We have held several other similar semi-interventions for him since then. That's probably a sign.

* * *

When Mike's mom was dying, he called me up. I went down to his mom's house in Laguna Beach to keep him company while he awaited the inevitable. For several days I did my best to distract him with idle chat while his mom was upstairs, approaching death. I felt for the guy. He wasn't afraid to let me see him cry from time to time, and I wasn't afraid to comfort him like a brother.

Regardless of what happened in Worcester and DC, there's a deeper bond between all of us as band mates that allows us to bury our differences in the past. I may not agree with every choice Mike makes, but I'll love the guy until the end. Whatever happens in the moment is never greater than the sum of all that has happened to us since we met. We've been through too much together.

103

Hefe

Mike still doesn't believe me when I tell him he pulled his pants down, bent over, and slapped his ass in front of the Worcester crowd. But he did. We played badly on that whole tour, but in Worcester I was watching people walk out of the show. Everything after the first four songs was a total embarrassment to all of us.

Smelly was pacing in the dressing room afterwards, ready to kill.

"I feel like I want to fucking punch him!"

I tried to calm him down. "Dude, just go to your room. I know you're pissed, and you have every right to be . . . "

I told the crew to block the door and keep Mike out. I knew if the two of them saw each other it would go nuclear. Smelly had steam shooting out of his ears, and Mike had coke and booze shooting through his blood vessels. There was no way it was going to be a calm discussion from either end.

"I'm fucking ready to quit the band."

He wasn't kidding. After Smelly stormed out, we all wondered what the morning would bring. The crew tried to talk to Mike, but he was drunk, belligerent, and unapologetic. We honestly weren't sure if NOFX had just played its last show.

Smelly had warned Mike that he was becoming an addict years earlier, before cocaine was even in the picture. We were in Europe with the Vandals, and every night Mike would pop his Valium and drink his Lambrusco just to summon the energy to get on stage. Mike even said out loud that he couldn't play sober anymore and that he needed booze and pills just to have fun. Smelly explained patiently that wine and pills would eventually lead to something worse. He wasn't suggesting Mike would end up as a heroin addict, but he had enough experience with addiction to recognize the symptoms. Mike thought Smelly was overreacting. I had spent enough time with addicts to know that he wasn't.

After the brief "intervention" brought on by the Worcester show, Mike and Smelly settled their differences and found a way to be respectful of each other's space, but Mike still can't perform sober. I'm not saying it never happens. I've seen him go for a day or two here and there. But then we all hear about it: "Look, I just did this show sober. Hey, I'm sober today everybody. See? Sober!" If you have to broadcast it, it means you're trying to prove you don't have a problem.

And if you're constantly trying to prove you don't have a problem, you have a problem.

104

Mike

Brian Baker was part of the band that coined the phrase "straight edge" as shorthand for a person who doesn't drink or do drugs. These days he likes to mention that fact right before snorting a line of coke (and it's funny every single time!). When Bad Religion and NOFX were paired on various Warped Tours, Brian was always my pill/booze/coke/party buddy. If I'm on tour somewhere and awake in the small hours of the night whacked out of my skull, I will often drunk-dial Brian because chances are he will be equally awake and skull-whacked.

So when Brian Baker came to me after a 2006 show in Washington, DC, and said, "Dude, take it down a notch," I knew I had crossed a line.

I dialed back my drinking and drug use significantly after Darla was born, but whenever I was on the road I felt like I was off the leash, so I drank and drugged harder to make up for my sobriety at home. I was probably also indulging heavily to deal with the feelings stirred up by my father's illness, not to mention the slow dissolution of my marriage, about which I was still in denial. My drinking/drug routine on tour works nine times out of ten, but it's still a very delicate chemistry experiment, prone to failure when things like a lack of dinner allow more booze into the system or when a sprained ankle encourages me to take an extra pill or two. I was bound to get the math wrong sooner or later.

I was mixing 10 to 20 milligrams of Valium with four or five martinis every night on our 2006 U.S. tour, and I stopped eating dinner before shows. Somewhere around the middle of the set at our Washington, DC, show I decided it would be a good idea to smash one of my martini glasses over my head. And I thought it would be an even better idea to spread out several lines of coke on my amplifier and snort them with Melvin in front of the crowd, instead of doing it backstage.

Smelly didn't like that last idea. He was furious, and he had every right to be. He prized his sobriety and had made every effort to maintain it while the rest of us partied around him. He had learned by that point to avoid our pre-show warm-ups and our after-show parties, but here I was shoving it in his face on stage where he couldn't escape. After twenty-two years as a band, we were about to have our first real argument.

When I walked off stage he said, "Stay the fuck away from me" and disappeared. I didn't see him for the next three days, other than when we were on stage together.

The booze and pills were keeping me oblivious to everything anyway. When we hit Worcester three days after DC, I rolled out of my bus bunk in my pajamas and didn't bother changing before walking to a nearby bar. I got super loaded and went straight from the bar to our show, where I played horribly in between my endless, unfunny babbling. Toward the end of the set, I stumbled off the front of the stage and fell into the barricade, breaking the fall with my face and scarring my arm. The crowd thought it was funny, but it was actually pretty fucked up and scary.

The crew pulled me back on stage and we tried to plow through two more songs, but—strangely enough—they didn't go any better than the previous ones. Melvin closed the show with his accordion solo from our song "Theme From a NOFX Album," but I wouldn't leave the stage. Jay and the crew had to tackle me and drag me off, and I didn't go quietly. I was grabbing wires and monitors and kicking and squirming the whole way.

This was not rock bottom for me. But later that night, I was on the receiving end of my first intervention.

Some people, when they are intervened upon, try to fight their way out of it or shift the blame to others or take offense. I already knew I had been an asshole, so I immediately apologized and told Smelly he was right to be pissed at me. No one was demanding I go to rehab or quit cold turkey, they just wanted me to manage myself more responsibly, and it seemed like a reasonable request. I agreed to adjust the chemistry experiment by cutting my pre-show Valium dosage in half, balancing my food/booze intake, and watering down my drinks a bit. We also instituted a punishment/reward system: if I screwed up too much on stage, Jay would confiscate my drink. If I played three songs without a mistake, I could have it back. And we also decided that we would, from that point on, have a sober dressing room and a separate party dressing room backstage, so Smelly could relax and we could party and there wouldn't be any stress or guilt on either side.

It worked well and has kept our band, more or less, argument-free since then. There have been other nights when I've gone too far, and there have been other interventions. But hey: I'm no quitter.

105

Hefe

My mom was always a fighter. She kept her diabetes at bay for decades, but by the time she was in her 70s she went blind in one eye and had to go in for dialysis treatments three times a week. When I married Jen the doctors told me our first Christmas together would be my mom's last, so Jen agreed to celebrate Christmas in Sacramento with my family. We celebrated my mom's last Christmas for at least six or seven more Christmases. Like I said: she was a fighter.

My mom faced countless challenges over the years, but she ultimately led a happy, productive life. She raised a loving family and left a legacy in the form of the health clinic she founded. She got to see me achieve my dream of playing music for a living, and she got to meet her grandson before she passed. She liked to say my success was "a gem in her crown." I knew she was proud of me, and she knew I loved her. I was sad when she died, but at least I was able to make peace with it when it happened.

I wasn't, however, prepared for my brother to go before her.

One day I was watching TV, and some doctor from Berkeley was talking about Gulf War Syndrome and how some scientists had discovered a dangerous reaction between a standard anti-nerve-gas pill issued to American soldiers and DEET, the main chemical in most bug sprays. My older brother, Henry, was an army sergeant who had served in both Gulf Wars, so I called him to ask if he had taken any anti-nerve-gas pills during his deployment. He said he had. I asked him if he used mosquito spray while he was serving. Of course he had. And he had also signed some waiver that prevented him from being able to sue the government if the anti-nerve-gas pill had any ugly side effects.

I didn't hear much more about Gulf War Syndrome on TV after that, but it wasn't long before some of the guys in Henry's squad started getting sick and dying. The government blamed Saddam Hussein and insisted he had used chemical agents to poison our troops. They also insisted that the troops avoid civilian doctors and only share their medical concerns with the VA hospital.

I had just landed in Germany to begin a European tour when Jen called to tell me my brother had been diagnosed with oral cancer. He had surgery to remove part of his tongue, and we thought he was in the clear, but eight or nine months later the cancer came back with a vengeance and snaked its way under his jaw and back into his neck. The doctors tried to help, but there was nothing else they could do. My brother began the slow process of withering away.

It's impossible to say for sure whether Henry's cancer had anything to do with the pills or the DEET or something else the army or Saddam put in the air or just too much junk food. But something brought my brother down hard, and it was the ugliest and most evil thing I'd ever seen.

Henry went from a chiseled, military build to a fragile waif in no time. Within a few months of his diagnosis he was in constant, excruciating pain and confined to a wheelchair. His jaw and neck were so swollen he could barely talk, and he was sensitive to loud noises. Being the patriot he was, the Fourth of July was his favorite holiday, so the family got together for a party at his house, and we wheeled him outside when it was time for the fireworks. He couldn't take the noise for long, though. We wheeled him back into his bedroom, knowing they were the last fireworks he'd ever see.

Henry's last days were spent in the hospital, with a steady flow of morphine to ease his pain. When I went to see him he was knocked out, but when he heard my voice he picked up his head and opened his eyes. The nurses told me he hadn't moved like that since he was admitted. We had to whisper in his ear for him to hear us. He couldn't speak, but he could communicate a little by nodding. I told him I was there for him along with everyone else in our family. He was about to leave behind four children. I told him not to worry—we'd all be watching over them. He nodded in understanding.

I got the call a few days later. Jen came home and found me sitting by our piano, crying.

What made it all the more tragic was that my mom had to experience the loss of her son less than one year before her own death. If life were fair, the sequence would've at least been reversed. But then again, if life were fair my mom and my brother would still be here.

106

Mike

I was giving my mom and her seventy-year-old friend a tour of my house one day while a repairman worked on my TV. Somehow he pushed a button that turned on the DVD player, which happened to contain a volume from my vast library of kinky porn. On the TV screen a girl was tied to the ceiling while another girl whipped the shit out of her. My mom stood there and watched. Considering that it was the most embarrassing moment of my life, my voice was surprisingly calm when I said, "Dude, can you switch this off?" The repairman looked at the screen and said, "Oh shit!" as he fumbled with the remote and shut off the TV.

My mom and I never spoke about the incident—until years later when she was about to die.

Cancer, unfortunately, ran in my mom's family. Her mother and grand-mother both died of ovarian cancer, so when she was in her fifties the doc-tors told her she should get a hysterectomy, because it was a genetic inevitability that she would develop ovarian cancer, too. Every few weeks I bugged my mom, "We have to book your surgery," and every time she made an excuse to put it off. She had never had surgery before; she was just scared. After two years of nagging, I didn't have to nag anymore. She called me and told me the diagnosis we had been dreading had come in.

I was pissed. Really pissed. It happens so often in your life: You tell people what they should do, over and over, and they don't do it. And they pay the consequences. You can't force someone to do something, no matter how much it would help them. It's the most frustrating thing in the world. And you usu-ally just have to sigh and let it go. But this was a tough one to shrug off.

They tried the hysterectomy after they found the cancer, but the cancer came back. She underwent chemo for six months after the surgery—a year and a half later the cancer came back. More surgery and six more months of chemo—a year later the cancer came back. The cancer attached itself to my mom's digestive tract, so the doctors kept cutting away at the valves that controlled her bowel movements. After the third round of surgery/chemo, the doctors said the next round would mean having to install a colostomy bag. Within six months, the fucking cancer came back.

When you go through chemotherapy, you're exhausted and nauseous for days on end. You throw up and you can't eat. You lose your hair and your muscles deteriorate. Then the treatment starts to wear off and you're fine for a couple of days, which reminds you just how nice it is not to be in pain. And then the next treatment begins and everything hits you all over again. It's utter misery. After several six-month stretches of the whole fucking cycle, and with no end in sight, my mom had had enough.

She wanted to live out her remaining days—however many there were—as an adult. She declined the chemo and the colostomy bag and chose life. She came to NOFX shows and drank and smoked pot and fucked her boyfriend and enjoyed herself while she could. I visited her often and made sure she spent plenty of time with Darla.

Darla was only about three years old when my mom was dying, but she has vivid memories of her grandma. Erin's mom had seven grandkids total, but Darla was my mother's only grandchild, so my mom lavished crazy attention on her.

In the spring of 2007, Erin, Darla, and I all moved down to my mom's house in Laguna Beach because it was clear that her time was almost up. Her friends came by, my friends visited, her boyfriend was there, the beach was just outside; it was a warm and pleasant way for her to spend her last days.

After two weeks, she went downhill fast. She was still coherent, but her muscles and organs were giving out and it was visible to anyone who looked at her. Darla came into her room one day and innocently asked, "What's wrong with grandma's face?" I told Erin it was probably time for her and Darla to say their final goodbyes and head back home.

I stayed in Laguna and a few days later my mom asked me to kill her. I was hanging out with her and five of her friends, and she said she didn't want to suffer unconsciously for weeks on end if it came to that point. "I want you guys to end this." No one would agree to do it, but I said I would. She made it clear to the room so there was no second-guessing after the fact: "I give Michael permission to kill me. I might not be able to say anything then, so I'm telling you now." We all understood, and a few days later it was clear that I would have to keep my word to her.

The night before she died, her boyfriend and I stayed up all night with her, drinking Jameson and telling stories. She couldn't talk anymore, but I told her every crazy story I could think of. Every sex story, every drug story, every crime I committed as a pre-teen, every girl I snuck over to the house, everything I've talked about in this book and some stories that I would never dare to include. I reminded her about the time she caught me with the porn in the DVD player and the time she found a riding crop in my suitcase, and I finally explained that the locked door she always wondered about in my house led to a fully equipped S&M dungeon. I laughed harder and longer than I had in a long time as I confessed all my sins. I had managed to punch a hole in the cloud that had been surrounding us all since my mom declined chemo. And my mom had a smile on her face the whole time.

The next day she had difficulty breathing. I decided to breathe with her, to understand what she was going through. I lay in bed next to her and tried to match the pattern of her breaths. The inhales were short and sharp, the exhales were long and slow. After a minute I wasn't getting enough air, and I realized that she wasn't, either. She had stopped using oxygen because she thought she would go faster, but as her muscles gave out she started suffocating. The doctors said to keep her heavily sedated and hooked up to the machines and she wouldn't feel anything, but I was watching her drown. I started crying. I knew this was the moment. I said, very clearly, "Mom, I don't think you're getting enough air. Do you want me to kill you right now?"

She hadn't moved or spoken in two or three days, but she summoned every ounce of strength she had left. Her body lurched upward as she pushed out a gasp:

"hhhhYES!"

I talked with a doctor friend who told me to give her all the pills I could. Between that and the morphine she was already on, it should do the job. I crushed up a ton of pills and cooked up like ten shots. I didn't know what I was doing, but I called a friend who was a nurse to help me. The machine that delivered her morphine through an IV is locked and designed to only deliver small doses, so I tore open the bag and gave her another ten injections of morphine.

She didn't die.

Her eyes were closed, and she was making these horrible choking noises all night and into the next day. Doing this deed was hard enough, but failing at it made it worse. Her breath would get really slow and I would think, "Okay, it's gonna happen now," but it just wouldn't happen. I called my doctor friend when morning broke and explained what was going on. He said that her liver was probably still processing everything and that's why her heart wouldn't shut down.

It took thirty-six hours from that first so-called lethal injection until she finally let go. If I could do it all over again, I would have just put a pillow over her face. It would've been harder for me to muster the courage to do it, but it would've been over for her in five minutes. Instead I waited until she had drawn her last breath, and then put a pillow over her face just to cover her up. She didn't look peaceful. Her eyes and mouth were hanging half open. It was a face I didn't want to remember.

The rest of the afternoon was paperwork and phone calls. I didn't cry or wallow, I just took care of business. The hospital came to take back their equipment and asked what happened to the bag on the morphine IV machine. "It must have torn or something." They didn't ask any follow-up questions. They understood.

I was officially an orphan. Even though it was one of the saddest moments of my life, I felt proud. I was happy my mom's suffering had ended, and I was happy I got the chance to spend that last month saying goodbye and thanking her for raising me. Not many people are allowed that luxury. Not many people get to say what they really mean when it really counts.

If the shoe had been on the other foot and I had been on my deathbed with my mom at my side, I don't know what kind of stories she would've told. She was always so open with me, sometimes too open. Once she was dating a guy and considering breaking up with him. She said to me—to her son—"I don't know. His cock is so big, I just can't take it."

And people wonder where my sense of tact and social grace comes from.

107

Melvin

Around the time when my café was closing in the mid-'90s I finally opened up to my mom about being molested by our neighbor. I was seeing a therapist and practicing the skill of opening up and looking inside myself. My mom and I were hanging out at my house one day, and out of nowhere she apologized to me for being so strict when I was I a kid. She said she felt like she was mean to me and confessed that she felt bad for raising me with too many rules and boundaries. I, of course, forgave her. And then, since she had just shared her heaviest burden, I decided to share mine.

She didn't know how to take it. Like any parent she was shocked and saddened. I softened the blow by reminding her that I came through it okay, and that I was surrounded by good people and I was working through it. That made her feel a bit better.

Not long after our discussion, my mom was hospitalized with sticky platelet syndrome, which is a disorder that caused her blood to clot more than it should. She survived a cardiac arrest and had to undergo a blood transfusion, but she came through it all fine and was able to manage her condition with medication. When I heard the word "chemotherapy" years later I assumed the sticky platelets were acting up again and didn't think much of it.

I got married in the summer of 2007 and my mom was dancing and healthy at my wedding. But within a year I found myself driving her to chemotherapy appointments. I assumed it was simply a new treatment for her old problem. You would think at some point someone would have mentioned the word "leukemia." It's a heavy word, with ominous implications. But my mom had a way of suffering in silence; she didn't want us to fuss over her.

My parents should've been communicating what was going on, and I should've been communicating my fears and concerns. But instead we went on as we always did, conversing about practicalities and minutiae and never delving far enough below the surface to scratch up any emotion.

When I returned to L.A. a few months later I found my mom emaciated in a hospital bed. She was pale and bald from the chemo, but the most heart-breaking thing to witness was her exhaustion. She was always so sociable, but now whenever someone came to visit she would tire quickly from the effort of talking. I didn't need to hear the word "leukemia" anymore—I saw it right in front of me.

After a couple weeks in the hospital the doctors decided she could come home, as long as she had the proper medical equipment and supervision. I don't think I was naïve enough to believe she was going to get better, but I also wasn't processing the idea that sending her home meant her final days were upon us. My mom, on the other hand, was keenly aware of the end. My mother-in-law visited her in the hospital and told me later that my mom had told her, "You'll have to be a grandmother for both of us."

We cleared out the living room at my parents' house and put a hospital bed near the TV. A nurse came regularly and gave us instructions for which drugs to give my mom when, and what number to call if something hap-pened. I would wake up in the morning and make tea for both of us, and we would talk.

But she never said anything as heavy to me as she did to my mother-in-law. I suppose she didn't want to burden me, but we also never talked about the stuff we probably should've talked about. It was our last chance to finally say goodbye, and we both blew it. Most people aren't lucky enough to have that kind of warning before a parent passes away. It was a chance to finally open up to each other, to finally end the curse of emotional silence that we'd been perpetuating our entire lives. We just chatted about the weather and how she'd slept the night before and sipped our tea. The unfortunate truth is that a talkative person is not necessarily a communicative person.

In September 2008 NOFX had a show booked in Phoenix. Some radio festival thing with Pennywise and Rise Against. I didn't really want to go, but it was a huge show, and it was way too late to cancel. The band might have suggested I stay home if only I had been communicative enough to explain what I had been going through, but you know how that goes by now. The plan was to fly out, play, and fly home early the next morning. I would only be gone for twelve hours—it didn't seem like a big deal.

I flew out, played the show, and fell asleep. I woke up to a dozen missed calls from my dad. I never saw my mom again.

When I stepped on stage in Phoenix, I thought, "This one's for my mom." You would think I'd remember very little about the show with so much swirling through my head, but strangely my memories of the motor-home dressing rooms and the enormous outdoor stage and the sun setting as we played were more vivid than most of my tour memories from that era. I don't think I offered too many details about my mom to the guys in the band. I still wasn't really prepared for her to die.

I came home to an empty hospital bed in the living room. My parents had already made all the arrangements for her burial plot, so my sister, my dad, and I dealt with the cemetery people and squared things away. We picked a headstone and an inscription, and I did my best to keep my dad company (while never really talking about our grief or the simple fact that we missed my mom. What the hell is wrong with us?).

The loss didn't set in until her memorial service. It was a beautiful, perfect, sunny Los Angeles day. We were surrounded by a crowd of loving and supportive friends and family. Butterflies floated through the air. The tranquility took the edge off the somberness. I guess we were there to place her urn in the ground, but the whole day was such a blur that I don't even remember if that happened or not.

What I do remember is the moment they pulled the tarp off the burial plot. Just as they revealed the hole they had dug in the earth this little brown rabbit with white feet came bounding out of it and took off into the bushes. Some people let out a gasp; a few laughed uneasily at the release of tension.

My mom's friend Walter said, "That's Helaine right there." And I broke down into heavy sobbing.

I don't know what it was about those words, but after the hospital and the sickness and the six missed calls and the empty hospital bed and the hole in the earth, the dam finally burst. I cried my eyes out as the reality I'd been foolishly denying all along finally sunk in. My mom was dead.

+ + +

My son Eli was born two years after my mom passed, and my son Caspian was born a few years later. Not a week goes by without one of them doing something cute or silly or imaginative that makes me wish I could share it with her. They even remind me of her in some of their features, like Caspian's distinctive chin. Or the way Eli shows his lower teeth when he makes goofy faces for a camera, just like she used to do.

I've tried hard to block out the memory of my mom in that hospital bed. I've spent a lot of time looking at old photos, to remind myself of when she was active and healthy. I keep lots of pictures of her on the wall in our house, and I find myself talking to them all the time. I seek her advice, I vent my frustrations about parenting . . . it's sad to think that I have deeper conversations with her photos than I did with her when she was around. But she still manages to give me strength.

Sometimes I feel guilty for not being able to save her. I've since read up on diets and nutrition, and maybe if I had told her to stop eating sugar or caffeine or something it would've somehow made a difference. But who knows if that would've done anything? What would've made a bigger difference would've just been opening up to her. Telling her I cared. Thanking her for passing down her creative spirit. Thanking her for teaching me that we're never too old to learn something new. Thanking her for everything.

I took it for granted that she'd always be there. But maybe not every conversation with my mom needed to be fraught with emotion and gratitude and heavy revelations about the past. She was there. She was part of my life, and I was part of hers. I knew I was loved. She knew she was loved in return.

Maybe that's all that matters.

Helaine Melvin.

Hefe, Dad, and Henry.

Hefe and Mom.

Mike and Mom.

108

Smelly

Before I got clean I was living in a North Hollywood junkie house called "Funland." The name could not have been more misleading. The standout memory I have from that place was the time a bunch of FFF gangsters showed up to one of our keggers and started a 20-on-20 brawl with some other gang dudes at the party. I was in the driveway watching things get gnarly as my friend Chris went toe-to-toe with some big FFF dude, but I lost track of Chris when I heard the distinct sound of someone racking a pump-action shotgun behind me.

The FFF guy holding it shouted, "Anybody fucking want some?!" and half the party scattered. Then a dozen cop cars showed up and everyone else scattered. While the police patted me down, I noticed a pool of blood and a clump of Chris's hair left behind in the driveway.

When I came home from our 1992 European tour, I got a letter from the Van Nuys police department. One of my Funland roommates, Carina, had borrowed my car while I was away, used it in an armed convenience store robbery, crashed it into a telephone pole, and fled the scene. Thankfully I had my passport stamps to prove I wasn't in the country at the time.

Carina was pregnant when she went to jail for the robbery, and she gave birth to a heroin-addicted baby while serving time. Her ex-boyfriend, Duck (one of my other junkie roomies), got custody of the kid. Duck always had a bit of a dangerous, sketchy vibe to him, but overall he was a fun guy and a good friend. But one day I picked up a copy of the *L.A. Weekly*, and there he was staring back at me from the cover. The headline read "The Face of Evil." He subjected his poor son to regular, unspeakable physical abuse. When the kid was just over two years old, Duck beat him to death.

His case was so shocking it caused the state to re-examine its custody laws. The California legislature was taught a lesson that should've been obvious all along: junkies and kids do not mix well.

✦   ✦   ✦

I got married in 2000 to a woman I'd known for about four months. We did the Vegas runaway thing on impulse, and I thought I'd found "the one," but we ended up divorced in 2010. Looking back, the red flags started flying at full mast a few months after the elopement, when I got my first real glimpse of her extended family. All of them were fucked up in one way or another—strung out on drugs, living in squalor, surviving off SSI . . . total fucking trainwrecks.

My now-ex-wife's aunt was a junkie with a husband behind bars. I first met their daughter, Joey, when she was only three years old. She was a beautiful, innocent baby girl with matted, brownish-blonde hair who hadn't bathed or had a decent meal in who knows how long. Her sad, brown eyes pleaded for help.

I don't want to offer up too many details about the conditions Joey was living in with her mom, but in the previous pages of this book I've gone into detail about some of the foul, nauseating places where I rested my head during my heroin years. Imagine if I'd had a toddler with me.

Now imagine it being a hundred times worse than anything I've described.

My heart broke when I met Joey for the second time at age five and found that her living situation had not improved. A few years later her mom was arrested for child endangerment. We got the call from Child Protective Services and immediately offered her a place to live.

I was a father overnight. It wasn't how I'd pictured it happening, but being a dad was something I'd wanted since I was a kid. My own childhood was so shitty, I wanted the opportunity to show someone real, unconditional love. My dad had shown me what NOT to do. I couldn't wait to turn all of those negative experiences into something positive.

Joey had just turned eight and didn't know what to make of the whole situation. She had been living in tents and under freeways, or spending nights in by-the-hour motels. She had been passed around to various extended family members before, so she thought our house in Long Beach was yet another temporary situation. She was frightened and quiet, regardless of all the assurances that she was finally in a safe place. She would try to socialize with other kids, but her self-consciousness left her shaking and upset. She barely knew how to read, write, or even properly use a fork and knife.

I made a promise to myself and, silently, to her. I was going to love her. I was going to protect her. I was going to give her every ounce of emotional support that I never got. I was going to be there for her 110 percent. And if that meant quitting the band—if that's really what it was going to take—I would accept that.

A couple weeks after she arrived, we were walking into a Target. She does this funny little skip when she's happy, and she was doing it then. She skipped up behind me and, for the first time, took my hand and held it. It fucking melted my heart. And it let me know I was on the right path.

Over the next few months I watched this damaged soul, who had seen way too much for her age, actually become a kid. Riding a bike. Playing with other kids. Getting a somewhat normal life, which is all she ever wanted.

She entered school in October 2006 and was placed in the third grade, but she tested at below-kindergarten levels in math and reading. She was a sharp kid, but she had been robbed of an education. By June she had not only caught up to the level of her classmates, she had surpassed them. I put on a tie and attended an awards banquet at the end of the school year, where Joey was honored by the mayor of Long Beach with a plaque and the title of "Most Inspiring Student" in the Long Beach Unified School District.

But of course there were, and still are, hurdles. Her whole life she had been discarded wherever she went. Everything that had been given to her had been taken away or left behind. The sadness and alienation can be overwhelming sometimes.

Luckily, she has someone who can relate: my father.

The cracks in my dad's hardened exterior first appeared when he went sober, and they grew when I went sober, but when my dad met Joey the walls crumbled to dust. He had been abused and abandoned. He had moved from home to home and lived out of a suitcase. He and Joey were one and the same. When I told her about his past, it put her life into perspective. It showed her she wasn't alone, and it bonded them deeply. It helped her understand that even though we don't share blood we're still family.

The twist in the story is that while we were all so busy trying to heal Joey, she actually healed us. Having her around opened my dad up emotionally. He saw in her a second chance at his own childhood and a second chance to be a supportive parent. He takes her out cruising in his hot rod and shows her more affection than I ever saw from him when I was a kid. My mom always felt guilty for not standing up for me against my dad, so she gets a second chance at raising a kid without all the ugliness in the way. My mom and dad both get to feel a sense of pride from watching their screw-up son become a responsible, attentive father. And I get to bond with both of my parents by relating to their struggles, learning from their mistakes, and having them compliment me on how I'm handling parenthood.

Joey has become the nucleus of the Sandin family. She has soothed so many deep wounds. A couple years back, when the sadness of the past crept back into her mind, as it occasionally does, we were crying and hugging and talking it out when she asked me why I cared so much about her.

I said, "I may be making a difference in your life, but you're making just as much of a difference in my life."

She asked, "Why?"

I said, "You gave me purpose. I love you unconditionally, and my purpose is to make your life as good as possible. You gave me a reason to be on this planet."

It's all true. Even the rough times as a parent have been fulfilling. If it was nothing but the roughest of rough times with her for the rest of my life, I would still feel satisfied. If I had to, I would re-do my shitty childhood a thousand times over just to know what I know now to give Joey a good life. I would sacrifice my own happiness every time. I now know what true selflessness is.

Meanwhile, my dad still hasn't quite gotten the hang of expressing his feelings. His heart has definitely been unlocked, and he's warm enough to offer hugs these days, but I still have never heard him utter the words "I love you." I know he wants to say it; he just can't. Sometimes when my dad is over I'll take Joey aside and whisper mischievously, "Joey, tell Grandpa you love him."

She'll sweetly intone, "I love you, Grandpa!"

He'll grunt back over his shoulder, "Yeah, yeah, yeah" or "I heard ya" or "Whaddya want from me?"

But maybe someday.

Not that I'm one to talk. I've never told my dad I love him, either. But the truth is without him I wouldn't be who I am. He taught me about music, he taught me about the value of hard work. Things may not have been ideal when I was growing up, but I know now that our situation was just as tough on him as it was on me. I have total respect for him, and considering how well things have ultimately turned out I have to thank him for being the man he is.

It's easier to say these things in print than it is to say them to his face, of course. I wonder if I'll ever gather the courage to communicate, in person, just how much he means to me. For now, he'll have to read these words for the very first time in this book:

I love you, Dad.

109

Mike

One year, on my birthday, I was in our home dungeon when there was a knock at the door. It was Erin, dressed in a full, shiny, black-latex catsuit, complete with a hood that covered her entire face. She said, in a seductive voice, "Your wife sent me," and gave me a special and severe birthday beating.

Erin enjoyed S&M but never to the extent that I did. She went out of her way to indulge my perversities as much as she could, but there was still a wedge between us. I felt like she was playing a role I had written for her. I was living out my fantasies, but I knew she wasn't living out hers. That's not what I wanted. With a sexual disconnect added to the weight of our sinking marriage, it's no surprise we went under.

It was forty minutes before NOFX was supposed to take the stage in Philadelphia in the fall of 2008 when yet another phone argument with Erin spiraled into an unnecessarily big fight. It's an unwritten rule for people in relationships with people in bands: don't start shit right before they go on. They'll carry the fight with them and it will ruin the show for them and the crowd. This wasn't just a normal fight, though. This was the fight that made me decide to leave my wife.

I said I was done. I couldn't do it anymore. After the tour, I was going to move out. She was crying, and I was ready to break. I used whiskey to keep myself together. Lots and lots of whiskey.

After our whiskey-soaked show that night, I had a whiskey-fueled bus party with Paddy from Dillinger Four and Dave from the Loved Ones. I cranked up the music in the bus lounge and we started a three-man slam pit. Paddy was doing stage dives off the table. Dave and Paddy picked me up, and I was making footprints on the big mirror on the lounge ceiling. Then I grabbed the mirror and the whole thing came crashing down.

Jay entered the bus with his girlfriend. I didn't realize it at the time, but in my whirlwind of destruction I guess I slammed into her. Jay yelled at me and I told him to shut the fuck up. I said something like, "It's my bus, I'm going to fucking do what I want! You don't like it, go somewhere else!" And suddenly, I found myself in a chokehold.

I tried to struggle out of it, but Jay's pretty strong. I fought until I couldn't take it anymore, and then I went limp and gave up. I broke into tears. The party was over. Paddy and Dave awkwardly bailed. Jay let me go,

323

and I told him about Erin and the phone call before the show. It's a sign of true friendship when you can be a total asshole to your friend, he can choke you out, and you can still spend the rest of the night hanging out and crying. It was one of the darkest nights of my life. Even after the chokehold, I was really glad to have Jay there with me.

Before I left for that summer's Warped Tour I got a one-bedroom apartment. Which was pointless because as soon as I got home Erin convinced me to give our marriage another shot. We tried couples therapy, we tried living apart; we didn't give up without a fight. Or two. Or several hundred. We'd had a lot of good years together, and we got a great kid out of the deal. But it was time to call it quits.

◆ ◆ ◆

The silver lining of moving out and living as a bachelor again meant I could fully indulge in as much S&M debauchery as I could handle. During the 2009 Warped Tour I rented a dungeon in downtown Los Angeles and hosted a party with a bunch of friends and members of the Vandals, Sum 41, and Alkaline Trio and their girlfriends. The moment I stepped into the dungeon I knew which dominatrix was in charge. There were five hot dommes in leather and latex waiting for us, but one of them carried herself like she owned the place. And in fact she did. With bright red hair, socially offensive tattoos, and milky white skin, she reminded me of all my adolescent crushes. She was a cross between Wendy O'Williams, Becky Bondage, and Magenta from *Rocky Horror*. Her name was Goddess Soma.

Soma had a slave named Boi, a twenty-year-old lesbian who gender-identified as a male. Soma wasn't a NOFX fan, but Boi was, and he was also a huge Alkaline Trio fan (he had their logo tattooed on his arm), so when I walked in with Matt Skiba, Boi freaked the fuck out.

Soma beat up on a bunch of the girls but seemed to go out of her way to avoid disciplining me. She put some other dommes on me, and one of them sliced open a habañero pepper and shoved it up my ass. I was blindfolded and didn't know what was going on. I thought to myself, "That's one of the smallest butt plugs I've ever felt." And then the juice from the pepper hit my anal membranes.

Yep, they burn just as much down there.

It was a fucking great party. At one point I found myself standing naked in the kitchen, even though the other twenty people in the room were all clothed. You would think it would be like that nightmare we've all had about showing up naked at school, but it was just pleasantly weird. At the end of the night, Boi told me Goddess Soma wanted to see me in her bedroom. No one gets to go in Soma's bedroom—this was a sacred invitation.

When I went in, Soma ordered me to put my face between the legs of another domme, Mistress Suzette. While my face was being smothered by Suzette's panties, Soma strapped on an intimidating purple dildo, played the *Ziggy Stardust* album on her stereo, and fucked the hell out of me.

You tend to remember somebody when your first date involves David Bowie and ass rape. But Soma stayed in my mind mostly because after our session we sat and talked. I had visited other professional dommes before (Erin was okay with it as long as I never fucked anyone, and I never did), but usually I would go in for a session, pay, and then leave. This was the first time I was beaten by someone I could also hang out with. Soma was smarter and more well read than anyone I had met in the S&M scene (or any scene for that matter), and it didn't hurt that she was super fucking hot. She invited me to come and hang out at the dungeon whenever I was in town.

Erin and I were already separated, but we began official divorce proceedings in January 2010, and I moved in with Soma pretty soon after. We rented a pale yellow house perched on a hill in La Cañada that was built in the '70s and looked like something out of a Grimms' fairy tale. Soma and I took the master bedroom on the lower floor, Boi had a room upstairs, my friend Big John from the Warped Tour and his dominatrix girlfriend Nikki Nefarious moved into the guesthouse, and a kinky black dude named Culepepper lived over the garage. It was like a polyamorous version of *The Waltons*.

It was for sure the craziest and most hedonistic year of my life. Soma would bring home girls for both of us to party with. A couple of times, Soma and her goth girlfriend Drea beat the shit out of me and raped me (which may sound awesome, but was actually kinda rough!). Soma would ring a bell to summon Boi to her room and then command him to do the dishes, shine her boots, or help her dress. Film crews stopped by to shoot S&M photo sessions or videos featuring Soma and her friends. One night we had an orgy with Soma, Drea, Boi, and two other female submissives that went until nine in the morning when a film crew walked in and said, "Ahh, you guys started without us!"*

We spent plenty of long nights with our fetish-friendly friends at Soma's dungeon in downtown L.A. It was at that dungeon where Nikki Nefarious tied me to a table one night and Soma produced a scalpel. She lovingly carved a large, bold "S" into my inner thigh. She had pushed me to a new limit of pain and intimacy and had permanently marked me as her own. It was one of the most beautiful moments of my life and an emotional experience for everyone in the room—all of us were weeping by the end of it. Fuck

---

*In our orgies, Soma is always the one fucking all the girls. My penis is exclusively her plaything. (Aside from supervised hand or blowjobs now and again.)

all the paperwork and the lawyers: that incision was the moment when, for me, my divorce was truly final.

I now belonged to someone else.

◆ ◆ ◆

Polyamory is a fine way to live, but once the novelty wore off I started to find the other people in our bedroom a distraction. I wanted to be with Soma and no one else. After about a year Soma and I moved to a different house in Glendale, and everybody else went his or her separate ways.

I learned more about S&M over the next year or two than I had learned in the previous thirty. Nipple clamps became as much a part of my routine on stage as my line of coke before the encore. Soma came on tour with me and would cinch my balls with a rope during our set. At the Roskilde Festival in Denmark, they had easels set up near the backstage tents, so Soma was painting and I was licking her pussy out in the open. Later, I snuck into one of the catering tents and stole a spatula and a wooden spoon, and we found an empty tent with a couch and some tables in it. She beat me with the new tools and strangled my balls with a piece of twine she found in the tent. Three festivalgoers poked their heads in and watched us for a while—one girl even joined in on the spanking. When we played the Pukkelpop Festival in Belgium later that summer, Soma used a gas mask to cut off my air and latex mittens to bind my hands while she whipped me in our dressing room. The festival ended, and one of the organizers politely knocked on the door and asked us to clear out. When we got dressed and opened the door, we found ten security guards lined up and waiting for us. I still had the mittens on as they escorted us to our bus.

During the Folsom Street Fair—an annual gathering of BDSM fetishists in San Francisco that draws over four hundred thousand people—we were eating with friends at a Thai restaurant, and I went down on Soma under the table. (It was one of the only times I've ever seen Soma get embarrassed.) She borrowed ropes from Nikki, who was sitting with us, and tied me to my chair. My shirt was already off, so she snapped on some nipple clamps and then took the candle that was on the table and dripped hot wax on my chest while we waited for our food. The waiters were hardly bothered—they had probably seen plenty of crazy shit that day. Earlier in the day Soma had met a new submissive named Juliet, and we brought her home after the fair. We made her kneel beside our bed and read us erotic stories while we fucked. Soma cruelly mocked her as she read. She'd say, "You wish you were getting fucked," or "You'll never be loved by anyone." Then she leaned over and slapped Juliet across the face and said, "Read better." When we were finished we made her sleep in the closet.

Once, Soma and I were both flying to Chicago, but I had to fly from San Francisco and meet her at LAX before connecting. We decided ahead of time we would pretend not to know each other. She got on the plane first; I walked on five minutes later. It was a full flight and we were sitting in coach. I had the window seat, she had the middle, and an older guy in a business suit had the aisle. As the plane took off, I made small talk with Soma as though I was trying to pick her up, and she kept shooting me down like I was a nuisance.

"I play in this punk band, NOFX."

"Oh. I've never heard of you."

She was reading a book.

"What are you reading about?"

"S&M"

"Like what?"

"Well, I'm a professional dominatrix, and I'm doing some research."

I could tell that the businessman was starting to eavesdrop.

"What kind of things do you do?"

"You really wanna know?"

I nodded, "Sure."

She pulled her carry-on bag from under the seat and took out some rope. She tied my arms to the armrests, tied my legs together, blindfolded me, and on went the nipple clamps. I was wearing shorts, so she reached up my thigh and put clothespins on my balls.

The businessman hit the flight attendant call button. "Are there any other seats?"

Sorry. Full flight.

He buried his nose in a newspaper and turned away as much as he could while we made out next to him. After a while Soma put my travel pillow around my neck and I took a nap while still tied up, blindfolded, clamped, and clothespinned. You would think there would be some sort of FAA regulation against being tied up with clothespins on your balls on a flight, but none of the flight attendants said a word to us. I guess the FAA never considered that scenario when they were making up the rules.

◆   ◆   ◆

When I was a kid holding up a tape recorder to the TV speaker to record *The Rocky Horror Picture Show*, there was a lyric that always stuck with me: "Don't dream it. Be it." It ran through my head for years as I held myself back, ashamed of my fetishes, afraid of what people might think if I truly opened up.

And I'm not just talking about S&M.

One night when I was fifteen I slept over at my friend Chris Prettyman's house. His mom had to take him somewhere in the morning, and while they were out I went into his mom's bedroom and found a pair of leather pants. There was something about the smell and the sensation of the leather against my skin. And there was something about the femininity of it. I squeezed into the pants, locked myself in the bathroom (even though I was alone in the house), and jerked off as I looked at myself in the mirror.

I never told a soul. I didn't know what it all meant. At the time, the world—let alone the homophobic, gay-bashing L.A. punk scene—wasn't all that enlightened about cross-dressing. Anything vaguely feminine made you gay in most people's eyes. My dad always said if I ever came home with an earring he would rip it out of my ear, and he threw the word "faggot" around a lot. I didn't have any homosexual desires, but did wanting to wear women's clothes make me a "faggot?"

Cross-dressing wasn't an obsession or anything. Out of my top twenty fantasies it probably ranked somewhere around eighteen, so I left it unexplored for a long time. Bondage was one thing, but anything that feminized me still felt taboo. Fast forward twenty years later to when I was with Erin, and I was finally brave enough to put on latex stockings or maybe a PVC maid's outfit from time to time. She usually humored me, but one day we were arguing about something, and she hissed at me: "And by the way, you look stupid dressed like a girl."

It instantly crushed me. I said, "Do you know what you just did? I can never dress like that again." I had trusted her with my most vulnerable secret, and she had humiliated me with it. She didn't mean for her words to shatter my confidence the way they did, but the damage was done. She felt guilty and tried to get me to dress up on other occasions, but I was never able to emotionally trust her again. She thought I looked stupid . . . and maybe she was right.

So many people with secret fetishes feel shame or alienation. I didn't feel ashamed of my fetishes; I was fine with being a pervert. I felt ashamed of my own fear. I kept saying to myself, "You're a fucking coward. You're not living how you want to live." Even into my forties I kept hearing those *Rocky Horror* lyrics in my head: "Don't dream it. Be it . . . "

Years later, Soma helped me conquer my fear. Bit by bit she encouraged my cross-dressing: some high heels here, a corset there. And then one day I asked her what she wanted for her birthday and she said, "I want you to be my girlfriend for the weekend."

She shaved my body, dressed me, and did my makeup. She wouldn't let me look at myself the entire time. Three hours later, she put me in front of a mirror.

My knees went weak. My stomach flipped and my hand drew itself to my heart. I didn't cry, but I was close. I said, "I can't believe it. I look beautiful." Soma corrected me: "You look fucking gorgeous."

We had the best lesbian sex ever. It was supposed to be my birthday gift to her, but she had given an amazing gift to me.

I still held back from going public about cross-dressing. Getting beaten bloody or locked in a puppy cage? I would brag about that shit all day. But feminization was still something I was scared for others to know about. NOFX fans should've seen it coming: for years, if someone threw a bra on stage I would put it on. I would convince the band to dress in drag for our Halloween and New Year's Eve shows. I wore "kilts." But I was still a coward, hiding behind the safety of a joke.

Finally, in 2015, I wore a pink nightie during a show in Luxembourg with Lagwagon. It wasn't a costume, it wasn't a joke. It was me dressing the way I wanted to dress. And no one cared. Joey Cape told me I looked badass. Someone backstage poked fun at me and Melvin told them to shut up. When pictures of me hit the internet, Fletcher from Pennywise texted me: "That's punk as fuck."

From that night on, I was truly liberated. No more hiding. I walked through Heathrow Airport in drag and didn't give a fuck what people thought. Punks are supposed to shock people; my pink Mohawk doesn't get half as many stares as my pink nightie.

If you're a woman out there reading this, all I can say is that you should encourage your man to explore himself. Don't shut him down. Don't humiliate him. Wanting to wear lace or nylon or satin or latex doesn't make someone gay or transgender. All guys ever get to wear is cotton, and that's boring as fuck.

And if you're a guy out there torturing yourself over your desire to cross-dress or to try any other harmless fetish, you should know that you're not fucked up, and you're not alone. Talk it over with your partner, and if they don't accept you for who you are then find someone who will. You only live once. You owe it to yourself to explore what makes you happy.

Give yourself over to absolute pleasure.

Don't dream it.

Be it.

110

Melvin

Despite the fact that our album covers and T-shirt designs regularly featured images of dominatrixes, I was completely oblivious to Mike's love of S&M for almost two decades of our friendship. I didn't even think much of it when he first suggested visiting an S&M club in Sydney on our second tour of Australia.

Mike was so excited about the idea and kept talking to everyone we met about how to find it and what the details were while recruiting friends and members of the opening band to join us. I thought his interest in the club was the same as mine: it would be a change of pace. By that point we were sick of going to punk bars after every single show, so this seemed like a more unique way to spend an evening.

The club was similar to most nightclubs, aside from the people milling about in leather S&M outfits and the equipment designed for tying people up in the middle of everything. A dominatrix whipped willing members of the crowd, but I don't think Mike even participated in a beating that night. We all watched Ben from the band Bodyjar go up and get spanked and whipped instead (most likely at Mike's urging). It looked incredibly painful, but, as I'd hoped, it was a unique way to spend our evening.

We went to similar clubs in two other towns on the same tour. Mike never volunteered for a spanking, so I still didn't connect the dots. On our tour of Japan later that year, Mike found yet another club for us and our friends from the Swingin' Utters to visit. By that point I felt more comfortable in the clubs, and I thought I knew roughly what to expect. Always open-minded to new experiences, I volunteered for a beating.

I was bound, blindfolded, and ball-gagged before I knew what was happening. Once my hands were tied, the reality of not being able to move set in, and I wasn't comfortable with the situation anymore. But before I could process my own discomfort, the dominatrix undid my pants and yanked them down around my ankles, leaving me completely naked in front of all my friends (and quite a few strangers). It went from uncomfortable to seriously uncomfortable in a matter of moments.

And then she shoved a dildo up my ass.

I don't know how big it was, but as far as my rectum was concerned it seemed like the Guinness World Record Holder for Biggest Dildo Ever Manufactured in Human History. "Uncomfortable" was no longer applicable to the situation. "Violated" was more appropriate. The ball gag kept me from saying anything, the ropes around my hands kept me from doing anything. The blindfold and the loud music prevented me from knowing what else was going on around me, or what kind of reactions my friends were having to my humiliation.

I suffered through some spanking and whipping, and finally the dildo was extracted. I was untied and left to pull up my own pants as I rejoined my friends. There was no applause or laughter or any signal that what had just happened was all in good fun. People had a hard time making eye contact with me, or maybe it was the other way around. None of us spoke about it again. Ever.

The next time we returned to Japan, I saw Mike finally volunteer for a beating. And it finally clicked in my head what had been going on all along. Mike didn't just volunteer, he went all in. I was taken aback by how fierce of a whipping he was able to endure and how the same spanking and exhibitionism that had brought me such misery seemed to bring him such pleasure. This wasn't a random night of fun. This was his passion.

Over the ensuing years I've joined Mike at a bunch of S&M clubs and parties all over the world. I've seen so many whips and ropes and paddles and gags and needles and plastic wrap and dripping candles and nipple clamps and restraints and corsets and red handprints on Mike's ass that it's become normal to me. And after hearing so many stories about his sexual experiments with Erin, and later with Soma, it went beyond normal to mundane. I never much enjoyed picturing my buddy naked, so I tuned him out most of the time.

Although I must say the story about the saline injections definitely held my attention.

111

Mike

I never travel with drugs because I don't want to get caught at the airport, so if I ever have any coke or ecstasy left over after a night of partying I tuck it in the pages of the Bible in my hotel room. I like to picture someone alone in a strange city, lost and looking for answers, opening the Bible and having my leftover drugs fall into his or her lap. I consider it missionary work.

In 2010, Me First and the Gimme Gimmes played the Fest in Gainesville, Florida. I stayed up late after the show, bankrupting James from Against Me! in a poker game, but I had a flight to catch at 6:30 a.m., so I just stayed up all night. I had bought a bunch of drugs in anticipation of a large-scale party, and I had about a gram and a half of coke left over. Instead of leaving it in the Bible, I went to the hotel lobby to catch my cab to the airport and tossed it in a planter box on the way out. Then I tweeted that I had hidden drugs in the lobby and sent my Twitter followers on what I like to call a "treasure hunt."

I heard at least fifty people went searching for the treasure, but one of the guys from Municipal Waste was up really early (or really late) and got the tweet before the rest of the crowd, so he scored the prize. Nice job, Tony.

◆　◆　◆

My flight that morning was to Miami, where I would meet Soma and connect to a flight to Jamaica. We were headed to Kink in the Caribbean, a weeklong version of the Folsom Street Fair at an all-inclusive beach resort. I called Soma from the Gainesville airport to let her know I'd be boarding soon.

She asked me, "You have your toys with you, right?"

"Yeah . . . "

"Go to the bathroom. I want you to stick a butt plug in your ass and put nipple clamps on your tits until you see me."

When you enter into a dominant/submissive relationship, you discuss your limits early on. The agreement is that the domme gives the orders, and the sub can't refuse any order within those pre-agreed limits. The thrill of the relationship is trusting someone to push you to the very edge and catch you right before you go over. If the sub refuses the domme's orders, there's no trust, and it's no fun. So when your domme tells you to stick a butt plug up your ass before you board an hour-long flight, you go into the bathroom of the Gainesville Regional Airport and you lube the fuck up.

Did I mention she also made me put on a cock ring? Because after a gaggle of punks who had just been at the Fest bought me enough drinks on the plane, I certainly mentioned it to them. I told two kids sitting behind me that I had nipple clamps and an ass plug in, too. They didn't believe me until I pulled my shirt up and showed them the clamps. After that they took my word about the butt plug and the cock ring.

An hour is a long fucking time for all that stuff to be on—and in—your body, so when I met Soma at the Miami airport she mercifully allowed me to remove the butt plug and nipple clamps. But when we went through security to get on our flight to Jamaica, the metal detector went off. They wanded me down and it beeped at crotch level. I still had the cock ring on.

I explained what was going on, and they took me into a private room and made me take the ring off. The poor TSA guy had to take the cock ring in his rubber-gloved hands and inspect it closely to make sure I wasn't hiding anything dangerous. He showed it to a colleague and pointed at me. Once everything was cleared up and I put my clothes back on, the colleague asked for my autograph: he was a NOFX fan.

I've become more open about my sexuality, but some situations still make me uneasy. Kink in the Caribbean wasn't one of those situations. We walked into the resort, and the first thing I saw was a guy in a rubber sack and a gas mask coming down a waterslide. His domme caught him in the pool and graciously allowed him not to drown. I belonged here.

When we hit the pool ourselves, Soma and our friend Domina Angelina tied me up and dunked me under the water and then made me wear my fingerless rubber mittens and get drinks for them. Of course I spilled everything, and Soma made me walk around the pool and ask every domme there to slap me as punishment. Each slap was harder than the last: dominatrixes do not like being outdone.

There were about a hundred kinky people at the resort. Mostly couples in crazy rubber outfits and some infamous pro dommes. Every night there were S&M shows, fire shows, kinky cabaret shows, outdoor dungeon parties, and slave auctions. During the day there were latex-themed pool parties and some very informative classes. I studied proper bullwhip technique: it's all in the wrist.

After a week of pure debauchery, Soma and I were finishing our night up at 5 a.m. with our South African friends Paul and Joanne, watching the waves crash into a cement pier by the beach. An offshore hurricane had pushed in a huge swell. We walked to the end of the pier, where Soma tied me to a metal light post and Joanne bound Paul's hands behind his back. The waves swept over the pier as Soma whaled on me with her flogger and fucked me with a strap-on while Joanne repeatedly dunked Paul's head under water in a nearby cement trough. When the girls finally released us we all sat on the edge of the pier, holding hands and watching the sunrise. (And then a huge wave came in and nearly knocked us all into the ocean, and we retreated to safety.)

We were definitely never bored. S&M was never the same routine for us; Soma is a queen of improvisation. One day Soma said, "I'm gonna make you feel what I have to go through every month. I'm putting you on birth control." She's the domme. I had to say yes. I was so bummed as I watched her punch a pill out of her little circular package, but I was a good sub so I took my medicine.

After a while I started to worry. I had no idea what these things were doing to my body, and since I wasn't getting high from them it hardly seemed worth the risk. I finally freaked out after a couple days. "We don't know what these pills could be doing to me!" She looked at me with a sinister smile and said, "They're just sugar pills, sugar."

Every birth control packet has several placebo pills to coincide with the time when a woman is on her period—those were the pills she was giving me. But in my mind I was on birth control the whole time! S&M isn't all about whips and leather; it's about the mind fuck, and Soma is a mind fuck expert.

Once, we decided to do a role-play in which I would be one of Soma's new clients. I went to her website and filled out an application form and booked a session with her. I showed up to the dungeon on time, and she introduced herself and brought me inside. She asked me questions about what I liked and what my limits were, as if she hadn't been testing them for over a year. She tied me to a gynecological examination table, put my feet up in stirrups, blindfolded me, and made me snort a line of ketamine. Suddenly, I felt a needle pierce my ball sack, accompanied by a burning sensation. She had pierced my nipples with needles during our play sessions before, so I thought she was just going to another level by piercing my junk. When my hour appointment was up, she pulled off my blindfold and held a mirror up under my crotch. It wasn't a piercing.

She had injected 250cc of saline into my scrotum and blown it up to the size of a softball.

I tried to walk around, but it felt like there was a warm water balloon dangling between my legs. It went away over the course of the next twelve hours, but every now and then I'd forget about it, go to scratch my balls, and frighten myself.

It wasn't a turn-on; I couldn't have gotten a boner if I wanted to. It was just one of those beautiful mind fucks. Like punk rock, it was pointless self-destruction.

The mind fuck, however, goes both ways. After a show in Toronto on NOFX's 2011 Canadian tour, Soma and I were playing in our hotel room and we decided to switch: I would be the domme, she would be the sub. I tied her to a chair and blindfolded her and (thanks to some prior planning and perfect timing) Jay Walker entered the room. Soma freaked a little bit, "What's going on? Who's here?" It was a total loss of control for her, and she may have been somewhat self-conscious since her outfit was entirely transparent latex.

I pulled off the blindfold and showed her it was Jay. I reminded her about the "S" she had carved in my leg and told her that tonight it was my turn to mark her. Jay had brought his tattoo gun. I pulled down her bottom lip and (because I often play the Daddy role in our relationship) Jay inked the word "Daddy's" on the inside. I already belonged to her, now she belonged to me.

◆ ◆ ◆

At the end of that Canadian tour I hid four different packages of "treasure" around my hotel in Vancouver and tweeted that the hunt was on before heading to the airport to fly home.

While waiting for my flight, I was paged: "Michael Burkett, please come to gate ten." I thought I was getting a frequent-flyer upgrade, but at the gate were two police officers who took me to a back room. They said they had gotten an anonymous tip that I was holding drugs. They pulled my checked bags off the plane and went through everything with a fine-tooth comb.

I had gotten rid of my coke and ecstasy, but I forgot I had two small Percocets in a coat pocket in my suitcase. I had a prescription for them, but I didn't have the prescription on me, so I dreaded the trouble I was about to get into. Traveling with drugs is one thing, crossing international borders with them is another. Thankfully they missed the pills and I made it home, but the search took over an hour. I missed my flight and had to catch another one three hours later.

So that was the last-ever treasure hunt.

◆ ◆ ◆

I have been told (on enough occasions that I have written multiple songs about it) that I have a problem with drugs and alcohol. Maybe I do, but is it a bad enough problem that I actually have to (Goddess forbid) quit? I think I can handle it. But then again I'm sure that's what all addicts think. How does a successful guy know when he needs help? I've got enough money in the bank that it would take forever for drugs to bankrupt me. I've got friends and fans in every town on tour so I'm rarely without an excuse to party. And as much as my band mates might want to give me the same ultimatum I gave Smelly back in the day, it's pretty tough to replace the singer, the chief songwriter, the bass player,* and the label owner all at once.

On Christmas Eve 2011, Darla celebrated with me at my apartment in San Francisco, and then I dropped her off at Erin's so she could celebrate Christmas Day with her mom in the morning. Soma was down in L.A., so I was alone and bored. I did some coke. I drank a little. I jerked off. I took some Ambien, but the coke overpowered it and I couldn't sleep. It was the first time I stayed up all night on coke by myself. My head may have been a little cloudy, but it was enough to make me consider the idea that I had a problem. I went online and found out where the nearest AA meeting was.

---

*Well, that one's not so hard.

At 7 a.m., I drunkenly drove my Honda Odyssey minivan to a community center in Bernal Heights. Twenty people sat in folding chairs, telling stories about their addiction. I didn't really think of myself as one of them. I didn't need twelve steps. I just needed to dial things back a bit. And then toward the end of the meeting someone said, "Merry Christmas" and I remembered what day it was. Maybe a step or two wouldn't hurt.

When I'm home and around my daughter, I'm always able to put on the brakes. But it's hard for me to play a show these days without my Valium/vodka/coke combo. And sometimes it just makes sense to party, like when an old friend comes to town, or when a new band signs to Fat Wreck Chords, or when it just happens to be a nice, sunny afternoon. It's hard for me to see a reason to go sober when my doctor tells me I'm healthy and when some of my best memories spring from nights I barely remember.

Then I find myself at an AA meeting on Christmas morning, and I have to wonder if I really know what I'm doing or if my endless rationalizations will point me toward the same fate as Tony Sly.

Tony was the singer and lead guitarist for No Use For A Name and a very close friend for over twenty years. He wasn't a good guy—he was a great guy. In 2012 he took a lethal combination of painkillers and Xanax* before flying home to San Francisco after an acoustic solo show in Gainesville, Florida. He arrived at his house, called his wife to let her know he had gotten in, and fell asleep. He never woke up again.

I got a call at 7 a.m. from Matt, No Use For A Name's bassist, and I was sad, but those old walls were still up, and they kept the pain from hitting me for several more hours. I was eating a burger alone at a diner near my house when Eric Melvin called. I answered and said, "Melvin . . . Tony . . ." and then I completely came apart. It was probably five full minutes before I could get my tears under control and finish my sentence. I walked all the way to the Fat Wreck Chords offices, which is at least an hour on foot. When I got there I couldn't even walk through the door. Someone saw me outside, and everyone came out to see what was wrong. We all sat on the grass and mourned together. Whatever disconnect I'd always had inside, losing Tony connected it.

More than any intervention, more than any other consequence of my drug use, more than any other death, Tony made me re-examine my habits. When someone you know dies in a drunk-driving accident you may not stop drinking, you may not stop driving, but you at least reconsider the combination.

---

*Both prescribed by a doctor, who later lost his license and died a drug-related death.

There have been nights when I've gone into sweats and thought, "I hope tonight isn't the night . . . " I've tried to tone down my partying since losing Tony. And I've learned enough lessons to be careful about quantities and mixtures, but it's not an exact science. Maybe there's something I haven't learned. I never used to second-guess myself so much; now Tony is always in the back of my mind.

It could've just as easily been me. The last song Tony ever performed on stage was a cover of "Linoleum."

My stepdaughter Sidra, Darla, me, and Soma at the horse races on Derby Day.

From left: Ryan Harlin, Hefe, Jay, Smelly, and Jeff Alulis in South Korea, working on NOFX: Backstage Passport.

NOFX at the Dead Sea.

112

Mike

In the summer of 2003, we booked our first ever show in Iceland. The promoter warned us that no one really knew us out there, and he couldn't guarantee us much money, but we were in it for the fuck of it. When we arrived, we found out he wasn't exaggerating. We did a radio interview and the host had never heard of our band. We went to a record store and we weren't on the shelves. We played a bar in front of 200 curiosity seekers and maybe 40 of them knew the songs.

A lot of bands might complain about being plunged back into obscurity after playing a festival to 10,000 or so people two days before, but it was one of the funnest shows we'd played in years. We bought a bunch of bottles of some nasty-smelling 80 proof grain alcohol that the locals called "Black Death" and gave it out to the crowd. Kids were cupping their hands as I poured shots into them. It was their national independence day, so after the show we went bar hopping all night with some of our newest fans, and the sun never went down.

We ate whale with green peppercorn sauce* and Kent and I golfed while the rest of the band and crew went to the Blue Lagoon, a geothermal pool situated in a lava field. It was such a rad trip that we ended up giving the promoter his money back because we couldn't bear the idea of him taking a loss while we had all the fun.

That's where the idea for what would eventually become *NOFX: Backstage Passport* was born. We couldn't always afford to travel to strange countries and take a loss, but if we booked a tour of weird places, filmed a documentary about it, and put it out on DVD, maybe it would pay for itself.

Kent and I discussed the idea for a while and started talking to filmmakers. I had recently been interviewed for the documentary *Let Them Know: The Story of Youth Brigade and BYO Records* by a pair of guys named Jeff Alulis and Ryan Harlin, who had also directed a documentary called *Do You*

---

*Icelanders are allowed to hunt a certain number of whales each year for food, so it's legal there. It tasted okay, but definitely not worth killing a whale for. (And the puffin we ate wasn't much better.)

Remember? 15 Years of the Bouncing Souls that I thought was really well done. Everyone we talked to was jumping at the chance to make our documentary, but Jeff and Ryan were the only ones who said they could do the whole thing on the cheap with just the two of them and no other crew. That was important: We couldn't afford to drag too many extra people around the world with us, and even if we could we wanted the shooting to be as low-profile as possible. In the end, it's pretty amazing they got the footage they did with a team of only two covering the whole band and crew around the clock.

We officially began the tour in South America in the fall of 2006. If you've seen *Backstage Passport** you know the highlights: Kent falling down shitfaced on day one. The cops kidnapping our crew in Peru. The Colombia promoter getting death threats. The kids jumping off the balconies in Chile. And then there were moments that never made the cut, like me juggling three huge balls of cocaine in Brazil.

When the South America tour was almost over, Jeff said we probably had enough material to make a ninety-minute documentary based solely on those first two weeks, even though we still had months of touring and dozens of other countries on the horizon. Eureka: we would sell the project as a TV series instead of a documentary.

Fuse TV bought our pitch and Jeff, Ryan, and I oversaw the editing as the episodes came together.† Jeff and Ryan had shot more than six hundred hours of footage over the course of fourteen months. Most "reality" shows don't come close to that. They shoot for a couple weeks tops, usually with a story already in mind. We broke the rules of reality TV by actually filming reality. We went to plenty of places where nothing happened, but after enough time on the road with NOFX, the shit inevitably hit the fan: Kent puking on the Russian train, military security measures in Indonesia, busting Melvin's head open with my bass in Israel, black people and tiger cubs in South Africa . . .

We had to tweak a few things in order to tell a cohesive story, like saying that we played certain countries in a different order than we really did, or

---

*And if you haven't, it's available on DVD at www.fatwreck.com!

†People assume Fuse came up with the idea for the show, or that they were involved from the outset. We had actually shot everything except for our South Africa tour before we even had a deal in place with Fuse.

making it seem like we were on the road constantly when really we toured for two or three weeks at a time and came home for a few weeks in between. But ultimately the show was 90 percent reality and 10 percent massaging. Normal reality shows have those percentages reversed. The big stuff, the stuff that everyone asks about, like getting completely ripped off in Beijing and Bali, or the crew sneaking out of the Peru venue in an equipment truck, or the fight with the Israeli crowd, or anything else that was a major plot point was absolutely real, unexpected, and never staged. Yes, we did weird green drugs in Singapore and, yes, I was the highest I've ever been in my life. (Everyone asks what "the Green Dragon" was—the dealer told us it was half ketamine and half ecstasy, but who knows what got lost in translation.)

One thing to remember about editing is that it goes both ways: Not only was the Green Dragon footage not faked, but we cut out the footage of us later that evening doing even more of it in the stairwell of a parking garage. Not only did Hefe actually go missing before our show in Singapore, he went missing before our show the night before in Seoul as well and apparently had to flag down some random dude and get a ride to the club on the back of a motorcycle. We cut that out because we didn't think anyone would believe he got lost two nights in a row on the same tour.

The premiere of *NOFX: Backstage Passport* gave Fuse a 96 percent jump in ratings overall and a 200 percent jump in ratings for the 12 to 34 demographic in that timeslot. It remained one of their top-rated shows throughout its run and was among their top five rated shows for a while when they were showing reruns.

Backstage Passport captured the essence of NOFX in a way that music, print, artwork, and live shows never quite could. When I meet someone on a golf course or at a party and they show some interest in my band, I don't give them a CD, I give them a *Backstage Passport* DVD. You don't have to like us, or even punk rock, to enjoy it.

And when I think about touring any time after the mid-'90s, I never think about playing some random show in the Midwest or some festival in Europe. I think of Indonesia. I think of Israel. I think about wandering through Red Square in the middle of the night. I think about playing acoustic guitar in a hotel lobby in Peru. I think about how unthinkable all of those tours were before that Iceland show. It's a tangible example of why I lead a charmed life. I went the way I wasn't supposed to go, and I ended up playing in front of a thousand Malaysians while filming my own TV show.

I say it often, but never often enough: start a punk band, see the world.

113

Melvin

Looking out the window of the plane, I saw waves crashing into a black, volcanic shore and a conspicuous lack of trees. It felt more like we were landing on Mars than Iceland. I had been looking forward to the trip for months, excited to plant the NOFX flag in a new nation.

But the first day we were there, I caught a savage case of the flu and spent the whole day hovering over the toilet while everyone else swam in the Blue Lagoon. I did get to see the midnight sun and eat whale sashimi, but while Mike was inspired to venture to more uncharted touring locations by the fun he had, I was inspired by the fun I missed.

Somehow I got in touch with a girl named Karen who booked bands in Hong Kong, and I lobbied Mike and Kent to set up a show there en route to Japan in 2005. My heart was set on this new adventure, so I became actively involved with the booking, staying in direct contact with Karen and working out as many details as I could before letting Kent take over. A few months later I was on a plane, bound for redemption from my illness-spoiled opportunity.

Being in Hong Kong is like walking through a James Bond movie. Everything is moving and electric and exotic and disorienting, and at any minute you feel like some shady dudes in suits are going to start some shit. We were excited to taste authentic Chinese food for the first time, so our hosts talked our way into an exclusive restaurant. Inside, the glaring, uncomfortable fluorescent lights bounced off the renter's-white walls while we ate the blandest, most overcooked food we'd ever had. (And this was the "nice" restaurant?)

I don't think Mike finished his meal, but before he excused himself we learned that our show was crossing paths with the annual Rockit Music Festival. Thousands of people would be gathered to see bands in Victoria Park while we would be hosting three hundred kids at a community center housed in a Catholic church. The band wondered why we didn't try to book ourselves on the festival bill, or why we didn't at least try to book our own show a day earlier or later. I kept my head down and pushed my mushy food around my plate.

It can be a blast to play for smaller crowds in odd places, but when a third of the crowd is made up of British and American expat kids and most of the Chinese people are relegated to the back of the room (and not all that excited anyway), the show could be considered a disappointment. But the show was only part of the reason we had detoured to Hong Kong. I wanted to enjoy the type of cultural adventure I had missed in Reykjavik, so I coordinated a band/crew trip to see Hong Kong's famous Tian Tan Buddha statue.

I was under the impression that it was the largest Buddha statue in the world, but at some point during lunch our local guides corrected us and explained that it was the second largest. Second largest in the world still seemed like a big deal, but at some point during the one-mile hike (or maybe during the 268-step ascent up the mountainside) we were corrected further: it's actually the second largest *outdoor* Buddha in the world. Further research has since narrowed the honor down even further: it is in fact the second largest outdoor *seated* Buddha *made of bronze* in the world.

The sarcastic comments from the band and crew became more frequent as we neared the top of the mountain, but we were all still looking forward to at least touching history through this cultural relic from one of China's ancient dynasties. When we reached the statue, there was a plaque at its base.

It was built in 1993. My dreadlocks are older than the Tian Tan Buddha statue.

I don't think anyone in the band or crew blamed me for any of the glitches on our Hong Kong trip, but I felt responsible for all of them. I felt responsible for not knowing about the festival, I felt responsible for our mediocre dinner, and I felt responsible for dragging everyone to the First Most Disappointing Buddha Statue In The World. I was glad I had very little to do with the planning of our *Backstage Passport* tours the following year.

◆   ◆   ◆

For all the adventure we experienced on the *Backstage Passport* tours, I can't help but feel like I squandered some once-in-a-lifetime moments. When everything was getting ugly in Peru, I was vomiting up the excess Coca Pisco Sours I had downed earlier in the evening. When we were in the Philippines, I was too intimidated by the bomb squad inspecting our van when we arrived at the hotel to venture out into the city.

NOFX will probably never return to most of the places we played in *Backstage Passport*, and I doubt I'll be dragging my kids to places like Manila anytime soon. In the last few years I've become keenly aware of just how precious time is, and just how extraordinary it is that I get to go where I go and do what I do. But while I sometimes look back and wonder what I missed by staying in, I also marvel at the unlikely alignment of the universe that allowed my punk band to land me on top of the Great Wall of China.

I don't know how we ended up here. I think about it all the time. What if Smelly had never rejoined the band? What if Dave Allen had remained our singer? What if Mike's head had been crushed when that truck hit our van? What if Smelly had OD'd? What if Hefe had ended up in jail for counterfeiting? What if Chelsea and I had kept our baby? Or what if I had been decapitated by a train while trying to flatten a penny?

Or what if none of us had ever met in the first place?

Those are the questions that push any potential regrets out of my mind. I can't say I should've done anything differently, except maybe paying more attention to my guitar playing a bit sooner. Maybe I'd be fifteen or twenty years further along with my technical ability. Maybe I'd be helping our band's sound and songwriting process and live show.

But who would've ever thought that playing guitar was something I should've focused on?

114

Hefe

I don't know how to spell or pronounce the name of the capital of Iceland so I'm not going to try. The name is bigger than the town itself. You could walk around the whole place in ten minutes. That's not to say I didn't have a blast; I tripped out on all the volcanic scenery. We'd been all over the United States, Europe, Japan, and Australia, but Iceland was the first time I felt like I was stepping into a copy of *National Geographic*.

It was more of a vacation than a tour. We went to the Blue Lagoon geothermal pool and Limo and I slapped white mud all over our bodies. I don't know what the mud is supposed to do—it's good for your skin or something. But when some older tourist ladies asked us about it, I gave them a whole lecture about its miraculous anti-aging properties. As I rinsed the mud off my face I said, "You should've seen me before. I'm fifty years old." They oohed and ahhed. Limo shook his head and told me I was a bad man.

The *Backstage Passport* tours weren't exactly a vacation, but they were definitely an adventure. The moments of relaxation were rare because we were worried about cancellations and riots and losing money. But I got to float in the Dead Sea, ride through a safari park in South Africa, and steer a boat in St. Petersburg in between all the craziness.

I also went down a waterslide naked with the rest of the band in Bali, but that didn't make the cut. Nor did the cubed eggs the chef made us in Ecuador, or my tour of the back streets of South Korea—but then again that happened when there were no cameras around. I left our hotel in Seoul to walk to the show, which was only a couple blocks away, but I somehow ended up walking in the wrong direction and got completely lost. I walked into several businesses, pointing at the address of the club printed on my tour itinerary, but no one had any idea what I was trying to say to them. I think at one point I may have even wandered into someone's house (the lines between commercial and residential get a little blurry in some of those alleys). Finally, some dude on a moped rolled up next to me and said he was from the club. I hopped on, and he buzzed through the streets at what seemed like top speed. Neither of us were wearing helmets as he whizzed between cars and took gnarly turns. I wanted to close my eyes but I couldn't. We got to the club five minutes before stage time. I'm less surprised that I didn't die on that bike than I am that I didn't die of a heart attack after getting off it.

Even after all these years of traveling with the band, the *Backstage Passport* tours showed me how much else there is out there to see and experience. I mean, I saw a fucking warthog up close. I watched *The Lion King* however many times and saw that animated warthog do his thing, but there I was in South Africa with a real-deal warthog right in front of me. I had a lot of rock star fantasies back when I first started playing guitar, but none of them involved warthogs.

Hell, none of them even involved punk. I don't know how the fuck I ended up here. And I haven't the slightest clue where we're going.

I'm just riding the NOFX moped through traffic without a helmet. And hoping it doesn't kill me before I get wherever it is I'm supposed to go.

115

Smelly

When Jeff, one of the producers of *Backstage Passport* showed up at my door to film me packing, I asked him if he would be along for the whole South American tour. He said, "I'll be along for this whole year of traveling." I didn't understand what he meant.

"Where else are we going?"

"They didn't tell you? You guys are going all over the place. Israel, China, South Africa . . . "

No one tells the drummer anything. But I was stoked to hear about all the travel, and it turned out to be fourteen months of madness. In a good way, for once.

One of my friends happens to be Pearl Jam's tour manager. When he saw the first episode of *Backstage Passport* with Kent falling down drunk and flopping around on the ground in Rio, he said, "Fire him." He was dead serious, but I couldn't contain my laughter. There was no way to explain how ridiculous his suggestion was, because to him it made perfect sense: your manager shows up drunk, you fire him. That's how it's supposed to work. It showed me what an unusual place we occupy in the music industry. Kent is the heart and soul of our whole operation, but in the eyes of the big, major-label rock world he wouldn't have made it past day one of that tour. We're an anomaly that way. Our band's dysfunction is what keeps us functioning. I've never toured with another band, so to me the chaos is normal. I wouldn't know what to do if I was suddenly surrounded by so-called "professionals." It would probably kinda suck.

It may have been embarrassing having guys with cameras call attention to me in every town square across five continents, but when the show aired I really loved it. Not only was it a time capsule of some of our most exotic tours, it also gave me a sense of perspective. When I saw my band and my life from a third-person point of view it made me understand just how lucky I am to have what I have. After so many years of touring, the travel and the shows can become a routine. It's easy to take all those trips to Europe and Australia for granted, or to become jaded about releasing another album. But when I see myself on a TV screen petting a tiger cub or swimming in the Dead Sea I realize that my life has turned out to be really fucking cool.

◆ ◆ ◆

My fondest memory from the *Backstage Passport* tours was a moment that happened off camera. At the end of the Asian leg of our tour, Rugly and I hired a boat to take us on a surf trip around some of the small islands off Lombok and Sumbawa in Indonesia. It was just the two of us with a captain and a couple of deckhands bobbing around the ocean for two weeks. The crew would cast anchor in the morning and we'd surf until we got our fill. They would make us meals between sets and we'd spend the night sailing to the next break.

The meals were usually fresh-caught fish, right out of the water. There was a toilet for me and Rugly to use, but the crew guys had no problem dropping a deuce over the side of the boat while waving and smiling at us. It was refreshingly simple living.

One day we pulled into a bay near some microscopic, nameless island. There were a dozen or so grass huts on the shore and some water buffalo wandering along the beach. A handful of local kids hopped in a little boat powered by an engine that looked like a Weed Eater and buzzed out toward us. They jumped in the water, swam over, and climbed up onto our boat.

Their village was so far removed from society that they spoke their own dialect. Our Indonesian boat crew couldn't communicate with them any better than Rugly or I could, but they were so excited to have visitors, and we were happy to entertain them. We gave them cookies and hung out with them all day. We gave them a pen and it was as if we had handed them a magic wand. Their minds were blown as they wrote and drew and passed around their new toy.

It's tempting to think about walking away from everything and living simply in a place like that, isolated from the rest of the world. I've considered it very seriously. I don't need creature comforts or indoor plumbing. I still love Costa Rica, and have been back many times since my acid turtle experience, but even Costa Rica would be too on-the-grid. Maybe Nicaragua or El Salvador. Maybe I'll spend a year in one remote place and then the next year somewhere else. Maybe I belong in a grass hut somewhere off the coast of Indonesia.

Every now and then I'll look at the pictures I took of those kids on our boat. One of them is wearing a hat with the logo of a surf company on it that I gave him. I'm not sure if that's a mile marker of how far I've been or a signpost pointing me to an eventual destination.

I keep staring at it either way.

116

Mike

The first time an unsuspecting person ever drank my piss was at the South By Southwest Music Festival in Austin, Texas.

I had written a song called "Cokie the Clown," about a bitter birthday clown who gets out of rehab and takes petty revenge on his audience by dosing them with various drugs. Fat Wreck Chords had a showcase at SXSW at Emo's, and I decided to play a solo acoustic set in character as Cokie. I also decided to play a little joke.

Before the set I put on some sloppy, sad-clown makeup and a pair of floppy, oversized shoes and Ryan from *Backstage Passport* filmed me peeing into an empty bottle of Patrón. With the camera still rolling, Ryan followed me as I walked on stage with the bottle, poured shots, and offered them to the crowd. Everyone gulped them down without thinking twice.

At the end of the set Ryan hooked his video camera up to a TV on stage and pressed play. Everyone watched the unedited video and cheered at the sight of themselves drinking piss.

Music journalists and bloggers flipped out. It seemed like every review and article about the festival had at least some mention of Cokie the Clown and the pee-drinking stunt. The story was picked up by Austin's local news channels and even by TMZ, and the Austin Health Department launched an investigation. Poor Vanessa at Fat Wreck had to field a flood of unexpected calls from the press.

In so many ways the show was a total success. But the problem was that the pee prank overshadowed the rest of the performance.

After all these years, I've cultivated the reputation of Punk Rock Funny Man. I wanted to turn that image on its head with the Cokie performance, so in between songs, instead of my usual jokey banter, I told a selection of my most fucked-up stories. I told the crowd about Melvin and me watching those gangsters carry that girl into the basement and about my roommate who hanged himself. I sang "My Orphan Year" after telling them about my dad's awkward funeral and I sang an unreleased song about killing my mom.

Everyone kept waiting for a punch line that wasn't coming. Some were confused. Some were angry. Everyone was bummed out. People booed and yelled, "What's wrong with you?" and "That's fucked up!" And when I told the story about milking that girl in England someone shouted, "Bullshit!"

"Bullshit" was the one heckle that got me. I guess when a person tells one fucked-up story it sounds believable, but a series of fucked-up stories back to back sounds too weird to be true. Collectively, NOFX has enough fucked-up stories that no one ever knows what to believe about us.

It's hard to blame them. It wasn't even real pee in that Patrón bottle.

Months after the Cokie performance, we released a video that showed how Kent had deftly switched bottles off screen with some simple misdirection. But the truth never gained the same traction as the initial joke. To this day, people still think they drank my urine.

But when it comes to our history we don't make up or embellish our stories. Our memories for small details may not be photographic and we've changed a few names to protect the innocent, but everything you've read in this book is true.* Almost all of it can be confirmed by outside sources, and the parts that can't aren't worth fabricating. NOFX likes a good joke as much as the next band, but deep down our fans know that, in the end, NOFX will always tell you the fucking truth (whether you want to hear it or not).

But again, I don't blame people for doubting us. Even the Cokie "reveal" video is still not the whole story of that evening.

---

*Except for the part about killing my mom . . . according to my lawyer. (Happy now, Stacy?)

As I peed into that Patrón bottle before the set, everything was very rushed and tense. I only had one empty bottle and one full bladder and one shot at making the video look good. We were so focused on making a smooth switch and getting me on stage with the prop bottle that we left behind the actual Patrón bottle that was actually filled with my actual piss. Later on, when we went into the back bar area to retrieve it, it was gone. Someone at the show must've seen it, thought they scored a free bottle of tequila, and snuck off with it.

I left the show with my Weirdness Barometer still broken and a smile on my face. Because someone, somewhere out there, drank my pee.

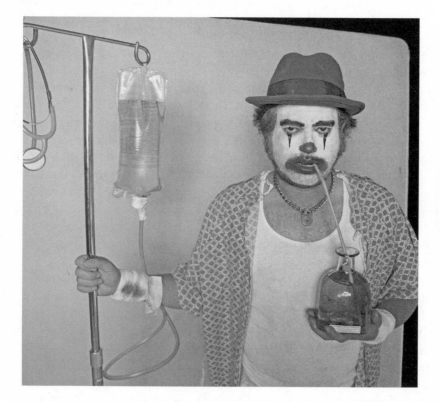

ACKNOWLEDGMENTS

NOFX

We would like to thank Roger Gastman for his valuable guidance, and for hooking us up with Marc Gerald at The Agency Group, who in turn we would like to thank for hooking us up with Ben Schafer and everyone at DaCapo Press, who in turn we would like to thank for their hard work and thoughtful collaboration on this book.

Thanks to Kristin Jamieson and Kuang Lee for taking the time to plow through the early drafts and offer first impressions; thanks to David Caplan for catching the first round of errors; and thanks to Katie Wech for her incisive notes and sincere encouragement.

Thanks to Oscar Moreno for transcribing endless hours of interviews and thanks to Harry Michaelson for transcribing a few as well. Thanks to DJ and Jay Walker for checking the facts from those hazy Wino days. Thanks to DrFaustusAU for his amazing Dr. Seuss parody cover art, which legal said we couldn't use; and thanks to Jennie Cotterill for the equally amazing lawyer-approved cover.

Thanks to everyone who helped us out by generously providing photos and images, particularly Jerry Riddle for access to his massive photo and flyer archive, and thanks to Scott Harding for his Photoshop assistance.

Our love as always goes out to Caspian, Darla, Eli, Flynn, Helaine, Jaden, Jen, Joey, Kat, Kalyn, Leslie, Liam, Sarah, Sidra, Soma, Stu, and of course Kent and The Team.

And while we're at it, thanks to everyone at Fat Wreck Chords, Stacy Fass, Dave Pollack at Destiny Tourbooking, Chris Moses and Blue Murder, Josh at Motor Studios, Zach, Cheryl, and Jake at Ziesler, Rusty at Taylor-Made-Adidas, Eric at Beats, Greg Crane at Yamaha Drums, Zildjian, Remo, Sennheiser, Mesa Boogie, ESP Guitars, Ernie Ball, Jim Dunlop Picks, Ultimate Ears, Thorndike Travel, Hurley, Vans, and our fans who are literate enough to read this far.

Jeff Alulis

Thank you, NOFX, for entrusting me with your story. I will forever be grateful for the chances you've taken on me, and for changing the course of my life by bringing me along on so many epic adventures. It has meant everything.

I can't possibly thank Gena, Paul, and Eric Alulis, Ryan Harlin, and Lisa Howe enough for their love and support over the years, on all projects up to and including this one. No amount of gratitude could ever repay them for what they've given to me. So just forget I said anything.

Thanks to my writing teacher, mentor, and fellow Skull Farmer Thom Williams for the endless inspiration and guidance. I wish I could've shared this one with you.

And thanks to all my other English and writing teachers over the years, particularly Barbara Giorgio, Tom McHugh, Brian Mooney, Ted Braun, David Howard, Paul Wolff, Nelson Gidding, Jack Epps Jr., Nina Foch, and all my other USC professors and classmates. And a special thank you to Jane McDevitt, my first grade teacher, to whom I long ago promised I'd dedicate my first book. (I don't know if this one is exactly what she had in mind . . .)

PHOTO CREDITS

All photos appear courtesy of NOFX and Jerry Riddle, except the following:

Page 72, photo © The Greenfield Family
Page 89, photo © Carol Hernandez
Page 119, photo © Chris Stavros
Page 124 and 194, photos © Epitaph Records
Page 163, photo © Dana McCarty
Page 230, photo © Dan Winters
Page 267, photo © Jimmy Mac
Page 286, 287, and 293, photos © Chapman Baehler
    (with special thanks to Alternative Press)
Page 322, photo © Magdalena Wosinska
Page 340 (bottom), photo © Guy Carmel
Page 348, photo © Jeff "Rhino" Neumann
Page 351, photo © Grumpy
Page 352, photo © Robert Granger
Page 258, 263, 264, 269, 330 (top), and 354,
    photos © Lisa Johnson